Lefty, Double-X, and The Kid

THE 1939 RED SOX, A TEAM IN TRANSITION

Edited by Bill Nowlin

ASSOCIATE EDITORS
Mark Armour, Maurice Bouchard, and Len Levin

an imprint of
Rounder Records Corp.
One Rounder Way
Burlington, MA 01803

ISBN-13: 978-1-57940-162-7
ISBN-10: 1-57940-162-7

Edited by Bill Nowlin.
Associate editors: Mark Armour, Maurice Bouchard & Len Levin
Lefty, Double-X, and The Kid: The 1939 Red Sox, a Team in Transition
1. Boston Red Sox (baseball team) 2. 1939 baseball season 3. Biography I. Nowlin, Bill.

First edition
Library of Congress Control Number: 2008941961

796.357'092

Design and composition by Jane Tenenbaum
Cover design by Francisco Gonzalez

Contents

1939

by Mark Armour

The Boston Red Sox have had a long and colorful past, detailed in many fine histories and biographies. The short version of their story goes something like this: After a run of success, including five World Series victories in their first two decades, the sale of Babe Ruth to the Yankees helped lead to 86 years of misery, which finally ended with championships in 2004 and 2007. Unfortunately, this legend ignores a lot of good teams and players, not all of whom played in 1949 or 1967. There was, for example, 1939.

Those Red Sox were led by five Hall of Famers—Jimmie Foxx, Lefty Grove, Joe Cronin, Ted Williams, and Bobby Doerr—who helped the team to 89 wins (their highest total since 1917) and a second-place finish behind the Yankees. It was above all a team in transition. Foxx, Grove, and Cronin had been acquired in the mid-1930s by Tom Yawkey, their new young millionaire owner, in a brazen attempt to turn a downtrodden franchise overnight into a champion. After this strategy did not pay off, Yawkey's general manager Eddie Collins began to acquire young players from established minor leagues, including Williams and Doerr, who would help lead some very strong teams in the 1940s. In 1939, these two philosophies overlapped, with all five of these players enjoying fine seasons.

The veteran Grove, in his 15th major league season and with 271 wins under his belt, could not pitch as often as he once did—generally getting the ball once a week in 1939—but was still the best pitcher in the league when he pitched. Joe Cronin joined the Red Sox in 1935, a year after Grove, and struggled for a few years to win the respect of his teammates and fans. By 1939 he was back at the top of his game, at least as a hitter. Foxx was acquired in 1936, and continued to be one of the great hitters in the game.

The season saw the sensational major league debut of Ted Williams, who caused a commotion both on the field--with his rookie-record 145 RBIs—and off the field. Showing supreme plate discipline, he walked over 100 times—extraordinary for a first-year ballplayer. His teammate Doerr built on the solid second season he'd enjoyed in 1938, and—though just six months older—acted as a mature ballast to the ebullient Teddy. These five men, along with several other good players young and old, engendered renewed optimism among Red Sox fans was as the season got underway.

So why didn't they win? The New York Yankees were too good—in Rob Neyer and Eddie Epstein's book *Baseball Dynasties*, the authors each conclude that New York had the greatest baseball team ever put together. Finishing second to the 1939 Yankees is no shame. The problem, Joe Cronin felt, was that the rest of the league (other than the Red Sox) rolled over for the Yankees. In 1939, the Red Sox won 11 of 19 games against the New Yorkers, including a memorable five-game sweep in Yankee Stadium in early July. The Yankees beat everyone else like a drum, with at least 13 victories against each foe, and romped to a 106–45 record.

So this book is about an interesting second-place team. There was no thrilling postseason, no tight pennant race, no real doubt about how things were going to turn out. But the players on the team were about as an interesting aggregation as one could find in the era, as a reading of their biographies will reveal. Heck, they even had a bonafide United States foreign intelligence agent in their midst. And they performed pretty well. The 1939 Red Sox won 59% of their games, finishing with a winning percentage just .004 behind their 2007 club, which won the World Series. They were led by a fiery manager, a cranky southpaw, a slugging first baseman, a gentlemanly second sacker, and a Kid in right field.

The Ballplayers

Jim Tabor, Tom Carey, and Boze Berger limbering up in Sarasota during the spring of 1939

ELDEN AUKER *by Robert H. Schaefer*

G	ERA	W	L	SV	GS	GF	CG	SHO	IP	H	R	ER	BB	SO	HR	HBP	WP	BFP
31	5.39	9	10	0	25	4	6	1	151	183	108	90	61	53	13	1	0	697

G	AB	R	H	2B	3B	HR	RBI	BB	SO	BA	OBP	SLG	SB	HBP
31	53	6	12	1	0	2	3	1	14	.226	.241	.358	0	0

Over a major-league career that lasted 10 seasons, Elden Auker played for Hall of Fame managers Bucky Harris, Mickey Cochrane (who called him "Mule Ears"), and Joe Cronin (who severely limited Auker's effectiveness by calling, from his shortstop position, each pitch Auker was to throw). Auker was a teammate of Hall of Famers Hank Greenberg, Charlie Gehringer, Goose Goslin, and Al Simmons on the Tigers; Jimmie Foxx, Lefty Grove, Bobby Doerr, and Ted Williams on the Red Sox; and Rick Ferrell on the St. Louis Browns.

Born in Norcatur (population approximately 500) in rural Kansas on September 21, 1910, Elden was an only child. Surrounded by farms sprawled out over the prairie, downtown Norcatur was just two blocks long. The town's only saloon shut down during Prohibition and never reopened. By the time he was six weeks old everyone in town knew Elden. His father, Fred, was the town's only postman, and his mother took him along on his father's route and introduced Elden to all the postal patrons. Initially Fred delivered the mail on horseback but before Elden was born he was using a motorcycle in the more temperate months and a horse-drawn wagon in the harsh winter. The family income was supplemented by marketing milk and eggs. Elden's mother was in charge of this effort. His first job was to deliver these products in his red express wagon. At an early age Elden had instilled in him by his parents a respect for the value of money.

Norcatur High School didn't have a baseball team, so beginning when he was 15, Auker played on the town team with the men. After graduating from high school in 1928, he attended Kansas Agricultural and Mechanical College (today Kansas State) in Manhattan, Kansas. Charlie Corseau, who recruited him, was the varsity basketball and baseball coach there, and arranged part-time jobs for Elden so he could pay his way. Auker's goal was to become a medical doctor and he took the appropriate courses in anatomy, physiology, chemistry, psychology, etc., to prepare for that profession.

Auker in 1939, uniform bearing the 1839–1939 Baseball Centennial patch

While in college, Auker played varsity football (quarterback), baseball (pitcher), and basketball (guard and team captain). He was voted All Big Six in all three sports. This resulted in a college nickname: Big Six. But in his autobiography, Auker wrote that no one in major-league baseball ever called him that.

Football was his favorite sport. Ironically, in his first college football game, Auker permanently injured his right shoulder. This prevented him from ever throwing overhand. To compensate for the shoulder separation, he learned to pitch with a slightly underhand motion.

Auker always took on extra jobs to earn money, which was in short supply in the 1930s. In the summer of 1931, he pitched for pay on a town team, the Manhattan Travelers, and faced Satchel Paige, who was pitching for the legendary Kansas City Monarchs. Auker beat Paige, 2–1, the Monarchs' only run coming on a home run by catcher T.J. Young. This loss broke the Monarchs' 33-game winning streak. Later that summer Auker played for another town team in Oxford, Nebraska, but under the name Eddie Leroy to preserve his college eligibility. Once more Auker's team faced the Kansas City Monarchs, but this time a pitcher named Andy Cooper was on the mound for the Monarchs. Auker threw a shutout, winning 1–0. Auker thought Cooper had a sharper curveball than Paige, and was at least as good a pitcher as Paige, if not better.

After graduation in 1932, Auker was scouted by football great Bronko Nagurski and turned down an offer of $6,000 from the Chicago Bears to play pro football. Instead he signed with the Detroit Tigers for $450. He decided to play baseball because his paychecks would start immediately instead of waiting until the fall, when the football season started. Auker's intention was to play pro baseball as a means of earning tuition money for medical school. But he made such good money at baseball that he couldn't afford to give it up. Besides, the Depression was in full force and both jobs and money were scarce.

At one of his first minor-league stops, Decatur of the Three-I League in 1932, his manager was Bob Coleman, who had caught perhaps the most famous submarine pitcher to ever work in the majors, Carl Mays. Coleman suggested that Auker modify his slightly underhand throwing motion even more and throw directly underhand. Before the 1933 season ended, Auker, who was 16–10 with Beaumont of the Texas League, was called up to the Big Show by the Detroit Tigers. He started six games and relieved in nine others, going 3–3 overall. He pitched a total of 55 innings.

Also in 1933, Elden married Mildred Purcell, a college classmate. In their senior year Elden was voted "Joe College," and Mildred "Betty Coed." Although they knew each other in college they didn't date until after graduation. Their only child, a son, James, was born in 1939. Their marriage was better than any Hollywood love story and Elden and Mildred were devoted to each other for their entire lives.

In 1934 Mickey Cochrane replaced Bucky Harris as the Tigers' skipper. Cochrane was a dynamic playing manager and he infused a winning spirit in the club by constantly exhorting his players to do better. The talent was there, and the club responded. The Tigers had an outstanding pitching staff, led by Lynwood "Schoolboy" Rowe and Tommy Bridges (24–8 and 22–11, respectively), and ably supported by Auker's fine 15–7 season, along with another 15 wins from Fred (Firpo) Marberry. The Bengals coasted to victory with a record of 101–53, seven games ahead of the aging Yankees.

The '34 Tigers were a powerhouse team and boasted an infield that combined to drive in an astonishing total of 462 runs. Four members of the team would be elected to the Hall of Fame—Cochrane, Charlie Gehringer, Goose Goslin, and Hank Greenberg.

In the National League, the St. Louis Cardinals won their fourth pennant since 1926—behind four different managers. The latest version of the Cards, known as the Gashouse Gang, was led by another playing manager, Frankie Frisch. The Cardinals' roster included five players destined for the Hall of Fame—Dizzy Dean, Leo Durocher, Frisch, Joe Medwick, and Dazzy Vance. They had a 95–58 record and the '34 season would be their finest moment, as the fabled Gashouse Gang never won another pennant.

The '34 Series opened in Detroit, and the Cardinals took the opener, 3–1, with Dizzy Dean besting Alvin "General" Crowder. In the second game, Schoolboy Rowe went all the way as the Tigers scored a run in the bottom of the ninth to pull out a 3–2 victory. Bill Walker took the loss for the Cards.

The Series shifted to St. Louis, where the Cardinals won the third game, 4–1. Paul Dean beat Tommy Bridges, who was knocked out in the fifth inning after facing three hitters without retiring anyone.

The Cardinals now led two games to one and the Tigers needed a win. Auker was matched against Dazzy Vance in the fourth game. Elden pitched a complete game as Bill Walker again took the loss. Auker gave up 10 hits and three earned runs in an 8–4 Tigers victory.

At the end of six games the Series was dead even. Auker started the crucial Game Seven at home, opposing Dizzy Dean. Auker pitched well enough for the first two innings, allowing three hits, but the Cardinals' Dizzy Dean kept the Tigers from scoring, too. After Auker got the first out in the top of the third, Dean doubled to left. Pepper Martin then beat out a slow roller to first, giving the Cardinals runners on first and third. Outfielder Jack Rothrock walked, loading the bases. The next batter was the switch-hitting Frisch. He fouled off four pitches and then doubled to right field, clearing the bases.

Cochrane removed Auker in favor of Rowe, who got Medwick to ground out to short. St. Louis kept hitting, though, and by the time the inning was over, the Cardinals had scored seven runs. It was quite a game, and Tigers fans displayed their frustration after Joe Medwick and Tigers third baseman Marvin Owen tangled in a fight on the field, pelting Medwick with bottles, food, and all sorts of trash as soon as he took his position in left field. The crowd was in such an uproar that the game had to be halted. Commissioner Kenesaw Mountain Landis, ordered that Medwick be removed from the game "for his own safety." The final score was 11–0, bringing the championship home to St. Louis.

Auker got some measure of revenge by winning the first major-league baseball players' winter golf tournament in Lakeland, Florida, in January 1935, defeating Dizzy Dean and Babe Ruth, among others.

The Tigers picked up in 1935 right where they left off in '34, winning the AL pennant with a record of 93 and 58. The team was largely unchanged, but General Crowder improved greatly over his '34 season, from 3–1 to 16–10. Auker also did better, going to 18–7 from 15–7, and led the league with a wining percentage of .720. It was his best season ever. In the World Series, the Tigers faced the Cubs, who had compiled a record of 100–54 under Charlie Grim.

With the Series tied at one game each, Auker started Game Three in Chicago against Bill Lee. Auker gave up a solo home run to Frank Demaree in the second, in addition to a scratch run. The Cubs squeaked out another run in the fifth, so going into the sixth the Tigers were down 3–1. The top of the seventh started with Marvin Owen flying out to right field. When utility infielder Flea Clifton walked, manager Cochrane saw a chance to ignite a rally and sent Gee Walker up to bat for Auker. Walker promptly hit into a double play, ending the rally and the inning. But in the top of the seventh, the Tigers scored four runs, getting Auker off the hook. They won the game by a final score of 6–5. It was Auker's only appearance in the '35 Series. The joy in Detroit knew no bounds when the Tigers went on to win their first-ever world championship. But that powerhouse Detroit team was not able to win another pennant until 1940. By then Auker was gone, shipped off to Boston

Auker's years in Detroit were happy ones. It was a closely knit team and produced lifelong friendships. But the idyllic situation came to an abrupt end when Auker was traded to the Boston Red Sox at end of 1938 season for third baseman Mike Higgins. Detroit felt this trade was necessary because Marv Owen was in poor health and was ready to retire. Over his five-plus seasons with Detroit, Auker started 136 games and completed 70 of them, compiling a record of 77 wins and 52 losses.

In Boston, according to Auker, manager and shortstop Joe Cronin called each pitch for all his pitchers except Lefty Grove. Auker didn't learn of this until well into the season. He complained bitterly about not being allowed to pitch as he thought best, but to no avail. Auker dealt with this situation by disregarding the catcher's signals. Cronin responded to this rebellious act by temporarily taking Auker out of the pitching rotation. Auker's performance suffered in 1939 as he lost 10 games while winning 9. He completed only six of the 25 games he started.

On the bright side of this unhappy year, Auker became lifelong friends with Ted Williams. They truly loved each other. Years later, at events hosted by the Ted Williams Museum and Hitters Hall of Fame in Citrus Hills, Florida, Williams and Auker would discuss the fine points of hitting and pitching. Whenever they disagreed on some particular, Ted would look Elden right in the eye and bellow out, "Goddammit Elden, pitchers are dumb, dumb, dumb." Elden didn't take this personally, as it was Ted's universal judgment of all pitchers.

Auker roomed with Jimmie Foxx while on the road in '39, and came to respect and admire Double-X so much that he named his only child James Emory in his honor. Fortunately, the child was a boy.

At the end of the 1939 season, Auker told Red Sox owner Tom Yawkey he couldn't play for Cronin and would retire if Yawkey didn't trade him. After being assured by St. Louis Browns manager Fred Haney that Auker could call his own game, Yawkey sold the pitcher to St. Louis for $30,000.

The Browns simply didn't compare with either the Tigers or the Red Sox. They were not contenders, and finished a dismal sixth in 1940 and '41. Luke Sewell

Elden on the road

took over as manager in 1942 and the Brownies rose to third place, winning 82 games. Auker won 14 of those games and earned a substantial salary. World War II was now raging, and Auker felt he had to devote full time to what up until then had been his off-season job.

Auker realized that his career as a ballplayer wasn't going to last forever. In 1938 he began to prepare himself for life after baseball. He and Mildred stayed in Detroit that winter instead of going to Florida to chase a little white ball around the golf links. A Detroit friend, Jim Jackson, offered him a job at his small firm, the Midwest Abrasive Company. Auker learned the abrasive industry from the ground up by working in all departments. The next year he moved into the sales department, and then learned how the abrasive was employed in the honing process that removed all the microscopic rough spots from the interior of 20mm and 40mm anti-aircraft gun barrels—a critical step in fabricating accurate gun barrels. By the end of 1942, Auker was a vital link in the production of defensive armaments for the Navy and he believed his country needed him more than baseball. Although offered a lucrative contract by St. Louis, he decided not return for the 1943 season. He was 32 years old, and was fully aware that by the time the war ended he would be too old to resume his career on the diamond.

Abandoning baseball and committing himself to the war effort was a noble, patriotic decision. It was also a very expensive one, as his annual income was greatly reduced. Ultimately, Auker was rewarded because by the time he retired in 1975, he had risen to be president of what was then the industry's second largest firm and was very well off financially.

As Auker rose up the executive ladder, he and Mildred were obliged to relocate to Massachusetts. There, in addition to his corporate responsibilities, Auker became the vice president of the National Association of Manufacturers and president and chairman of the board of the Associated Industries of Massachusetts, a manufacturers' trade group. In this role he met Joseph Kennedy (father of the president), Ronald Reagan, and Barry Goldwater, played golf with Gerald Ford and Tip O'Neill, and interacted with numerous other important people.

Immediately after his retirement in 1975, Auker was hired by Dresser Industries, the parent company of the division from which he had retired, as a consultant to evaluate its Washington office. He and Mildred had just purchased a home in Vero Beach, Florida, but Auker accepted the offer and commuted by air each weekend to Florida for a year.

Auker and Mildred became full-time residents of Vero Beach when he completed the consulting agreement in 1977. In his 80s, he joined the Society for American Baseball Research in 1997 and attended every meeting of the Central Florida Chapter. Andy Seminick, a resident of Cocoa, Florida, also became a chapter member. In 1998 the chapter was renamed the Auker-Seminick (alphabetical order) Chapter in their honor. The chapter celebrated Elden's 90th birthday in 2000 and hosted a party for him. When asked how he spent his time, he replied that he played golf two or three times a week. Naturally, someone asked him about his score. With a smile Elden softly said, "It's less than my age."

Typically, a chapter meeting was centered on one of the members making a presentation of their latest research findings. Following this, the meeting took the form of an open discussion. Both Auker and Seminick freely participated and candidly shared their baseball experiences. Elden's tales from the diamond were enthralling, as was his entire life story. Just possibly the experience of talking about his career, and the enthusiastic reception to it, led him to write his autobiography, *Sleeper Cars and Flannel Uniforms.*

In his book, Auker made it quite clear that he didn't put up with cheaters, or rule violators like Pete Rose. Although Elden was a soft-spoken and gentle man, it was evident that he was made of iron when it came to his moral code.

It was also clear that he thought current pitchers were not up to the physical standards of his day. Typically, Auker reported, the day after pitching a game he would do some easy throwing and a lot of hard running in the outfield. The following day he would throw batting practice from the mound. And Auker threw hard stuff, no creampuffs or meatballs. He worked to improve the command of his pitches, and didn't care to be hit hard by his teammates. A teammate had to earn a solid hit, even if it was just BP. After throwing batting practice, Auker would do more hard running in the outfield. He religiously ran hard every day. He was convinced that a pitcher's strength came from his legs. Simply doing wind sprints didn't improve leg strength and Auker was an advocate of running as hard as possible.

The major change Auker observed in pitching technique had to do with brushing back a hitter. He said emphatically, "The plate is mine. If a batter gets into my territory I'm going to make him eat dirt." Auker said he never threw to hurt a hitter, but plunking him in the ribs to back him off the plate was acceptable. In Auker's opinion, the rule change that prevented a pitcher from doing this tipped the balance sharply in the hitter's favor.

When Tiger Stadium was "retired" at end of the 1999 season, Auker participated in the solemn ceremony. As the senior Tiger in attendance he stood at the head of a line of 60 Tigers players, arranged in order of seniority, anchored at the other end by the current team captain, catcher Brad Ausmus. Auker's remarks over the public address system clearly indicated that in his heart and mind he was still a Tiger. The flag was lowered, folded, and passed from the center-field flagpole from one player to the next until it reached home plate. It was then put into storage until Opening Day of the 2000 season, when the process of passing the flag from home plate out to the center-field flagpole was repeated by the same players at the new home of the Tigers, Comerica Park. Elden's son, James, arranged to get a copy of the video and Elden showed it at the next meeting of SABR.

Another honor came to Auker on May 27, 2000. His home town of Norcatur dedicated a park in his name. The land was donated by Jim Nelson, a boyhood buddy of Elden's. It was a very emotional moment for Elden and Mildred, as the entire town turned out for the ceremony, highlighted by a band playing the national anthem as the flag was raised.

Elden had a long history of heart problems—he was on his third pacemaker—and on August 4, 2006, Elden passed away from heart failure. A memorial service celebrating his life was held at the First United Methodist Church of Vero Beach. It was attended by a huge throng of relatives, friends, business associates, and fellow SABR members. His son, James, and two grandsons eulogized Elden. Their tender, loving words moved the audience greatly. Immediately following the service his family hosted a reception in the Christian Life Center Fellowship Hall.

Sources

Auker, Elden, with Tom Keegan. *Sleeper Cars and Flannel Uniforms.* Chicago: Triumph Books, 2001.

Bucek, Jeanine, ed. *The Baseball Encyclopedia.* Tenth Edition. New York: Macmillan, 1996.

Cohen, Richard M. & David S. Neft. *The World Series.* New York: The Dial Press, 1979

Levenson, Barry. *The Seventh Game.* New York: McGraw-Hill, 2004

Schaefer, Robert. Personal notes taken at meetings of the Auker-Seminick SABR Chapter, 1996–2006.

Van Brimmer, Kevin. "Auker was 'Treasure to Game, Humanity.'" *TC Palm* (Obituary), August 5, 2006.

JIM BAGBY *by Jim Elfers*

G	ERA	W	L	SV	GS	GF	CG	SHO	IP	H	R	ER	BB	SO	HR	HBP	WP	BFP
21	7.05	5	5	0	11	5	3	0	80	119	66	63	36	35	7	2	2	388

G	AB	R	H	2B	3B	HR	RBI	BB	SO	BA	OBP	SLG	SB	HBP
21	34	10	10	2	0	1	4	0	1	.294	.314	.441	0	1

Jim Bagby, Jr. was a second-generation major leaguer, his career neatly echoing that of his father, James "Sarge" Bagby, Sr. Both were right-handed pitchers; both at various times led the American League in innings pitched; and both spent the bulk of their careers with Cleveland. Both compiled some memorable seasons. Twice Jim's pitching merited his selection to the All-Star Game. When Jim Bagby, Jr. toed the rubber for the Red Sox in the 1946 World Series, the Bagbys became the first father and son to appear in a World Series. However, Jim's greatest fame came in 1941 when he ended Joe DiMaggio's consecutive game hitting streak at 56.

James Charles Jacob Bagby, Jr. was born in Cleveland, Ohio, on September 8, 1916, while his father was in mid-career with the Indians. Jim grew up in Atlanta, Georgia, where his father had settled after playing with the Atlanta Crackers of the Southern Association. Eventually the family re-located to the prosperous Atlanta suburb of Marietta, where both father and son resided until their deaths. The family was small but close. There were three children, Jim and his older sisters, Betty and Mabel, who was named after her mother, the former Mabel Smith. The bond between father and son was especially close.

As a child, Jim Jr. avidly followed his father's career and he virtually grew up at Ponce de Leon Park, home field for the Crackers. When not watching his father play, Jim spent many hours playing catch with his dad. It wasn't long before the younger Bagby learned all of his father's pitches. Jim's mother disapproved. Her thoughts, echoing those of so many baseball wives of the generation, were highlighted in a *Liberty* magazine profile that quoted her talking to her husband:

> The conversation was repeated many times. Often enough to impress Jim Bagby Jr., young as he was. "I don't know why you want him to grow up to be a baseball player," his mother would say. "What has baseball ever done for you, Jim? You worked hard in the minor leagues for years, and then you were in the majors for a spell, and here you are in the

Jim Bagby, Jr.

minors again. After all those years what do you have to show for it? First I want our boy to have a good education, and then a job in some reliable business."

The talk would die down, and then, when his mother had left the room, his father would ask, "Ready, Jim?" And Jim would nod eagerly and the two would go out behind the little house in Atlanta and play ball.[1]

Young Bagby's course to the majors was not a straight line from childhood to adulthood. There came a time in his adolescence when he came close to giving up on baseball completely. As a 12-year-old he was the best pitcher on the Atlanta area sandlots but then mysteriously, *Liberty* recounts, his arm "went lame." His mother's emotions were mixed but young Jim felt that she was secretly glad of the situation.

For three years Jim didn't touch a baseball. Things changed when he turned 15. Starting slowly, he ultimately rediscovered his old form. The team he played on tied for the city of Atlanta championship game but lost the playoff. The re-emergence of his son's talent elated his father. The elder Bagby knew the owner of a semipro team in Montgomery, Georgia. Beginning in 1932, the son pitched semipro ball in Montgomery and was winning consistently.

In the spring of 1935 the senior Bagby finagled a tryout for his son with Cincinnati. Amid the hubbub of Chuck Dressen's first full season as manager of the Reds, the gangly 19-year-old attracted almost no attention. Embittered, he left the Reds spring training camp on his own volition after three disheartening weeks. A pep talk from his father soon revived his spirits. When the Boston Red Sox played in Atlanta as they barnstormed their way north to open the season, the father tried something else.

Gaining the ear of Red Sox manager Joe Cronin, he arranged another tryout for Jim. Cronin liked what he saw and wired Eddie Collins to find a position for the 6-foot-2, 175-pound pitcher with great stuff and a solid assortment of pitches. As a result Jim found himself in the ranks of professional baseball as a member of Boston's Piedmont League farm club, the Charlotte Hornets.

With the Class B Hornets he compiled a 13–9 record while appearing in 40 games and pitching 218 innings. Showing a maturity beyond his years on the mound, Bagby possessed a wicked curve, a fantastic changeup taught to him by his father, a sinker, and his main weapon, blinding speed. In 1936, Charlotte dropped out of the Piedmont League and the Red Sox switched their affiliation to the new team in Rocky Mount. Bagby was assigned there.

But Rocky Mount was a bit of a setback; Bagby compiled a 9–12 record while pitching 169 innings in 39 games with an ERA of 5.11. Despite the mediocre season, Jim was promoted to the 1937 Single-A Hazelton (Pennsylvania) Red Sox (New York-Pennsylvania League), where his talents emerged. He went 21–8 in 37 games (his 21 victories led the league) with a stellar ERA of 2.71 to earn not just league MVP honors but also a promotion to the majors.

Jim made his debut in a way that every kid in America dreams about. He started on Opening Day, April 18, 1938, against the world champion New York Yankees, the most potent lineup in baseball. When he arrived at Fenway, Jim had no idea he would be on the mound to kick off the season. In what was also the first major-league game he had ever seen, Jim found himself inserted as the starter by Joe Cronin. Cronin made the conscious decision to not tell Bagby sooner because he did not want the 21-year-old to mentally "pitch himself out" with distraction.[2] Bagby pitched six innings and earned the win. The game was tied, 4–4, when he was lifted for a pinch-hitter and the Sox rallied to take an 8–4 lead. The lead held up and Jim Bagby, Jr. had the first of his 97 major-league victories.

Jim compiled a 15–11 record in 43 games, 25 as a starter. He had 10 complete games but achieved only one shutout that season, a tight 2–0 home win over the visiting Philadelphia Athletics on August 18. His ERA stood at 4.21 with 73 strikeouts—but 90 walks. He surrendered 218 hits and 110 runs. It was a fairly decent start for what became a successful career.

Once he made the majors, Jim and his father only argued about one issue: who was the better hitter. Both were good hitting pitchers, and Jr. actually was used as an occasional pinch hitter. His lifetime average of .226 was eight points higher than his father's. The two were profiled in *The Sporting News*, the article ended thus: "But Junior is certain of one thing: that he can outhit the old man. The old man will grant him only one thing—that

Bagby takes in a game from the stands in 1939

he probably gets more distance. 'But look what he's got to hit?' says Pop, 'Who couldn't knock the rabbit ball a country mile?'"[3]

For Jim another life adventure began in the off season. On October 13, 1938, he married 21-year-old Leola Hicks in the pastor's office of the Druid Hills Baptist Church in Atlanta. The two had met two years previously at a local basketball game. In a small, simple ceremony, Jim's sister, Mabel—herself married for only a short time—served as the matron of honor. The marriage would last the rest of his life.

Perhaps he had played over his head in 1938, perhaps he was distracted by the responsibilities of being a new husband, but whatever the reason, Bagby came out flat in the 1939 season. He amassed a 5–5 record with an ERA of 7.09. The Red Sox decided that he needed to be sent down to the minors to get his game back, so he was sent to the Little Rock Travelers of the Southern Association. The Southern Association was Class A1, just a notch above his most recent minor-league assignment, in Hazelton.

The demotion had exactly the effect the parent club desired. Bagby pitched to a 7–6 record and a 3.54 ERA with Little Rock. Whatever the Red Sox were looking for in him, Jim found it. He was back in the majors to stay in 1940, although at first it didn't look that way. His 1940 numbers were nothing to get excited about: a 10–16 record in 36 games. His ERA of 4.73 was a tad high, although he began to work relief on a regular basis. The combination was good enough to keep Bagby in a Sox uniform.

On August 24, he found himself involved in perhaps the oddest moment of Ted Williams' long career in Boston. Although Ted liked to say, "The only thing dumber than a pitcher is two pitchers." Ted had been pestering Joe Cronin to let him pitch. Ted liked to brag about his youthful pitching exploits and when the first game of a doubleheader against the Tigers turned into a 11–1 blowout, Cronin decided that it was time for Ted to put up or shut up.

Jim Bagby, who was on the mound, was moved to left field and Ted came in to pitch the final two innings. Ted faced nine batters, allowing three hits and one run. The highlight was striking out Rudy York on three pitches. Interestingly, the catcher was Joe Glenn, who had also caught Babe Ruth's last major league pitching performance.

Jim stayed in a Red Sox uniform until December. The one thing the Sox lacked in 1940 was a quality catcher;

at the league winter meetings, Joe Cronin, at the behest of Eddie Collins, rectified that problem. In a complicated deal to get Frankie Pytlak from Cleveland, Cronin "sold pitchers Fritz Ostermueller and Denny Galehouse to the St. Louis Browns for $30,000. Purchased Pete Fox from Detroit for an unannounced sum. Swapped Roger "Doc" Cramer, his veteran outfielder, to Washington for Gerald "Gee" Walker, and immediately turned over Walker, pitcher Jim Bagby and catcher Gene Desautels to Cleveland, receiving in return Pytlak, pitcher Joe Dobson, and infielder Odell Hale."[4]

The deal was initially unpopular in Cleveland, as Pytlak was a fan favorite and the Indians seemed to get the worst of the deal. Bagby was perceived in Cleveland as a mediocre pitcher at best. It turned out that the Lake Erie air would eventually turn out to be just the tonic Jim needed.

The deal was, however, considered shrewd by most of the experts. *The Sporting News* ranked the Indians' rotation of Bob Feller, Al Smith, Al Milnar, Bagby, and Mel Harder as "best in [the] loop."[5] Bagby's season was not spectacular by any standard, but he did find a home with Cleveland.

With the Tribe, Jim started 27 games but finished only 12; he won nine games while losing 15. His ERA was a pedestrian 4.04, but was an improvement over 1940. Interestingly, the same man who signed his father's checks when he was with the Indians signed Jim's as well. Indians bookkeeper Mark Wanstall had been with the club for 25 years. *The Sporting News* observed, "It happens only once in a lifetime, and can certainly occur only once in the history of major league ball in Cleveland."[6]

Cleveland also offered some important off-field impact on his life. No doubt aware of his mother's fears of a baseball career being an economic dead end, Jim enrolled in art school. Jim took morning classes at a Cleveland school; his long term goal was that of becoming a professional artist.

The highlight of his 1941 season would ensure that his name would live forever, if only as the answer to a trivia question. It is almost impossible to convey the atmosphere and the national mania that was singularly focused on July 17, 1941. For the previous 56 games, Joe DiMaggio had hit safely at least once. The streak was the centerpiece of the nation's newscasts; it was followed breathlessly by newspapers and fans to the exclusion of all else. Attendance for Yankees games both at home and on the road soared. Some 67,000 fans turned out at Cleveland's Municipal Stadium that night to see if "Joltin' Joe" could extend the streak.

Cleveland starter Al Smith pitched the first seven innings. He walked Joe once, then got some exceptional help from third baseman Ken Keltner, who made two stellar grabs to retire DiMaggio his next two times up.

Bagby came in to work the eighth inning. For years afterwards he would tell all who asked what he pitched that night. Most reporters over the years usually asked about that night in 1941 when the country watched him end DiMaggio's streak. Jim loved to tell and retell the story. "Just fastballs," Bagby said when asked about pitch selection by interviewer John Holway. Bagby continued, "Joe hit one of them hard but he just hit it at somebody."[7] DiMaggio hit into a 6-4-3 double play, Boudreau to Mack to Grimes, which just beat Joe to the bag. Ultimately the Yankees won the game, 4-3, but that was distinctly an anticlimax for the evening.

Jim achieved some professional highlights in 1942 and 1943. In both years he led the American League in games started. In 1942 he compiled a 17-9 record in 38 games. The 1942 season was Jim's single greatest season. He started 35 games and recorded 16 complete games with 4 shutouts, both professional bests. His outstanding ERA of 2.69 was also his personal best. Jim was a natural selection for that July's All-Star Game. In 1943 he returned to the All-Star Game but in neither year did he see action. His 1943 numbers were 17-14 in 36 games while leading the league in innings pitched with 273. His ERA of 3.10 however, was closer to his final major league average of 3.96. (His father led the American League twice in games, and once each in victories, complete games, and innings pitched.)

In 1944 Jim appeared in just 13 games before leaving baseball for a one-year stint in the Merchant Marine. His hitch was uneventful and perhaps left Jim with a desire for more. Early in 1945 Jim took the Army physical but was rated 4-F because of his harelip. He returned to the Indians for the final year of World War II and had an 8-11 record. He started 19 games and worked 6 in relief. On December 12, 1945, the fifth anniversary of the trade from Boston, he was traded back to Boston for pitcher Vic Johnson and cash.[8]

With Boston he was used almost equally as a starter and as a reliever. Bagby built a 7-6 record, he started 11 games and completed six with one shutout. He also relieved in 10 games. The highlight of his career came in October when the Red Sox went to the World Series against the St. Louis Cardinals. In Game Four, after Tex Hughson surrendered three runs in the second inning and two more in the third inning without recording an out, Bagby was called upon to face Enos Slaughter with Stan Musial stationed at second base. Bagby got Slaughter to ground out and Whitey Kurowski to foul out before Joe Garagiola singled to drive in Musial. Bagby struck out Harry Walker to end the uprising. In three full innings of work, Jim gave up one earned run on six hits and a walk. Jim flied out to center field in his one Series at-bat, falling short of his father's 1920 feat: a pitcher hitting a home run in a World Series. Jim, Sr. was the first pitcher to homer in the fall classic.

On February 10, 1947 the Pirates bought Bagby from

the Red Sox for slightly over the $10,000 waiver price.[9] It turned out to be his last big-league season. In another parallel with his father, the Pirates were the last major-league team for both Bagbys. With the Buccos, his record was 5–4 in 37 games with an ERA of 4.67. He started six games and finished two of them, as he was used almost exclusively in relief.

His big-league career was almost the same length as that of his father. "Sarge" played nine years, while his son hung on for one more year, making an even decade in the bigs.

The 1948 season found Jim in the Triple A American Association with the Indianapolis Indians, trying to pitch his way back onto the Pirates' lineup. He amassed an impressive 16–9 record in 31 games but it wasn't enough to get him back to the smoky Steel City. At the end of the season, the Pirates gave Jim his outright release.

As a free agent in 1949, Jim latched on with the Atlanta Crackers. He was pitching in his hometown, in the same stadium he had grown up in as he watched his father's professional baseball life begin to sputter down. In 30 games he completed a 10–14 record in 178 innings, not quite good enough at age 33 for someone to pick up his option.

The story was even more interesting in his final year as a professional baseball player. With the Class B Tampa Smokers of the Florida International League he put on an impressive show with a 9–1 record in 26 games and 114 innings pitched. Not bad at all for a 34-year-old. His final big-league career record was 97–96 with an ERA of 3.96. He recorded 84 complete games and 13 shutouts.

With the conclusion of that season, Jim adjusted to life without baseball. He settled in Marietta and began working as a draftsman in the aircraft industry. Those old art school classes he had taken in Cleveland paid dividends. This job lasted until he retired in the 1980s. He also began playing golf seriously. He had started golfing as a player but now had time to work on his game. He became adept enough at golf to turn professional, playing in tournaments on weekends or while on vacation from the airplane factory. These jobs paid him more than baseball had. A life-long smoker, Jim's cancerous larynx was removed in 1982. From that point on he relied upon Leola to communicate with the world, as she became an accomplished lip-reader.

Jim's cancer re-emerged in 1988 and killed him on

Bagby warming up in 1946

September 2, just days before his 72nd birthday. Completing the pattern set in childhood, he was buried not far from his father in Atlanta's Westview Cemetery. Jim followed his father posthumously in still another way in 1992. Ten years after his father had been enshrined, James Bagby, Jr. joined him in the Georgia Sports Hall of Fame.

Notes

1. Graham, Frank, "Bagby and Son." *Liberty*, September 26, 1942, p.21
2. Clifford Bloodgood "Beginner's Luck" *Baseball*, April 1941, p.487
3. Troy, Jack "Bagby, Jr, Just Like His Pop, Even to Ability to Sock, Happy with tribe for Whom Father had 31 wins in '20" *The Sporting News* February 27, 1941, p. 3
4. "Bosox Chief Lack Plugged by Pytlak In Three-Way Deal" *The Sporting News* December 19, 1940, p.1
5. McAuley, Ed, "Cleveland Pitching Keeps Its Date with Best In Loop Rating" *The Sporting News* April 24, 1941, p.1
6. "Once in a Lifetime" *The Sporting News* February 20, 1941, p.8
7. Holway, John B. "A Mystery Man in the End to DiMaggio's Streak" *The New York Times* July 15, 1990, p. S1
8. *Who's Who in Baseball* 1947, p.60
9. Doyle, Charles J. "Hank Quit When Bucs Snubbed His Bid For Release" *The Sporting News*, February 19, 1947, p.3

Sources

Graham, Frank "Bagby and Son" *Liberty*, September 26, 1942, p.21
Bloodgood, Clifford "Beginners Luck," *Baseball*, April 1941, p. 487
Troy, Jack "Bagby, Jr. Just Like His Pop, even in the ability to Sock, Happy with Tribe for Whom Father had 31 wins in '20" *The Sporting News*, February 27, 1941, p.3
"Bosox Chief Lack Plugged by Pytlak in Three Way Deal" *The Sporting News*, December 19, 1941, p.1
"Cleveland Pitching Keeps it Date with Best in Loop Rating" *The Sporting News*, April 24, 1941, p.1
"Once in a Lifetime" *The Sporting News*, February 20, 1941, p.8
Holway, John B. "A Mystery Man in the End to DiMaggio's Streak" *The New York Times*, July 15, 1990 p. S1
Who's Who in Baseball 1947, p. 60
"Hank Quit When Bucs Snubbed His Bid for Release" *The Sporting News*, February 19, 1947, p. 3
Statistics come from: Palmer, Pete and Gillette, Gary, *The Baseball Encyclopedia* (New York: Barnes & Noble, 2004)
Additional data from www.retrosheet.org and the Georgia Sports Hall of Fame and Museum website: http://www.gshf.org/site/

MOE BERG *by Ralph L. Berger*

G	AB	R	H	2B	3B	HR	RBI	BB	SO	BA	OBP	SLG	SB	HBP
14	33	3	9	1	0	1	5	2	3	.273	.314	.394	0	0

Casey Stengel, an eccentric man himself, called Moe Berg "the strangest man ever to play baseball." Dark, handsome, erudite, fluent in many languages, charming, and shadowy—just who was this man who was a professional baseball player and a so-called master spy? Who is the real Moe Berg? He epitomizes frustration for any biographer.

Moe Berg was destined to be not a slayer of dragons but a maverick who went beyond the borders of ordinary life. Berg had a nervous vitality about his person. His movements were animal-like. He appeared to be a person out of sync and out of sympathy with his environment. Moe Berg was in a world by himself, passionately interested in knowledge for its own sake. He was also quick to share this knowledge with anyone who cared to listen to him. In essence he was a free spirit. John Kieran, a former sports columnist for the *New York Times*, called Moe "the most scholarly athlete I ever knew."

What was the real mystery of Moe Berg? Was he really a spy? Was he a complex human being? No revelations can touch his innermost secrets. A complex yet simple man, he was said to have asked minutes before he died, "How did the Mets do today?"

Morris Berg, allegedly master of 12 languages, was born in a cold-water tenement on East 121st Street in Manhattan on March 2, 1902, to Russian-Jewish immigrant parents, Bernard Berg, a druggist, and Rose Tashker. Bernard Berg arrived in New York from the Ukraine in 1894 and found work ironing in a laundry. Rose arrived two years later. Bernard had set aside enough money to open his own laundry on the Lower East Side. He had higher ambitions, though, and attended night school at the Columbia College of Pharmacy. By the time Moe was born, joining older siblings Samuel and Ethel, Bernard was a pharmacist.

At nine months of age Moe moved with his family to the Roseville section of Newark, New Jersey, where Bernard Berg opened his own pharmacy. It was for the Roseville Methodist Episcopal Church that Moe played his first organized ball. As he was Jewish, he invented a new name for himself, Runt Wolfe. His father worked for 30

Moe Berg

years so that his children would have a college education. Samuel became a medical doctor, Ethel a schoolteacher. The family felt that Moe should become a lawyer. And so he did.

Moe attended Barrington High School and was an all-city third baseman with a rifle arm. He graduated from Barrington at the tender age of 16 and a year later went to New York University. One year later he transferred to Princeton University. Most of the students attending Princeton were Protestants from wealthy families. Moe, Jewish and not affluent, hovered around the periphery of that closed society. He was a loner and perhaps this contributed to his mysterious ways many years later. At Princeton Berg studied classical and Romance languages: Greek, Latin, French, Spanish, and Italian. He also studied German and even Sanskrit.

Because he was Jewish, Moe ran into some awkward moments at Princeton. One such incident came about when one of his teammates was nominated for membership in one of the prestigious dining clubs then so essential to social life at Princeton. The teammate accepted on the condition that Moe Berg also become a member. The club acceded to those wishes on the condition that Berg not attempt to bring any more Jews into the club. Moe Berg said no, thanks, to this requirement. His teammate also declined to join. Moe, feeling responsible for his teammate's refusal to join, talked him into becoming a member. Left with a bitter taste in his mouth about Princeton, Berg never returned for any class reunions.

Baseball gained Berg something like acceptance, as he started for the Princeton nine for three years. His last year, he was captain and a star shortstop. That team was the best Princeton ever had, winning 18 straight games and handing Holy Cross star pitcher Ownie Carroll one of his two losses as a college pitcher. Moe graduated with honors in 1923, 24th in a class of 211.

After graduation, Moe Berg signed with the Brooklyn Robins of the National League. He also entered Columbia Law School, eventually receiving his law degree in 1930. At this point in life he encountered Dutch Carter, an eminent lawyer who advised him to keep playing professional baseball. Carter had wanted a baseball career himself, but his family had persuaded him to follow the law, and he still regretted it. He told Berg that he would have plenty of time to practice law after his baseball career was over. Berg followed his advice, also turning down a position at Princeton to teach Romance languages.

In 49 games with the Robins in 1923, shortstop Moe Berg batted a puny .186. After the season, he sailed to Paris, where he enrolled for classes at the Sorbonne. Back in the US in 1924, he was with Minneapolis and Toledo in the American Association, playing third base and short-stop with a combined average of .264. In 1925 he was with Reading of the International League as a shortstop, batting .311 with 124 RBIs. Finally making it back to the majors in 1926, he played in 41 games for the White Sox, batting .221. It was in 1927 with the White Sox that he inadvertently became a catcher. Ray Schalk, manager of the White Sox and their first-string catcher, was out with a broken thumb. Ray Crouse was also injured. Then in a game in Boston Harry McCurdy had his hand slashed ac-cidentally by a Boston batter.

Schalk was in a panic. Looking up and down the bench, he said, "Can any of you fellows catch?" Moe said he used to think he could. Schalk asked: Who said Moe couldn't? Moe's answer: "My high-school coach." Schalk assured Berg that he'd be obliged if Moe could prove his high-school coach wrong.

Moe strapped on the so-called tools of ignorance and proved that indeed he could catch. Schalk was so delighted with Berg that after the game he hugged and kissed him. There was no turning back. The brightest man in base-ball was now wedded to the tools of ignorance. Berg was an excellent defensive catcher. Possessing a strong arm, he could gun down the swiftest baserunners. His hitting left something to be desired. Berg batted only .243 with six home runs lifetime. But his baseball acumen in call-ing games and his knowledge of the hitters put him in great demand around the league. Moe went on to play for Cleveland, Washington, and Boston in the American League until his retirement after the 1939 season. In all he spent 15 seasons in the majors mainly because of his defensive skills and his knowledge of baseball.

When Ted Williams was in his second year with Red Sox, he sought out Moe Berg for advice. Williams wanted to know about what made great hitters like Lou Gehrig and Babe Ruth. Berg replied, "Gehrig would wait and wait and wait until he hit the pitch almost out of the catcher's glove. As to Ruth, he had no weaknesses, he had a good eye and laid off pitches out of the strike zone. "Ted," Moe said, "you most resemble a hitter like Shoeless Joe Jack-son. But you are better than all of them. When it comes to wrists you have the best." Whether at this early stage of Williams's career Moe was being honest or just trying to pump up Ted's confidence is debatable; what Williams went on to do is not.

In 1934 Berg's career took the turn that made him the stuff of legend.

Now a member of a team of Americans who toured Japan, he is said to have walked the streets of Tokyo dressed in a long black kimono. He entered St. Luke's Hospital carrying a bouquet of flowers intended for Am-bassador Joseph Grew's daughter (Mrs. Cecil Burton), who had recently given birth to a daughter. He introduced himself as a friend of Mrs. Burton but instead of going to her room, he went up to the roof and, using a motion pic-ture camera, shot the skyline and other important parts of Tokyo. He never visited Mrs. Burton. In 1942, General Jimmy Doolittle's pilots viewed Berg's photos before their famous raid on Tokyo. However, the pictures were too old to be useful to the pilots.

Berg retired as a player after his 1939 season with the Red Sox, but stayed on as a bullpen coach for two seasons. During this time, *Atlantic Monthly* published an essay of his, "Pitchers and Catchers," which is considered a clas-sic study of the strategies of baseball. In August 1943, he was recruited into the Office of Strategic Services (OSS), the forerunner of the CIA, by General William "Wild Bill" Donovan, former commander of the Fighting 69th Reg-iment in World War I. Berg had just finished a tour of South American countries to secure cooperation between them and the United States in the war against the Axis.

One of Berg's first assignments with the OSS was to parachute into Yugoslavia to inquire into the relative strengths of the Chetniks, a royalist group who were led by Draza Mihajlovic, and the Communist partisans led by Josip Broz (Tito) in their fight against the Germans. After talking to both leaders and analyzing their relative strengths, Berg reported, he felt that the partisans under Tito were superior and had the backing of the Yugoslav people. Thus the greater aid went to Tito.

On another mission, Berg posed as a German busi-nessman in Switzerland. His order from the OSS was to carry a shoulder-holstered pistol and assassinate Werner Heisenberg, a German physicist suspected by the Allies to be working on an atomic bomb (if indeed the Germans were moving ahead on the A-bomb). Heisenberg divulged nothing. Berg, who was to shoot him on the spot and then take cyanide to avoid capture, concluded that the Ger-mans were nowhere close to an atomic bomb. Heisenberg and Berg were to live another day.

Generally serious, Berg had a lighter side. With the Washington Senators, his roomie was Dave Harris, a slow-moving Southerner who once was deputized as a sheriff to track down some men who had stolen a mule. One day Harris was feeling a bit sickly and told his room-mate Moe that he was "doin' poorly." Moe said, "Stick out your tongue." Harris complied and Moe told him, "Dave, you are suffering from a bit of intestinal fortitude." The next day Harris informed reporters that he had shaken off that little bit of intestinal fortitude. But Harris had the last laugh: "Moe, I can drive in more runs in a month than you smart guys can think across the plate all season."

One day in Philadelphia, the temperature reached about 100 degrees. Moe dutifully put on the equipment and stoically went out to catch, the perspiration coming out his body profusely. Berg was catching Earl Whitehill, a fast but wild lefty, that day. In the seventh inning, Doc Cramer came to bat and got into a battle with Whitehill over who was going to outstare the other. Meanwhile, Berg was crouching every time he gave a signal and getting up while the two were staring at each other. This went on for quite some time with Moe going up and down like a yo-yo. In disgust, Berg peeled off his chest protector, shin guards, and mask and laid them neatly on home plate. He then turned to Bill McGowan, the home-plate umpire, and said, "I'll return when those two guys decide to play baseball. Right now I'm going to take a shower."

One of Berg's many eccentricities involved newspapers. He would not let anyone touch his newspapers until he had read them. If anyone did touch them, Berg considered them dead and would go out and buy the papers again. Even in a snowstorm, Berg would go out to buy papers if someone had touched them before he did.

Moe was a proud man. When he was asked to write his biography, he angrily refused when his co-author mistakenly thought he was Moe of the Three Stooges. Berg also supposedly refused the Medal of Merit from the United States government when he was told he could not explain to friends why he earned it. His sister accepted it after his death.

Berg and an acquaintance

Notwithstanding living in a cold-water flat, the entire Berg family was intelligent and sought learning. The genes must have been there in Moe for intelligence and learning. So what made Moe seek a life of baseball and spying? Why did he never marry? Why did he have the knack of suddenly appearing and then disappearing at a moment's notice? We know that when he attended Princeton, he was on the fringe of that society of wealthy Protestant students and was never fully accepted into their world. Did his experience at Princeton have anything to do with his being on the fringe of society in his everyday life? If his experience at Princeton had been one of acceptance, would it have changed his makeup and the extent of his participation in the broader society? Loners are often thought of as dangerous people. But Moe was charming and interesting.

He was a loner yet was sought after as company. How do we explain this paradox? By now we have mostly only questions and only mere suppositions about Berg.

Marriage seems to have been out of the question. The closest Berg came to marriage was his involvement with Estella Huni, whose father owned the New Haven School of Music. Tall, beautiful, and sophisticated, she was an intellectual match for Moe. They had much in common—opera, art, books, and witty conversation. Early in 1944, Moe was sent to Europe, and his correspondence with Estella was sparse. She braved it out for a while, but then his letters stopped altogether, and she gave up the dream of marrying him. She eventually married a naval officer.

Berg's uncanny knack for appearing and suddenly vanishing came from his days at Princeton and from his personality, which demanded utter secrecy where his inner life was concerned. He wanted to be mysterious, to make himself the intriguing figure his psyche demanded.

Moe Berg's whole family, especially his brother, Sam, and his sister, Ethel, was somewhat enigmatic. Dr. Sam, as he liked to be called, never married and could be cruel. Ethel aspired to be an actress but settled upon being a schoolteacher and also never married. Ethel became an excellent kindergarten teacher and was given the responsibility of instructing other kindergarten teachers. She was also noted for roller-skating down the corridors of her school. Dr. Sam and Ethel detested each other and did not speak for 30 years. Moreover, his father, Bernard, chose not to live in a Jewish section of Newark. He preferred to live among a more Gentile population. Accordingly, Moe lived on the fringe of society at a young age and continued doing so at Princeton. The Bergs also felt they were superior to their other relatives and looked down upon them. At family gatherings they would stand apart from other members, living on the fringe of their own extended family. Did this come into play for Moe? It would seem so.

Bernard Berg didn't approve of Moe's baseball career. Despite Moe's pleadings, he never attended a baseball game, let alone one in which Moe was playing. He was vehemently opposed to sports because he felt they were distractions in one's life. Moe's father tried but failed to discourage his son's athletic leanings. Asked if he felt he had wasted his life, Moe always replied, "I'd rather be a ballplayer than a Supreme Court justice."

Rose, on the other hand, exulted in the fame it brought her son. When Moe was playing baseball at Princeton, he and his father exchanged acrimonious letters over his athletic activities. Meanwhile, Dr. Sam always felt that he was the neglected one in the family and was jealous of the attention that came Moe's way. Ethel, caught in the middle of all this, was probably the one most neglected.

Moe would appear from nowhere and just as suddenly disappear. It was his nature. He wanted to be free of obligations such as deep relationships with other people. Granted, he was charming and witty, but he always shrouded himself. He was the perfect man to be a spy because he revealed little about himself. His innermost feelings were as thoroughly classified as his spy activities.

Some people considered him a leech who invited himself to affairs that others paid for. Some sought him out passionately for his wide-ranging knowledge and ability to relate facts and figures to all who cared to listen. But did he ever reveal himself? Did he ever divulge his innermost feelings and thoughts to someone? He was like the spy who came in from the cold. Staying on the fringe of society, free to roam wherever he wanted, from time to time he still needed the warmth of human society to bolster him.

His brother, Samuel, with whom he lived for a while, said that after the war Moe became a bit moody and snappish. Moe seemed a lost soul. He appeared directionless, living only for his books. He would show up at Mets games, usually sitting alone in the right-field stands, wearing his customary black suit and carrying a Neville Chamberlain black umbrella. After almost 17 years of having Moe live with him and with papers and books piling up to the point that it was driving him insane, Sam finally asked Moe to leave. Moe did not budge. Dr. Sam had lawyers draw up eviction papers to get Moe out of the house.

Moe wound up living out his life in Ethel's home in Belleville, New Jersey. Things were not always good there, either. One time when a relative came to visit Moe, he offered to take her to see the writer Anita Loos. Ethel, upon hearing this, rushed out of the house and began tearing up weeds out of the garden. She said, "That son of a gun never asks me to go with him to meet Anita Loos and now he asks you."

Whenever anyone would ask any question that Moe felt uneasy about, he would put a finger to his lips and utter, "Shhh." Was this shushing a shield against not only his spy activities but also his innermost feelings? Or was it part of a vivid fantasy life?

Adding to all this was a business loss that Moe suffered from a company in which he had invested $4,000. The company, which manufactured stationery, had done well, and Moe was reported to have made profits of about $250,000. However, the profits were plowed back into the business when it expanded. Unfortunately, the expansion did not work out. The company went bankrupt, and Moe never realized his profits. Moe, it seemed, never complained to anyone over this financial loss; he seemed to worry more about all the people who lost their jobs when the firm went under. There were debts to be paid, and Moe, with the help of friends, paid them. His reaction was to plunge more deeply into his world of books and study.

Moe Berg was not of his time. Perhaps he saw himself as a throwback to more chivalrous centuries, when loyalty, honesty, and courtesy were valued. Maybe he was the knight-errant who bravely fought on when he knew he was doomed, or the lone cowboy who would ride into town, root out the bad guys, and ride into the sunset. The townsfolk would be grateful but would never make him sheriff. In any case, he lived out his life never really having a solid relationship with anyone.

Little about Moe Berg adds up. How did he last so long in the majors, continuously from 1926 to 1939, when he was no better than a mediocre player? He may have been a fine catcher, but he was a weak hitter in an era of heavy hitters, when weak hitters didn't last long. His more or less exact contemporaries in the American League alone include Gehrig, Gehringer, Grove, Lyons, Cochrane, Dickey, and other players of similar caliber. Was he kept on major-league rosters at the behest of the government for his undercover abilities? Maybe, but the Tokyo episode, in which he supposedly passed himself off as Japanese, has the implausibility of a bad spy novel or movie. Perhaps he did everything claimed for him, but perhaps he had an overly romanticized fantasy life and was a master con; the finger pressed to the lips is a masterful touch. He was intelligent, to be sure, but it's also possible he was just plain unbalanced or wanted to make himself appear more important than he was.

Moe Berg died on May 29, 1972, in Belleville, New Jersey, after a fall at his sister's home. His brother and sister survived him.

Sources

BaseballLibrary.com. www.baseballlibrary.com

Dawidoff, Nicholas. *The Catcher Was a Spy: The Mysterious Life of Moe Berg.* New York: Pantheon Books, 1994.

Horvitz, Peter S., and Joachim Horvitz. *The Big Book of Jewish Baseball: An Encyclopedia and Anecdotal History.* New York: S.P.I Books, 2001.

James, Bill. *The New Bill James Historical Baseball Abstract.* New York: The Free Press, 2001.

Kaufman, Louis, Barbara Fitzgerald, and Tom Sewell. *Moe Berg: Athlete, Scholar, Spy.* Boston: Little, Brown, 1974.

Morris Berg File at the National Baseball Hall of Fame and Museum in Cooperstown, New York.

New York Times. Obituary. June 1, 1972.

Seidel, Michael. *Ted Williams: A Baseball Life.* Chicago: Contemporary Books, 1991.

Shatzkin, Mike, ed. *The Ballplayers.* New York: William Morrow and Company, 1990.

BOZE BERGER *by Anthony Basich*

G	AB	R	H	2B	3B	HR	RBI	BB	SO	BA	OBP	SLG	SB	HBP
20	30	4	9	2	0	0	2	1	10	.300	.323	.367	0	0

Prospects who don't fulfill their promise are a dime a dozen throughout baseball history. Boze Berger could be the epitome of that kind of prospect. While his major-league service was not exemplary, Berger had a flexible glove in the field, giving him some value to a few American League teams. After spending three seasons with the Cleveland Indians and two with the Chicago White Sox, Berger capped his big league career with one season on the bench for the 1939 Boston Red Sox. Often described as an athletic, tall, and rangy youngster with a pleasant personality and a sheepish grin, the right-handed Berger went from a star college athlete to highly touted prospect to a career military officer.

Louis William Berger, also called "Bozie," "Bosey," or "Boze," was born on May 13, 1910, on an Army post in Baltimore, Maryland, and grew up in Arlington, Virginia.

His father, also Louis Berger, was a career Army man, a noncommissioned officer, who served in France during World War I. Berger's mother was Mary E. Daywalt of Baltimore. Boze also had a twin sister, Elizabeth.

Berger graduated from McKinley Technical High School in Washington and the University of Maryland, in 1932. At Maryland he was an all-American athlete excelling at baseball, basketball (he was the university's first All-American basketball player), and football. A star halfback on the football team, he scored two touchdowns in his first varsity game at Yale, forcing a 13–13 tie with the Ivy League school.

University of Maryland athletic director H.C. Byrd said Berger possessed the greatest competitive spirit of any athlete he had seen. In his honor, the university started a Bozie Berger Cup during his rookie year in the major leagues, annually awarded to an outstanding University of Maryland athlete.

A member of the Omicron Delta Kappa fraternity,

Boze Berger, 1939

Berger was the vice president of the Student Government Association and participated in the Army Reserve Officers Training Corps, achieving the cadet ranking of major. After graduating, he held a reserve commission in the Army while he pursued a career in professional baseball.

As the third baseman for the Maryland Terrapins, Berger batted .365 in his senior season and had a .978 fielding percentage, making him a widely sought after prospect coming out of the college ranks. According to Cleveland scout Bill Bradley, Berger had as many as a dozen scouts watching him at a time. He was considered one of the most skillful fielders among college baseball players of the day.

The decision came down to Cleveland or Detroit, but Indians general manager Billy Evans told Berger's coach that the youngster would have a much better chance of rising quickly to the major-league club, because the Tribe was being rebuilt with young prospects, while the Tigers had a roster populated by veterans. Just before he received his bachelor's degree in economics, Berger signed with Cleveland for the same salary that Detroit offered. He reported to the team on June 15, 1932, and stayed with the big-league club for a few weeks before being sent to the minors. He appeared in just one game, on August 17. He had one at-bat, a strikeout.

With the exception of that one at-bat, Berger spent his first three seasons in the minors. His first stop was with the Williamsport (Pennsylvania) Grays of the Class B New York-Pennsylvania League during the summer of 1932. In 21 games, playing mostly third base and some at second and shortstop, Berger batted .298 in 84 at-bats, hitting one home run and driving in 10 runs. He impressed Cleveland enough that he earned a promotion to the New Orleans Pelicans for the following season. He did not fare as well with the Pelicans in the Class A Southern

Association, but impressed with his glove by playing every infield position. Berger played in 78 games, but hit only .240 in 225 at-bats with two home runs, 31 RBIs, 12 doubles, four triples, and three stolen bases.

In 1934, Fordham baseball coach Art Devlin, a veteran of John McGraw's New York Giants teams, told a sportswriter that Berger was the best fielder he'd seen since he coached Frank Frisch at Fordham, and thought he would hit over .300 in his first year with Cleveland. Cleveland general manager Billy Evans was also excited by the young Berger, saying he was a "can't miss" star in waiting. Yet observers said Berger had a lot of trouble hitting curveballs as a result of standing too close to the plate and holding his hands too close to his body, not allowing himself to reach for balls breaking on the outside corner of the plate.

Berger also impressed Cleveland manager Walter Johnson during spring training in 1934. He used the young prospect throughout much of the exhibition season. Second base was a spot of uncertainty for the Indians. Odell Hale, the leading candidate for the position, was a natural third baseman, while Berger showed proficiency at all infield positions. Ultimately Johnson felt the young Berger needed more seasoning in New Orleans before he could join the big-league club, and Hale won the starting second-base job. Berger was sent back to New Orleans with instructions for Pelicans manager Larry Gilbert to rectify his inability to hit the curveball.

At New Orleans, Berger showed enough improvement at the plate at earn Most Valuable Player honors. He batted .313 for the pennant- and Dixie Series-winning Pelicans. He had a .471 slugging percentage and tied for the league lead in base hits (190). Hitting in the second spot in the lineup, he drove in 94 runs, scored 105 times, and hit 42 doubles, 10 triples, and 11 home runs. He had 11 stolen bases. He also proved a standout defensively at second base, recording 990 chances, one short of the league record, and participated in 112 double plays.

Sportswriter Sam Murphy said that Berger was able to improve by simply watching other batters in the league. He developed a crouch and began hitting the curves swooping toward him. When opposing pitchers adjusted by throwing fastballs high and inside, forcing Berger out of his crouch, he went into a half-crouch and found that he was successfully able to hit anything hurled at him, Murphy wrote.

Berger on deck

Berger earned another cup of coffee with the big-league club at the end of the 1934 season, but never entered a game. However Johnson announced that Berger would make the 1935 team either at second or at third.

The spot opened for Berger when Cleveland moved Odell Hale to third base. Before the season began, Berger was told he would probably also see action in right field because of his strong right arm. "For combined strength and accuracy of throwing, probably no man in the American League outshines him," Gordon Cobbledick wrote in the *Cleveland Plain Dealer* on April 8, 1935. Johnson had high hopes for the rookie; he even told a sportswriter in January that Berger held the destiny of the 1935 Indians in his own hands. As for Berger, he said, "I know it is a great responsibility, but I really haven't given thought to it. I'm going to do the best I can and if that isn't good enough it'll be just too bad for me."

Pelicans manager Larry Gilbert told Cobbledick on February 25, "In the field he can do anything any second baseman can do. He's so good that—if he hits .260 or .270 he will be a valuable man, but I believe he'll do better than that." Sportswriter Charles L. Dufour agreed, writing in the *New Orleans Item* that Berger was one of the greatest baseball heroes in the history of the Pelicans. "If second base strength is all you need to be a pennant winner you've got it," he wrote.

As the starting second baseman for the 1935 Indians, Berger played 124 games and committed 27 errors, more than average for the era, but he handled many more chances that most at his position. He was, perhaps, an above-average defensive player. He played in 124 games, but might have played in more if he had swung the bat better. He recorded a .258 batting average, only 5 home runs, and 43 RBIs. According to Billy Evans, big-league pitchers were finding they could get Berger with the curveball.

Manager Johnson told Boston sportswriter John Drohan in May, "The trouble with Berger is that he's trying too hard. But he may snap out of it anytime." Johnson had big expectations for the Indians, but they could muster only an 82–71 third-place finish.

Berger lost his starting job to rookie Roy Hughes after hurting his arm while making a fast underhanded throw. Hughes played 40 games at second. In retrospect, wrote Gordon Cobbledick in the *Cleveland Plain Dealer* in March 1936, "Much—undoubtedly too much—was expected of Berger in spring training last year. He looked pitifully weak at times, but never allowed his weakness to get him down."

During the 1935–1936 offseason, Berger spent time at his Rosslyn, Virginia, home resting his injured arms and coaching the Fort Myer Army post basketball team. He was confident going into the 1936 season that he could win back the starting job at second. He had signed a new contract that included a salary increase.

But Hughes was handed the starting job. Berger appeared in only 28 games. He had 52 at-bats and connected for only nine base hits, for a measly .173 batting average.

In the offseason the Indians placed Berger on waivers, and just as the 1937 season began, the Chicago White Sox picked him up. While replacing an injured Tony Piet at third for 40 games, Berger once again failed to impress with his fielding as he committed 10 errors. In 130 at-bats, he hit 5 home runs, drove in 13 runs, and batted .238 with a .322 on-base percentage.

At the start of the 1938 season, Berger got his chance to prove himself with the White Sox after starting shortstop Luke Appling was injured. Berger accumulated the most plate appearances in his career that season with 470 at-bats and 43 walks while filling in mostly at second base and shortstop. But he hit only .217 and made 21 errors in 67 games at shortstop and 15 errors in 42 games at second base. He hit three home runs and had 36 RBIs.

On December 21, 1938, the White Sox traded Berger to the Boston Red Sox for infielder Eric McNair. McNair went on to have a successful season, playing mostly third base for the White Sox and batting .324 with 82 RBIs. Berger meanwhile spent most of the season on the bench. He accumulated only 30 at-bats in 20 games, rapping out nine hits for a token .300 batting average. He played 10 games at shortstop, five games at third base, and two at second base.

With highly touted rookie Jim Tabor getting most of the action at third base, Berger was "wearing the seat of his pants thin" by riding the bench, according to Boston sportswriter Vic Stout. He had appeared in just two games without any at-bats when presented with an opportunity in June. Tabor was briefly benched by manager Joe Cronin. Berger was so excited by the opportunity that an hour before Red Sox batting practice, he went out to the diamond, stood at third, and had grounders batted to him. That day against the Washington Senators, Berger went 1-for-2 with a double, a fly out, and a sacrifice bunt. His second-inning RBI became the game-winner as Lefty Grove pitched a 3–0 shutout. Tabor retained his job however and had a successful rookie season.

For Berger, 1939 was his last major-league season.

On December 26, the Brooklyn Dodgers purchased his contract from the Red Sox for the $7,500 waiver price. The Dodgers signed him as a utility infielder, and he went to spring training in 1940 with hopes of making the big-league club. But he faced a big obstacle: a young, up-and-coming rookie by the name of Pee Wee Reese. The underweight shortstop asked Berger how he could quickly put on weight. Berger took Reese to dinner and instructed the rookie to eat everything the experienced veteran ate. Reese was sick for three days.

Before Opening Day, Berger was sent to the Dodgers' Montreal farm club in the International League, where he spent the entire season. He played in 134 games, and hit only .232 in 435 at-bats, with 25 doubles, 6 home runs, and 50 RBIs.

Before the 1941 season, the New York Yankees acquired Berger from the Dodgers for first baseman Jack Graham. That season, he played for four minor-league teams: Newark, Kansas City, Toledo, and Seattle. At Kansas City and Toledo in the International League, he batted only .209 in 91 at-bats. While playing for Seattle, Berger was able to contribute to the team's Pacific Coast League championship, hitting .246 in 130 at-bats with one home run and 17 RBIs. It was during this season that Berger married the former Mary Jean Lowe.

Although he signed on with the International League's Baltimore Orioles as a player/coach for 1942, Berger was unable to assume those duties. The United States entered World War II after the Japanese attack on Pearl Harbor on December 7, 1941, and Berger was activated as an Army officer. He reported for duty on February 3, 1942. He went on to serve for 20 years, first as an Army officer, then with the Air Force. He retired as a lieutenant colonel.

Berger had been looking forward to playing for and coaching the Orioles, since he was from the area, but he was also eager to serve his country. "Baseball was a lot of fun but it wasn't a very steady job," he told the *County Advertiser* of Montgomery County, Maryland, in 1983. "With a wife and child on the way, I wanted something a little more secure." Berger never played professional baseball at any level again, although he did participate in a Service All-Star game in 1942.

During World War II, Berger served in China. After the war, he became a United Nations observer. During the Korean War, he was the commander of Iwakuni Air Force Base in Japan. Later he commanded Bolling Air Force Base in Washington. He was awarded the Bronze Star for his service. After retiring from the Air Force in 1962, Berger worked as the director of building services at the University of Maryland until 1974.

Boze Berger died of a heart attack on November 3, 1992. He was 82 years old. He is buried in Arlington National Cemetery, outside Washington. Shortly after his death, his wife, Mary Jean, wrote in a note found in his

Hall of Fame file that if he could live his life all over again, he would do it the exact same way—only he would be a switch-hitter.

Sources

Most statistical information about Berger's career comes from www.retrosheet.org, www.baseball-reference.com, and www. baseball-almanac.com

Berger's file at the National Baseball Hall of Fame library contains unidentified clippings.

Graham, Dillon. "Berger Coaches Army Cagers; Says Arm Is in Good Shape." Associated Press, January 25, 1936.

Cobbledick, Gordon. "Extra Man Role May Aid Berger." *Cleveland Plain Dealer*, March 6, 1936.

Cobbledick, Gordon. "Bill Rapp, Who Discovered Ferrell, Tipped Off Indians on Bozo Berger." *Cleveland Plain Dealer*, April 1, 1935.

Cobbledick, Gordon. "Berger Draws Praise of Old Nats' Speeder." *Cleveland Plain Dealer*, November 25, 1934.

Cobbledick, Gordon. "Berger "Can't Miss as Star, Says Evans." *Cleveland Plain Dealer*, March 17, 1934.

Cobbledick, Gordon. "Berger Groomed to Play 'Em Off Wall." *Cleveland Plain Dealer*, April 8, 1935.

Cobbledick, Gordon. "Berger Joins Batterymen in 1st Drill." *Cleveland Plain Dealer*, February 25, 1935.

Associated Press. "Indians Put Finger on 2d Sacker." January 10, 1935.

Rossomondo, Bob. "Bosey's Baseball." *The County Advertiser*, Montgomery County, Maryland, July 27, 1983.

TOM CAREY *by Trey Strecker*

G	AB	R	H	2B	3B	HR	RBI	BB	SO	BA	OBP	SLG	SB	HBP
54	161	17	39	6	2	0	20	3	9	.242	.265	.304	0	2

A "flashy infielder" known for his fancy defensive work rather than his bat, Tom Carey played eight major-league seasons with the St. Louis Browns and the Boston Red Sox, retiring with a .275 batting average, 2 home runs, and a .972 fielding percentage in 466 games. According to St. Louis sportswriter J. Roy Stockton, the infielder was "agile as a cat, with nimble fingers, an accurate arm and the ability to throw quickly from any position."

Thomas Francis Aloysius Carey was born in Hoboken, New Jersey, on October 11, 1906. Carey understated his age during his playing career, shaving two years by claiming he was born in 1908 rather than 1906.[1] According to the 1910 Census, his father, Patrick, was a laborer who emigrated from Ireland to the United States in 1889, a year after Tom's mother, Mary, arrived from Ireland. Patrick married Mary about 1892, and they had seven children, five of whom survived, Annie (born in July 1893), William (December 1896), Patrick (May 1899), Peter (1904) and Thomas, the youngest. The father died while Tom was a child, so he lived with his brother-in-law, his sister, and their three children. In 1920, Patrick, Peter, and Thomas were living with their widowed mother at 807 Willow Avenue in

Tom Carey

Hoboken. In 1930, Patrick (by then a policeman), Peter, and Thomas were living with their mother at 1118 Park Avenue. After attending Hoboken's Our Lady of Grace grammar school, where he played basketball as well as baseball, Carey went to work in one of the city's industrial shops, but he continued to play ball.

Known as "Scoops" or "The Hoboken Harp," the 5-foot-8, 170-pound right-hander began his professional baseball career in 1928, sticking briefly with Jersey City in the International League before he was released. The next year, Carey caught on with the West New York and New Jersey semi-pro club, a strong team that played the Bushwicks, the Cuban Giants, and Philadelphia Giants.

Carey was playing semipro ball in New York in 1930 when Yankees scout Paul Krichell signed him to play shortstop for the pennant-winning Chambersburg (Pennsylvania) Young Yanks of the Class D Blue Ridge League. Carey hit .306 with 10 home runs in 107 games. Near the end of that season, he was transferred to Scranton of the Class B New York-Pennsylvania League, where St. Louis Cardinals scout Charley Kelchner acquired him to play with Houston in the Texas League the following year. At Houston, Carey starred at shortstop behind Dizzy Dean

(Paul Dean, Billy Myers, Tex Carleton, and Joe Medwick were also on that team), batting .240 with 15 doubles and 8 triples. In 1932, he played in 142 games for Houston and 20 for Columbus in the American Association. His average with Houston jumped to .270 but in his 68 at-bats for Columbus, he hit only .191.

In 1933, Scoops was transferred to Rochester of the International League, where he had three strong seasons. After he hit .297 and .287 in his first two seasons, the Cardinals took him to spring training in Bradenton, Florida, in 1935, but sent him back to Rochester, where he became the team captain. In July 1935, Carey, batting .301, was purchased from Rochester by the St. Louis Browns to replace the disabled Ollie Bejma at second base.[2] A Browns publicist described Carey as "the outstanding prospect among minor league infielders." Although he was a light hitter, Carey "never failed to sparkle on defense," and he was regarded as "an aggressive, fighting player who will go after any ball and run out the weakest of pop flies."

Carey's major-league debut on July 19 with Rogers Hornsby's Browns came as a surprise. When the 28-year-old infielder reported to the Browns manager at Yankee Stadium, Hornsby growled, "You were supposed to be here yesterday," and told the rookie that he would play second base. In the minor leagues, Carey had played only shortstop, but he became adept at the new position after committing a league-high 25 errors in 1936.[3]

He broke in nicely, going 2-for-4 with two doubles and a run batted in as the Browns beat the Bronx Bombers, 7–6. Carey's most productive day that year was probably the August 11 doubleheader, when he was 1-for-4 and 4-for-5. Although the Browns finished seventh in 1935, Carey hit .291 in his rookie season, with 22 extra-base hits (no homers) and drove in 42 runs, while playing second base in 76 games.

He had two productive seasons in St. Louis: In 1936, he played a career-high 134 games, hitting .273 with 27 doubles, 6 triples, 58 runs scored, and 57 runs batted in; the next year, he hit .275 with 24 doubles, 54 runs, and 40 RBIs in 130 games. He hit two home runs in his career, both solo shots, on August 2, 1936, and June 16, 1937. Even though Hornsby had played only occasionally since the 1931 season, his biographer nonetheless noted Carey's arrival on the scene in the spring of 1937: "Hornsby . . . sat down in favor of Tom Carey, and from then on, regardless of front-office wishes, he was willing to play only when it wasn't cold and the ground was dry."[4]

The Browns had a new manager in 1938, Gabby Street, and after two seasons as a full-time player, Carey was optioned to the Pacific Coast League's Hollywood Stars, where he played shortstop and batted .297 in 157 games. During the 1938 season, the Browns acquired Don Heffner from the Yankees to replace Carey at second base, and on December 6, 1938, St. Louis traded Carey to the Boston Red Sox for pitcher Johnny Marcum. In Boston, Scoops served as a utility infielder; manager Joe Cronin called Carey "an excellent infield insurance policy." During spring training, Edwin Rumill of Boston's *Christian Science Monitor* commented, "Tom Carey played a sparkling defensive game at second base. . . . Too bad he doesn't hit."[5]

Backing up second baseman Bobby Doerr and shortstop-manager Cronin in 1939, Carey appeared in only 54 games—the most he ever played in a single season with the Red Sox. Carey accumulated 161 at-bats (he averaged .242) and drove in 20 runs. In 1940, he had only 62 at-bats, mostly filling in when Bobby Doerr pulled a muscle in early June and when Cronin benched himself with a severe head cold in mid-July. Carey drove in seven runs (one of them a single in the 13th inning to win the September 10 game), and batted .323, but there just wasn't the room for him to play more regularly. With the addition of utility man Skeeter Newsome to the Red Sox in 1941, he hit .190 in 21 at-bats without an extra-base hit and without driving in a run—though he scored seven.

Carey saw his already limited playing time dwindle to two innings in 1942, leading one newspaper wag—exactly who is uncertain because the newspaper article is incomplete—to label him "baseball's Forgotten Man" and note that Fenway Park patrons saw him play only during infield practice: "A member of the Red Sox in good standing, he has spent 99.44–100 per cent of his time on the bench." During his brief appearance on the field that year, the Forgotten Man had one hit in a single at-bat, drove in a run, and fielded one chance cleanly—a perfect 1.000 performance. Nevertheless, the Associated Press (which called him "Boston's $5,000-a-hit player") argued that Carey's "backstage activities"—warming up pitchers and throwing batting practice to the regulars, earned his $5,000 salary.

With Johnny Pesky in the Navy after the 1942 season, it looked as though Carey would get a shot at shortstop, but on the very day—Valentine's Day—that he received his contract for 1943, he also received notice of reclassification as 1A in the draft and was ordered to report for his physical.

Carey served in the Navy from 1943 to 1945, primarily as baseball coach at the Sampson Naval Training Base in upstate New York. He returned to the Red Sox briefly as a player for their pennant-winning 1946 season. Rosters were swollen in the first year after the war to permit clubs to accommodate returning servicemen, but many saw little playing time. It would not be surprising if Carey, then 37 and having lost three years of major-league-caliber baseball, were a little rusty. But Tom declared himself in better shape than ever, having lost weight and kept fit. "I don't see any reason why I couldn't go for five more years," he said. "I mean that." The *Monitor*'s Ed Rumill observed that Carey "has been out-playing, out-hustling, and even out-hitting most of the younger infielders in camp."

Carey had experience at second, third, and short and offered a steady backup. From spring training, Rumill praised him in print: "A more popular team ballplayer has never had a locker at Fenway. And he is a good hustler. A man who fits in with your team spirit and can step in and play three of the four infield positions is a handy weapon when you are on the prowl for the pennant. History insists that a contender is no stronger than its reserves, and Carey has, in the past, been an ideal reserve." Rumill foresaw another possible role: "If Cronin feels that he no longer has room for Carey on the varsity . . . he has the experience and intelligence to fill a coaching or even a managerial berth."

After the opening bell, Carey got little playing time. He had just one single in five at-bats, usually as a late-inning substitute during games that had become lost causes. In midseason, Rumill wrote, "Cronin had so many infielders, even before the arrival of [Don] Gutteridge, that some of them had to dress in the room adjacent to the regular Sox clubhouse."[6] Carey was indeed made a coach on the team. "I'd like to stay in baseball, naturally," he said. "But that's up to the Red Sox. I'm ready to take any job they give me."[7]

On October 30, 1946, Boston released the 40-year-old Carey, along with Mace Brown, Mike Ryba, and Charlie Wagner, hiring all four in other capacities. Carey was sent to Wellsville, New York, where he managed the Red Sox' farm team in the Class D PONY League in 1947 and 1948. In 1949 and 1950, he coached for the Red Sox Birmingham, Alabama, affiliate in the Southern Association.

We know almost nothing about Carey's life after baseball. He died from liver disease on February 21, 1970, at Highland Hospital in Rochester, New York. He is buried in Rochester's Holy Sepulchre Cemetery. He was survived by his wife, Grace M. Carey, who died in 1998.

Notes

1. Tucker, Walter Dunn. "How Old Is That Guy, Anyway?" *Baseball Research Journal* 36 (2007): 94–98.
2. Alexander, Charles. *Rogers Hornsby*. New York: Henry Holt, 1995: 199.
3. Shatzkin, Mike, ed. *The Ballplayers*. New York: Arbor House, 1990: 158.
4. Alexander, op. cit.: 211.
5. *Christian Science Monitor*, March 30, 1946. Carey's playing weight may have increased by the time he got to Boston. Rumill dubbed him a "chubby veteran" when he signed his 1942 contract and later a "pleasant-faced New Yorker, on the roly-poly side."
6. Ibid.
7. Ibid.

Sources

Alexander, Charles. *Rogers Hornsby*. (New York: Henry Holt, 1995).

Ancestry.com.

Baseball-reference.com.

Carey, Thomas. Clipping File. National Baseball Hall of Fame.

Shatzkin, Mike, ed. *The Ballplayers*. (New York: Arbor House, 1990).

The Sporting News.

Tucker, Walter Dunn. "How Old Is That Guy, Anyway?" *Baseball Research Journal* 36 (2007): 94–98. This article asserts that Carey claimed a 1909 birthdate, but since all other sources—including contemporary ones—cite 1908, we have elected to keep that date.

DOC CRAMER *by Donald J. Hubbard*

G	AB	R	H	2B	3B	HR	RBI	BB	SO	BA	OBP	SLG	SB	HBP
137	589	110	183	30	6	0	56	36	17	.311	.352	.382	3	2

Like many businessmen in the aftermath of the 1929 stock market crash, legendary Philadelphia Athletics manager Connie Mack took a beating financially and, as a result, he dealt his star outfielder Roger "Doc" Cramer to the Boston Red Sox. Cramer joined other Athletics stars such as Lefty Grove and Jimmie Foxx in the exodus to Boston, whose much more financially secure Sox owner, Tom Yawkey, reaped the benefit.

Born in Beach Haven, in southern New Jersey, on July 22, 1905, Roger Cramer earned the appellation "Doc" because of his friendship while growing up with a local physician named Joshua Hilliard. Cramer religiously accompanied his friend and mentor on his house calls to patients, often traveling on a "one-hoss dray" in nearby Manahawkin, where he and his family moved to when he was very young. He liked people calling him "Doc" but hated his other nickname, "Flit," given to him supposedly by a sportswriter. Cramer's parents Eva and John R. Cramer (a butcher) had six children, though one died young. The Cramers were mainly of Dutch extraction, with some German, and while Doc Cramer did not pursue medicine, he did apprentice as a carpenter. Even during his major-league career, he built houses as a union man during the offseason, always earning more than he made in any year he played professional baseball.

By the age of eight, Doc had begun to follow baseball obsessively, playing it as often as possible and watching many local games. He probably did not see any major-league games as a child or teenager, as his father did not share in his passion for the game. Perhaps Dad could not figure out why his son threw right-handed and batted left-handed; to his family, this remains a mystery.

Doc Cramer first played baseball on the Beach Haven sandlots with his brother, cousins, and friends, and when he wasn't making rounds with Dr. Hilliard he played ball constantly. When he was in high school (where he was an A student), he and family members even formed a baseball team of their own, the Sprague and Cramer club. Doc also starred on the Manahawkin High varsity team; when not pitching, Doc played center field, second base, and catcher. He married his childhood sweetheart, Helen, on the day after Christmas in 1927 and they raised two daughters together.

Currently, most major-league teams favor having two catchers on their rosters instead of three, in order to carve out another spot for a relief pitcher, but in the 1930s, teams often carried three catchers.

Still, Connie Mack, a former catcher himself, must have commiserated with the plight of his third-stringer, Cy Perkins, because on July 4, 1929, he permitted Perkins to take a day off and umpire a semipro doubleheader in southern New Jersey. All that Mack asked in return was that if Perkins saw any talented athletes, he let the Athletics know about it. With that caveat in hand, Perkins slipped off to a twin bill between the Manahawkin and Beach Haven clubs.

Perkins had advance knowledge that a special young man named Cramer might help out the major-league club. It seems that some time earlier, Perkins and his teammate Jimmy Dykes had stopped by the office of a realtor named Van Dyke to look for some vacation property, and Van Dyke tipped them off to the local phenom. Doc did not disappoint on July 4, and at the end of the second game, Perkins approached the young prospect and asked, "How would you like to come to Philadelphia tomorrow morning and see Mr. Mack?"

Cramer shot back, "What time does Mr. Mack reach the park?"

"About 9 o'clock," replied Perkins.

"I'll be there at 8:30," Cramer promised, and the next day he arrived at Shibe Park to meet Connie Mack wearing a suit his brother Paul had bought him for the occasion. Doc's father tried to persuade him not to go, but he did not listen and headed off for his tryout with his cousin Chris Sprague driving him there. Mack signed up the eager youngster and assigned him to the Martinsburg team in the Blue Ridge League.

It was there that in 1929, Doc Cramer began his

Roger "Doc" Cramer

professional career, in a Class-D minor league consisting of teams primarily from western Maryland. He hit .404 and won the batting championship, beating out future Red Sox teammate Joe Vosmik in the final game of the season. Vosmik needed to have a slightly better day at the plate to win the title. Although he had thrown 30-some innings over the course of the season, Cramer was a fixture in the outfield. An oft-repeated tale, perhaps apocryphal, has Cramer copping the batting crown for himself when his manager started him on the mound for that final game; Cramer kept Vosmik at bay by walking him each time he came to bat.

Apparently Connie Mack liked what he heard about the Blue Ridge batting champion because he secured him to serve as a reserve outfielder for the rest of the major-league season. Cramer debuted on September 18 in a ninth-inning pinch-hit role against the visiting St. Louis Browns. An 0-for-5 game starting in left field against the Senators was his only other appearance. In all, Cramer came to bat six times without a hit in 1929.

Doc accompanied the Athletics to spring training the next year but did not make the cut when the A's broke camp, being optioned to Portland in the Pacific Coast League. Years later Cramer related to Peter Golenbock a spring training incident between himself and the Hall of Fame hurler:

"I remember spring training my first year with the A's. I hit a home run off [Grove] in an intrasquad game. I came up to hit the next time, and Mickey Cochrane said, 'Look out, he's going to throw at you.' He hit me in the ribs. I went into the clubhouse, and after he finished his three innings, he came in and he said, 'You didn't hit that one, did you rookie?'"

Luckily for Cramer, he became "a great friend" to the notoriously moody and taciturn Grove.

Doc hit so well at Portland (.347 in 74 games) that Mack called him up to for another viewing in midsummer.

For the rest of the 1930 season, Cramer was a utility outfielder, working his way into 30 games and chipping out a .232 batting average. Playing the field for Philadelphia proved most frustrating for Doc, as the A's had three pretty fair veterans standing ahead of him on the depth chart: Al Simmons in left field, Mule Haas in center field, and Bing Miller in right. Otherwise, it was a pretty heady time for Doc to play for the team; besides the legendary manager and starting outfielders, Jimmie Foxx manned first base, Mickey Cochrane caught, and Lefty Grove, George Earnshaw, Eddie Rommel, and Rube Walberg pitched. Cramer did not play in the 1930 World Series, which the Athletics won in six games over the Cardinals.

In 1931, Cramer played on one of the last of the great Philadelphia Athletics teams and his playing time incrementally increased—65 games and 223 at-bats for a .260 average. He hit his first major league home run, a solo shot, on August 16 off Sarge Connally at Cleveland's League Park, contributing to a 6–4 Philadelphia win. Earnshaw and Walberg had 21 and 20 wins respectively, and Waite Hoyt came over from Detroit during the season and helped the club win the pennant with 10 wins. Grove remained the ace of the staff with a 31–4 record. To round out this wonderful season, Doc came to bat twice in the World Series that year, getting one hit and two runs batted in as the Athletics lost to the Cardinals in seven games.

In 1932, the Athletics failed to repeat, winning 94 games but finishing second to the Yankees. Mack permitted Cramer to pick up considerably more playing time, at the expense of Bing Miller, and Doc responded with a .336 average in 92 games. His time had finally arrived, but his limited at-bats in his first few seasons undoubtedly cost him a shot at 3,000 hits and an almost certain election to the Hall of Fame.

The country continued to suffer in the '30s under its seemingly intractable Depression, and no team suffered more financially, despite relatively good attendance, than poor Connie Mack's Athletics—despite their excellent rosters and contending teams. Beset with financial issues, Mack began to sell or trade his stars to more prosperous clubs, or at the least more adventurous owners. Outfielders Simmons and Haas both went to the White Sox. The development helped Cramer, who received more playing time. In 1933 he worked in 152 games and batted .295, but the team, shorn of some of its key stars, slipped to mediocrity. In a strange statistical quirk, Cramer, a singles hitter extraordinaire, registered a career-high eight home runs that season.

Lefty Grove departed after the '33 campaign, and in the next year the club really felt the pinch by sliding into the second division, although again Cramer took advantage of his opportunities by batting .311. In 1935, Doc excelled again with a .332 average on a team increasingly unable to protect him in the order. With Jimmie Foxx, he dominated the team's offensive categories. As a reward, he was named to the American League All-Star team for the first time, although he did not get a chance to bat in that year's Midsummer Classic.

Chronic economic difficulties continued to plague the franchise, compelling Mack to deal Jimmie Foxx and talented pitcher Johnny Marcum to the Red Sox. Soon

thereafter, Mack traded Cramer and then-promising shortstop Eric "Boob" McNair also to the Red Sox in exchange for $75,000 and throw-ins Hank Johnson and Al Niemiec. McNair had a couple of good seasons for the Red Sox and one very productive season for the White Sox in 1939, when he batted .324, good for 10th in the league. Cramer was voted onto the American League All-Star team each year from 1937 through 1940. He never forgot his first major league manager, though; Doc loved Connie Mack, always considering him a second father.

Philadelphia may have run out of money, but it launched Cramer's career and in his last year there, the club brought onto its roster a catcher named Paul Richards from Waxahachie, Texas, one of the greatest baseball minds of all time and Doc's best friend in baseball.

In 1936, his first season with the Red Sox, Doc had a .292 average, although he hit no home runs that year and did not hit any for almost five years afterwards. He did improve his batting average though, with a .305 mark in '37 and a .301 campaign in '38.

On a personal level, Cramer flourished in Boston, his favorite city. His daughter Joan remembers birthday parties with the players and their children in attendance. In one of her more memorable parties, the young Joan saw Ted Williams walking toward her with his tan pants and brown and white sports coat and in a fit of mischief grabbed a garden hose and sprayed the Splendid Splinter from head to toe. Ted was furious, but he never did catch her.

Another time Doc went to visit a jewelry store in Boston and found it closed. Turning to leave, he stepped on a bag in the foyer, which upon inspection revealed dozens of uncut diamonds. The store had closed for the day, but Cramer contacted the store's owner the next morning and to the merchant's great relief, returned the bag to the grateful owner—so grateful that he supplied the Cramer family with bracelets and rings free for years thereafter.

No matter how famous or well-known Cramer became, he never forgot the times in his own youth when his family did not have money, so each year before Thanksgiving and Christmas, his wife would buy several bags of groceries and load them into the family's 1937 Chevrolet pickup truck. Then, Doc and daughter Joan drove to folks in town having a tough go of it. Obeying her father's instructions, Joan would go to each house and drop off the groceries on the front porch, never knocking or ringing the bell, and from there they would go to the next needy family until their rounds were complete.

In 1939, it was thought that the Sox might finally overtake the Yankees and win the American League pennant, a hope fostered greatly by the emergence of Ted Williams. No one had to tell Williams how great he was, but on one occasion Doc took exception to the rookie's cockiness and threw a punch at him in a vain attempt to inject him with humility. As a seasoned veteran, Doc could be expected to replicate his usual production, and if the pitching held and this Williams fellow fulfilled his hype, pennant fever would embrace the Hub.

Unfortunately, Doc began the season feebly, swatting away at virtually everything without success, and until mid-May his batting average hovered below .200. Exhibiting his frustration, he attempted to attain superhuman feats in the field, throwing himself into the center-field screen in a vain attempt to snare a Hank Greenberg drive on May 4, and then days later performing a somersault in catching a "fierce liner" off the bat of Rudy York.

Finally, in a game against the Senators on May 14, he went 3-for-7 at the plate, raising his average to .213, thereafter becoming the Doc Cramer of old, with multi-hit games following swiftly after the breakthrough. By the end of the month, he had raised his average close to .300, but by then manager Joe Cronin had taken him out of his customary leadoff spot, supplanting him with a slugging young second baseman named Bobby Doerr.

Cramer on dugout steps awaiting action

Yet it was a game against Detroit on the second of June, which seemed to exemplify Doc's year, and indeed his entire career, in a microcosm. In an 8–5 loss, Doc went a perfect 5-for-5 at the plate, a pretty rare feat, and yet the next day's Sox headline in the *Globe* lauded the team's manager/shortstop, trumpeting the fact that CRONIN POLES 2. Like Rodney Dangerfield, Doc got no respect, and his singles hitting paled in the face of power hitting every time.

Although the Yankees pulled away from the Red Sox and clinched the pennant in September, Cramer continued to play hard in what became, at best, a race for second place. His devotion paid off as he finished the season with a .311 average, a truly impressive statistic given his glacial start at the plate.

As the threat of World War II increased the Sox gathered for the '40 campaign, and Doc

Cramer was never a prolific base stealer despite being highly-regarded as a swift runner in the outfield. Some have wondered why Doc did not steal more, although catchers threw him out frequently (he stole 62 bases but was caught 73 times). He was well-known as a singles hitter; one also wonders if he often did not try to go for the double and held up at first instead. During the remainder of the summer, Doc had his typical year: strong defense, swift running in the outfield (but woeful in consummating steals), plenty of hits, but no home runs. The *Boston Globe's* Mel Webb credited him with saving five runs by himself in a game against the Yankees on September 7, and he stoically stayed in a game against St. Louis on September 19 after he tripled home teammate Red Nonnenkamp. On the latter occasion, the Browns' Johnny Berardino had thrown the ball from the outfield to his third baseman but inadvertently hit Doc, who was, in the words of sportswriter Gerry Moore, "so stunned from the blow on the head he was unable to get up and score himself when the ball caromed clear to the grandstand wall off the Cramer cranium."

batted .303, but the winds had shifted at Fenway, with the advent of another pretty slick outfielder named Dom DiMaggio. Fenway has always been friendly to power hitters but less enamored of singles hitters, and as he grew older, the home park became less tolerant of Doc's style.

Cramer loved Boston and wanted to keep playing there, but after 1940 the Red Sox traded him to the Washington Senators for Gee Walker. Doc always felt that Cronin traded him out of spite, as the two strong personalities never got on. The same day, the Red Sox packaged Walker with pitcher Jim Bagby and catcher Gene Desautels in a deal with the Cleveland Indians for catcher Frank Pytlak, infielder Odell Hale, and pitcher Joe Dobson. Initially the trade seemed to work out a bit better for the Indians as Bagby won 17 games for them in 1942 and 1943, but Dobson proved to be a very good pickup for the Sox, for whom he won more than 100 games through 1950.

Without the luxury of batting in the same lineup with Williams, Foxx, and Doerr, Cramer saw his offensive levels drop off and he never hit over .300 again (he did hit .300 on the nose in 1943). Although many ballplayers joined the armed forces in World War II and the talent pool was diluted significantly during the war years, Cramer, by now in his late 30s, did not really capitalize on this phenomenon and he never made the All-Star Game after the trade.

Cramer's stay in Washington lasted only one year and he hated every minute of his time there, preferring to play in Boston. Although Cramer had led the American League in hits the year before the trade, as a Senator in 1941, he had 20 fewer hits in one less at-bat and his average dropped from .303 with Boston in 1940 to .273 in Washington. In the offseason, the Senators traded Cramer and Jimmy Bloodworth to Detroit for Frank Croucher and Bruce Campbell. Campbell had been a good hitter in the '30s with more power than Cramer, but he played for the Senators only in 1942 and did not play again.

With the Tigers, Cramer experienced more frustration at the plate in 1942, batting only .263. But he rebounded nicely the next year with an even .300 mark. He hit well in 1944, too, tallying up a .292 average. And that year Paul Richards came out of retirement to be reunited with Cramer, and they had a much longer run as teammates than the first time as they played together with the Tigers for the next four years.

Having played for a World Series team early in his career, Doc received one last opportunity to play in another Fall Classic in 1945 when the Tigers won the last crown of the war years. During the regular season, Doc continued to range center field while batting .275, even managing to swat six home runs, turning 40 years old in July. In the World Series against the Cubs, Doc got much more of an opportunity to play than his first time, playing in all seven games, batting a lofty .379 with 11 hits, and even stealing a base as the Tigers bested the Cubs.

In 1946 and 1947, Doc played sparingly, and in 1948, he rounded out his playing days with no hits in four at-bats, although he did walk three times. He closed the book on his career with a .296 batting average and 2,705 hits, only 37 of them being home runs. He had two 6-for-6 games at the plate during his career. He coached for the Tigers in 1948 and when his best friend Paul Richards, now managing the Chicago White Sox, asked him to coach there, he switched to Chicago's South Side from 1951 through 1953, helping to tutor a young Latin star named Minnie Minoso. Parenthetically, Cramer also had very brief stints in the minor leagues in 1949 and 1950, playing in 65 games for Buffalo in the IL in 1949 and two games for the Seattle Rainiers in 1950.

After '53, Cramer left major-league baseball, spending most of the rest of his life as a carpenter; he even built his own house in Manahawkin. He enjoyed watching baseball and tried each year to attend a Phillies game. He also enjoyed attending as many old-timers games as he enjoyed meeting up with old acquaintances, and also stayed in touch regularly with Hank Greenberg, Lou Finney, Paul Richards, Pinky Higgins, Rudy York (who often donated cocker spaniel puppies to the family), and Ted Williams. He always had mixed feelings about the Splendid Splinter, believing that the influence that his old friend Ted exerted over the Veterans Committee kept him out of the Hall of Fame.

A very popular and humble man, he constantly had old ballplayers like Jimmie Foxx over to his house. Babe Ruth was a frequent guest of the Cramers and the Babe often carried a flask of alcohol with him in his shirt pocket. Once Doc asked him to visit a young local boy who had recently lost a leg, and Ruth drove over with Cramer to visit the thrilled youngster.

Doc Cramer died on September 9, 1990, after honoring 12 mailed requests for his autograph, in his beloved Manahawkin, where a street is named after him today.

Sources

Interviews with Joan Cramer, March 8 and April 17, 2008. Letter from Joan Cramer dated May 9, 2008.

Boston Globe

National Baseball Hall of Fame Doc Cramer file, reviewed March 7, 2008. The first meeting with Perkins is noted in an unidentified article by Harry Edwards.

Golenbock, Peter, *Fenway, An Unexpurgated History of the Boston Red Sox*, Peter Golenbock (orig. New York: G.P. Putnam's Son's, 1992, paperback reprint, North Attleboro, Massachusetts: Covered Bridge Press, p. 81.) The author thanks Peter Golenbock for sharing his time with him to talk about Cramer and giving his permission to use stories about Cramer from *Fenway*.

The fight between Williams and Cramer was related to the author by Richard A. Johnson, who has revealed the incident previously in his *Red Sox Century*, co-written with Glenn Stout.

JOE CRONIN *by Mark Armour*

G	AB	R	H	2B	3B	HR	RBI	BB	SO	BA	OBP	SLG	SB	HBP
143	520	97	160	33	3	19	107	87	48	.308	.407	.492	6	0

Star player, manager, general manager, league president—only one man in baseball history has followed a career path like this one. Joe Cronin, one of the greatest shortstops in the game's history, spent 50 years in baseball without being fired or taking a year off. Every job was a promotion, and he came within a whisker of being baseball's commissioner in 1965. Late in life, reflecting on all his contributions and responsibilities over the years, Joe made it clear where his heart lay. "In the end," said Joe, "the game's on the field."

Joseph Edward Cronin was born in San Francisco on October 12, 1906, six months after the great earthquake and fire that devastated his home city. His father, Jeremiah, born in Ireland in 1871, had immigrated to San Francisco in either 1886 or 1887 in search of an easier life, but had found mostly hard work in the years since. His wife, Mary Carolin, was a native of the city, and the couple had two other boys—Raymond (b. December 1894) and James (b. July 1896). Jeremiah had a team of horses, which came in handy when it came to rebuilding the city. The family lost its home in the fire and was living with Jeremiah's sister when Joe was born. In early 1907 they moved into a new house in the Excelsior District in the southern part of the city.

The Cronins were Irish Catholics, and preached the virtues of family, hard work, and church. Joe's brothers being much older, he was blessed with a lot of time to play sports, which neither of his brothers had done. San Francisco had a well-established system of playgrounds, with directors responsible for organizing teams in different sports, and playing games against other playgrounds. The Excelsior Playground, as luck would have it, was one block from the Cronin house.

Joe, a strong youth who grew to nearly 6 feet tall as a teenager, played soccer, and ran track. He won the boys' city tennis championship in 1920. But baseball was his first love, as it was for most athletes in the city. Though there were no major-league teams west of St. Louis, the San Francisco Seals of the Pacific Coast League became like the major leagues for the patrons of the city. In addition, many San Franciscans had played for the Seals and then made good in the majors, including George Kelly, Harry Heilmann, and Ping Bodie, one of Joe's early heroes. Joe dreamed of someday playing for the Seals himself.

In 1922 Joe teamed up with Wally Berger to help win the city baseball championship at Mission High. Soon after this event the school burned down, and while it was

Cronin served the Sox as player/manager

being rebuilt, Joe transferred to Sacred Heart, a Catholic school a few miles north of his home. Joe starred in several sports at his new school, and his baseball team won the citywide prep school title in 1924, his senior year. By this time, Joe was also playing shortstop with several summer club teams and for a semipro team in the city of Napa, north of San Francisco.

Although Cronin had long dreamed of playing for the Seals, he passed up an offer to join the San Francisco club by taking a higher offer from scout Joe Devine of the Pittsburgh Pirates in late 1924. In the spring, Joe trained with the Pirates in Paso Robles, California, but soon joined the Johnstown club of the Middle Atlantic League, hitting .313 with just three home runs but 11 triples and 18 doubles in 99 games. At the end of the season, Joe and his friend and roommate Eddie Montague joined the Pirates, working out with major leaguers and sitting on the bench while Pittsburgh beat Washington in the 1925 World Series.

The Pirates were a strong club, especially at the positions Joe would most likely play. Shortstop Glenn Wright and third baseman Pie Traynor were among the best at their positions in the game, and the 19-year-old Cronin had very little hope of playing much in 1926. He traveled with the team early in the season, pinch-running four times and scoring two runs, before being assigned to New

Haven in the Eastern League. This club was operated by George Weiss, near the start of a long career in the game that would eventually land him in the Hall of Fame. By midsummer, Cronin was hitting .320 and earned another recall to the Pirates. In the latter stages of the season Joe played 38 games, mostly at second base, a position he had never played. He hit .265 for manager Bill McKechnie, a promising start for the youngster.

After the season McKechnie was fired, and the new manager, Donie Bush, moved George Grantham from first to second base, blocking Cronin's best path. Joe stuck with the 1927 club the entire season, but played just 12 games, hitting 5-for-22 (.227). The Pirates won the NL pennant again, but Joe had a miserable time and hoped to play in the minors rather than sit on the bench again. After spending spring training of 1928 with the team, he was sold by the Pirates to Kansas City (American Association) in early April. He was back in the minor leagues.

With Kansas City, Joe played mostly third base and struggled to regain his batting stroke after a year of playing so infrequently. In July he was hitting just .245 and feared he might be sent to a lower classification club. Instead, Joe's ship suddenly came in. Joe Engel, a scout for the Washington Senators, was making a scouting trip in the Midwest when he discovered that Cronin, whom he remembered from the Pirates, was available. The Senators, it turned out, needed an infielder, and Engel made the purchase.

Joe reported to Washington in mid-July. When Engel brought him to meet Clark Griffith, the Senators' owner, they first had to meet Mildred Robertson, Griffith's niece and secretary. In fact, Engel had sent a telegram to Mildred before his arrival, warning her that he had signed her future husband. As it turned out, Joe and Mildred soon began a long courtship before being married after the 1934 season.

The Senators needed a shortstop, oddly, because of an arm injury suffered by their left fielder, Goose Goslin, which kept him from throwing the ball more than a few feet. Goslin was such a great hitter that the club needed his bat, so the shortstop, Bobby Reeves, had to run out to left field to retrieve relay throws. Though hitting well over .300 in June, Reeves began to lose weight rapidly, and at the very least the team needed a capable reserve. Cronin began as Reeves' backup, but eventually manager Bucky Harris began playing Joe most of the time. He hit just

Shortstop Cronin with the Red Sox

.242 in 63 games but played an excellent shortstop and became a favorite of his manager.

After the season Harris was fired and replaced by Walter Johnson. Johnson was a longtime Senators hero, but was not familiar with Cronin at all and said he'd keep an open mind. The next spring Johnson moved Ossie Bluege from third base to shortstop and installed Jackie Hayes at third, but an early-season injury to Bluege gave Cronin an opening, and his strong play forced the recovered Bluege back to third base. In 145 games, including 143 at shortstop, Joe hit a solid .282 with eight home runs and 29 doubles. His 62 errors, due mainly to overaggressive throwing, did not cause alarm. Turning 22 that fall, Cronin was one of the brightest young players in the game.

In 1930 Cronin took his game up another notch, becoming the best shortstop and one of the best players in baseball. Joe hit .346 for the season, with 203 hits and 126 runs batted in. In fact, the baseball writers voted Joe the league's MVP, ahead of Al Simmons and Lou Gehrig. It was not until 1931 that the writers' award became the "official" MVP award, but Cronin was recognized in the press as the recipient in 1930. *The Sporting News* also gave Cronin its Player of the Year award. The Senators' 94 wins were eight shy of the great Philadelphia Athletics' 102–52 record.

Other than baseball, the principal excitement in Joe's life was his relationship with Mildred Robertson. Per Joe Engel's prophesy, Joe and Mildred had taken to each other right away, but it was anything but a whirlwind romance. Joe began by dropping in to the office more often than he needed to, but their courtship became more traditional in the spring of 1930 during spring training. As her uncle's secretary, Mildred accompanied the team to their spring camp in Biloxi, Mississippi, every year. By the time the Senators returned from spring training to Washington in 1930, Joe and Mildred were dating twice a week when the team was home. Joe was adamant that the relationship remain a secret lest people write that Joe was trying to get in good with the boss.

On the field, Joe maintained his new plateau of excellence. In 1931 he hit .306 with 12 home runs and 126 runs batted in, as his club won 92 games, again well back of the Athletics. The next year he overcame a chipped bone in his thumb, suffered when he was struck by a pitch in June, to hit .318 with 116 runs batted in and a league-leading 18 triples. His club won 93 games, its third straight 90-win season and the third best record in team history. Nonetheless, after the season, Clark Griffith fired Walter Johnson, the team's greatest hero. Griffith surprised everyone by selecting Cronin, just turning 26, to replace him. Not only did he have to gain the respect of the veterans, he still had to worry about hitting and playing shortstop. Of course, there was the extra financial reward.

Cronin silenced all of the doubters in 1933 by continuing his fine play on the field (.309 with 118 runs batted in and a league-leading 45 doubles), while simultaneously managing his team to a pennant in his first season, still the youngest manager in World Series history. The Senators finished 99–53, and held off the Babe Ruth- and Lou Gehrig-led Yankees by seven games. In the World Series, they ran up against the New York Giants and their great pitcher Carl Hubbell, and fell in five games.

The next season, 1934, was a difficult one for Cronin and the Senators. The club dropped all the way to seventh place, at 66–86, and Joe took several weeks to get on track. At the end of May his average had dropped to .215, before he finally began to hit. He got his average up to .284 with 101 runs batted in, but as the team's manager he was more distressed by the showing of his club. On September 3 he collided with Red Sox pitcher Wes Ferrell on an infield single and broke his left forearm, finishing his season. Cronin spent a week away from the bench, but returned on the 10th. A few days later, at the urging of Clark Griffith, Joe and Mildred pushed up their planned wedding to September 27 with a few days left in the season. After the ceremony, Joe and Mildred boarded a cruise ship for a honeymoon trip through the Panama Canal to Joe's hometown of San Francisco.

When the Cronins landed in California, Joe had an urgent message to call Griffith. The news was a shock. The Red Sox had offered $250,000 plus Lyn Lary for Cronin, and had agreed to sign Joe to a five-year contract as player-manager at $30,000 per year. It only needed Cronin's OK. Joe realized what this would mean for Griffith, and also for himself and his new wife. He told Griffith to take the deal.

Two hundred fifty thousand dollars? In 1934, during the height of the Great Depression, this was an unfathomable sum. Cronin was the Alex Rodriguez of his time—his purchase price and contract became part of his identity. Stories about Cronin long after he had retired mentioned his 1934 purchase price.

When Cronin joined the Red Sox, dubbed the "Gold Sox" or the "Millionaires" by the nation's press corps, the club was expected to win. When they did not win, the fans and press around the country typically blamed the high-priced help, including Cronin. Even worse, many of the veteran players Yawkey had acquired—ornery men like Wes Ferrell, Lefty Grove, and Bill Werber—did not like or respect their manager. This should not have been a big surprise; Grove did not like Connie Mack telling him what to do, and he certainly was not prepared to listen to the rich kid shortstop. The team was filled with temperamental head cases, and Cronin was younger than most of them.

On April 26, 1935, just a week into Cronin's first season in Boston, the Senators beat Grove, 10–5, thanks to five Boston errors, three by Cronin, which led to eight unearned runs. Grove did not hide his irritation at each bobbled ball, or his anger when Cronin removed him in the seventh. When Cronin came to bat the next inning the Fenway Park crowd showered him with boos, causing Mildred to leave the park in tears. Cronin tripled, which provided a temporary respite.

It was not always this bad, but it was often bad enough. In July 1936, Ferrell called Cronin to the mound and told him he would not throw another pitch until the pitcher warming up in the bullpen sat down. A month later he stormed off the mound and back to his hotel room after a Cronin error. When informed by a reporter of his $1,000 fine, he shot back, "Is that so? Well, that isn't the end of this. I'm going to punch Cronin in the jaw as soon as I see him." A month later, Werber cursed at Cronin during a game and was ordered off the field. Cronin was not yet 30 years old when all this was going on.

Yawkey and Collins were no help. Lefty Grove hunted and drank with the owner, who looked the other way when his star pitcher openly blasted Cronin in the press. Ferrell apparently never paid his fine for storming off the mound. The Red Sox continued to acquire controversial veterans, players who had had trouble with managers over their careers, and invariably they caused trouble with Cronin. When Collins finally succeeded in dealing Ferrell (along with his brother Rick, who caused no trouble) in 1937, the club acquired Bobo Newsom and Ben Chapman, two of the bigger managerial challenges in the game.

Joe Cronin's defensive ability was a major subplot of the 1930s Red Sox. His fine reputation in Washington deteriorated steadily in Boston, largely due to the complaining of Grove and Ferrell. Cronin had a couple of poor defensive seasons (1935 and 1936) before recovering for a few years until he gradually slowed down. Pictures of Cronin in the 1930s show a large man growing alarmingly larger, and his weight did garner comment in the press. Joe still made plays, partly due (as the manager and player with the strongest arm) to taking all of the infield pop flies, the discretionary tags at second base, and all outfield relays he could, even balls to right field. His real range at shortstop was actually steadily eroding.

After a fine year at bat in 1935 (.295 with 95 runs batted in), Joe suffered through a frustrating season in 1936. The acquisition of Jimmie Foxx and others from the Athletics made the Red Sox a supposed pennant contender, but Joe's injury-plagued season (a broken thumb limiting

Jake Wade, Cronin, and Denny Galehouse during 1939 spring training

hit .285 with a career-high 24 home runs in 1940, then .311 with 95 runs batted in 1941.

Ironically, after his All-Star season in 1941, he quietly stepped aside for rookie Johnny Pesky in 1942. Perhaps Cronin wanted it to be his idea. Even with Pesky in the Navy for three years beginning in 1943, Cronin was mainly a utility infielder and pinch-hitter (setting a league record with five pinch home runs in 1943) during the war years. In April 1945 he broke his leg in a game against the Yankees, missed the rest of the reason, and hobbled away from his playing career.

In the heavily Irish culture of 1930s Boston, the Irish and personable Cronin remained personally popular with the fans and press. Even otherwise critical stories invariably mentioned what a swell guy he was. By the 1940s, Cronin was no longer the young upstart manager, but was a veteran on a team that was developing young talent. The new generation, men like Ted Williams and Bobby Doerr, admired and respected Cronin. The internal incidents ceased.

Cronin started seven All-Star games, including the first three, and would have started a few more had the game existed earlier in his career. In the famous 1934 game, when Carl Hubbell struck out five Immortals in succession, Cronin was the fifth victim—after Babe Ruth, Lou Gehrig, Jimmie Foxx, and Al Simmons. Less remembered today is that Cronin managed the AL team, and that the AL won the game.

With his stars back and Cronin a full-time manager for the first time in 1946, the Red Sox cruised to the pennant but lost a seven-game World Series to the Cardinals. With most of the star players save Williams having off-years or hurting in 1947, the club fell back to third place. At the end of the season, Cronin took off his uniform for good, replacing the ill Eddie Collins as the club's general manager.

In Cronin's first act in his new role, he hired Joe McCarthy as his new manager. He followed that up with two big trades with the Browns that netted the club Vern Stephens, Ellis Kinder, and Jack Kramer, at the cost of a few players and $375,000. These deals catapulted the

him to 81 games and a .281 average) helped the Red Sox finish a disappointing sixth. At this point many observers thought Joe, overweight, struggling in the field, and injured, might be through at just 30 years old.

Instead, Joe rebounded to hit .307 with 18 home runs and 110 RBIs in 1937, then .325 with 94 RBIs and a league-leading 51 doubles in 1938. In the latter year, the Red Sox finished in second place with 88 wins, their most as a team in 20 years. On May 30 in Yankee Stadium, Joe got in a famous fight with Jake Powell on the field that carried over into the clubhouse runway after they had both been ejected. The runway was behind the Yankee dugout, and Joe had to hold off most of the Yankee team.

In 1938 Yawkey purchased the Louisville minor league club, mainly in order to secure the rights to their young shortstop, Pee Wee Reese. After watching him play in a couple of exhibition matches against the Red Sox the next spring, Cronin was apparently not impressed and in July the Red Sox sold Reese to the Dodgers. Cronin was still a good player, and would be a better player than Reese for a few more years. That Cronin appeared to be ordering the sale of a competitor for his job is a decision that haunted him later.

The Red Sox won 89 games in 1939, and Joe had another fine year—.308 and 107 runs batted in. Joe's biggest problem in these years was the Yankees, who were one of history's greatest teams. It was not any great shame to finish second to the Yankees in this era, and the Red Sox did so four times in five seasons beginning in 1938. Joe team back into contention again, but they lost two heart-breaking pennant races in 1948 and 1949.

During Cronin's 11-year tenure running the franchise (as general manager, president, and eventually treasurer), the team evolved from a contender to a middle-of-the-road club. The biggest problem, though by no means the only one, was the club's failure to field any black players. The Red Sox famously had first crack at Jackie Robinson in 1945, and at Willie Mays in 1949. By 1958, Cronin's last season as general manager, more than 100 blacks (either African-Americans or dark-skinned Latins) had played in the majors, 11 of whom went on to the Hall of Fame. None of the 100 played for the Red Sox.

Joe and Mildred had four children—Thomas Griffith (named after Yawkey and Clark Griffith, born 1938), Michael (1941), Maureen (1944), and Kevin (1950). They bought a house in Newton, just outside the city of Boston, in 1939 and settled there. In 1946, they bought a second house in Osterville, on Cape Cod, where the family spent most summers once the children got out of school. When Joe was no longer managing, he would work in the team offices during the week and spend most weekends on the Cape with his family.

During his years as GM, he had to deal with occasional controversies with Ted Williams, the mental breakdown of outfielder Jimmy Piersall, and the shocking death of young first base star Harry Agganis. He also had to deal with rumors that the Red Sox were going to move to San Francisco, or that he wanted to take over an expansion team in his native city. Joe would protest these rumors, saying that Boston, not San Francisco, was his home, the only home his children had ever known.

Meanwhile, Cronin's power within baseball continued to grow. While running the Red Sox, he also served on the major-league rules committee, pension committee, and realignment committee, and represented Yawkey at all the league meetings. When AL President Will Harridge was first rumored to be stepping down in October 1956, Cronin was thought to be the obvious successor. When Harridge finally quit two years later, Cronin was quickly hired to succeed him.

In deference to Cronin, the league office was moved from Chicago to Boston. Cronin scouted the new offices himself, settling on a location in Copley Square. His principal role was to preside over league meetings, building consensus to solve the problems of the moment. The leagues had much more power than they do today—leagues had their own umpires, could expand or move teams without consulting the other league, could have their own rules, their own schedules. During his 15 years running the American League, Cronin oversaw the league's expansion from eight to 12 teams, and orchestrated the relocation of four teams.

In 1966, while league president, Cronin hired Emmett Ashford, the first black major-league umpire, nearly seven years before the National League integrated. In a later interview with Larry Gerlach, Ashford praised Cronin for having the guts to hire him: "Jackie Robinson had his Branch Rickey; I had my Joe Cronin." History, alas, is complicated.

Cronin was twice a leading candidate for the commissioner's job: in 1965, when Ford Frick resigned, and again when William Eckert was forced out in 1968. Cronin ran the American League until 1973, the year the league introduced the designated hitter rule, a rule he did not like but which he helped write. Commissioner Bowie Kuhn wanted to move the two league offices to New York, where the commissioner's offices were. Cronin did not want to move, and he chose to retire instead. At the end of his final season, he was given the ceremonial title of American League chairman.

Joe spent a life in the game, and he was renowned for his good works outside the game. He set up the Red Sox' initial connection with the Jimmy Fund, which became the team's signature charity after its original sponsor, the Boston Braves, left town, and worked with the fund for many years. He received dozens of honors for his work outside the game.

Joe Cronin entered the Hall of Fame in 1956, with his longtime friend and rival Hank Greenberg—they were rivals as players, and at the time of induction they were rival general managers. The Red Sox retired his number 4 on May 29, 1984; on the same rainy evening they retired Ted Williams' number 9—the first two numbers the Red Sox officially put out of service. Joe was dying of cancer, and the ceremony was pushed ahead to ensure that he could attend. He made it to that park that night, but was only able to wave to the crowd from a suite high above the field.

Williams was there, and praised his former manager and longtime friend. After waving to Joe, he told the crowd how important Cronin was to him. "Joe Cronin was a great player, a great manager, a wonderful father. No one respects you more than I do, Joe. I love you. In my book, you are a great man."

After a long battle with cancer, Joe passed away on September 7, 1984, leaving his beloved Mildred and their four children. He may be the least known of the honorees on Fenway Park's right field façade, but no man had a greater impact on Red Sox history than Joseph Edward Cronin.

Sources

This article is derived from ongoing research for a full-length book on Joe Cronin, to be published by the University of Nebraska Press in 2010. Principal sources include Cronin's Hall of Fame file, many articles from *The Sporting News* and *New York Times*, and the online reSources at Baseball-Reference.com and Retrosheet.org.

GENE DESAUTELS *by Bill Nowlin*

G	AB	R	H	2B	3B	HR	RBI	BB	SO	BA	OBP	SLG	SB	HBP
76	226	26	55	14	0	0	21	33	13	.243	.340	.305	3	0

Eugene Desautels, a right-handed-batting catcher and protégé of Crusaders coach Jack Barry, jumped directly from Holy Cross College to the major leagues in 1930 without a stop in the minor leagues. He'd been a high school football star and was admitted to Holy Cross on an athletic scholarship, but his plans to play college football were scotched when the athletic department concluded that he was too valuable working behind the plate. Worcester, Massachusetts, native Desautels was fortunate to play for a couple of truly stellar teams under Barry, and he was quick to credit Barry as an important influence.

In 1929, the Crusaders reeled off 20 wins in a row. It's not surprising that scouts flocked to watch the team. The 20th consecutive win was on June 11, 1929, and Desautels hit two triples in the game and stole a base. The Crusaders finished the year with a 28–2 record. They'd been 19–3 in 1928 and were 17–3–1 in 1930, winning the Eastern Championship each of the three seasons. When "Red" Desautels was inducted into the Holy Cross Varsity Club Hall of Fame in 1981, he was celebrated as the best catcher in Holy Cross history. His batting average increased each year, from .368 to .423 to .484. It was Detroit Tigers scout Jean Dubuc who signed Desautels.

Eugene Abraham Desautels was born in Worcester, Massachusetts, on June 13, 1907, to Victor William "Willie" Desautels and Mary "Dollie" Willette. Willie was born in Quebec and moved to the Quinebaug Village section of Dudley, Massachusetts by 1890. Dudley, a town located 18 miles south of Worcester on the Connecticut border, attracted many French-Canadians to work in its textile mills. Willie (1877–1967) worked as a laborer and later was foreman in a satinet mill (satinet is a *faux* satin made mostly from cotton). Dollie, also of French Canadian descent, was born in Massachusetts around 1880. She and Willie, who were married at age 16 and 19 respectively, had six children together, four boys, Ernest William (b. 1898), Alfred Loyd (b. 1900), Armand (b. 1903), Eugene and two daughters, Pearl A. (b. about 1902) and Viola L. (b. about 1912). Sadly, Dollie died at an early age, sometime between 1912 and 1918.

Gene Desautels

Gene had played baseball by the age of six. His brother Fred wanted to be a pitcher and drafted Gene to catch for him; Gene never had a chance to try another position. By age 14 he was helping out as batting practice catcher for Rockdale in the Blackstone Valley League. The team played three games a week, and during a game against East Douglas (the team featured a young Hank Greenberg at the time), a dispute arose and umpire Bill Summers tossed out Rockdale's catcher. "You can't do that!" yelled the manager. "All I have left is a three-dollar catcher." The three bucks was what Gene took home. Summers said he didn't "give a damn if he was a 10-cent catcher." And Gene found himself in the game. Jack Barry was at the game and he liked what he saw. Gene had entered a vocational school, planning to specialize in textile dyes, but Barry talked him into going to high school and later to Holy Cross.[1]

After graduating with his bachelor of philosophy degree in June 1930, "Red" Desautels joined the Tigers and made his major-league debut in the second game of a June 22, 1930, doubleheader against the Red Sox. He was 0-for-1 at the plate, with a successful sacrifice, in a game called after six innings due to Boston's Sunday closing law that required games to be over by 6 p.m. The Tigers took both games. Desautels collected his first hit on the 24th off Red Sox righty Hod Lisenbee. Ray Hayworth, Detroit's main man behind the plate, played in only 77 games that year. Pinky Hargrave was the most-used reserve backstop, with 55 games, followed by Desautels who appeared in 42 games. Gene's batting was anemic, however, just .190, with nine RBIs to his credit.

That was the story throughout his career. Except for his 1938 season with the Red Sox, Desautels was valued much more for his catching talents and work with the pitchers than for his bat.

Years later, Joe Cronin, the former Red Sox manager but by then president of the American League, was asked in testimony before the Senate Antitrust Subcommittee if he'd even seen a player win an argument with an umpire. Yes, he told the senators: "Gene Desautels, then a rookie catcher with Detroit, was a cocky young fellow and was giving umpire Cal Hubbard a hard time. On a play at second, Desautels slid in and Hubbard called him out. I think Hubbard was hoping Desautels would complain so he could throw him out of the game, too. Desautels said sweetly, 'You can't call me out.' Hubbard blustered, 'Oh, no? Why not?' 'Because I'm sitting on the ball.'" [*Washington Post*, February 19, 1964]

Come 1931, Desautels dropped down a notch and became the fourth catcher on the Tigers depth chart. Ray Hayworth remained No. 1, with the recently added Johnny Grabowski and Wally Schang sharing backup roles. Gene was seen (in the *Washington Post*) as "a clever youngster who is not any too effective with the stick." Consequently, he played most of the year for Columbus of the American Association and got some work in; he hit .273 in 275 at-bats, driving in 32 runs. Gene got into three September games with the big-league club, managing just one single in 11 at-bats.

He played in Detroit for the next two years, again in a reserve role sharing duties with Muddy Ruel in 1932 with Hayworth playing a little more than half the games. Gene was with the ballclub but sat on the bench for a full 100 games before getting his first start. Desautels got the nod as second-string catcher for 1933, but his hitting held him back from seeing more work. He caught in 30 games in 1933, a couple more than Johnny Pasek. The stick work was still problematic; he hit .236 in 1932 but only .143 in 1933, and drove in but six runs in the two years combined. Though he was not used as much as he would have liked, Desautels told interviewer Brent Kelley that manager Bucky Harris "did more for me than anyone."

When Mickey Cochrane took over as catcher-manager for the Tigers in 1934, Hayworth dropped to second string, and it was back to the American Association for Desautels. He was optioned to Toledo in early April. He spent the full year catching for the Mud Hens and fared better against American Association pitching, hitting .268. Then he headed west, sold to Hollywood on November 28, 1934. He got in a full year of work with the Hollywood Stars in 1935. Manager Frank Shellenback had quite a team, with Bobby Doerr, George Myatt, Vince DiMaggio, and more. And Gene found himself a Hollywood Star on the silver screen, too. The final scene in the 1935 motion picture *Alibi Ike* was shot at Los Angeles' Wrigley Field, starring Joe E. Brown and Olivia DeHavilland, but included more than a dozen ballplayers including Desautels. In regular season action, Desautels had 426 at-bats and showed some power with six home runs, batting .265. When the Coast League franchise Stars moved to San Diego and became the Padres in 1936, Desautels really picked it up, hitting at a .319 clip in 480 at-bats over 148 games.

Eddie Collins of the Red Sox had a good relationship with, owner Bill Lane of the Padres. On September 4, 1936, the Boston Red Sox purchased Desautels for 1937

delivery. Joining Gene from San Diego on the 1937 Red Sox roster was Padres second baseman Bobby Doerr. Collins kept in close touch with Desautels, who lived in San Diego the winter of 1936–37. Collins had seen Ted Williams with the Padres and was immediately impressed, getting a handshake agreement that Lane would offer him the chance to sign Williams when the time came. Desautels wrote Williams' biographer Michael Seidel that Collins had called him and asked him to "keep tabs on Williams." Ted asked Desautels to pitch to him throughout the winter months after the 1936 season and Gene did, "by the hour that winter . . . willing enough but not at the pace Williams desired." He later advised Collins to purchase the option on Ted.

A few days before the 1937 season opened, Gene Desautels returned to Worcester and saw his Red Sox shut out the Holy Cross Crusaders, 5–0. After Rick Ferrell was traded to the Senators in June, Desautels became Boston's first-string catcher, backed up by Moe Berg. He played in close to two-thirds of the games and batted .243. He drove in 27 runs. The Sox finished in fifth place.

Desautels moved and took up residence in Quinebaug, Connecticut. He enjoyed playing for New England's major-league team. In 1938, with Johnny Peacock as his backup, Gene did even better, and he surprised his manager; before the 1938 season Cronin said, "We're a little weak in catching. Gene Desautels, he's a corking receiver, and a grand boy, but he doesn't hit much." Wearing number 2 now that Rick Ferrell had been traded to Washington, Gene had his best season, batting .291, driving in 48 runs and even hitting his first two major-league home runs. The first came on April 26 in Washington, an inside-the-park blast to Griffith Stadium's deep center field off former Red Sox pitcher Pete Appleton (previously known as Pete Jablonowski), and the second was hit on May 14 off knuckleballer Dutch Leonard, also of the Washington Senators.

There was an unusual incident that occurred in either 1937 or 1938, when Desautels may have helped save Joe Cronin's life—or Eric McNair's! Peter Golenbock quoted a player who preferred to remain anonymous as saying that he and Desautels were sitting in the Book Cadillac Hotel and heard a noise outside their seventh- or eighth-floor window. It was Eric McNair outside on the ledge. He was "stiff as a hoot owl. And he had a gun in his hand." He told the two ballplayers, "I'm going to kill Cronin." It took them about 45 minutes, but they eventually talked McNair back inside. "That ledge wasn't very wide," Desautels told Golenbock, "and we were afraid he might fall off and kill himself, because he had been drinking. If he had slipped, he would have been dead." [*Red Sox Nation*, pp. 99–100]

Desautels was never a star backstop. The Red Sox simply lacked great catchers in these days. Entering 1939, Harry Ferguson of United Press offered the assessment that "Gene Desautels and John Peacock make up an adequate but not brilliant catching staff." The left-handed-hitting Peacock pushed his way into a platoon situation, garnering 274 at-bats compared to Gene's 226. Peacock hit .277 and Desautels .243, matching his 1937 mark and distinctly down from the .291 he'd hit in '38. Gene started the season dismally, hitting well under .200 for the first couple of months, but was considered a solid defensive catcher in whom the pitchers had confidence.

A July 2 game against the Yankees showed some of his grit. In the first inning of the day's doubleheader, Tommy Henrich collided at home plate and knocked Gene cold—but he held onto the ball and Henrich was out.

Jack Malaney of the *Boston Post* paid Gene a real tribute in the August 17, 1939, *Sporting News*, noting that "Gene Desautels caught all of the 12 victories Lefty Grove had pitched without ever once shaking off his catcher." Gene came up with a "lame arm" in mid-August, though, and had to take a few days off for treatment.

Looking back on Red's tenure with the team over his first three seasons, owner Tom Yawkey nodded in his direction while sitting in the stands in Sarasota in March 1940 and said, "There's a man who does not get the credit that belongs to him. Gene may not hit as hard as some other catchers you could name, but for my money there is nothing wrong with his catching. He is one of those steady workmen who does everything easily and gracefully, with the result that not too much attention is paid him." [*The Sporting News*, April 4, 1940] Joe Cronin agreed, calling Gene "the most underrated catcher in the American League." Desautels worked hard, too, and worked "as hard and as faithfully as if he were a rookie trying to earn a job," the newspaper said.

Desautels caught one more year for the Red Sox, in 1940, with both he and Johnny Peacock beating back a challenge for the catcher's slot from George Lacy of Minneapolis; Gene played more than Peacock but still fell short on offense, declining further at bat, hitting just .225. Cronin was never fully satisfied with either. SABR's Mark Armour notes that the role of catcher had become such a sinkhole for the team that Jimmie Foxx volunteered to catch to allow Lou Finney the chance to play first base. Foxx was the regular catcher for six weeks or so, and appeared in 42 games behind the plate. After the 1940 season, the Sox helped engineer a three-team trade in December that saw Desautels, Jim Bagby, and Gee Walker go to the Indians, while catcher Frankie Pytlak, Odell Hale and Joe Dobson came to Boston. The Red Sox had shipped Doc Cramer to the Washington Senators, acquiring Walker so they could package him in the deal. The Indians felt that Gene would be "every bit as good as Pytlak" as their second-string catcher. Desautels declared, "Thank goodness I won't have to face that Bob Feller again." He thought it was a good trade for Cleveland. Jim Bagby, in a subtle slap at Joe Cronin, said he thought that playing "under different management" would benefit him. "I didn't pitch my own game in Boston," he said.

The *Washington Post*'s Shirley Povich found the trade fascinating, but didn't think the Red Sox improved themselves any. It was Walker who was the key to the deal for the Indians, he wrote. "Desautels and Bagby scarcely figure to bolster the Cleveland club. . . . Desautels is a nice sort of lad, but he has been the chief reason why the Boston catching staff was never rated highly and why, finally, Jimmy Foxx was called behind the bat last season. The Indians will hardly use Desautels much." The Indians had Rollie Hemsley as their first-string catcher but he was showing signs of self-limitation, both in terms of age and alcohol. In early January, the Tribe picked up George Susce as a backup, but Desautels got into 66 ballgames and was kept busy. He was a hard worker who generally got good marks for his catching, but really struggled with his hitting. To his credit, he kept trying. Arch Ward led a March 1941 column in the *Chicago Tribune* by noting that, despite 12 years in baseball, he "still asks other players to help him improve his hitting."

It wasn't long before Desautels began to make a good impression on the field. Bill Cunningham wrote a May 21 column in the *Washington Post* praising Hemsley ("one of the most notorious bottlemen in all baseball") for his success with sobriety, and added, "Desautels . . . seems ideal as Hemsley's understudy and Cleveland is delighted with him." There were very few outstanding games, though. On July 5, he was 2-for-4 and drove in two. He had his third and last big league home run on May 14 at Yankee Stadium off future Hall of Famer Red Ruffing. By year's end, though, Gene had pretty much matched his 1940 totals—17 RBIs but a lower average, just .201. There was one embarrassing moment for him on July 26, at Fenway Park, when he looked to have singled to right field but Lou Finney played the ball so quickly that he threw out Gene before he reached first base.

After the season, Cincinnati purchased Hemsley from Cleveland. The Indians planned to count on prospect Otto Denning, with Desautels as a backup. Shirley Povich wrote that the Indians could carry Desautels "because he is a good catcher." He improved his average considerably in 1942, but didn't get nearly as much work as had been planned due to a fractured fibula—a broken leg—suffered in a collision while blocking the plate against Detroit's Billy Hitchcock on May 10. He was expected to be out about six weeks, and the Indians called up Jim Hegan. It was nearly 10 weeks, though, before Desautels returned, catching two innings of a game and singling. Hegan replaced him as a runner and saw the game through to the 12th inning, when Hegan singled in the winning run. In the first game of two on August 11, Gene set a major league record for the longest game played in which a catcher had neither a putout nor an assist—a

14-inning game that ended in a 0–0 tie. Al Milnar had a no-hitter through 8⅔ innings until Doc Cramer broke up his bid—but he didn't strike out even one batter all game long. In December, the Indians acquired Buddy Rosar from the Yankees, presumably to make him the first string catcher. However, manager Lou Boudreau claimed in April 1943 that Rosar would be backing up Desautels. Denning had become a first baseman, and Hegan had entered the Coast Guard. In fact, Rosar earned his way and played most of the games, hitting .283 while Desautels finished the season with his usual 60-some games, this year batting just .205.

At the end of the season, Desautels was ordered to report for induction into the United States Army on January 5, 1944. Gene and his wife, Josephine Connolly of Detroit, had two children at the time (a third was born later), and he was working in the offseason at the Heywood-Schuster Shoe Company in Douglas, Massachusetts, but there was a war on. He was living in Dudley, near Douglas, at the time. When due to report, he received a deferment for a month, but made a move of his own and enlisted in the Marines on February 29. He reported to the Parris Island training center in South Carolina—and by August was reported the leading hitter on the Parris Island baseball team. During the winter months, PFC Desautels was named basketball coach of the Parris Island Marines team. He managed the baseball team for two summers—his first time as a manager.

Desautels was discharged from the Marines on July 28, 1945, and was clearly in the best of shape; he was back in the game for the Indians just a week later, playing the second game of their August 5 doubleheader. He didn't play much the rest of the season, though, getting in just nine at-bats and only one hit. In mid-September, not even waiting until season's end, the Indians placed him on waivers and he was claimed by the Philadelphia Athletics on September 17.

Athletics manager Connie Mack, slated Buddy Rosar, who had been traded from Cleveland before Desautels, as Philadelphia's top catcher, with Jim Pruett (who'd hit .303 with Toronto in 1945) as second. Gene was third. On March 29, though, the situation brightened as Mack sold Pruett to the Giants and said he'd go with just Rosar and Desautels. This proved to be the case, though the team results weren't at all favorable—the Athletics finished last, 55 games behind the Red Sox. Gene hit .215 in his last season of major-league ball, driving in 13 more

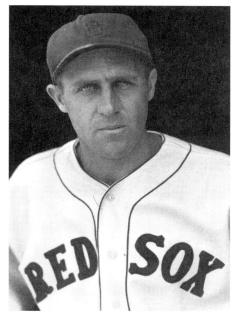

Eugene "Red" Desautels

runs. One of them was a nice one to remember in the years ahead—a bases-loaded single he hit in the bottom of the ninth to win a 1–0 game in Philadelphia on August 29 against the Indians. He was given his unconditional release by the Athletics during the offseason.

Desautels had performed one last service as a major leaguer, though. He was Philadelphia's "player rep" to a meeting held in Chicago on July 29, 1946. The players recommended the implementation of a pension plan, a minimum salary, provisions for players to receive a percentage of money during a waiver deal or trade, a provision for spring training per diems payments, and a grievance committee—all in all, an early step on the road to collective bargaining between an organized players' group and owners.

Desautels caught for the Toronto Maple Leafs in 1947, but could only hit .188 against International League pitching, in 208 at-bats. He did hit five home runs, but it was not a good showing. That was his last year as a player, though he assigned himself 50 times at bat in 16 games while manager of the Class A Williamsport Tigers of the Eastern League. He was appointed Williamsport's manager in December 1947 and served for the 1948 and 1949 seasons. At the end of 1949, Gene swapped positions with Jack Tighe, who'd managed the Class A Flint, Michigan, Tigers farm club—Tighe taking over Williamsport and Desautels taking over Flint. The area appealed to him and he made Flint his residence until his death in 1994, even though he managed the Flint ballclub just the 1950 season. In December, he was named manager of the Double A Little Rock Travelers and worked in Arkansas for one season, 1951, leading the team to its first Southern Association pennant in nine years.

He moved on to manage the Indianapolis Indians of the American Association in 1952, at the request of Indians GM Hank Greenberg. It was not a good season for Indianapolis, which finished sixth and drew poorly. Gene put himself in one game. Gene was named to his fifth club in five years, when hired on November 1 to skipper the Sacramento Solons in the Pacific Coast League for 1953. It had been a last-place team under Joe Gordon, who became a scout for the Tigers, and Gene's first year saw the team destined to go nowhere. The team surprised at first, starting off hustling, though losing several one-run games. In the end, the Solons sank to the bottom once more. Gene did his part for the team, taking part in egg-throwing contests before a game or two, and getting into it a couple of times with umpires, but the staff had two 17-game losers and—as predicted—finished last. Discouragingly, there were few moves made to try to improve the club over the winter. Again, the 1954 team started off better than expected, and this time did well for the first month or so, but then had dropped to seventh place by July, prompting Gene to resign on July 12, 1954. One of the reasons was likely the lack of support; the July 28 *Sporting News* referred to the Solons as "suffering from a shortage of operating capital, leading some observers to believe a change in ownership might take place there before next year." The way Gene put it to Brent Kelley: "They were operating on a shoestring. They couldn't afford to buy anybody or get anybody, and that was it for managing."

Desautels got himself a position as athletic consultant working with the Charles Stewart Mott Foundation in Flint. The Holy Cross graduate used his position with the Mott Foundation to urge players to broaden themselves as individuals. "Too many players . . . depend too much on baseball," he said. "So many never reach the majors and these are the ones who are not ready to meet the challenge when they reach the 35-year mark. During the last few years that I managed I urged all young players to prepare themselves for the day they were through with baseball, so they wouldn't have to start from scratch when they reach the end of the road as active players. Many count on getting some kind of baseball job as coach, scout, or manager. However, these jobs are limited and the game is unable to care for everyone who reaches the inevitable age of 'too old to play.'"

The National Amateur Baseball Federation named Desautels as one of its three vice presidents. He hosted an annual tournament in Flint for several years in the late 1950s. In 1956, he invited the Red Sox' Ted Williams and Jimmy Piersall, and the Tigers' Charlie Maxwell to compete in a June 18 hitting contest as a benefit for the boys baseball program in Flint; Williams hit 25 drives out of Atwood Stadium.

He also helped do some scouting for the Tigers, running an area tryout camp in 1958. Gene was married early in his career but was a widower when he met Mildred Kramer, who became his second wife in 1960. He was working as school counselor at Southwestern High School in Flint, a position he held until retirement. She was a former legal secretary, retired by the time they met and, at the time of our interview, 104 years old.

Gene and Mildred enjoyed taking what they called "gypsy trips." Mildred said they'd "just start out and go.

Put the golf clubs in the back seat, and swimming suits, and away we'd go. We'd start out, nothing in mind, and just go. Especially in Canada. We liked to go across Canada. We had no time to get back. If we liked a place, we'd stay and if we didn't, we'd move on."

They enjoyed a number of cruises, to Scandinavia, to Japan, to Hawaii. Gene's widow didn't think he had a favorite team, but there was one thing he'd had enough of in baseball and that was travel by rail. "He liked the fellows he played with at each place. He got tired of riding trains, though. We went someplace and I decided we'd take the train across Canada into California. He put his foot down to that. He said, 'I've had enough of that train ride in baseball.' They practically lived on trains. That's how they traveled. It was too much togetherness. That's the one time he vetoed what I'd had planned."

None of his children showed interest in baseball, nor had his first wife. Gene Junior became a health-care provider and works as a surgeon in Chico, California. His daughters, Joanne and Diane, both lived in California as well.

Gene Desautels died on November 5, 1994, in Flint. He was 87 and had enjoyed a good and productive long life. "He died of a heart attack while he was shopping at the city market," his widow explained. "He was paying for something—buying, I think, a cauliflower—and he just dropped over. That was it."

Notes

1. McAuley, "So the Three-Dollar Catcher Went to College," an unidentified article signed with just a surname, dated February 23, 1941, found in the Desautels player file at the National Baseball Hall of Fame. Dick Farrington in *The Sporting News* says that Desautels was on the East Douglas team.

Sources

Interview with Mildred Desautels on May 26, 2007.

Drohan, John. "Desautels Rates High With Cronin" Unidentified article found in the Desautels player file at the National Baseball Hall of Fame. May 17, 1940.

Farrrington, Dick. "Desautels Began Catching at 12 for Brother; Ump's Thumb Gave Him Semi-Pro Chance," *The Sporting News*, August 4, 1938.

Golenbock, Peter. *Red Sox Nation*. (Chicago: Triumph Books, 2005)

Kelley, Brent. "Gene Desautels," *Sports Collectors Digest*, January 25, 1991.

Unidentified article by McAuley found in the Desautels player file at the National Baseball Hall of Fame. February 23, 1941.

Thanks to Rod Nelson, Dick Daly, Francis Kinlaw, and James Wrobel/Holy Cross.

EMERSON DICKMAN *by Jon Daly*

G	ERA	W	L	SV	GS	GF	CG	SHO	IP	H	R	ER	BB	SO	HR	HBP	WP	BFP
48	4.43	8	3	5	1	23	0	0	113⅔	126	70	56	43	46	10	3	3	507

G	AB	R	H	2B	3B	HR	RBI	BB	SO	BA	OBP	SLG	SB	HBP
48	36	2	2	0	0	0	1	2	13	.056	.105	.056	0	0

A prewar pitcher, Emerson Dickman was a fastballing, curveballing right-handed reliever for the Red Sox.

Born George Emerson Dickman on November 12, 1914, to George Emerson Dickman Sr. and Mary (Hagen) Dickman, Emerson came from Irish and German stock. A younger sister, Joan, completed the family. The elder George was connected with Fox Films, selling its movies to theaters. Fred Lieb, who profiled Dickman in *The Sporting News*, wrote that he started pitching in grammar school and continued at Nichols Prep School in his hometown of Buffalo, New York. He also took up football and hockey there. Lieb also compared Emerson's looks to those of Robert Taylor, a Hollywood leading man of the day. This earned him some ribbing from the bench jockeys of the American League. In addition to team sports, Dickman was also a squash player.

A childhood friend, Jack Cook, who captained the baseball team at Washington and Lee University in Lexington, Virginia, recruited Dickman for the team. There, Emerson was a two-sport star and belonged to the Lambda Chi Alpha fraternity. During his sophomore year, he won eight games and struck out 73 as the squad won the Southern Conference championship. In the summer, Dickman pitched for the Buffalo Blue Coals, a semipro outfit that went to the National Baseball Congress tournament in Wichita.

The New York Yankees almost signed Dickman after his junior year in 1936. Ivory hunter Paul Krichell was schmoozing with Dickman's father in a Buffalo hotel when he received a call from Ed Barrow to drop everything, travel to Maryland, and go after Charlie "King Kong" Keller.

The 6-foot-2, 175-pound Dickman signed instead with the Boston Red Sox after his junior season. Supposedly contenders, the 1936 Red Sox had a fractious clubhouse

Emerson Dickman at Fenway Park

that proved to be too big a barrier. They were called the "Millionaires" after owner Tom Yawkey's free spending ways. They did their share of drinking. The pitching staff didn't get along with manager Joe Cronin, who was more offensive-minded than defensive-minded. The team craved young pitching, signing Chicago schoolboy Frank Dasso, Dartmouth's Ted Olson, and Dickman. Dickman's career, such as it was, was the best of the three.

Emery, as the Boston newspapers called him, was supposed to meet the team in Buffalo as their train made its way west but didn't join them until June 16, when they started a western trip in Chicago. Dickman warmed up that first day with polymath-catcher Moe Berg. "The finest prospect I've seen in a long time," enthused Berg, "He looks fine. I predict something for that fellow." It was the first time Dickman had picked up the ball in a month.

Lefty Grove and Wes Ferrell helped coach Herb Pennock work with the younger pitchers that year. After Dickman threw batting practice, Ferrell hustled him to the outfield, telling him that he needed to shag flies to get in shape. Ferrell started that night but failed to run out a grounder to shortstop that the Chicago White Sox' Luke Appling airmailed wide of the bag at first. "Don't take that as an example, Dick," some Sox said to the young hurler.

Dickman stuck with the team for the road trip. Farm director Billy Evans felt it would be a good experience for him to get into a game before being assigned to a minor-league team. Dickman appeared in his first game on June 27. Wes Ferrell started against his old team in Cleveland, but the Tribe beat the Red Sox, 14–5. Neither Jack Wilson nor Rube Walberg did the job in relief, and Cronin gave the ball to Dickman to pitch the eighth. He struck out two, walked one, gave up two hits, threw a wild pitch, and gave up two runs, one earned. It proved to be his only appearance until 1938. The next day, there was a small Buffalo contingent at the game and they presented Dickman and Cleveland's Frank Pytlak (another native of their city) with gifts.

As Evans had intended, Dickman spent some time traveling with the big club and working with pitching coach Pennock before being sent to Rocky Mount, North Carolina, of the Class B Piedmont League. At Rocky Mount, the tall, wiry right-hander pitched 63 innings in nine games, going 5–0 with a 1.86 ERA. In 1937, he was assigned to Little Rock of the Class A Southern Association. He went 16–8 with a 4.04 ERA for Doc Prothro's Travelers and helped them to the Southern Association championship before wrenching his back.

Dickman spent the next 3½ years with Boston, mainly in the bullpen. In 1938, he was able to crack the rotation in July after some relief success. He appeared in 32 games, starting 11, and posted a 5–5 record. The lifetime .145 batter also hit his only career home run, off Chubby Dean in Philadelphia on July 2. He finished the season with a 5.28 ERA. He threw his one and only career shutout on July 25, a 4–0 win over the Indians in the first game of a Fenway doubleheader.

Dickman's best year was 1939, when he appeared in 48 games, all but one in relief, and had five saves and an 8–3 record. Though saves were not officially tracked in those days, his five would have been good enough to rank sixth in the American League. (The Yankees' Johnny Murphy led with 19 and Dickman's bullpen mate, veteran Joe Heving, had seven.) Dickman had an ERA of 4.43; which was pretty good keeping in mind that Fenway was his home park. He also had career highs in wins, IP, appearances, strikeouts, and a career-low ERA

Highlights of Emerson's 1939 season included a win against the Yankees on July 7. He entered the game in the sixth with the game 3–3 and runners on second and third. Dickman intentionally walked King Kong Keller to load the bases, then struck out the next two batters to retire the side. This started a five-game sweep of the Yanks that brought the Bosox within striking distance of the New Yorkers (6½ games.) Dickman garnered another win with another long relief stint in the series.

He had a win against Cleveland on July 15. After the Tribe knocked Fritz Ostermueller out of the box in the fifth, Dickman held them scoreless the rest of the way. This extended the Bosox winning streak to 10 games, though it ended the next day when they split a doubleheader with Detroit. Dickman also had a game in St.

Dickman on the road

Louis against the Browns where he replaced Jack Wade in the second and went 7⅔ innings to get the win. They don't use relievers like that 70 years later!

Dickman started 1940 in the rotation, but lasted only a month before returning to bullpen duty. He appeared in 35 games (8–6, with three saves). That year, his ERA crept over 6.00. He saw little duty in 1941, getting into only nine games (three starts), and posting a 1–1 record. His final major-league appearance was on June 26, 1941. Emerson gave up a triple to Roy Weatherly—the two had debuted in the very same game in 1936—and let him score on a wild pitch in the last inning of an 11–8 Red Sox loss to Cleveland. Dickman's major-league career had lasted one day less than five years. After that game he was assigned to Louisville. Nevertheless, 1941 was not a bad year for him. He met his future wife, a cover girl named Connie Joannes. He was in Valdosta, Georgia, en route to Sarasota for spring training with a friend from home, Bill Farnsworth. Bill knew a woman who was there with Connie. They were either shooting a Lucky Strike ad or on a nationwide tour for Coty perfume. Bill set up Em and Connie. Dickman married the 19-year-old New Jerseyite in the fall. (Incidentally, Farnsworth went on to marry Alan Ladd's ex-wife.)

Dickman might have made it back to the majors. His stats weren't great, but he was hardly over the hill at 27 when the attacking Japanese navy sounded the tocsin of war at Pearl Harbor, Hawaii.

On January 19, 1942, just six weeks after the attack, Dickman enlisted in the Naval Reserve. Dickman started his naval career as a storekeeper third class. He spent most of the war at King's Point, New York, home of the United States Merchant Marine Academy but was recruited by Lieutenant Commander Jimmy Powers, erstwhile sports editor of the *New York Daily News* to serve along with some other athletes in the Morale and Athletics Department which Powers commanded. Dickman earned his commission as an ensign and rose to the rank of lieutenant during the war.

Dickman was a physical training instructor, keeping cadets fit, he said, with "Gene Tunney tactics." He also coached baseball at the academy. It was a nine to five life. He'd leave their apartment in nearby Great Neck and head to the academy. Connie would go into New York City for modeling assignments. They couple had two sons (Emerson and Robert) during the war. Before the war ended, he was transferred to Hawaii for a period of time.

Dickman told a reporter from *The Sporting News* that he wanted to get into advertising after the war. In a feature article on his wife, he told the writer that he wanted to open a restaurant or a sporting goods store. What he didn't do was return to professional baseball, but he did play semipro ball in the New York City area.

Dickman coached baseball at Princeton from 1949 to 1951. The Tigers won the Eastern Intercontinental Baseball League all three years. They made their only appearance in the College World Series in 1951 before losing to USC and Tennessee. Dick Sisler was among Dickman's players and thought that coaching was more of an avocation than a job for the former pitcher.

Dickman left after the 1951 season to concentrate on his career as a radio/TV salesman; first at Capehart-Farnsworth, then at Stromberg-Carlson; both manufacturers of the day. Connie continued to model for household products after the war; brands such as Ipana toothpaste, Resistab cold tablets, and Super Starlac powdered milk. She was later the "Avon lady" for many years. The couple had a daughter, also named Connie, during the 1950s.

Emerson's wife described him as a friendly man, which was an asset for his career in sales. Yet he had a sense of modesty and wouldn't bring up his baseball career unless someone else brought it up first.

Dickman took interest in his kids playing sports. Second son Robert played in the Astros' minor league system as a catcher despite suffering from polio as a child. Dickman also golfed after his career and helped Fred Corcoran set up tournaments for the PGA. His last job was with the Yankees. He was a group and season sales representative from 1975 until he retired in 1980.

Dickman died on April 27, 1981, at the Sloan-Kettering Cancer Center in New York City. He is buried in George Washington Memorial Park in Paramus, New Jersey. In 1996 he was inducted into the Washington and Lee University Athletic Hall of Fame.

Sources

Interview with Dick Sisler on January 9, 2008.
Interview with Emerson Dickman III on May 9, 2008.
Interview with Connie Brescia on May 10, 2008.
baseball-reference.com
Ladies Home Journal, Boston Globe, Boston Herald, Boston Post,Hartford Courant, New York Daily News, New York Times, The Sporting News
Stout, Glenn, and Richard A. Johnson, *Red Sox Century* (New York: Houghton Mifflin, 2000)
Special thanks to Rod Nelson.

BOBBY DOERR *by Bill Nowlin*

G	AB	R	H	2B	3B	HR	RBI	BB	SO	BA	OBP	SLG	SB	HBP
127	525	75	167	28	2	12	73	38	32	.318	.365	.448	1	1

It was Ted Williams who dubbed Bobby Doerr "the silent captain of the Red Sox" and a more down-to-earth Hall of Famer might be hard to find. A career Red Sox player, Doerr's fame enjoyed a renaissance in 2003 with the publication of David Halberstam's book about him and his famous teammates.

Born in the city of Los Angeles on April 7, 1918, Robert Pershing Doerr was one of the four Sox from the West Coast who starred in the 1940s—Williams from San Diego, Doerr from Los Angeles, Dom DiMaggio from San Francisco, and Johnny Pesky from Portland, Oregon. Doerr was born to Harold and Frances Doerr. His father worked for the telephone company,

The Silent Captain

rising to become a foreman in the cable department, a position he held through the Depression. The Doerrs had three children—Hal, the eldest by five years, Bobby, and a younger sister Dorothy, who was three years younger than Bobby. Doerr told interviewer Maury Brown, "If she'd have been a boy, she'd have been a professional. She was a good athlete."

Baseball came early. "We lived near a playground that had four baseball diamonds on it and when I got to be 11, 12 years old, I was always over at the ballpark practicing or playing or doing something pertaining to baseball. And when I wasn't doing that, I was bouncing a rubber ball off the steps of my front porch at home." Manchester Playground attracted a number of kids from the area, and a surprising number of them went on to play pro ball. Bobby's American Legion team, the Leonard Wood Post, boasted quite a team. The infield alone boasted George McDonald at first base (11 of his 18 seasons were with the PCL San Diego Padres), Bobby Doerr at second base (14 seasons with the Red Sox), Mickey Owen at shortstop (13 seasons in the major leagues), and Steve Mesner at third (six seasons in the National League.) That was quite a group of 14-year-olds.

Bobby's older brother Hal played professionally as well, a catcher in the Pacific Coast League from 1932–1936. It was Doerr's father who helped bring about Owen's transition from shortstop to catcher in the winter of 1933. The team they put together for some wintertime ball didn't have a catcher so Harold Doerr urged Owen to give it a try. Mr. Doerr helped out in other ways, too. During these miserable economic times, rather than lay people off, the telephone company reduced many people's hours to three days a week—which at least provided some income. "It was just Depression days," Bobby explained. "Sometimes he would buy some baseball shoes for some of the kids, or a glove. Things were tough. Kids couldn't afford to get it themselves, and he had a job. . . . He tried to help when he could from time to time; some of those kids were even having a hard time having meals at home."

Wintertime play was important—unlike Legion ball, the games included people of all ages, including some players who had played minor league ball but wanted to pick up a little extra money playing semipro on the playgrounds. "So when I was 15 and 16, I got to play against pretty good professional ballplayers." That gave Bobby some valuable experience. It also got him noticed.

Doerr told author Cynthia Wilber that his fondest memory as a child was winning the 1932 American Legion state tournament on Catalina Island, winning a regional tournament in Ogden, Utah, then coming within a game in Omaha, Nebraska, of playing for the national title in Manchester, NH.

Bobby played high school ball for two years at Fremont High, in 1933 and the first part of 1934, but he'd been working out some with the Hollywood Sheiks and they offered to sign both him and George McDonald.[1] Both were 16 at the time, and in high school. Bill Lane was the owner of the ballclub and Oscar Vitt was the Sheiks' manager. Hal was playing for the Portland Beavers at the time. The Sheiks offered an ironclad two-year contract guaranteeing they would not send Bobby out. Bobby's father let him sign, "but I had to promise that I'd go back to high school in the wintertime and get my high school diploma." He did. Bobby understands that more professional ballplayers came out of Fremont High than any other high school in the country.

Doerr played 67 games for Hollywood in 1934, batting

.259, all but six of the 16-year-old's 52 hits being singles. In 1935, Bobby acknowledges he "had a pretty good year"—he hit for a .317 average and added some power, hitting 22 doubles, eight triples, and four home runs. He drove in 74 runs, playing a very full 172-game season.

That winter, the Red Sox purchased an option on the contracts of both Doerr and teammate George Myatt, paying a reported $75,000. Bill Lane moved the Hollywood team to San Diego early in 1936, where they were renamed the San Diego Padres. In July, Eddie Collins came to look over the pair while the Padres were playing in Portland, and took Doerr's contract but declined Myatt. Collins also noticed a young player named Ted Williams and shook hands on the right to purchase Williams at a later time. Doerr improved again in his third year in the Coast League, batting .342 with 37 doubles and 12 triples, though just two home runs. He led the league with 238 hits and scored an even 100 runs.

Doerr was 18 years old when he headed east for his first spring training with the Red Sox, traveling across the country to Sarasota, Florida, with Mel Almada. Doerr made the team in 1937, batting leadoff on Opening Day and going 3-for-5. He had won the starting job and held it until he was beaned by Washington's Ed Linke on April 26; the ball hit him over the left ear and bounded over to the Red Sox dugout. In Wilber's book, Doerr says, "It didn't knock me out, but I was out of the lineup for a few days and Eric McNair got back in. He was playing good ball, so I didn't play too much that first couple of months. The last month of the season I got back in and I played pretty well for the rest of the year." Eric McNair played most of the games at second but by season's end, Bobby had accumulated 147 at-bats in 55 games.

Though he batted just .224, he took over second base fulltime beginning in 1938. The right-hand hitting Doerr (5'11", 175 pounds) batted .289 in 1938, with 80 RBIs, playing in 145 games. He led the league in sacrifice hits with 22. Defensively, he helped turn a league-leading 118 double plays. Only once more did he hit less than .270—he batted .258 in 1947, driving in 95 runs.

Doerr explained to Wilber, "I never did work in the off-season, and I never did play winter ball or anything else. I think it was good for me to get away after a full season. . . . In those days, I don't think anyone ever got too complacent. Even after I played ten years of ball, I still felt like I had to play well or somebody might take my place. They had plenty of players in the minor leagues who were good enough to come up and take your job, and I think that kept us going all of the time. I hustled and put that extra effort in all of the time."

In 1939, he upped his average to .318 and added some power, more than doubling his home run total with 12 roundtrippers. Though his average slipped a bit in 1940 (to .291), he became a more productive hitter, driving in 105 runs, with 37 doubles, 10 triples, and 22 home runs.

Again, he led the league in double plays, again turning 118 of them. His 401 putouts also led the AL.

Doerr was named to the first of nine American League All-Star teams in 1941; he played in eight games, starting five of them, and his three-run home run in the bottom of the second inning of the 1943 game, off Mort Cooper, made all the difference in the 5–3 AL win.

Though his RBI total dropped to 93 in 1941, he bumped it back up to 102 the following year, the second of six seasons he drove in more than 100 runs. He led the league in fielding average, too. Come 1943, he played in every Red Sox game all year long (and the All-Star Game), and though his RBI total slipped to 75—a function of greatly weakened team offense—Doerr excelled on defense, leading the American League in putouts, assists, double plays, and fielding average.

Doerr anchored the second base slot for Boston through the 1951 season, missing just one year (and one crucial month) during World War II. The month was September 1944. When the war broke out, Bobby was exempt because he and his wife Monica had a young son, Don. He'd also been rejected for a perforated eardrum. As the war rolled on, the military needed more and more men and the pressures on seemingly-healthy athletes intensified. After the 1943 season, Doerr took a wintertime defense job in Los Angeles, working at a sheet metal machine shop run by the man who had managed his old American Legion team. When he left the defense job to play the 1944 season, he received his draft orders and was told to report at the beginning of September. By the time September came around, the Red Sox were in the thick of the pennant race, just four games out of first place—and both Doerr (.325 at the time, his .528 slugging average led the league) and Hughson (18–5, 2.26 ERA) had to leave. The team couldn't sustain those two losses and their hopes sputtered out.

Bobby's .325 average was second in the league, just two points behind the ultimate batting champion, Lou Boudreau, who hit .327. Doerr was named AL Player of the Year by *The Sporting News*.

Because of the war, Doerr missed the entire 1945 season. He had made his home in Oregon and so reported for induction in the United States Army in Portland. He was first assigned to Fort Lewis and a week later reported

Doerr in the springtime

for infantry duty at Camp Roberts. After completing the months of training, word began to circulate within his outfit that they were being prepared to ship out to Ford Ord, and then overseas for the invasion of Japan. President Truman brought the whole thing to a halt by dropping two atomic bombs on Japan.

After the war, Staff Sergeant Doerr changed back into his Red Sox uniform and returned to the 1946 edition of the Red Sox. He drove in 116 runs, his highest total yet—thanks to the potent Boston batting order. Bobby once again led the league in four defensive categories, the same four as in 1943: putouts, assists, double plays, and fielding percentage.

The Red Sox waltzed to the World Series, but lost to the Cardinals in seven games. Doerr led the regulars in hitting, batting .409 with nine hits in 22 Series at-bats. Babe Ruth, asked who was the MVP of the American League, said, "Doerr, and not Ted Williams, is the No. 1 player on the team."

He averaged over 110 RBIs from 1946 through 1950, with a career-high 120 RBIs in the 1950 campaign. That last full season, he led the league a fourth time in putouts and a fourth time in fielding average. His .993 in 1948 was the Red Sox record for second basemen until Mark Loretta surpassed it with a .994 mark in the 2006 season.

Doerr hit for the cycle twice (May 17, 1944 and May 13, 1947); he is the only Red Sox player to do it more than once. In a June 8, 1950 game, he hit three homers and drove in eight runs. Despite the power demonstrated by his 223 career home runs, his fielding was at least as important. He was always exceptional on defense, more than once running off strings of over 300 chances without an error. He led the league 16 times in one defensive category or another and wound up his career with a lifetime .980 mark—at the time of his retirement, he was the all-time major league leader.

On August 2, 1947, Doerr was given a night at Fenway. He received an estimated $22,500 worth of gifts including a car.

In early August 1951, in the midst of another excellent year, Bobby suffered a serious back problem. He'd hurt it a bit bending over for a slow-hit ground ball; he felt something give, but continued the game. Quite a while afterwards, he woke up one morning and found he could hardly get out of bed or put on his shoes. He got some treatment but missed nearly three weeks before returning to play. He got in only a few more games. The problem persisted, and he had to bow out after just one at-bat in the first game of the September 7 doubleheader. Fears that it was a ruptured disc proved not the case and surgery was ruled out, but Doerr was told to rest the remainder of the season.

At season's end, Doerr could look back on 1,247 RBIs, a career batting average of .288 and the aforementioned home run and fielding totals, and some 2,042 major league base hits.

Bobby had played most of his career for just two managers: Joe Cronin and Joe McCarthy. He felt Cronin was "firm, but he patted you on the back; he always encouraged you in different ways. That was when I was younger, and was a big help to me." McCarthy was a "much firmer disposition kind of guy" who was admittedly "a little more difficult to play for"—but Bobby recognized that he played some of his best seasons for McCarthy.[2]

He'd played 14 seasons in the majors and had a good career. Though only 33, he didn't want

Doerr as an instructor at Winter Haven in 1992

to risk more serious injury and decided to retire to his farm in Oregon. Over time, the back fused itself in some fashion and he found himself able to lift bales of hay and sacks of grain. He began raising cattle, fattening steers for resale, but there was almost no profit in it for the small herd of 100 or so that he could hold on his spread. When Bobby returned to Boston for a night to honor Joe Cronin in 1956, he was asked if he might like to manage in Boston's system. He declined, but did take a position that he describes as "kind of like a roving coach in the minor leagues" beginning in 1957. He is listed as a Red Sox scout for the years 1957–66. He did a lot of traveling, checking out Red Sox prospects in Minneapolis, San Francisco, Seattle, Winston-Salem, Corning, and other locations.

Doing this work for several years, Doerr came to know Dick Williams, particularly after Williams took over as manager of the Toronto farm club. "I got to know him pretty good when he was with Toronto. I have to say that seeing him operate in the minor leagues coaching and managing, and then three years at the Red Sox level, he was the best manager that I saw. Now Joe Cronin was very good. I loved Joe Cronin, to play for. But if I had

to pick a manager to take a team that was potentially a winning team, Dick Williams someway was able to put something together, and I thought he was one of the best managers I saw."

After he was named Red Sox manager for the 1967 season, Dick Williams asked Bobby to serve as his first base coach. He served for the three seasons that Williams managed, 1967–1969. Doerr agrees that Williams "wasn't the most liked guy. He didn't tolerate easy mistakes. Some way or another, though, the players never got uptight playing for him. He kept a tight ship and to take that club in '67 and put it into a pennant winner, there were so many things he did that he was the best guy I saw." They did not have frequent coaches meetings. "He said what you're supposed to do and he let you do it. You worked with the batter. Nobody ever interfered with what I was supposed to do." Doerr's job was to work with the hitters, as well as coach first. He was familiar with most of the young hitters, having seen them while doing his work as a roving instructor. Eddie Popowski had the same store of experience, and both offered a stable, almost paternal influence to an exceptionally young ballclub. Dick Williams told interviewer Jeff Angus, "He helped me out quite a bit when I was in Toronto. In '67, he was a buffer between people, a soft-spoken guy who could help get the message across."

Second baseman Mike Andrews of the 1967 Sox told the *Boston Herald*'s Steve Buckley, "Bobby Doerr was my mentor. When I was in the minors, I always seemed to improve when he came along. I had so much faith in him that if he told me I'd be a better hitter if I changed my shoelaces, I'd have done it."

After Williams was fired late in 1969, incoming manager Eddie Kasko brought in his new staff for the 1970 campaign.

Several years later, Doerr was named coach for the Toronto Blue Jays, and served them for a number of years as the team's hitting coach. "I really didn't want to go back into baseball," he says, "but they made it so nice for me. Pat Gillick was really good to work with. Peter Bavasi. I was there '77 through '81 and then I worked a couple of years in the minor leagues. More or less spring training, up to Medicine Hat with the rookie team. I didn't do much after '82, '83."

In 1986, Bobby Doerr and Ernie Lombardi were named to the Hall of Fame by the special veterans committee, and were inducted with Willie McCovey in August that year. On May 21, 1988, the Red Sox retired Bobby's uniform number, #1.

Bobby's son Don Doerr later played some college ball at the University of Washington and went into the Basin League in the middle 1960s, pitching for the Sturgis club against future major leaguers like Jim Lonborg and Jim Palmer. Bobby rated his curve ball of major league caliber, but says he "didn't have quite enough fast ball . . . didn't have quite enough to go far in professional ball."

In his later years, Doerr devoted his life to care for his wife Monica, wheelchair-bound for much of her later years due to multiple sclerosis. Mrs. Doerr suffered two strokes in 1999 and then a final one which brought about her passing in 2003.

Bob Doerr splits his time now between his two properties in Oregon, and has been able to enjoy more time with his son, now retired himself after a successful career as a manager with the accounting firm of Coopers and Lybrand, based in Eugene. Bob visits Boston two or three times a year now, such as for a reunion of the remaining 1946 Red Sox that kicked off the 2006 baseball season in Opening Day ceremonies.

Notes

1. The Hollywood ballclub of the period was popularly known as the Sheiks, though one can find references to them as the Hollywood Stars. Dick Beverage, author of *The Hollywood Stars*, reports of Doerr's timeframe, "The players I've talked to from that era to a man referred to the club as the Sheiks.

Doerr with a young Wade Boggs

That was the most popular name. But they were sometimes called the Stars in the papers."

2. Doerr's remarks were made in an interview for the Oregon Stadium Campaign in 2002.

Sources

Interviews with Bobby Doerr, May 8 and 23, 2006.

Maury Brown interview with Bobby Doerr, November 13, 2002.

Steve Buckley, "The Silent Captain Still," *Boston Herald*, May 22, 2005.

Wilber, Cynthia J., *For the Love of the Game* (NY: William Morrow, 1992)

Thanks to Jeff Angus, Mark Armour, Dick Beverage. Maury Brown, Dan Desrochers, Bobby Doerr, J. Thomas Hetrick, and David Paulson.

LOU FINNEY *by Doug Skipper*

G	AB	R	H	2B	3B	HR	RBI	BB	SO	BA	OBP	SLG	SB	HBP
95	249	43	81	18	3	1	46	24	11	.325	.385	.434	2	0

Lou Finney was a tough man to strike out. A fast, feisty left-handed hitter with line-drive power, Finney made contact often enough and was versatile enough in the field to play an important role first for Connie Mack's Depression-era Philadelphia Athletics and later for Joe Cronin's World War II-era Boston Red Sox.

A scrappy, curly-haired Alabaman who spoke with a Southern drawl, Finney stood 6 feet tall and weighed 180 pounds; batted from the left side; and threw from the right. He spent 15 years in the major leagues between 1931 and 1947, and fanned just 186 times in 4,631 at-bats, or only once for every 24.9 official turns, one of the 50 best ratios in major-league history.

A .287 career hitter who hustled whenever he was on the field, the fiery Finney slugged just 31 big-league home runs, but hit 203 doubles and 85 triples. Although he could scamper around the bases, he was not a strong basestealer and swiped just 39 sacks in 84 tries. A top-of-the-order slap hitter, Finney scored 643 runs and drove in 494. He collected 1,329 career hits and walked 329 times to post a .336 on-base percentage.

At his best in his natural position, right field, Finney also played first base for Mack and Cronin. "What almost clinches a post for Finney is the fact that he can play first base like a regular," James Isaminger wrote for *The Sporting News*. "He is great on ground balls and handles all kinds of throws. He really is an artistic first sacker. A man who can play both first and the outfield as Finney does is too good to be turned loose." Most often a reserve, Finney still appeared in 100 or more big-league games in seven seasons.

He was highly competitive—Jimmie Foxx once said, "He's a guy that'll cut your heart out to win a ballgame"—and loved to needle opponents. *Sporting News* editor J.G. Taylor Spink recalled in a story about player superstitions, "Bobo Newsom, the garrulous Senator slinger, also has an allergy for small pieces of paper. It was worked to the limit one day by Lou Finney, who, along with the rest of the Athletics, was being mesmerized by Bobo's fast ball. As he took the field one inning, Finney stuffed a newspaper in his pocket. Out in right field, he tore the thing to little bits, and spilled them all over the mound as he came into the dugout after the third out. Newsom went into a tantrum; park attendants had to be called to clean up the wind-blown bits before Buck would agree to pitch again. By that time he was well cooled out again and the A's hitters knocked him out of the box."

A fine all-around athlete "who never has any winter weight to melt," Finney continued his career as a passionate player-manager in the minors when his major-league career ended. Later, he returned home to Alabama to run a small business with his older brother, Hal, a former National League catcher.

Louis Klopsche Finney was born on August 13, 1910, in Chambers County, Alabama, the fifth of Charlie and Mary (Wilson) Finney's 10 children. The Finney family came to America from Scotland before the Revolutionary War and members of the clan served under the Stars and Bars on the side of the Confederacy during the Civil War. Charlie and Mary were of Scottish and Irish descent, were both native Alabamans, and were both educated. They married in 1902. A year later, daughter Ida was born. Their first son, Harold, nicknamed Hal, followed in 1905 (though some Sources list 1907). Jack was born in 1906, daughter Rebecca arrived in 1908, and Louis (listed in both the 1920 and 1930 United States Census as "Lewis"), two years after that. Mary had read an inspirational biography of German author Louis Klopsche, a German immigrant who founded the *Christian Herald*, and tagged her son with the unwieldy moniker. After Louis arrived, Sarah, John, May, Bettie, and finally William, who was born in 1924, followed.

Lou's birthplace is listed as Buffalo, and Hal's as La Fayette (often spelled "Lafayette"), though it is possible both were born on the 1,200-acre cotton and oats farm the family owned in White Plains, a short distance from each town. Buffalo, a half-mile north, was the Finney family's mailing address and La Fayette, five miles to the south, is the Chambers County seat and the 1914 birthplace of boxing legend Joe Louis. Chambers County is located in the middle of the eastern edge of Alabama, along the Georgia border, and between Montgomery, Alabama, and Atlanta, Georgia. Charles and Mary's children

Lou Finney

attended school five miles north and east at Five Points. Oldest brother Hal went on to play baseball at Birmingham Southern College, about 120 miles west and north of the family home. Jack, perhaps the finest athlete in the Finney family, played football for Birmingham Southern, though injuries cut his career short. Lou left high school to follow his brothers to the college, but quit after he fractured both legs in a football game. He returned home and earned his diploma from Five Points High, where he starred as a third baseman for the baseball team and lettered in football and basketball.

Finney played semipro baseball at Akron, Ohio, in 1929, but when the 1930 Census reached the Five Points Hamburg Region of Chambers County in April, "Lewis" was back on the family farm and at work at a rubber plant. Legend suggests that he was seated behind two mules in late June 1930, when a neighbor informed him that the Carrollton (Georgia) Champs of the Class D Georgia-Alabama League needed an outfielder. Finney answered the call. Just 19 years old, he launched a barrage on the league in his first season in organized baseball. He batted .389 with 17 doubles and 7 home runs before Carrollton and Talladega, the league's cellar dwellers, disbanded on August 14.

By that time, he had been spotted by Ira Thomas, a scout for Connie Mack's Athletics. Philadelphia purchased Finney's contract after the 1930 season and assigned him to the Harrisburg (Pennsylvania) Senators of the Class B New York-Pennsylvania League for 1931. However, he failed to impress the Harrisburg manager and was transferred to the York (Pennsylvania) White Roses in the same league. At York, he resumed his assault on minor-league pitchers. He batted .347 for manager Jack Bentley and earned *The Sporting News'* All-NYP honors.

Mack purchased the young Alabaman's contract for the season's final weeks. Just a month past his 21st birthday, Finney made his big-league debut for the Tall Tactician on September 12, 1931, against the St. Louis Browns. The Athletics were in the midst of a 19-game home stand, and Finney appeared in nine games—all at Shibe Park—and rapped out nine hits, including a triple, in 24 at-bats. He scored seven runs and drove in three in his three-week stint.

Finney spent the 1932 season with the Portland Beavers of the highly competitive Pacific Coast League. Often called the Third Major League, the PCL boasted a number of future and former major leaguers. Two of the best in 1932 were Finney and fellow Philadelphia farmhand Michael Franklin "Pinky" Higgins, both of whom made *The Sporting News'* All-PCL team. One or the other was among the league leaders in every offensive category to propel Portland to the PCL pennant with a 111–78 record. Finney slapped 268 hits and batted .351 with 7 triples, all team highs, and finished third in the league's Most Valuable Player voting. *Sporting News* correspondent "Beaver-Duck" reported that "Lou Finney is just about the sensation of the league in right field. In batting, fielding, and throwing, but above all in pepper and hustling spirit, this 22-year-old looks like a certain major leaguer. He loves to play, does his best work in the pinches, and does it with the eager enthusiasm of a youth to whom winning the game for his team means much more than base hits for his individual average."

Still 22 years old, Finney rejoined the Athletics and his Portland teammate Higgins, who was Philadelphia's third baseman in 1933. Finney enjoyed a splendid spring training and was viewed as a replacement for Al Simmons, one of baseball's all-time great outfielders, whom Mack had traded to Chicago before the season. Finney was "emulating Ty Cobb of a quarter-century ago with his base-running," Bill Dooley gushed in *The Sporting News*.

"I think Finney will not be long in making Mack forget Simmons," Dooley wrote. "Not a slugger like the great Milwaukeean, Finney is none the less a sharp hitter and a lot faster than Simmons. Here is a lad whose baserunning will open a lot of eyes. He is not only fast on the basepaths, but alert and daring. Any fielder who loafs in returning one of Finney's hits to the infield will find him taking an extra base."

Dooley was also impressed by the "Alabama flychaser's" desire to improve. "Finney didn't know how to slide into a bag when he reported to the Athletics this spring. One of the first requests he made of the coaching staff was a sliding pit. He practiced in it day after day until he learned." When the regular season started, Finney was still hot. But he was nervous and quickly cooled off, and Mack sold his contract with the right to recall the outfielder on 24 hours' notice, to Montreal of the Double A International League. There, Finney hit .298 with 23 extra-base hits in 65 games. His second home run for the Royals came on his last at-bat, on August 15, after Mack notified Montreal to return Finney to Philly. The sudden recall derailed the Royals' playoff hopes and created friction between Montreal and Mack. Back in Philadelphia, Finney continued to hit well.

For the season, he played 63 games as an outfielder, appeared in 11 additional games as a pinch hitter, and batted .267 with 12 doubles and 3 home runs in 240 at-bats.

Between seasons, there were rumors that Mack would trade the youngster to Boston, but when the 1934 season opened; he was Philadelphia's fourth outfielder behind Indian Bob Johnson, Doc Cramer, and Ed Coleman, and sometimes spelled slugger Jimmie Foxx at first base, roles he reprised the next year. Finney played in 201 games in 1934 and 1935, batted .276, and though he hit just one homer in the two seasons, he smacked 22 doubles. In the early summer of 1934, he fell ill and while he was away from the team, and rumors circulated that he was really a Polish player named Louis Klopsche. Finney felt compelled to assure his teammates on his return that the reports were errant and writer James Isaminger told for the first time the story of Finney's naming. The Alabaman was a valuable stopgap for Mack in those two seasons. When Higgins was hurt in 1934, Foxx moved to third and Finney held down first, and when rookie Wally Moses crashed into a fence and was injured in 1935, Finney moved back to the outfield. In 1935, Mack sent Foxx behind the plate 26 times and played Finney at first, but a spate of Athletics injuries nixed the experiment.

In June 1935, soon after teammate Merritt "Sugar" Cain was traded to St. Louis, he and Finney fought fiercely before a game at Sportsman's Park. Cain, a Georgian, first knocked Finney down, and then the Scotsman from Alabama bounced up and decked Cain twice, then pounced upon him. *The Sporting News* described the intensity, but not the reason for the brawl. Shortly after the grudge match between the two—who had been teammates not only with the A's but with Carrollton—Finney was hit by a batting-practice line drive that fractured his left thumb and he missed 10 days.

Mack continued to feel the effects of the Depression and declining attendance at Shibe Park, and dealt the powerful Foxx to Boston before the 1936 season for players and cash. Rookie Alfred "Chubby" Dean (77 games) shared the first-base duties with Finney, who also played the outfield in 73 games. Playing nearly every day for the first time, he batted .302 in 151 games and collected 37 extra-base hits, though just one was a home run—an inside-the-park effort. The AL leader in at-bats with 653, he scored a career high 100 runs and drove in 41. On July 27, he collected five hits in a 15–8 win over the White Sox. Finney's fifth hit came in the ninth when the Athletics scored seven runs off two Chicago pitchers, the second his old nemesis Cain. Erroneously, the Associated Press article in the *New York Times* reported that it was Hal Finney (who didn't manage a single hit that summer in 35 at bats for the Pirates in his fifth and final major-league season) who collected the four singles and a triple for Philadelphia.

Despite Finney's fine season, he and Dean split the first base duties in 1937. (Dean, a lifetime .274 hitter, later unwisely moved to the mound and compiled a 30–46 record and a 5.08 ERA as pitcher.) Finney did play 50 games at first in 1937, made the only appearance of his career at second base, where he recorded an assist, and played 39 games in the outfield. Bouncing around the lineup and battling an ailment he picked up in Mexico in spring training, a hernia, a chronic sinus infection, and later, appendicitis, he saw his average slip to .251. He hit another round-tripper, again inside the park, his sixth home run in six major-league seasons. With 10 days left in the regular season, Finney, with Mack's consent, returned home to Alabama and underwent surgery on his sinuses, had a hernia repaired, had the inflamed appendix that had bothered him for months extracted, and had his tonsils removed.

Healthy in 1938, the 27-year-old "Alabama Assassin" enjoyed a power surge when he slugged 10 home runs—with nine of them clearing the fences. He finished fourth in the AL with 12 triples and smacked 21 doubles. He split time at first base with Dick Siebert, Nick Etten, and others, served as a fourth outfielder behind Johnson, Moses, and Sam Chapman, and played in a total of 122 games.

In 1939 Siebert started at first base and Finney batted just .136 in nine games before Mack sold him to Boston on May 9. Detroit and Boston had both claimed Finney on waivers; Mack dealt him to the Red Sox, who paid $2,500 more than the $7,500 waiver price. He joined a Boston team that boasted former teammates Foxx, Cramer, and Lefty Grove, along with 20-year-old Ted Williams, who had made his big-league debut 18 days earlier. The Alabaman enjoyed great success as a pinch-hitter—he led the AL with 13 pinch hits in 40 at-bats—then finished the season at first base after Foxx underwent an appendectomy.

For the Red Sox, Finney flourished under manager Joe Cronin and veteran scout and hitting instructor Hugh Duffy. He credited Duffy, the legendary New Englander,

for teaching him to snap his wrist. The results were immediate. Finney batted .325 in 249 at-bats in his 95 games with Boston, with 22 extra-base hits, including a pinch-hit home run at Sportsman's Park. The next spring, he praised Duffy to the *Boston Traveler's* John Drohan, among others: "I was with the Red Sox for a week or so when Hughie Duffy, who led the National League in batting way back in 1894, asked me if I were willing to take some advice from a 76-year-old man (Duffy was actually 72 at the time). As I realized I was not going anywhere, I told him I was more than willing. Consequently, Hughie, who was one of the Red Sox coaches and batted grounders in the infield practice despite his age, converted me from a choke hitter into a batsman who grabbed his bat way down at the end and swung from the hip. He also changed my stance in the batter's box, spreading my feet a trifle further apart. He also told me to put more wrist into my swing like Ted Williams. Well, I was not hitting my weight when I left the Athletics and I wound up the 1939 season with a mark of .310, the best I ever had." The Red Sox posted an 89–62 record and finished second to the Joe DiMaggio-led Yankees, who methodically captured their fourth straight AL pennant despite the loss of Lou Gehrig to the illness that would tragically cut short his life.

In spite of a broken finger in spring training, courtesy of Cincinnati's Johnny Vander Meer, and a nagging cold, Finney enjoyed another fine season in Boston in 1940. He played in the outfield in place of the injured Dom DiMaggio, and hit so well that the Red Sox postponed DiMaggio's return, before Finney himself suffered a leg injury. When he came back, he moved to first when Foxx injured his knee in a collision. When Double-X returned, Cronin asked his team captain to play catcher for the injured Gene Desautels, which allowed the Boston manager to keep both Finney and DiMaggio in the lineup. In either position, Finney hit well. He was the first major-league player to record 100 hits that season, ranked among the league batting leaders through the summer, and finished with a .320 average, ninth best in the AL. Finney and New York's Charlie "King Kong" Keller tied for second in the league with 15 triples, four behind league leader Barney McCosky of Detroit. The 15 triples were a career best for Finney, who also achieved personal highs with 31 doubles and 73 runs batted in. He scored 73 times and was the AL's toughest man to strike out, fanning just once per 41.1 at-bats, well ahead of runner-up Charlie Gehringer of Detroit, who struck out once every 30.2 AB's. "Finney has been tremendous for us," Cronin said in June. "His hitting has won him the right-field job and I'm going down the line with him. He's a great team player. Never squawks and does a great job every day."

Finney continued to credit Duffy, and attributed some of his success to a trip to the Louisville Slugger factory. "I never had a bat I liked in my life," Finney told United

Press writer George Kirksey. "So last May when the Red Sox played an exhibition game in Louisville, I went out to the bat factory to get the kind of stick I wanted. I saw some old Max Bishop models stuck away and I picked up one of them. I liked the feel of them so I had a model made up with a few minor changes. Right away I began to hit better. Then I began to watch Ted Williams and with coaching from Hughie Duffy, I learned to copy Ted's wrist action and follow-through."

Finney, Foxx, and Desautels

Duffy, who had hit .440 for the Boston Beaneaters in 1894 (SABR members' research resulted in the figure being raised from .438), was somewhat modest. "Finney goes around telling everybody I made a batter out of him, but he's exaggerating," Duffy told the *Traveler's* Jack Broudy. "It's true I saw several things he was doing wrong when he came to the Red Sox and we worked on them together until he straightened them out, but that doesn't mean I should get the credit for it. Lou is a fine boy and very appreciative." Duffy told another writer, "Sure I told him about the bat swing, but he worked hard in changing his style and it was by his own perseverance that he improved."

In July, Finney made his only All-Star Game appearance, and coaxed a walk from Carl Hubbell in the NL's 4–0 win. On May 11, he hit one of his two career grand slams, off Marius Russo at Yankee Stadium, to help Boston send New York to a defeat, the Bronx Bombers' eighth straight. Though never again an All-Star, he continued to provide valuable depth for the Red Sox the next two years. In 1941, Finney banged out 24 more doubles and 4 home runs, and batted .288. In 1942, he hit .285 in 113 games for the Red Sox at the age of 31. He was particularly adept in night games, collecting 14 hits in 35 after-dark at-bats between 1939 and 1941—a .400 average, even better than the .324 mark Williams posted in 34 at-bats.

By 1942, World War II was changing the face of baseball. Players began to leave the game to enter the military or to work in industries vital to the war. After the season, Williams entered the Navy, where he served as a fighter pilot. Finney, who had applied for a chief specialist rating in the Navy at one point, returned home to the 171-acre cotton farm near White Plains, Alabama, that he and his wife, the former Margie Griffin, owned in Chambers County. Finney, who was 32 years old and had no children, had received his draft notice, and had to choose between entering military service and staying on his farm to grow food, an occupation deemed critical to the war effort. On January 11, 1943, the *New York World Telegram* reported, "Lou Finney, Red Sox outfielder, was told by his Alabama draft board to remain on his farm or be inducted." He voluntarily retired from the game and sat out the entire 1943 season and the first months of the 1944 campaign. In June, two weeks after the Allies invaded France on D-Day, Finney left Alabama and returned to baseball and Boston, though *The Sporting News* noted he weighed a hefty 225 pounds when he reported. After a week of conditioning, Finney was activated on June 25, and batted a respectable .287 in 68 games. At the end of the season, his teammates voted him a full share, $241.87, of their fourth-place money.

However, his Alabama draft board tracked Finney to Boston in August, and delivered notice that he had been called to active duty and was required to report for a medical examination. Again Finney returned to his farm. *The Sporting News* reported, "Now Lou must stay on the farm until the war is over, which may be too late for him to resume his play."

While Finney farmed through the first half of the 1945 season, the Allied nations subdued Germany in May, and moved closer to victory in the Pacific over Japan. Once again, Finney journeyed north to rejoin the Red Sox. Cronin, who broke a leg on April 19 and hadn't played since, inactivated himself to open a roster spot for Finney on July 15, but used the Alabaman just twice, both times as a pinch hitter, before the Red Sox sold his contract to the defending American League champion St. Louis Browns on July 27, 1945. Finney spent time at first base and in the outfield, though Pete Gray, who had lost an arm in a childhood accident, served as the fourth outfielder for manager Luke Sewell. Finney also played one game at third base, and handled one of two chances successfully. In 58 games, he collected 59 hits, including 8 doubles, in 213 at-bats, a .277 average. On August 1, he smacked a grand slam off Dizzy Trout at Briggs Field (later called Tiger Stadium), and on September 9, he scampered around the bases for the final home run of his major league career, an inside-the-park circuit clout against Washington's Alex Carrasquel at Griffith Stadium.

At 35, he returned to the Browns at the start of the 1946 season. But the war had ended the previous year, and many of the veterans had started to return to organized baseball. And though Finney collected nine singles in 30 at-bats, a .300 average, the Browns released him on May 29.

That summer, Finney returned to his roots and played 45 games at first base and in the outfield for the last place Opelika Owls and later the second-place Valley Rebels, who represented the tri-city area of Valley and Lanett, Alabama, and West Point, Georgia, in the Georgia-Alabama League. He batted .299 and clubbed six home runs for the two teams.

Finney took one more shot at the brass ring when he pinch-hit unsuccessfully four times for the Philadelphia Phillies, his only at-bats in the National League, before the Phillies released him on May 13, 1947, at the age of 36.

Less than a week later, with his major-league career done, Finney returned to the minors, this time with St. Petersburg in the Class C Florida International League. With the Saints floundering in last place and 17 games behind in the standings, his old teammate Jimmie Foxx was fired on May 17. Finney took over a few days later as a player-manager and guided St. Pete to a 71–80 record, good for fifth in the eight-team league. Primarily a first baseman, he continued to spray the ball around. He hit .308 with 26 doubles, 9 triples, and 2 home runs.

Before the 1948 season started, Finney visited the Red Sox spring training camp, where he watched rookie lefty Mickey McDermott pitching. *The Sporting News* reported that Finney said, "I remember hitting against him last spring. He loaded the bases in the first inning with none out, then fanned the side. I was the third one. I worked him down to 3 and 2 and took a toe-hold for what I expected to be the fast one. He broke off a Bob Feller jug that nearly unhinged my back when I swung. He fanned seven of us in the three innings he worked. I wonder if Cronin would let me have him? I'd guarantee St. Pete a pennant."

Though he didn't land McDermott or win a pennant, the Saints posted a 78–73 record in 1948 and improved to fourth with a full season under Finney. St. Petersburg's attendance of nearly 137,947 was more than 23,000 better than the year before, the second best in the league behind league champion Havana. Finney played first base and in the outfield. He hit .314, with 27 doubles, 4 triples, and 8 homers. The fiery Finney not only drew fans to the park, he got them fired up. After a 1948 doubleheader, *The Sporting News* reported, "The fans' ire was fanned when manager Lou Finney was tossed out of both contests. The umpires were given a police escort to their quarters, but some 500 gathered outside and refused to leave. Finally, the arbiters rode out in a police car, while policemen made way with a flying wedge through the crowd."

At the baseball meetings after the season in Minneapolis, wealthy new West Palm Beach owner Lucius B. Ordway lured Finney away from St. Petersburg, which then slumped to seventh under four different managers in 1949. Finney piloted West Palm Beach to a fifth-place finish in the league, which had moved up to Class B. The Indians posted a 74–78 record, 4½ games better than the previous year, and enjoyed an attendance increase of 8,000. Finney played in the outfield, more sparingly than in the previous year, but still batted .286 with 14 extra-base hits. And in 226 plate appearances, he did not strike out once.

Despite his success, when Ordway entered into a working agreement with Philadelphia, the Athletics picked a new manager for West Palm Beach for 1950. The Indians finished seven games worse than in 1949 and attendance fell by more than 24,000. Finney managed to catch on with Temple (Texas) of the Class B Big State League. Temple had finished last the year before, and Finney again turned things around on the field and at the gate. The Eagles improved by 17⅔ games, to 74–70 in 1950 and attendance leapt up to 105,081, nearly 32,000 more than the year before and the best in the league. Finney batted .345 in 68 games for the fourth-place Eagles, who lost in the playoffs to regular-season champion Texarkana.

In December 1950, Finney was appointed to manage the Raleigh Capitals of the Carolina League, but resigned in February 1951 to devote time to his business in Chambers County and was replaced by Joe Medwick.

Two years later, Finney left Alabama to manage the Lincoln (Nebraska) Chiefs, a Milwaukee Braves farm team in the Class A Western League. The Chiefs managed nine more wins than they had the previous year and drew 26,000 more fans, but in the final month of the season, Finney resigned in order to again to join his brother Hal in the family feed and grain business, and was replaced by Walter Linden.

With that, Finney's baseball career came to an end. Lou ran the family firm for the remainder of his life with Hal. Like Lou, Hal broke into the major leagues in 1931. That year he played 10 games; six at catcher and four as a pinch-hitter, for the Pirates. He played 31 games the next year, and 56 in 1933, when he hit his lone homer and drove in 18 runs. He played in five games in 1934, spent the rest of that season in the minors with the Albany (New York) Senators in the International League, missed the 1935 season because of a fractured skull and an eye injury suffered in a tractor accident and started the 1936 season without a hit in 35 at-bats before the Pirates released him. The brothers worked together in Chambers County until April 22, 1966, when Lou, at the age of 55, suffered a coronary thrombosis, a blockage of a coronary artery, and died at the Chambers County Hospital in La Fayette. He was buried in the Finney family plot of the Chapel Hill Cemetery, just outside of White Plains. Hal, who died on December 20, 1991, is also buried at Chapel Hill.

Sources

www.baseball-almanac.com

www.baseball-reference.com

www.baseballlibrary.com

www.georgiaencyclopedia.com

www.retrosheet.org

The Tattersall-McConnell Home Run Log, *The SABR Baseball Encyclopedia.*

Daniel, W Harrison. *Jimmie Foxx: The Life and Times of a Baseball Hall of Famer, 1907–1967* (Jefferson North Carolina: McFarland, 2004)

Golenbock, Peter. *Red Sox Nation.* (Chicago: Triumph Books, 2005)

Looney, Jack. *Now Batting, Number . . . The Mystique, Superstition, and Lore of Baseball's Uniform Numbers.* (New York: Black Dog & Leventhal, 2006)

McConnell, Bob, and David Vincent, ed. *SABR Presents The Home Run Encyclopedia: The Who, What, And Where of Every Home Run Hit Since 1876.* (New York: Macmillan, 1996.)

Hardball Times, vol. 9: 293–301.

Stars and Stripes, The Sporting News, Boston Globe, Boston Post. Boston Traveler, New York Times, New York World Telegram, Philadelphia Evening Ledger.

Lou Finney Hall of Fame File.

Certificate of Death #10955, State of Alabama.

American League Service Bureau, Associated Press, and United Press.

JIMMIE FOXX *by John Bennett*

G	AB	R	H	2B	3B	HR	RBI	BB	SO	BA	OBP	SLG	SB	HBP
124	467	130	168	31	10	35	105	89	72	.360	.464	.694	4	2

As he had done many times in recent years, Jimmie Foxx chose to spend the afternoon of July 21, 1967, with his younger brother, Sam. The two men lived close by one another in Miami, and often got together to reminisce about the elder Foxx's legendary baseball career, in which he slugged 534 home runs, won three MVP awards, and was elected to the Hall of Fame. Foxx's second wife, Dorothy, had passed away in 1966 and his family saw him becoming more lonely and depressed. More and more, the time with his brother seemed to be the only thing to bring a smile to a man renowned for his generosity and good nature.

During dinner, Jimmie Foxx collapsed with an apparent heart attack (he had suffered two others in recent years) and was rushed to Miami Baptist Hospital, where attempts to revive him failed. An autopsy later revealed that Foxx had choked to death, in a fashion similar to that of his wife several months earlier. Broken-hearted, Sam Foxx died just a few weeks later. The sad end to Foxx's life does not diminish what is in many ways a classic American story. He rose from a Maryland farm boy who came from little to reach the heights of fame, and fell back to earth again. However, throughout it all he was able to retain the personality and appeal that still drew praise from his former teammates long after they played with him.

Foxx with Bobby Doerr

James Emory Foxx was born in Sudlersville, Maryland, on October 22, 1907. His parents, Dell and Mattie, were moderately successful tenant farmers. Dell Foxx had played baseball for a town team in his youth and instilled a love for the game in his eldest child (brother Sam would arrive in 1918). According to family legend, Jimmie attempted to run away and join the army at the age of 10, after hearing about his grandfather's military exploits in the Civil War. Young Jimmie did reasonably well in school, but truly excelled in athletic pursuits, including soccer and track as well as baseball. His many hours of work on the family farm would build up a fabled physique that belied his average-sized 5'11" frame. He set a number of local records in track events as a schoolboy, and always retained deceptive foot speed; teammate Billy Werber, an ace base stealer himself, maintained that Foxx was always one of the faster runners in the league.

In 1924 the expansion of the Eastern Shore League brought a team to nearby Easton. The franchise attracted additional attention due to its player-manager, Frank "Home Run" Baker, a future Hall of Famer and local hero from Trappe, Maryland. Foxx's baseball exploits for Sudlersville High quickly came to Baker's attention, and he invited Foxx for a tryout. Showing up in a pair of overalls, the high school junior told Baker he could catch for him if he needed him to do so, and was signed for a salary estimated at between $125 and $250 a month. Foxx played for Easton throughout the summer, hitting .296 with 10 home runs. At the end of July, the Philadelphia Athletics purchased his contract, and he even went up to the big club to watch the end of the regular season from the bench. After the season, he returned to Sudlersville and his senior year of high school—after all, the young slugger was only 16!

The schoolboy athlete did not finish that senior year, leaving in the winter to attend spring training with the Athletics. Foxx stuck with the team as a pinch hitter and reserve catcher, singling in his major-league debut against Washington's Vean Gregg on May 1, 1925. To get him some more playing time, manager Connie Mack sent Foxx to Providence of the Eastern League, where he hit .327 despite missing time with a shoulder injury. He returned to the team in September, although injuries continued to keep him on the bench. Still, he had a nifty .667 batting average in his first 10 major-league games, certainly an auspicious debut. He stuck with the Athletics for the 1926 season, but again saw little playing time. The team already had a gifted young catcher in Mickey Cochrane, which relegated Foxx to pinch-hitting and spot duty in the outfield.

By 1927 Connie Mack was beginning to build a powerhouse. The Ruth/Gehrig Yankees still reigned supreme, and the Athletics were only able to finish a distant second that season. Mack had carefully acquired younger players such as Foxx, Cochrane, pitcher Lefty Grove, and outfielder Al Simmons, and brought in veterans Ty Cobb (in 1927) and Tris Speaker (in 1928) to provide experience and guidance to his youthful stars. Foxx again spent most of the season on the bench, hitting .323 in a limited role. However, this season was significant in that he began playing first base most of the time. Foxx settled in at first base for the bulk of his career, and was an underrated fielder with better than average range. He also caught occasionally and sometimes manned third base,

a position he played in several All-Star games because of the presence of Lou Gehrig at first. In 1928 the A's, a mixture of young stars and old, gave the Yankees everything they could handle before falling just short of the pennant. Foxx became a regular at last, playing first and third and getting off to a torrid .407 start by June. He cooled off in the second half of the season, settling for .328, but was now clearly a rising star. In the offseason he celebrated the turn in his fortunes in two ways He bought his parents a new farm outside Sudlersville, and he eloped with girlfriend Helen Heite, with whom he would have two sons and a tempestuous 14-year marriage.

In 1929 the Athletics blossomed into a legendary juggernaut, romping to an easy pennant, finishing 18 games ahead of the Yankees. Foxx, playing mostly at first base now, had his first wonderful season. Throughout August, he was leading the league in hitting at .390 and running neck-and-neck with Ruth and Gehrig for the lead in home runs. A September slump cost him the batting title to Lou Fonseca (Foxx ultimately finished fourth), but he still pounded the ball to a .354 tune with 33 round-trippers. His on-base percentage of .463 led the league. The A's advanced to the World Series to face the Chicago Cubs.

Foxx's first child, Jimmie Jr., was born just before the Series and he told the press that he would hit a home run for him. He kept that promise by homering for the A's first run of the Series in Game One, and also went deep in Game Two. Foxx delivered a key single in the famous 10-run rally that won the fourth game, and the A's went to win the Series in five games. The championship season brought plenty of attention to the 21-year-old slugger, and he was feted royally in Sudlersville in celebration.

The 1930 season brought more of the same to Foxx and the Athletics. The team took a bit longer to put away its competition, this year coming from Washington, but it repeated as American League champions. A torrid early season was again the fashion for Foxx, as he hit 22 home runs through June and had a 19-game streak in July when he hit .446. He finished the season with a .335 average and 37 home runs, and was one of four A's players to have an on-base percentage over .420.

The 1930 World Series pitted the A's against the St. Louis Cardinals, and they battled to a 2–2 tie going into Game Five at Sportsman's Park. The game was scoreless into the top of the ninth inning. With one on, Foxx announced to his teammates that he would "bust up the game right now." He then proceeded to hit a Burleigh Grimes pitch in the left-center-field bleachers, giving the A's the win and providing the impetus for them to wrap up the Series in Game Six. The game-winning home run gave Foxx one of his proudest moments and he later cited the blow as one of the greatest moments of his career.

Off the field, Foxx continued to enjoy his favored childhood pastimes of hunting and fishing. He often took extended hunting forays with his teammates in the off-season, between barnstorming trips. Some newspapers reported Foxx to be a moderate eater who watched his diet during the season, but he also was known to tip the clubhouse boy famously for bringing him huge meals before and after games. When he returned home to Maryland, he frequently indulged in backwoods country feasts, including lifelong passions for Virginia ham and home-made peach ice cream. He enjoyed movies and collected autographed photos from his favorite stars, with Katharine Hepburn tops on the list. (In 1996, a Philadelphia newspaper ran an article linking Foxx romantically to actress Judy Holliday, but this was later revealed to be a hoax.)

The press took a liking to Foxx, dubbing him with various nicknames—"Double X," "The Maryland Strong Boy," or simply "The Beast." He was often depicted as a simple country boy, unaffected by the bright lights of the big city. Nonetheless, he did develop some expensive big-city habits. Foxx spent large sums on the best clothes money could buy, a tendency shared by wife, Helen. He also had a fondness for personal grooming, frequently visiting his manicurist during the season. As his salary grew, so too did his generosity and profligate spending. The star slugger gave handsome tips to everyone from the bellhop to the batboy, and he insisted on picking up the entire tab at every dinner and outing. He was known to literally give the shirt off his back if someone asked him for it. Many years later, Foxx's former teammates and opponents still spoke with reverence of his personal kindness and good will.

After winning consecutive World Series, the Athletics had an even better regular season in 1931. The team won 107 games and cruised to the pennant easily despite competition from a Yankees team that scored nearly seven runs per game. Foxx continued to play a key role, but was hampered by serious knee and foot injuries, as well as the beginnings of sinus trouble that would haunt him in later years. Still, he hit 30 home runs and had 120 runs batted in, the third of 12 consecutive seasons of over 30 home runs. In the World Series, the A's again faced the Cardinals, but this time Philadelphia was upset mainly because the storied exploits of Cards outfielder Pepper Martin. Foxx hit .348 in the Series and smashed a ball completely out of Shibe Park in Game Four. In his three postseason appearances, Foxx hit .344 with four home runs. However, the 1931 World Series was the last one for Foxx and the Philadelphia Athletics.

The 1932 campaign did not bring another pennant to Philadelphia, but Foxx thrilled fans home and away by making an epic run at Babe Ruth's single-season record of 60 home runs. By the first week in May he had belted 19 round-trippers, and he reached 41 by the end of July, a month ahead of Ruth's pace. In August, Foxx injured his thumb and wrist in a household accident, and although

he played through the injury it hampered his power output. Going into the last weekend of the season, Foxx had hit 56 homers, and he tried his best, hitting two more in the final two games. His total of 58 fell just short of the Babe's mark—but it is important to note that conditions for Ruth were a little easier in 1927. In the intervening five years, screens had been erected in St. Louis, Cleveland, and Detroit that reduced the number of home runs in those ballparks. In an interview with Fred Lieb after the season, Foxx stated that he had lost 6 home runs to the screens in St. Louis alone. In any event, 1932 stands as the peak year of Foxx's career. Aside from his 58 round-trippers, he led the league with 169 runs batted in and narrowly missed the batting title with a .364 mark. After the season, he was named the American League's Most Valuable Player.

After the season, Mack began the dismantling of his championship team. Declining attendance and personal financial woes due to the Depression left Mack desperate for money, and he was forced to sell off the only valuable asset he owned: the stars of his ballclub. Al Simmons was the first to go, followed by Grove, Cochrane, and other starters from the three pennant-winning teams. Only Foxx remained through the first three seasons of Mack's fire sale, and he put up three more great seasons throughout it all. In 1933, the Athletics still had enough left to finish third, helped in large part by Foxx's second straight MVP campaign. Playing through a series of leg ailments, Foxx hit 48 home runs with a .356 average and 163 runs batted in, giving him the Triple Crown that had narrowly evaded him in 1932. He was selected to play in the first All-Star game, and he hit for the cycle against Cleveland on August 14. After the season, Foxx battled with Mack over a pay raise (he eventually received a slight increase, to $18,000) and published a book, *How I Bat.* The ghost-written volume attributed his batting success to developing his wrist muscles and getting plenty of practice.

The Athletics further eroded in 1934, but again Foxx provided them with most of their season's highlights. For the third straight year, he hit over 40 home runs, and even stole a career high 11 bases. The most significant events of 1934 for Foxx came after the season. In an exhibition game in Winnipeg, a pitch thrown by minor-leaguer Barney Brown struck Foxx on the forehead and knocked him unconscious. He spent four days in the hospital and was considered "recovered" when released. However, he suffered from sinus problems for the rest of his life, which in turn led to extreme difficulties on and off the field. Despite this setback, Foxx was allowed to accompany Babe Ruth, Lou Gehrig, and other all-stars on a historic tour of Japan in November.

To help cover the loss of Cochrane, Foxx returned to his original position behind the plate to start the 1935 season. He had a strong arm and by all accounts handled pitchers well, but eventually moved back to first and third because of injuries to other players. The Athletics fell all the way to the cellar, but not without another strong year from its last remaining star. Foxx tied Hank Greenberg for the league lead with 36 homers and finished only three points behind in the batting title race. After the season, the long-rumored trade of Foxx finally came to fruition. Boston Red Sox owner Tom Yawkey, who had already purchased Grove from Philadelphia and player-manager Joe Cronin from Washington in recent years, paid Mack $150,000 for Foxx and pitcher Johnny Marcum (two minor players, Gordon Rhodes and George Salvino were also included in the deal). Foxx reacted positively to the deal, no doubt helped by a $7,000 increase in salary.

First baseman Foxx caught 42 games for the Red Sox in 1940, and pitched once in 1939

The highlight of Foxx's first season in Boston came on June 16, when he hit a ball completely out of Comiskey Park. (In later years, pitchers Lefty Gomez and Ted Lyons enjoyed spinning yarns about the tape measure shots Foxx hit off them.) This was one of 41 home runs that season, and although he did not lead the league in any of the power categories, Foxx's performance was one of the bright spots of a disappointing season for the Red Sox. In 1937, sinus problems brought his performance down dramatically. Foxx went through homerless streaks of 16 and 24 games, and hit a mere .285, the lowest average of his career up to that date. Although he topped his Comiskey Park blast by hitting a ball out of Fenway Park to the right of the center field flagpole against the Yankees on August 12, speculation began that his career was on the downslide.

In 1938, Foxx silenced his critics with one of his greatest seasons. He proved that his power had not diminished by hitting five home runs in the last week of the exhibition season. In May, he hit 10 home runs and drove in a whopping 35 runs. Other highlights followed, including a game on June 16 in which he was walked six times, tying a major league record. The Yankees eclipsed the Red Sox in the standings, and Foxx's home run totals came in second to Hank Greenberg's run at Ruth's record. Still, when the dust had settled over the 1938 season, Foxx had won two-thirds of another Triple Crown, batting .349 and driving in 175 runs, the fourth highest total all time. Thirty five of Foxx's 50 home runs were hit at friendly Fenway Park, establishing what was then a record for homers hit at home. His RBI totals still stand as a Boston Red Sox team record, and his home run total was not surpassed by a Red Sox player until David Ortiz in the 2006 season. After the season, Foxx beat out Greenberg in the voting to take home his third American League MVP award.

The 1939 season brought a new star to the Red Sox, a raw rookie named Theodore Samuel Williams. Williams had boasted to his new teammates, "Wait until Foxx sees me hit!"—but he also looked to the veteran slugger as a mentor and even a father figure. In later years, Williams told his younger teammates stories about Foxx's slugging, and pointed out places in ballparks where Foxx had hit tape-measure home runs. The friendship between the two men lasted until the end of Foxx's life, and Ted remained close to his teammates' family until his own death in 2002. Together the two sluggers formed a powerful left/right combo that brought the Red Sox into pennant contention for most of the 1939 season. Foxx enjoyed another superb season, batting .360, second in the league, and leading the AL with 35 home runs. His great year concluded a remarkable decade in which he was arguably the game's dominant hitter. From 1930 through 1939, Foxx slugged 415 home runs and drove in 1,403 runs.

During his years with the Red Sox, Foxx moved into a hotel and was separated from his family for long periods. It was during this period that the first signs of his drinking problems appeared. Although known to imbibe occasionally, he was never reported to be a heavy drinker during the early years of his career. After his beaning, his sinus problems brought him acute pain—a pain that subsided with alcohol. Roommate Elden Auker recalled several nights when Foxx would be plagued by severe nosebleeds. His ample free time in Boston led to increased after-hours activities, and he bragged to Ted Williams about the amount of scotch whiskey he could consume without being affected. A teammate with the Chicago Cubs remembered that a walk back from the ballpark to the team hotel with Foxx was fraught with dangerous opportunities, as the veteran enjoyed visiting each of his favorite taverns along the way.

Although his drinking problem is a matter of record, it is important to point out that Foxx was never noted for violent or aggressive behavior. To the contrary, he was known as a gentle peacemaker, often mediating disputes in card games and making sure rookie roommate Dom DiMaggio got to bed on time. Tom Yawkey enjoyed Foxx's company and shared many of his favorite activities. According to one story, the player avoided a fine from Joe Cronin for missing a curfew when he returned to the hotel lobby in the early morning with the owner in tow. Some have surmised that the length of Foxx's career was curtailed by his drinking, and it certainly did not help. It seems much more likely that it was a diminished batting eye caused by the beaning and related sinus problems that led to his decline. Foxx also frequently played through injuries that would have sidelined other players, and eventually this took a toll as well.

Foxx remained an all-star slugger in 1940 and 1941, driving in over 100 runs both years and hitting a total of 55 home runs. His triple allowed longtime teammate Lefty Grove to win his 300th game in 1941. Foxx had been eclipsed by Williams as the team's star and was showing signs of slowing at the plate and in the field. His sinus problem became more acute, and he began to wear eyeglasses off the field to combat a decline in his vision. In addition, he grew more critical of player-manager Joe Cronin. Although Foxx got along well with everybody, he never had the respect for Cronin that he had for Mack, and some tension developed (to his credit, Cronin interceded in Foxx's life in later years with offers of employment and financial assistance). When the 1941 season ended, it was no secret that Foxx's days with the Red Sox were coming to an end.

Off the field, Foxx's marriage to Helen had unraveled. According to Elden Auker, she constantly harassed Foxx via phone over financial issues, while all the time carrying on an extramarital affair. Their divorce became final in early 1943, with Helen accusing Foxx of selfishness and other forms of mental cruelty. The acrimonious divorce resulted in a long estrangement between Foxx and his two young sons, James Emory Jr. and W. Kenneth. Both were sent to military schools, and seldom if ever spoke to their father. Kenneth did not reunite with his father until his stepmother's funeral in 1966, and Jimmie Jr. essentially disappeared in the 1950s after serving in the Korean War. For many years his family believed that he was deceased; however he resurfaced in the Philadelphia area and renewed contact with his siblings just a few years prior to his death in 2006.

As the 1942 season began, Cronin told Foxx that he would have to win the first base job from young Tony Lupien. Despite breaking a toe in spring training, Foxx outhit Lupien and started the season as a regular. Just as he was beginning to hit again, a freak batting practice injury resulted in a broken rib. On June 1, the Red Sox placed Foxx on waivers, and he was sold to the Chicago Cubs for a mere $10,000. The move caused great regret and sadness for both Boston players and fans, but Foxx's days as a productive player were over. He hit only .205 for the Cubs the rest of the year, and announced his retirement at the end of the season.

He stayed out of baseball during 1943, a year highlighted by his second marriage, to Dorothy Yard. Foxx and Dorothy enjoyed a warm and committed relationship through thick and thin until her untimely death in 1966, and he became a true father to her two children, John and

Nanci, as well. In 1944, Foxx volunteered for the military, but was rejected due to his sinus condition. He returned to play a handful of games as a player-coach for the Cubs and also became interim manager of Portsmouth in the Class B Piedmont League.

The final go-round for Jimmie Foxx's major league career came in the city where he had starred for so long-Philadelphia. This time it was with the Phillies, who were looking to fill out their roster in the tight wartime era. Foxx was invited to spring training and after hitting several long home runs made the team as a pinch-hitter. By this time, he was having increasing difficulty with his eyes, and also suffered from shin splints and bursitis. Tony Lupien, who had followed Foxx at first base for the Red Sox, also played for the Phillies in 1945 and remembers Jimmie as being particularly down on himself in this period. However, another teammate, Andy Seminick, remembers Foxx as his usual fun-loving, generous self all year, often inviting Andy to his home for big fried chicken dinners.

Foxx hit the last seven home runs of his career for the Phillies, but what made his final season unique was his turn on the pitching mound. Volunteering to help the team out in any way he could, Foxx pitched 23 innings, with a 1–0 record and 1.59 ERA. His high point on the mound came in the second game of a doubleheader on August 19, when Foxx pitched five no-hit innings in an emergency start. (He had pitched once very briefly while with the 1939 Red Sox.) His last major-league at-bat came against the Dodgers on September 23. At the close of the season Foxx retired for good, with a .325 lifetime batting average, 2,646 hits, and 534 home runs—a total that was second only to Ruth until 1966. His total of 1,922 runs batted in still ranked as eighth all time in 2008.

The end of his playing career represented a dramatic transition in Foxx's life. He was now happily remarried with a new son, also named Jimmie Jr., but his divorce from Helen had been damaging to his finances, and he had lost thousands in an investment in a Florida golf course that closed because of World War II restrictions. For the rest of his life, he struggled mightily at times to find a steady career outside baseball, yet his teenage rise to the majors had left him with little preparation to do so. He took a turn in the Red Sox radio booth in 1946, but his Maryland accent did not win over many listeners. He also spent brief periods as a minor-league manager and coach in St. Petersburg in 1947 and Bridgeport, Connecticut in 1949, and worked for a trucking company and beer distributor.

Foxx had received Hall of Fame votes as far back as 1936, when active players were eligible (he came in fourth then among active players behind Rogers Hornsby, Mickey Cochrane, and Lou Gehrig.) However, he fell short of the needed vote totals in six other regular and run off elections until 1951. Foxx was named on 79.2% of the ballots, and earned election along with leading vote

Foxx out hunting after the 1939 campaign

getter Mel Ott. In a brief speech, he merely noted that he was proud to be a member, and proud to have his old manager, Connie Mack on hand. After the ceremony, he spent most of his time under a tree signing autographs. Foxx generally enjoyed giving autographs throughout his life, although toward its end he sometimes had to use a rubber stamp to keep up with all of the many requests forwarded to his home. His family remembers frequent occasions when he would leave the table at restaurants to accommodate his fans.

Foxx got back into baseball in 1952 in an unusual manner when he was invited to manage the Fort Wayne Daisies—a team in the All-American Girls Professional Baseball League. He succeeded fellow Hall of Famer Max Carey, who had become the league president, and was offered a $3,600 salary with bonuses. By all accounts, Foxx's time with the Daisies was an enjoyable one. With daughter Nanci helping out as a batgirl, the team had improved attendance and made the playoffs. In 1992, the film *A League of Their Own* based its main character (played by Tom Hanks) loosely on Foxx, although the women who played for him remember him only as a true gentleman in every way. Foxx did not return to the Daisies for the 1953 season, with his only complaint being the many long bus rides.

After his turn with the Daisies, the retired slugger

continued to drift from job to job. At various times, he worked as a car salesman, for an oil company, and even as a coal truck driver. An ambitious venture in which Foxx was to do public-service work with inner city youths failed to get off the ground. In 1956, he returned to Florida and spent two seasons as a head baseball coach at the University of Miami and as a hitting instructor for the minor league Miami Marlins. After the 1957 season, he was let go from both positions, and found himself bankrupt and unemployed. Invited to speak at the Boston Writers Dinner in January 1958, Foxx admitted that he was broke and unable to pay his way there. All his baseball earnings, he announced, were long gone. After his financial problems were disclosed, Foxx received many offers of employment and even cash donations (which he then donated to the Jimmy Fund). Soon, a good fit was found. After a meeting with Cronin in Boston, Foxx accepted a job as the hitting instructor for the Red Sox's Triple A farm team, the Minneapolis Millers.

Although he seldom took batting practice, saying that he "couldn't do it" anymore, Foxx was well liked and admired by the Millers players. One player he befriended was Bill Monbouquette, a young pitcher on the brink of a solid major-league career that included a no-hitter for the Red Sox in 1962. Monbouquette remembers Foxx as a generous and giving man, "one of the nicest people I've ever met." Both pitchers and hitters picked his brain constantly for tips and advice, and Foxx was always glad to advise. During the season, Foxx surprised Monbouquette's parents with a visit to their home in Massachusetts while on the way to a Fenway Park old-timers game. "I just wanted to let them know you were doing okay," Foxx told the young pitcher on his return.

However, Foxx's tenure with the Millers lasted only a single season. Art Schult, the Millers catcher, recalled that the players "idolized" Foxx, but that he did not get involved in the politics of the game with management. During the season, he was twice hospitalized with high blood pressure and other ailments. Expecting to return to the Millers for 1959, Foxx was instead given his release by the Red Sox at the end of the 1958 season. The official reason given was that the team, for financial reasons, wanted to hire someone to do double duty as a player and coach.

The real reason, however, had more to do with Foxx's off-the-field habits. Gene Mauch, the Millers' manager in 1958, recalled jumping at the chance to hire Foxx, a boyhood favorite, and felt he could help out the team's hitters. Sadly, things did not go as planned. According to Mauch, "By then, Jim had a bad drinking problem, and was seldom at the park on time to be of help. I idolized the man, and kept him away from scrutiny. At the end of the season, Cronin gave him his money and sent him home—it was so sad." Foxx's drinking habits were also rumored to have led to the end of his coaching in Miami and may have affected his employment elsewhere. His alcohol use may have stemmed from his sinus injury, and been worsened by his good-time lifestyle in Boston. However, at this point Foxx's drinking was related as much as anything to the loss of his baseball career. Daughter Nanci believes his drinking problems had a lot to do with the emptiness he felt in adjusting to normalcy once his playing days had ended.

The ill-fated season in Minneapolis was Foxx's last job in baseball. He did occasionally appear at old-timers' games, and was interviewed when Willie Mays passed him on the all-time home run list (Foxx applauded Mays, saying it was great to see it done by a fellow right-handed hitter). A restaurant bearing his name in Illinois quickly went under, and he continued to move around, bouncing from work with a sporting goods store in Lakewood, Ohio, to several part-time jobs in Florida when he returned there for good in 1964. His son, Jimmie Jr. II, stayed in Ohio to pursue an athletic career at Kent State University. Health problems continued to plague the elder Foxx; he suffered two minor heart attacks and his mobility was lessened by a back injury suffered in a fall.

In May 1966, he suffered a terrible personal blow when his wife, Dorothy, died of asphyxia. Throughout the good years and bad, the two had a strong and devoted marriage, and after her passing, depression seemed to get the better of Foxx. He returned to Maryland one last time in August 1966 to surprise a fan, Gil Dunn, who had written him concerning a memorabilia display in his drugstore near Sudlersville. The aging slugger gave Dunn a variety of uniforms, equipment, and trophies, and with brother Sam in tow made the rounds of his old hometown one final time. The locals had turned a cold shoulder to Foxx in his retirement years; a strong indication of this came when several local establishments refused to cash a $100 check, later proven good in a neighboring town. Less than a year later he was dead at 59, and was buried next to Dorothy in Miami's Flagler Memorial Park Cemetery.

In the years since Foxx's death, a gradual re-appreciation of his achievements has elevated his status. As a member of baseball's 500 Home Run Club, Foxx memorabilia fetches top dollar on the collector circuit. The Babe Ruth Hall of Fame and Museum has devoted exhibit space to Foxx, thanks in part to donations from Gil Dunn. In the past few years, Foxx has been honored by the Oakland Athletics and was inducted into the Boston Red Sox Hall of Fame, each time with daughter Nanci proudly on hand to accept for him. He was one of the first players chosen by old teammate Ted Williams to be enshrined in his own Hitters Hall of Fame. Foxx even made it on to a U.S. postage stamp in the summer of 2000. In September 2006, Foxx returned to the Fenway limelight once again. David Ortiz, another perpetually smiling Red Sox slugger, broke his 68-year team home run record with Nanci in attendance.

Perhaps the greatest tribute though, came from his hometown of Sudlersville, Maryland. A monument to Foxx was erected in celebration of his 80th birthday in 1987, and after 10 years of fundraising, a bronze life statue was unveiled on October 25, 1997 in the center of his hometown. The Maryland Strong Boy had come home for good.

Sources

My research on Jimmie Foxx's life began about the same time I joined SABR in 1993. Writing this biography entailed the use of primary, secondary, and interview sources. In addition, I am grateful to the assistance of Mark Armour, Harrison Daniel, Peter Golenbock, Bob Gorman, Mark Hodermarsky, Bill Nowlin, Fred Schuld, and Dick Thompson (among others) in the preparation of this narrative.

Primary and Secondary Sources

Auker, Elden. *Sleeper Cars and Flannel Uniforms.* (Chicago: Triumph Books, 2000)

Canaday, Nanci (as told to John Bennett). "My Dad—Jimmie Foxx," *The National Pastime,* Number 19, 1999

Daniel, W. Harrison, *Jimmie Foxx: The Life and Times of a Baseball Hall of Famer.* (Jefferson NC: McFarland, 1996)

DiMaggio, Dominic and Bill Gilbert. *Real Grass, Real Heroes: Baseball's Historic 1941 Season.* (Kensington, 1991)

Golenbock, Peter. *Fenway: An Unexpurgated History of the Boston Red Sox.* (Douglas Charles, 1991)

Hall of Fame Files, Jimmie Foxx (volumes 1, 2, 3), National Baseball Hall of Fame and Library, Cooperstown, New York.

Gorman, Bob. *Double X: The Story of Jimmie Foxx, Baseball's Forgotten Slugger.* (B. Goff, 1990)

Linn, Ed. *The Great Rivalry.* (Ticknor and Field, 1991)

Millikin, Mark. *Jimmie Foxx: The Pride of Sudlersville.* (Scarecrow Press, 1998)

Williams, Ted, with John Underwood. *My Turn At Bat: The Story of My Life.* (New York: Fireside, 1988)

Werber, Bill. *Memories of a Ballplayer.* (Cleveland: SABR Press, 2001)

In particular I wish to cite the three biographies of Jimmie Foxx, all of which have their own special strengths. They were extremely useful resources and should be the first place for a Foxx enthusiast to go.

I was able to interview the following former players by phone or mail, and/or in person between 1993–200?, several of whom are directly quoted within:

Elden Auker, Dom DiMaggio, Bob Doerr, Bob Feller, David "Boo" Ferriss, Tom Heinrich, Tony Lupien, Gene Mauch, Lenny Merullo, Bill Monbouquette, Johnny Pesky, Art Schult, Andy Seminick, Charlie Wagner, Bill Werber, and Alma Ziegler.

Last and certainly not least, I wish to personally note and thank the assistance of Jimmie's daughter, Nanci Foxx Canaday, who has been instrumental in my research on Foxx for 10 years now. Along with her husband, Jim, she welcomed me into her Florida home for an interview on June 30, 2000, and continues an annual correspondence. Nanci provides living proof of Jimmie's best qualities, and none of my work would have happened without her help.

FABIAN GAFFKE *by Bill Nowlin*

G	AB	R	H	2B	3B	HR	RBI	BB	SO	BA	OBP	SLG	SB	HBP
1	1	0	0	0	0	0	1	0	0	.000	.000	.000	0	0

Before he died, Fabian Gaffke frequently told his family, "I hope when I'm off this earth, they play ball in Heaven." Gaffke was "a sturdy Pole" (in the words of *Milwaukee Journal* sportswriter Sam Levy), born in Milwaukee's South Side to John and Agnes Gaffke on August 5, 1913. John worked in a coke plant near the Allen-Bradley works and Agnes was a homemaker. There were three other children in the family—sisters Nory (Eleanor—who died of a brain hemorrhage in her 20s) and Sophie, and a younger brother, Gilbert, who also tried his hand at professional baseball.

As a youngster, Fabe was always playing baseball, with the strong encouragement of his father, who urged him to practice and practice. There was some baseball in the family; Fabe's uncle Ray Gaffke was "a semipro star of the first water for many years" according to a clipping from a Milwaukee paper. Only illness held Ray back from the big leagues, the paper claimed.

In junior high, Fabian made the team at the age of 14 and, by 15, was also active as a catcher and outfielder with the Nowicki All-Star American Legion team, which won the Wisconsin state championship and the Midwest championship, and in the national tournament at Colorado Springs was the runner-up for the national title. He also made time to become proficient on the saxophone and clarinet, playing in the school band and with a combo of his own dubbed The Rusty Four.

Fabe also played semipro ball for Saint Stanlislaus P.R.C.U. (Polish Roman Catholic Union) in Milwaukee's Municipal Minor League in 1930 and 1931. His .491 average for the Stans led the league in 1930.

In 1932, Gaffke played with the Kosciuszko Reds and led the Southeastern Wisconsin State League with a .525 average. He caught the eye of a couple of White Sox scouts, who wasted little time in getting an option on him after spiriting him away for a week of workouts under the direction of White Sox coach Johnny Butler at Comiskey Park. In doing so, the White Sox scooped the Cubs, as Kosky Reds owner Leo Ryczek had planned to surprise

Fabian Gaffke

Fabe by taking him to Wrigley Field the very next weekend for a tryout.

That summer, Fabian appeared as a right-handed-hitting outfielder and second baseman with Waterloo (Class D Mississippi Valley League) under manager Doc Bennett; he played in 41 games for the Iowa team (163 at-bats), batting .221 and driving in 13 runs. On August 28, the Chicago White Sox exercised his option and that of two other players. His contract was formally purchased in November. Ed Gaffke, as he was known by some at the time, was sent on option to the Texas League's Galveston Buccaneers in January 1933. In March, John H. Murphy of the *Galveston News Tribune* took note of his early play for Galveston: "Gaffke is being called a second Joe Medwick by the fans. He takes a terrific cut at the ball and hits long line drives."

The second Joe Medwick didn't get much baseball in, though. Galveston had a veteran Texas League outfielder who kicked into high gear and held onto his spot on the Bucs. After Gaffke appeared in four games, with just one single in 10 at-bats, he was cut on April 25. Fabe returned to Wisconsin and played semipro ball once more, getting in enough at-bats with Kewaskum (Badger State League) playing shortstop to win the batting title with a .440 average.

In 1934, he wrote for a tryout with Des Moines in the Class A Western League, was accepted, and got in a full year: 123 games, 524 at-bats, an average of .311 with some power (27 doubles, 17 triples, 15 homers). The "Pulverizing Pole" drove in 93 runs. The team won the Western League title.

Moving up to the American Association, Fabe was still growing, listed as 5'8" tall and a stocky 190 pounds. His listed major-league playing height was 5'0"; his weight 185. Gaffke played for Minneapolis in 1935 and 1936, and legendary Twin Cities sportswriter Halsey Hall was impressed. On June 13, 1935, Hall wrote in *The Sporting News*, "The play of 20-year-old Fabian Gaffke in center field has won him recognition as one of the choice first-year men of any season. . . .'"

Gaffke grabs a ball in front of Fenway's left-field scoreboard

The "South Side Hercules" hit .302 with 19 homers in 1935 (76 RBIs). He missed a couple of stretches due to appendicitis in midseason, so perhaps it was not a surprise when he greatly exceeded those totals in 1936 and when he played in the American Association All-Star Game at center field. Impressed as well was Millers owner Mike Kelley, who said during spring training 1936, "Gaffke is the best centerfielder in the Association, fielding, hitting and throwing. He had three separate appendicitis attacks last summer that he kept secret, but after the season he had his appendix removed and right now he has just about everything in the way of baseball ability. He is a sure-fire major league prospect."

On September 8, 1936, Gaffke was acquired by the Boston Red Sox, brought up from Minneapolis along with pitcher Archie McKain (in December the Red Sox sent Dusty Cooke and Mike Meola to Minneapolis to complete the deal). The Red Sox made the easy call; Gaffke had hit .342 for the Millers, with 25 home runs and 47 other extra-base hits, driving in 132 runs. It was reportedly a rich deal for the day, paying Kelley $25,000 cash.

Gaffke got his first chance to play the next day. Looking ahead to that September 9 game, there was a bit of a shakeup in the works. Manager Joe Cronin recalled Babe Dahlgren from Syracuse to play first base and sent Jimmie Foxx to play left field. The *Boston Herald* wrote that Gaffke had been the unanimous choice of the American Association baseball writers as the league's outstanding center fielder. "If he lives up to this reputation," the paper opined, "the job will be his for keeps." It wasn't a magical debut. Gaffke was 0-for-4 in a 13-inning loss to the White

Sox—batting cleanup and playing right field. His second game came on September 11 and he batted leadoff, again going 0-for-4, but this time he scored three runs. His first hit came in his third game, a third-inning home run into the Sportsman's Park bleachers driving in Fritz Ostermueller ahead of him. It gave him his first real taste of glory but was the only bright spot in a 1-for-9 day.

While with Boston, Fabe bounced around up and down in the lineup; in some games, he batted sixth or seventh. He played both right and left fields (his .982 fielding percentage had led the American Association), and even kicked off a triple play on September 20, catching a fly ball, then firing it to Dahlgren at first, who relayed to Cronin to get the runner sprinting from second.

Heading into the 1937 season, the Red Sox had Doc Cramer set to play center field, but expected a lot from Buster Mills, Dom Dallessandro, and Fabian Gaffke as flycatchers. All were newcomers. "Judging by last year's records, at least one of this trio should make good," said Joe Cronin. Mills, Gaffke, and Doerr were listed in the *New York Times* as "three of the finest players produced in the minors last year." Gaffke came on really strong in the last week of spring training, and in a City Series game against the Boston Bees, he went 4-for-5 with a double, home run, and two singles. He got the nod.

Playing major league ball wasn't easy, and Gaffke seemed to strike out in key situations several times early in the year. He "had a hard time getting started," commented the *Christian Science Monitor*. He pulled a muscle in May and Mel Almada filled in for him for a couple of weeks; he made his return with a pinch-hit RBI double on May 22. His hitting came around, perhaps the best day coming on July 14 in St. Louis when he went 4-for-5 with a double and a triple and a stolen base, and scored five runs—the only player to do so in 1937. A few days later, nearly 1,000 fans from Milwaukee took buses and cars, and a special train, to Comiskey Park to watch their compatriot play two against the White Sox.

The Red Sox had acquired Ben Chapman in mid-June, though, and Chapman became the regular right fielder. Not being used as frequently, Fabe became less effective at the plate. On August 3, Gaffke was optioned to Minneapolis for the balance of the year. He was batting .274 at the time. Newspaper reports say that Mike Kelley pleaded with Red Sox general manager Eddie Collins for a right-handed-hitting outfielder and Gaffke fit the bill. He was brought back up to Boston on September 22 and got in one more excellent day: He hit a home run in both games of a September 30 doubleheader.

With Minneapolis, he had a very strong year, batting

.325 in 41 games and placing third in American Association MVP voting behind Rudy York and Lou Fette. While with the big-league team, Fabe had raised his Red Sox average to .288, with six homers and 34 RBIs. But his star seemed to somehow be waning, and the Red Sox projected newly-acquired Joe Vosmik, Doc Cramer, and Chapman as their outfield. By February 1938, Gaffke was described, with Leo Nonnenkamp, as "held-over spare outfielders." [*The Sporting News* February 2, 1938]

Leo Nonnenkamp got the nod as the backup outfielder in 1938 so Gaffke spent most of the season with the Minneapolis Millers—rooming with another outfielder, Ted Williams. Gaffke hit .293 for the Millers, but got into only 24 games. He was called up to Boston again, late in the season, and added another 10 at-bats to his resume but only one single and one RBI.

One of the more celebrated moments in Ted Williams' early days with the Red Sox came in Atlanta in an early April 1939 exhibition game. Ted went after a foul ball but overran it and was unable to make the catch. Frustrated, he kicked the ball, then picked it up and heaved it out of the ballpark. Cronin, playing shortstop, shouted back to the Boston bench, "Gaffke, you're playing right field." That's the story of the time Fabe took Ted Williams' place.

In 1939, Gaffke opened the season with the big-league club but on April 26, when the season was but six games old, he was farmed out to Louisville. After a disagreement with Mike Kelley in 1938, the Red Sox sought another high minor league affiliate and purchased the Louisville Colonels, transferring all the players they had under contract to Louisville. The Millers became an unaffiliated ballclub.

This left the Red Sox with just four outfielders, but Cronin said the Colonels were in "dire need" of a right-handed-hitting outfielder and that it would be good for Gaffke (who had been sharing the utility role with Nonnenkamp), to play more regularly. Gaffke had just one Boston at-bat in 1939, on April 25, a pinch-hit grounder that was misplayed by Washington's Cecil Travis, allowing the Red Sox to score their third run of the inning. For the second year in a row, he collected one major league

Gaffke, the "sturdy Pole"

RBI. He had a subpar season with the Colonels, hitting .240—though the team did win the 1939 Junior World Series. The Red Sox signed him for 1940, and in October, he married Alice Sokolowski of Milwaukee.

Alice and Fabe had met at a dance in December 1936 and Alice acknowledged later that "I was always crazy about baseball and I didn't know Fabe was a ballplayer until the following spring when he told me he had to leave for training camp with the Boston Red Sox. I was really stunned." [*Minneapolis Star-Journal*, June 22, 1941]

In April 1940, Fabian's brother Gilbert Gaffke signed with the LaCrosse Blackhawks for a tryout as an outfielder. Gilbert had started as a catcher and was a .400 hitter in Legion ball but apparently didn't get too far in the pros; he doesn't turn up in minor league records.

Fabian played the full 1940 season for Mike Kelley's independent Millers ballclub. He hit a solid .294, with 12 homers and 52 RBIs. Despite a bit of a rocky start in 1941, which saw him battling to hold an outfield job, he made the team and was voted onto the All-Star squad. Nicknamed "the Angel" by some of his teammates, he compiled a league-record streak of 118 games without an error in the outfield, and batted .305 with 97 RBIs helped by 21 home runs.

War was looming, and Cleveland outfielder Clarence "Soup" Campbell was expected to be called up by his draft board, so the Indians needed a backup outfielder, and on August 13, 1941—even though he'd been slumping at a .209 pace over the previous three weeks—the Indians purchased Gaffke's contract. He appeared briefly in four September games, with one single in four at-bats, but before spring training began in 1942 the Indians declared that they planned to give him a real chance. He got off to a slow start in spring training. On April 2 *The Sporting News* acknowledged that Gaffke "has not exactly overwhelmed the Tribesmen with his possibilities."

Fabe started the 1942 season with the Indians and contributed early on; his two-out, two-strike pinch-hit single in the bottom of the ninth won the April 18 game against the White Sox, the fifth game of the year and Cleveland's second win. Unfortunately, he would manage just two more RBIs in his remaining at-bats. Gaffke was hampered by an arm injury that, by August, required surgery to remove bone chips from his right arm. After 40 games and 67 at-bats, he was out for the season.

When he reported to Cleveland's camp the following March, *The Sporting News* reported he "still is under doctor's order not to throw too hard." The Indians needed better than that, so Gaffke left his hotel room in the early morning hours, leaving behind a note for manager Lou Boudreau: "When you read this, I'll be on my way home. I'm no good for anything but a bush league, playing about once a week. I'm going to work." [*Milwaukee Journal*, February 1992] The war was on in earnest, and after an operation on his right elbow, Gaffke retired and found a position for the next three years doing defense work as an expeditor for the Allen-Bradley Company in Milwaukee. The full-time position offered a measure of security for his wife and daughter Judith as well.

On January 21, 1946, Gaffke decided to give it another go and returned to baseball's active list. The Indians released him officially early in 1946 so he could take the center field job with Minneapolis, and he played in 18 games but was released from the Millers in the first half of May. Gaffke then chose to retire.

Gaffke resumed his work with the Allen-Bradley Company, this time as a receiving clerk. He had been active during the war years with the company's industrial baseball team and continued after the war. In his first six years the company team won three championships and a semipro tournament. After 1949, Gaffke stopped playing and turned to umpiring in County League baseball for the next 15 years. Other sideline activities included bowling in shop leagues and golf in company jamborees. Beginning in 1960, he worked for Allen-Bradley as an electrical wireman on special control panels, putting in a total of 34 years with the company.

After retirement in 1977, his daughter recalls, "He loved gardening. That was just like baseball to him; he loved gardening. Grandpa Fabe made all the Little League games of Judith's son Greg Magerowski. His favorite team was the hometown Brewers, though he did a little scouting for the Angels. That lasted only a very short time, before he had to tell them, "I'm not going on planes and going around the country." They asked him to watch the boys around Milwaukee, and there was one he recommended, but most of the time he was involved in company and community events. A member of the Loyal Order of Moose, active on church committees and in the Holy Name Society, he'd occasionally tend bar at a function and maybe break out his sax or his clarinet. He was named to the Wisconsin Baseball Hall of Fame in 1982.

Fabian Sebastian Gaffke died at 78 on February 8, 1992, in Milwaukee. He'd once told writer William Janz of the *Milwaukee Journal*, "I got to the major leagues, got a few steaks, didn't make that much money, but had a lot of fun. When I quit, I missed it very much." Alice Gaffke added, "He still misses it until this day." He was buried with his baseball glove and a bat in his casket, and was followed to the cemetery by a procession of 124 motor vehicles. One hopes he's found they do indeed have baseball diamonds in Heaven.

Sources

Interview with daughter Judy Magerowski, April 15, 2007.
Interview with Ed Gaffke, April 11, 2007.
Fabian Gaffke player file at the National Baseball Hall of Fame.

DENNY GALEHOUSE *by Glenn Stout*

G	ERA	W	L	SV	GS	GF	CG	SHO	IP	H	R	ER	BB	SO	HR	HBP	WP	BFP
30	4.54	9	10	0	18	6	6	1	$146\frac{2}{3}$	160	84	74	52	68	6	1	2	639

G	AB	R	H	2B	3B	HR	RBI	BB	SO	BA	OBP	SLG	SB	HBP
30	47	0	3	1	0	0	1	6	20	.064	.185	.085	0	1

Denny Galehouse was born on December 7, 1911, 30 years to the day before Japan bombed Pearl Harbor. For Red Sox fans, however, Galehouse is a reminder of another day of infamy—October 4, 1948, the date of the infamous playoff game between the Red Sox and Cleveland Indians to decide the American League pennant. For despite a 15-year major league career with the Cleveland Indians, St. Louis Browns, and the Red Sox during which the right-handed pitcher won 109 games and lost 118, he is best remembered in Boston for being the starting and losing pitcher in the playoff game against Cleveland. Ironically, until that game, Galehouse had a well-deserved reputation as a pitcher who thrived in the pressure of the postseason.

A native of Marshalltown, in northeastern Ohio, Galehouse grew up in nearby Doylestown, just southwest of Akron. After graduating from Doylestown High School in 1928, Galehouse pitched for several local semipro teams before being signed by scout Bill Bradley of the Cleveland Indians. Galehouse began his professional career in 1930 and spent two seasons with Johnstown in the Mid-Atlantic League, improving dramatically in 1931. He pitched for the Fort Wayne Chiefs of the Central League in 1932 and his 136 strikeouts led the league. His 14–6 record earned him a promotion to the New Orleans Pelicans of the Southern Association in 1933.

Galehouse went 17-10 for New Orleans that season and emerged as a top-flight pitching prospect. In the postseason playoff he defeated the Memphis Chicks twice, the second time by a shutout, as the Pelicans captured the Southern League title. Then, in the Dixie Series against Texas League champion San Antonio, Galehouse pitched three times in six days, starting and winning two games, to finish the season with a total of 21 victories.

During spring in 1934, Galehouse impressed Indians manager Walter Johnson and earned a spot on the Cleveland roster. He made his major league debut on April 30 against the White Sox in Chicago, pitching one inning of relief in a 20-10 Cleveland loss, giving up two hits, a walk, and two earned runs while facing seven hitters. After that single appearance he was returned to New Orleans.

Despite a 12-10 regular season record in 1934, Galehouse had a slightly better earned run average and again emerged as a postseason star for the Pelicans, shutting out Galveston, 2-0, in the finale of the Dixie Series as New Orleans captured its second consecutive Series title. Before the start of the 1935 season, Galehouse was loaned to Minneapolis of the American Association in a deal that landed the Indians outfielder Ab Wright. Galehouse was 15-8 for Minneapolis, and later got into five games for the Indians, including the first start of his major league career, on September 29, earning a 7-4 win in the first game of a doubleheader against the Browns for new Indians manager Steve O'Neill.

In the spring of 1936, Galehouse was out of options and reached the major leagues for good. Although he didn't throw hard, he was an early practitioner of the slider and a pitcher whose success depended upon control. For the bulk of his career he served as a back-of-the-rotation starter and swingman, capable of both starting and relieving. Galehouse went 8-7 in 1936 with a 4.85 ERA in 36 appearances while starting 15 games, and in 1937 was 9-14 while starting 29 games and throwing 200$\frac{2}{3}$ innings, second in both categories to teammate Mel Harder.

On December 15, 1938, Galehouse was traded to the Red Sox along with Tommy Irwin in exchange for outfielder Ben Chapman, the first of Galehouse's two stints as a member of the Red Sox. Galehouse went 7-8 in 1939 and 9-10 in 1940 before being sold to the St. Louis Browns.

Denny Galehouse

In St. Louis, Galehouse put together the best seasons of his career. In 1942, pitching against rosters depleted by the war, he picked up a career-high 12 victories and 24 decisions. In 1943, Galehouse had a career-low 2.77 ERA, going 11-11 for manager Luke Sewell.

After the 1943 season, Galehouse went to work six days a week at the Goodyear Aircraft plant in Akron, Ohio, earning a deferment from the draft because he was over the age of 26, married with a child, and his job was classified as essential to the war effort. He kept in shape by serving as pitching coach for the Cuyahoga High School baseball team and made an occasional appearance pitching for a local semipro team. As he told author William Mead in *Baseball Goes to War*, in addition to his work on the assembly line, Galehouse worked with the Selective Service "trying to get draft deferments for employees. It was my job to determine who was essential and who was not."

In mid-May of 1944, the Browns, in need of pitching, persuaded Galehouse to become a so-called "Sunday pitcher." For the next three months, Galehouse left Akron after his Saturday shift, traveled all night by train to wherever the Browns were playing, pitched the first game of the Sunday doubleheader, then immediately returned to Akron and put in another full six-day work week at the factory before repeating the process the following weekend. In July, when it became clear that the Browns had a chance to win the pennant, Galehouse learned that if he quit his job at the Goodyear plant he was unlikely to be drafted until the fall. He joined the Browns full time for the balance of the season and helped St. Louis capture the pennant and earn the right to play the Cardinals in an all-St. Louis World Series.

Galehouse was manager Sewell's choice to pitch Game One and he didn't disappoint, scattering seven hits to beat Mort Cooper, 2-1, in a complete game, losing his shutout with two outs in the ninth inning on a sacrifice fly. In Game Five, Galehouse pitched nearly as well, striking out 10 and again going the distance but losing 2-0 after giving up solo home runs to Ray Sanders and Danny Litwhiler. Cooper struck out 12 in the game, and the combined 22 strikeouts, which Cardinals shortstop Marty Marion blamed on the number of fans in Sportsman's Park's center-field seats who wore white shirts that day, stood as a World Series record for 19 years before being broken by Sandy Koufax and several Yankees pitchers in

Game One of the 1963 World Series. Unfortunately for Galehouse and his teammates, the Browns fell to the Cardinals in six games.

Galehouse was drafted into the Navy in April of 1945 and spent most of 1945 pitching for the Great Lakes Naval team in Chicago, which was coached by his old Cleveland teammate Bob Feller. Galehouse rejoined the Browns in 1946 and after a slow start was purchased by the Red Sox on June 20, 1947. Over the next three months, he was terrific for manager Joe Cronin, going 11–7 with a 3.32 ERA.

In 1948, under new manager Joe McCarthy, Galehouse resumed his accustomed role at the back of the rotation for the Red Sox, making 26 appearances and 14 starts with an 8–7 record. But when the Red Sox and Indians ended the regular season tied for first place, Galehouse was destined to pitch one more game. One day after the end of the regular season, on October 4, 1948, the Red Sox and Indians met in a one-game playoff in Fenway Park to decide the American League pennant.

One day earlier, after the Red Sox beat the Yankees, 10–5, behind Joe Dobson and several relievers, Boston manager Joe McCarthy told the Boston *Herald*, "Frankly I don't know who I'll pitch [in the playoff]. . . . We had men working in the bullpen all afternoon. I'll have to find out who did what, who was ready." Most observers expected McCarthy to pitch either Mel Parnell, who had three days' rest, was 15–8 for the season and had already beaten the Indians three times in 1948. Ellis Kinder, 10–7, was also well-rested and had won four of his last five starts. In many subsequent interviews, Parnell has said that when he arrived at Fenway that day he expected to pitch, only to be told by McCarthy that the manager had changed his mind and decided to pitch Galehouse, something Parnell always believed was a "total surprise" to Galehouse.

But in a 1989 interview, Galehouse's first ever about the playoff game, he told the author that he "had a pretty good idea the night before" that he was going to pitch. According to Galehouse, McCarthy sent "another player" around to talk to several Sox pitchers about starting the playoff game. "I'm not at liberty to say anything and I never will about who was asked to pitch," he said. "But the others that were asked all had some little reason maybe why they thought they weren't able to do it. They shall remain nameless. I was the only that said, 'If he wants me to pitch, I'll pitch.'"

Birdie Tebbetts admitted to the author that he was

Galehouse during his second stint with the Red Sox

that player sent around by McCarthy, but refused to give any details about what was said to him that evening. "I've never told that story and I don't intend to," he said. "I'm gonna be avoiding it until I write it myself. I've got it on tape." But neither Galehouse nor Tebbetts ever revealed before either died what truly happened that night.

When Galehouse arrived at Fenway Park, he found the ball placed in his glove, McCarthy's traditional method of letting a pitcher know he was starting that day. Despite the fact that Galehouse was, at best, Boston's fifth starter that season, there was some logic to McCarthy's decision. Galehouse had been successful in the postseason and earlier in the year, on July 30, he had pitched 8⅔ innings of two-hit relief against the Indians in Cleveland.

Joe McCarthy later told author Donald Honig that his other pitchers were "all used up" following a grueling regular season and that Galehouse "had pitched a great game against the Indians the last time we were in Cleveland." In fact, however, Galehouse had made two subsequent appearances against the Indians and been hit hard. Moreover, over the final two weeks of the season he had pitched only twice and been belted each time.

Neither was Galehouse well-rested. As the Red Sox outlasted the Yankees on October 3 to earn the right to meet Cleveland in the playoff, Galehouse recalled that McCarthy had sent him to the bullpen in the fourth inning and told him to stay loose. "So I threw six innings [in the bullpen] the day before. . . . That's something that hasn't been brought out at all."

Whatever led McCarthy to make his decision, Sox fans know what happened next. In the first inning Galehouse retired the first two Cleveland hitters and then Lou Boudreau hit a wind-blown home run into the net over the left field wall to give the Indians a 1–0 lead. Then Boudreau led off the fourth inning with a single, Joe Gordon followed with a hit, and Ken Keltner hit a home run to give the Indians a 4–1 lead and chase Galehouse. Cleveland pitcher Gene Bearden and his knuckleball held Boston at bay and the Indians went on to win, 8–3, to capture the pennant.

Galehouse, despite becoming, in the minds of some fans, the "goat" of the game, had no regrets. Despite warming up the day before, he felt he had good stuff that day, saying, "I did the best I could."

Just a few weeks into the 1949 season the Red Sox, as if trying to erase the memory of the loss, released Galehouse. He pitched the remainder of the 1949 season with

Seattle in the Pacific Coast League, going 10–12 with a 4.09 ERA, then went 6–7 (4.38 ERA) for Seattle in 1950 before retiring.

Galehouse returned to his home in Doylestown, where he was often referred to in the local press as "the Pride of Doylestown" and to his wife, Elizabeth, two sons, Denny Jr. and Jerry, and his daughter, Jan. He was hired by the Red Sox as a scout covering the Midwest, a position he held for the Red Sox, Tigers, Mets, Cardinals, Dodgers, and Padres for the next 48 years, often driving 40,000 miles or more each year in search of prospects. "It's not enough for a fellow to be able to hit, run, throw, and field to be a ballplayer," Galehouse once said of his approach. "He's got to have the heart that goes along with being a great competitor."

One of his most notable signings for Boston was St. Louis high school pitcher Frank Baumann. The most sought-after player in the nation in 1952, Baumann was persuaded by Galehouse to sign with Boston for a bonus of $85,000. Unfortunately, Baumann never fulfilled his promise.

Although Galehouse was disappointed to have lost the playoff game, before Boston lost the 1978 playoff game to the New York Yankees, the 1948 playoff game against Cleveland was rarely brought up by baseball historians or anyone else except in passing—no one interviewed him on the topic until 1989. Most published profiles of Galehouse gave greater weight to his performance in the 1944 World Series. But after the 1978 playoff game and, particularly, after the publication of Dan Shaughnessy's *Curse of the Bambino* in 1990, that changed. Thereafter Galehouse readily admitted to reporters that "When people find out who I am, that's [the playoff game] all they want to talk about."

Yet he was hardly haunted by his performance. Galehouse took great pride in his play during the 1944 World Series, his 11 grandchildren and six great-grandchildren, and in the fact that he earned a paycheck from the game of baseball for nearly 70 years.

Galehouse passed away from heart disease on October 14, 1998. The San Diego Padres, for whom he worked for the final 18 years of his career, still honor their top scout each year with the Denny Galehouse Award.

LEFTY GROVE *by Jim Kaplan*

G	ERA	W	L	SV	GS	GF	CG	SHO	IP	H	R	ER	BB	SO	HR	HBP	WP	BFP
23	2.54	15	4	0	23	0	17	0	191	180	63	54	58	81	8	1	0	798

G	AB	R	H	2B	3B	HR	RBI	BB	SO	BA	OBP	SLG	SB	HBP
25	67	3	9	0	0	1	5	9	26	.134	.237	.179	0	?

Lefty Grove may have been baseball's greatest all-time pitcher. He was certainly its most dominant. No one matched his nine ERA titles, and his .680 winning percentage (300–141) is the highest among 300 game winners (eighth best overall). After winning 111 games in a minor-league career that delayed his major-league debut until he was 25, Grove led the American League in strikeouts his first seven years, pitched effectively in hitter's' parks (Shibe Park, Fenway Park) and starred in three World Series. Few, if any, pitchers threw tantrums on a par with the 6'3", 190-pound Lefty, who did everything big. He even led all pitchers by striking out 593 times as a batter.

Robert Moses Grove was born to John and Emma Grove on March 6, 1900, in the bituminous-mining town of Lonaconing, Maryland. His father and older brothers preceded him into the mines,

Lefty Grove

but Lefty quit after two weeks, saying, "Dad, I didn't put that coal in here, and I hope I don't have to take no more of her out."

Lefty drifted into other jobs: as a "bobbin boy" working spinning spools to make silk thread, as an apprentice glass blower and needle etcher in a glass factory, and as a railroad worker laying rails and driving spikes. In his spare time, he played a kind of baseball using cork stoppers in wool socks wrapped in black tape, and fence pickets when bats weren't available. He did not play genuine baseball until 17, nor genuinely organized baseball until 19, when Dick Stakem, proprietor of a general store in nearby Midland, began using him in town games on a field sandwiched between a forest and train tracks. "Bobby never pitched a game [for Midland] until Memorial Day, 1919," Stakem told the *Philadelphia Bulletin*'s John J. Nolan. "He pitched a seven-inning game which was ended by rain. He fanned 15 batters, walked two men, hit two, and made a wild pitch.

"Here's the scorebook to prove it.

"Bob's best game was a postseason series against [the Baltimore & Ohio railroad team in] Cumberland, the big team around here. . . . We went down there with Bobby and he held them hitless, fanned 18 batters, and the only man to reach first eventually got around to third. The reason he got there was because Bobby told me he let him steal second and third as he was so sure he could fan the next batters and the runner wouldn't steal home. The score was 1 to 0, the other pitcher allowing just one hit."

The B & O manager supposedly wanted Grove, and the next year Bob was cleaning cylinder heads of steam engines for B & O in Cumberland, Maryland. Before he could put in a baseball season there, a local garage manager named Bill Louden, who managed the Martinsburg, West Virginia, team of the Class C Blue Ridge League, offered him a princely $125 a month, a good $50 more than his father and brothers were making. With his parents' blessing, Lefty took a 30-day leave from his job, signed a contract on May 5, got a roundtrip rail pass from his master mechanic and was driven across the mountains in a large car supplied by the Midland team. While Grove was going 3–3, with 60 strikeouts in 59 innings, word reached Jack Dunn, owner of the International League (Double-A) Baltimore Orioles. Dunn sent his son Jack Jr. to watch Grove. As it happened, the Martinsburg team had started the season on the road because it lacked a fence around the home field. Dunn bought Grove for a price in the $3,000-$3,500 range that satisfied Louden. "I was the only player," Grove said later, "ever traded for a fence."

According to some accounts, the Orioles signed Grove just ahead of overtures from the Giants, Dodgers, and Tigers. It will forever be debated how many major-league games Grove would have won if he hadn't spent five seasons with the Orioles. We'll never know the answer, but we do know that Grove enjoyed playing for the Orioles. Starting at $175 a month, he won his debut, 9–3, over Jersey City, prompting owner Dunn to say he wouldn't sell Lefty for $10,000. In 1920–24, Grove was 108–36 and struck out 1,108 batters for a minor-league record, though he was often wild and went 3–8 in postseason play. By his last season in Baltimore, however, Grove was certainly pitching like a major leaguer. He went 26–6 despite missing six weeks with a wrist injury, struck out 231 batters in 236 innings and reduced his walks from 186 to 108. Moreover, Grove routinely struck out between 10 and 14 major leaguers in exhibition games (they may have been reluctant to dig in against him), told Babe Ruth "I'm not afraid of you," and made good his boast by whiffing the Bambino in nine of 11 exhibition at-bats.

With no minor league draft in the 1920s, Dunn could wait for the best offer before selling Grove to the majors. By the 1924–25 offseason, he couldn't resist. The Cubs

and Dodgers offered $100,000, according to the *Philadelphia Evening Ledger*, but Dunn sold Grove to an old friend, Philadelphia owner/manager Connie Mack, for $100,600. The extra $600 supposedly made it a higher price than the Yankees had paid the Red Sox for Babe Ruth after the 1919 season—higher if you discount notes, interest on notes and a $300,000 loan that swelled the Yankees' cost to more than $400,000.

The much-ballyhooed sale backfired on Grove, who was called the "$100,600 Lemon" when he went 10–12 in 1925 and led the American League in both walks (131) and strikeouts (116). He was too pumped up and overthrowing as he had in the postseason with Baltimore. "Catching him was like catching bullets from a rifleman with bad aim," the Athletics' catcher Mickey Cochrane told sportswriter Frank Graham years later. Nonetheless, Mack stuck with him, and Grove, taciturn and sullen dur-

Grove sizing up the opposition

ing the season, returned home with a mission. "Huh, so I'm the wild guy of the league?" Grove said to the *Evening Bulletin*'s Nolan, who had taken an 11-hour train ride from Philadelphia. "I'll show 'em something next year. See that chalk mark on the barn door. I measured off sixty feet. I reckon it is, and at six o'clock every morning I hit the chalk mark twenty times before I quit. Then I tramp the hills hunting and cover about twenty miles a day."

Up at 5:30 AM, asleep by 9 PM, Grove was rested and ready for spring training. Though he was only 13-13 in 1926, his ERA dropped from 4.75 to a league-best 2.51, his walks dropped from 131 to 101 and his strikeouts climbed from 116 to an AL-best 194. A victim of non-support, he was shut out four times in the season's first two months. To Yankees manager Miller Huggins, Grove was night-and-day improved over 1925: "Now he has wide, bending curves, better control, is mentally fit, has a lot of confidence and plenty of natural ability," Huggins said. "He mixes his speed and curves and he's the speediest pitcher in baseball." Huggins could afford to be generous, because Grove failed to beat the Yankees when they pulled away from the pack in September. It was a pattern that would repeat.

Grove led the league in strikeouts the next five years and won 20 or more games for the next seven. Alas, there was no catching the 1927 Yankees, and Grove lost six of his last seven decisions to them in a heartbreaking 1928. A Babe Ruth homer in a decisive September tilt especially victimized Grove. However, both he and the Philadelphia club, 2½ games back of the Yankees at 98-55, were poised for greatness.

In 1929, the Athletics broke through. Grove was 2-1, with two saves, against the Yankees, 20-6 overall, and the A's won the pennant. Apparently fearing the Cubs' right-handed hitters, Mack declined to start either Grove or fellow lefty Rube Walberg in the World Series, but Grove made his mark in relief. After Howard Ehmke won the opener, 3-1, Grove replaced a struggling George Earnshaw in Game Two with two outs in the fifth, two men on base, and the A's leading, 6-3. Grove fanned Gabby Hartnett on five pitches and finished with six strikeouts, three hits, one walk and no runs allowed over 4⅓ innings. For some reason, Earnshaw was given the win; Grove had to enjoy the greatest long-relief save in Series history. "How can you hit the guy," Hartnett asked, "when you can't see him?"

In historic Game Four, when the A's rallied from an 8-0 deficit to win, 10-8, Grove pitched the last two innings in relief. The A's took the Series, four games to one, and Grove struck out 10 batters in 6⅓ innings. "When danger beckoned thickest," Heywood Broun wrote, "it was always Grove who stood towering on the mound, whipping over strikes against the luckless Chicago batters."

Thanks to Mack, who had convinced Grove to move some of his money to a bank that wasn't later closed down, Lefty survived the stock market crash. Indeed, he spent $5,700 to build Lefty's Place, a Lonaconing establishment with three bowling alleys, a pool table, and a counter filled with cigar cases, candy, cigarettes, and soft drinks. Terse at tributes in his honor, Grove quietly employed his brother Dewey, out of work since the glass factory burned down, and his physically challenged

brother-in-law, Bob Mathews. Lefty was always more comfortable with the homefolk than city dwellers.

Grove returned to spring training in 1930 as truculent as ever. When a rookie named Doc Cramer doubled against him in an intra-squad game, Grove whacked him in the ribs the next time Cramer batted. While the first-place A's went 102-52, Grove won the Triple Crown of pitching by leading the league in wins (28), strikeouts (209), and ERA (2.54), the latter an incredible 0.77 ahead of the next best pitcher. He also led the league with nine saves, though the stat wasn't tabulated until years later. He was excelling in the clutch, not just rolling up big numbers. In what the *Philadelphia Inquirer* called "a copyrighted situation"—the A's up 3-2, two outs, two on and Babe Ruth at the plate in the ninth—he fanned Ruth on a 2-2 pitch, hushing the crowd in Yankee Stadium on September 1.

In the World Series, the A's faced the National League champion St. Louis Cardinals, who had batted .314. The entire NL batted .303 for 1930 season, with the Cardinals' .314 only third best (the Cards scored the most runs/game). Only two of the six NL teams didn't hit at least .300 and they each hit .281 for the season. Grove won the opener, 5-2, while throwing 70 strikes and just 39 balls, fanning five and allowing nine hits. After George Earnshaw, Lefty's polar opposite (right-handed, sharper-breaking curve, slower fastball, a party boy), throttled the Cards, 6-1, in Game Two, St. Louis beat Rube Walberg, 5-0, and got by Grove, 3-1, on two unearned runs. Lefty relieved George in the eighth inning of a scoreless Game Five and won it, 2-0, on Jimmie Foxx's two-run homer. Whereupon Earnshaw returned on one day's rest to end the series in Game Six, 7-1. For the series, MVP Earnshaw was 2-0, with 19 strikeouts in 25 innings and a 0.72 ERA, while Grove was 2-1, with 10 strikeouts in 19 innings and a 1.42 ERA.

Grove still had not had his best year. By August 23, 1931, he was 25-2 for the season and tied for the American League record with 16 straight wins. The first-place A's were 84-32. Their opponent: the hapless St. Louis Browns. It didn't seem to matter that the A's were a little nicked up. Among other things, left fielder Al Simmons was in Milwaukee being treated for a sprained, blistered and infected left ankle. A rookie named Handsome Jimmy Moore replaced him. With 20,000 sweltering fans creating an unusually large crowd at Sportsman's Park, Grove faced Dick Coffman, who, with his 5-9 record, was nearly released three weeks earlier but had saved his job by winning three straight.

Grove and Coffman kept the game scoreless through two innings. Then came an event for which Grove would forever be remembered. After Fritz Schulte's two-out bloop single in the third mildly annoyed Grove, Oscar (Ski) Melillo unnerved him. Melillo hit what appeared to be a routine liner to left. Partially blinded by the sun,

Moore raced in, realized he had misjudged the ball, and reversed course. The shot nicked his glove and rolled to the fence, with Schulte scoring on the double.

Grove slapped his glove against his side in disgust, got out of the inning and returned to the dugout in muttering retreat. He righted himself to finish the game, a neat seven-hitter with six K's and no walks. Unfortunately, Coffman was even better, getting his usually problematic curve over and yielding just three hits. In stark reversal of his season-long fortunes, Grove lost, 1–0, in only an hour and 25 minutes.

Moore never used the sun as an excuse. "If I'd stood still, I'd have caught it," he told the *Boston Globe*'s Harold Kaese 34 years later. Grove didn't blame Moore. Instead, he raged at the absent Simmons for a good 20 minutes. In what was probably an unprecedented display of postgame pique, Grove tried to tear off the clubhouse door, shredding the wooden partition between lockers, banged up the lockers, broke chairs and ripped of his shirt, buttons flying. "Threw everything I could get my hands on—bats, balls, shoes, gloves, benches, water buckets, whatever was handy," he told author Donald Honig. If Grove couldn't break one record, he might as well break another.

Quickly enough, Lefty righted himself. Responding to Yankee bench-jockeying ("kicked over any water pails lately?") on August 29, he struck out eight of the first 10 batters he faced. By season's end, he was 31–4; only three innings of grooving the ball in a final-day Series warmup cost him an ERA under 2.00 (he finished at 2.06). Winning his second straight Triple Crown with 175 strikeouts, he was named the American League's Most Valuable Player. The Athletics won the pennant again, this time in a walk. At 107–45, the A's were 13½ games better than second-place New York.

With a blister on a throwing finger, Grove yielded 12 hits in the Series opener but got good fielding support and won, 6–2. "Nah, the blister didn't hurt," said Grove, who had to rely on curves and slowballs, "but them dinky hits they made got me mad. I started thinking my control was too good. You know I was putting them right over the plate.

"I started thinking, and you know what happens when a lefthander gets to thinking. Well, I began to chuck up slow ones and a little curve. Every time I tossed one the Cards got ahold of it. From now on, they won't see nuthin' but fastball pitching."

The Cardinals won Game Two, and a rain delay gave Grove several days to heal his blister. He still wasn't sharp. Allowing 11 hits and four earned runs in eight innings, he lost Game Three, 5–2. Earnshaw evened the Series, but then Pepper Martin got three hits and drove in four runs, the Cardinals winning Game Five, 5–1. With the A's on the brink of elimination, Grove won, 8–1, on five hits and one walk. In this, his last Series appearance, he was "pitching at the very peak of his form for the first time in

Young admirer with Grove

this intersectional warfare," wrote the AP's Alan Gould. Grove was poised for another outing, warming up on the sidelines, when a ninth-inning A's rally fell short in Game Seven and the Cardinals took the clincher, 4–2.

In his three World Series (1929 through 1931), Grove went 4–2, with a 1.75 ERA, 36 strikeouts in 51⅓ innings and two saves. In these same seasons, he was 79–15 in regular-season play. It was the high-water mark for both Grove and the Philadelphia Athletics, though neither seemed to be drowning in 1932 when the second-place A's won 94 games and Grove went 25–10. Used extensively in relief the next season and totaling an exhausting 275⅓ innings, Grove still had a 24–8 record and led the league with a .750 percentage and 21 complete games, but his strikeouts declined from 188 to 114. As the A's finished third in 1933 with a 79–72 record, the word went around the league that Grove's arm had gone south on him.

Soon Grove was headed north. Stung by poor attendance in the Depression, Mack began unloading his roster and traded Grove to the Boston Red Sox. Years later, summing up Lefty's performance with his club, Mack said Grove had been a "thrower" and never really learned how to pitch until later. Others praised him, but as a one-pitch pitcher. "When planes take off from a ship, they say they catapult," Yankee shortstop Frankie Crosetti said. "That's what his fastball did halfway to the plate. He threw just plain fastballs—he didn't need anything else."

These evaluations didn't quite describe Grove's

pitching. Though he relied on his fastball, he moved it around smartly, and his curve was strong enough to spot. As he showed in the '31 Series, he could even win when his fastball wasn't working.

Grove arrived in Sarasota, the 1934 Red Sox spring training camp, anointed as team savior. They had won 43 and 63 games in the previous two seasons, but newsmen called them contenders. Grove promptly announced he wouldn't train on Sundays—why not, when young owner Tom Yawkey was in thrall to him? Indeed, alone among Red Sox, he got a single room on the road. Unfortunately, Lefty developed a sore arm in mid-March, struggled all season and went 8–8 with a 6.50 ERA while the Sox limped to fourth at 76–76. The improvement of 13 games and the record 610,640 home attendance didn't satisfy the naysayers, too many of whom blamed Grove. Once again, he was a lemon.

Yet he didn't sour. As wily and ingenious as ever, Grove spent three weeks at Hot Springs, Arkansas, during the offseason, playing 36 holes of golf a day or using a rowing machine when it rained. He pitched only four innings against major leaguers in spring training and proclaimed himself fully recovered for 1935. With a new approach of "curve and control," Grove, now 35, went 20–12 with a league-leading 2.70 ERA. The curve became his major out pitch, Grove explained, because he had lost his fastball. "I actually was too fast to curve the ball while with Baltimore and Philadelphia," he said. "The ball didn't have enough time to break because I threw what passed for a curve as fast as I threw my fastball. I couldn't get enough twist on it. . . . Now that I'm not so fast I can really break one off and my fastball looks faster than it is because it's faster than the other stuff I throw." He paused and added, "A pitcher has time enough to get smarter after he loses his speed."

Grove won three more ERA titles in the next four years while winning 17, 17, 14, and 15 games and mellowing in his behavior. That is not to say he was a model citizen. Grove had no respect for Red Sox manager Joe Cronin and wasn't above saying so. In one unforgettable instance, Cronin ordered Grove to walk Hank Greenberg with two outs, a man on second and the Sox leading the Tigers, 4–3, in the top of the ninth. After grudgingly complying, Grove gave up three straight singles to trail, 6–4, at inning's end. Leaving the field, Grove threw his glove into the stands, ripped off his uniform and smashed one of Cronin's bats before heading into the clubhouse.

Grove in 1941

Amazingly, Boston won when Wes Ferrell, pinch-hitting for Grove, hit a three-run homer. When the happy winners told the steaming Grove the news, he silently rolled a bottle of wine over to Ferrell.

He slipped to 7–6 in 1940, but he had won 293 games and no one doubted he'd reach 300 in 1941. Oh, what a strange season it was! In April, all baseball eyes were on Grove, but they refocused on the pennant races and Joe DiMaggio's 56-game hitting streak before watching in awe as Ted Williams went 6-for-8 on the last Sunday to hit .406. All this while Americans were awaiting the latest word on approaching war clouds.

Meanwhile, Grove labored to get the big one. He had six wins by mid-season. On July 25, Red Sox manager Joe Cronin told Grove, "Pop, this is a nine-inning game. I'm not coming out to get you." Cronin didn't, and Grove survived a rock-'em, sock-'em slugfest to beat the Indians on 12 hits, 10–6, with his best friend in baseball, Jimmie Foxx, getting the decisive two-run triple. His final win was no pathetic last gasp, some descriptions notwithstanding. Grove threw only 38 balls and walked just one batter. The 12th 300-game winner, the first since Pete Alexander in 1926 and the last until Warren Spahn in 1961, he had earned his place in history. He was roundly toasted at a champagne dinner party he threw for teammates that night.

All too soon, Grove lost his last three decisions while Boston writers told him to quit. "A nice lesson in irony these days is to see reporters, photographers and feature writers stumbling over such fading stars as Foxx, Cronin and Lefty Grove in their haste to get at Ted Williams," Harold Kaese wrote in mid-September. While the Sox played the A's on the last day of the season, Grove was honored between games of a doubleheader. "Well, he's a better guy now," said an unnamed Athletic. "All he used to have was a fastball and a mean disposition." Connie Mack said, "I took more from Grove than I would from any man living. He said things and did things—but he's changed. I've seen it year by year. He's got to be a great fellow."

Grove quietly told owner Yawkey that he was retiring while they walked through Yawkey's hunting preserve in South Carolina in early December. The news was upstaged by the Japanese bombing of Pearl Harbor. Though he suffered reverses in retirement that would have soured many—getting divorced, outliving his only son, needing financial help from baseball—Grove nurtured the kinder, gentler side of his character long suppressed. He outfitted Philadelphia sandlotters, sent two youngsters through college and coached kid teams around Lonaconing. He was elected to the Hall of Fame in 1947, his first year of eligibility.

Grove was a boisterous presence in his appearances at Cooperstown. "When he saw the other old players, like Joe Cronin, he would just haul off and sock them," says Grove's friend David Schild. "If he considered you a friend, he would punch you in the stomach or slap you on the back. If he really liked you, he'd hit you both ways."

After his ex-wife Ethel died in 1960, Grove relocated to his daughter-in-law's home in Norwalk, Ohio. He died there on May 22, 1975, at the age of 75. He is buried at Frostburg Memorial Park in Frostburg, MD about nine miles from his hometown.

Sources

Kaplan, Jim. *Lefty Grove: American Original* by Jim Kaplan (Cleveland: Society for American Baseball Research, 2000)
www.baseball-almanac.com
www.retrosheet.org
www.baseballlibrary.com

JOE HEVING *by Bill Nowlin*

G	ERA	W	L	SV	GS	GF	CG	SHO	IP	H	R	ER	BB	SO	HR	HBP	WP	BFP
46	3.70	11	3	7	5	26	1	0	107	124	65	44	34	43	8	2	3	471

G	AB	R	H	2B	3B	HR	RBI	BB	SO	BA	OBP	SLG	SB	HBP
46	32	5	6	1	0	0	3	0	4	.188	.188	.219	0	0

Joe Heving was born four years later than his brother Johnnie, but made his major league 10 years afterwards. John was a catcher who played professional ball from 1919 to 1945, including five years with the Red Sox during the 1920s. Joe Heving heaved for a living—he was a right-handed pitcher, an early relief specialist who led the league in relief work in 1939 (11 wins and just three losses) and again in 1940. During his time in major-league ball, he compiled an excellent 76–48 record, often pitching for teams that weren't that strong. His career ERA was 3.90.

The Hevings hailed from Covington, Kentucky, just across the Ohio River from Cincinnati. Joe's daughter-in-law recalled that the Hevings had Swedish and American Indian ancestry, though both players' questionnaires at the Hall of Fame mention only German background. There were four boys in the family: Ben (born in 1891, a carpenter), Frank (born in 1894, a saw filer), John (born in 1896, who worked as a machinist for the Maxwell Motor Co. of Newcastle, Indiana, at the time of his registration for the World War I draft), and Joe—who gave his formal name as Joe William Heving, when he himself completed his draft registration card. Joe was born on September 2, 1900, and was working as a hat tacker in a Cincinnati factory at the time of his own 1917 registration.

After the war, and service in the United States Army

Joe Heving

in 1918, it was John who first found a job playing pro ball, as catcher for the Battle Creek, Michigan, ballclub of the Class B Michigan-Ontario League in 1919. He made the majors for one at-bat in 1920, but his first full season was with the Red Sox in 1924, when he batted .284 in 109 at-bats as Boston's third catcher. He played with Boston for five seasons, and the Athletics for two more with 1932 his final year.

An October 1936 *Sporting News* story says that Joe Heving had become a candy store proprietor and sold the business when he had the opportunity to play baseball. Joe began his professional career in 1923, playing in Oklahoma for the Bartlesville Bearcats in the Class C Southwestern League. He appeared in three games as a pitcher, throwing 12 innings and giving up two runs, finishing the season with a 1–0 record. But the pitching was an aberration, and he didn't pitch again until 1926; Joe was primarily an outfielder for the Bearcats, and accumulated 428 at-bats, with a .292 average.

With Mexia in the Class D Texas Association in 1924, he struggled, hitting just .224 in 98 at-bats. Later in the year, he played for Grand Rapids in the Michigan-Ontario League, batting .281 in a limited 32 times times at bat. Joe hit .281 again in 1925, getting in a full season with Topeka of the Class D Southwestern League with 513 at-bats in 130 games. It was in 1926 that the transition occurred.

Joe was again with Topeka. He hit .259 but also threw 121 innings in 16 appearances, with an 8-6 record.

In both 1927 and 1928, Joe split the season between Portsmouth (Virginia League) and Asheville (Sally League), with most of '27 in Portsmouth (12-8) and most of 1928 with Asheville (13-5). He was just 1-1 with Asheville the first year, but 8-1 with Portsmouth in 1928, for a combined 21-6 season. He got a workout in 1929, pitching 221 innings in the Southern Association for the Memphis Chicks under manager Doc Prothro; he posted a 3.30 ERA with 14 wins against 10 losses.

The New York Giants purchased Heving in late 1929 and he made their major league roster in 1930; he was seen as a raw rookie and groomed from the start for relief work. His debut came on April 29, 1930, at the Polo Grounds and it was a terrible one. The Brooklyn Robins scored twice in the top of the first, and when Giants starter Larry Benton was roughed up in the top of the second, too (he was tagged for five hits and walked two in 1⅓ innings), the Giants called on Hub Pruett to take over. He faced four batters and every one of them got a hit. The ball was handed to Heving, who didn't fare much better—he gave up three hits and walked a batter and, like Pruett, never retired a man. Before the inning was over, Brooklyn was ahead 13-0. The game was a mess all the way around, though, the final score being Robins 19, Giants 15—and so Heving's horror perhaps didn't stand out as much as it might otherwise have.

There were a couple of standout incidents that seaon— Heving's nose was broken by a ball during batting practice on June 27, and on August 24 he was on the mound during another bad moment in front of a massive overflow crowd of 47,000 watching the Cubs play the Giants in Chicago. The Cubs were up 2-1 and the Giants pulled Freddie Fitzsimmons for a pinch hitter in the top of the eighth, in vain. Heving retired the Cubs in the bottom of the eighth without a fuss, and then the Giants tied it with a run in the top of the ninth. Tension built in the bottom of the ninth, until reaching the ultimate: The bases were loaded with two outs. Cubs manager Joe McCarthy let his starting pitcher, Guy Bush, bat. Heving got two strikes on Bush. Focused on the plate, he never saw Danny Taylor steal home to win the game, as he went into a windup and threw the ball just wide of the plate.

The following spring, Giants manager John McGraw had pitching coach Chief Bender work with Heving on

Reliever extraordinaire Heving, the only grandfather in baseball at the time

the art of keeping runners on base. John Drebinger of the *New York Times* noted that Giants catchers were "lavish in their praise of Heving's pitching talents but frankly confess he has harried them no little in the past with a prolonged wind-up that allowed runners to take no end of liberties on the bases."

Despite the bad moments in 1930, though, by year's end Joe had appeared in 41 games (just two starts) and finished 22 of them. He had six saves and a 7-5 record. It was the one season when both brothers, Johnnie and Joe, were in the majors at the same time, but they played in different leagues and never really stood a chance of facing each other.

Joe's 1930 ERA was a mark he improved on somewhat in 1931, driving it down to 4.89, though his W-L record was a disappointing 1-6 and he worked only half as many games and half as many innings. The lengthy windup remained a problem and McGraw just didn't seem to trust him, and in August McGraw sent him down to Rochester. A note in *The Sporting News* said, "The big fellow failed to make good and was returned by Manager Southworth. The trouble with Heving was his delivery." After the 1931 season, the Giants had seen enough and he was released to Indianapolis in the American Association as part of a deal for Len Koenecke.

Joe spent 1932 with Indianapolis, and won 15 games while losing nine. He gave up only 74 runs in 173 innings and struck out 91 batters. The Chicago White Sox took him from Indianapolis in the Rule 5 draft at the end of September. Playing the full year in the American League, Joe had a very good year with an excellent 2.67 ERA (7-5) in 118 innings. He started six games and had three complete games, his best outing being a 4-0 shutout of the Red Sox on August 22.

By contrast, 1934 was a poor year. Though Heving threw 88 innings, he lost his first seven decisions and didn't win his first game of the year until September. It was in Chicago, in late relief, with the White Sox facing Lefty Gomez. Gomez had entered the game 24-3 and riding a 10-game win streak, but he walked Luke Appling and Jimmy Dykes doubled in the go-ahead run, while Joe held on for his first (and only) win of the year, throwing the final three innings. In late October, he was released outright to Louisville. He was expected to excel for the Colonels, but refused to report. "There wasn't much hope for Heving joining Louisville," reported *The Sporting News* in December. He lost a year, and Louisville traded his contract to Milwaukee for Wayne LeMaster on the condition that he report.

He reported. Heving threw a career-high 256 innings with Milwaukee in the American Association in 1936, winning 19 games and losing 12, with a 3.48 earned run average. In mid-June, *The Sporting News* termed him "the most effective relief pitcher in the business." His prime pitch was his sinkerball. The day they clinched the American Association pennant, September 3, 1936, the Brewers sold him to the Cleveland Indians for 1937. It would be his third shot at the major leagues. He made the club with Cleveland in the spring and he was 8–4, used exclusively in relief and working in 40 games with a 4.83 ERA. In 1938, Joe began the year with Cleveland, and was 1–1 while only working six innings (and giving up six earned runs) for the big-league club. By May, he wasn't looking nearly as good as he had and consequently Cleveland placed him on waivers. He was purchased for $7,500 by Milwaukee and spent most of the season there (8–8, 4.60) until the Brewers sold him to the Boston Red Sox on August 1.

Jack Malaney of the *Boston Post* wrote in the August 11 *Sporting News* that "not too much is to be expected" of Heving. Heving made an impression his first month on the job, shutting out the A's, 5–0, in the second game of an August 17 doubleheader sweep that put a stop to a six-game Red Sox losing streak. It was his first start for the Sox, and he allowed seven hits, and also initiated all three Red Sox double plays in the game. Despite what Malaney reported, Joe had success, starting 11 of the 16 games in which he appeared and finishing the last couple of months of 1938 at 8–1 (3.73). Malaney wrote six months later, in February 1939, "Heving proved a life-saver when he was brought up from Milwaukee last summer. His side-arm sinker-ball pitching proved effective. . . . [Manager Joe] Cronin found that Heving was more effective as a starter than as a relief man and will continue to work him that way." Cronin, instead, continued to use him in relief.

As noted above, he led the American League in relief work both in 1939 and 1940, at one point winning seven games in a row in relief for the Red Sox in 1939 (11–3, 3.70). He appeared in 46 games and put his name in the record books with one of the wins. On July 13, the Red Sox played the first night game in team history, in Cleveland. The game went 10 innings and the Red Sox won it, 6–5. The winning pitcher was Joe Heving. He was a holdout in the spring of 1940, the last player signed, but again served primarily as right-handed relief. His first start of the year was on August 15, and he threw a three-hitter. Joe appeared in another 39 games the year he turned 40. Each year he threw over 100 innings, and Peter Golenbock quotes Joe's teammate Doc Cramer as saying, "Cronin wanted to use him every day, and Joe Heving couldn't stand it. He was too old for that."

An Associated Press article hinted that it might have been that Cronin and Heving didn't get along: "Why Heving was given up by the Red Sox was obscure. On the 1941 Cleveland roster, he joins Jim Bagby, another pitcher who didn't get along with Boston's manager, Joe Cronin." The Red Sox were ready to move on, but Heving's career was far from over. Boston sold him to Cleveland in early February 1941, and he stuck with the Indians for four seasons. He showed the Red Sox a bit of comeback, shutting them out on six hits on July 27. Ted Williams kept his quest for .400 alive, though, with a 2-for-3 day. Heving posted ERAs of 2.28, 4.89, 2.75, and 1.95, winning 19 games and losing 9 for the Indians over the four years. He missed a little time in mid-1943 after being struck by a car outside the hotel in Cleveland, but still got in 72 innings that year. It was a remarkable year; early on, it was revealed that he was not only one of the older players in baseball at the time; he was already a grandfather! His one and only win of the year came on the final day, an 11-inning win over the Philadelphia Athletics. Grandfatherhood may not have set well with Joe; he was divorced from his first wife in the fall of 1943. A more likely reason is that he'd met Nancy Pearl Palmer, a beauty queen who sang country music on a radio show in Irvine, Kentucky. Nancy was 23, and the two were married in May 1944. His final season for the Tribe was an excellent one, particularly for a 44-year-old, 8–3 with the aforementioned 1.95 earned run average. He appeared in 63 games, setting a major-league record at the time (the old record was 61). The record stood until Ellis Kinder broke it in 1953.

In 1945, after holding out in the springtime, Heving was released by the Indians on May 21. He was signed by the Boston Braves two days later and finished his career with a few more months in Boston. He appeared in only three games, and threw only five innings, though he wound up with a 1.000 winning percentage (1–0). The Braves gave him his release on August 9, 1945.

At the plate, Joe was a career .170 batter, with 41 hits (the only extra-base hits were eight doubles), and 18 RBIs to his credit. He scored 20 runs.

After baseball, Joe took up a completely different trade, working as an ironworker. He had three children in all, all from his first marriage: Joe Jr., who was himself a welder and ironworker; Jolene, a medical technologist; and Evelyn. At various times during his later years, he indicated that he was a steelworker and car loader for Acme Newport Steel and a pipefitter for the Southern Railway. Heving died at St. Elizabeth's Hospital in Covington on April 11, 1970.

Sources

Joe Heving's player file at the National Baseball Hall of Fame.
www.retrosheet.org.
Thanks to Nancy Heving, Mary Sterling, and Wayne Tucker.

BILL LEFEBVRE *by Bill Nowlin*

G	ERA	W	L	SV	GS	GF	CG	SHO	IP	H	R	ER	BB	SO	HR	HBP	WP	BFP
5	5.81	1	1	0	3	2	0	0	26⅓	35	17	17	14	8	2	0	0	122

G	AB	R	H	2B	3B	HR	RBI	BB	SO	BA	OBP	SLG	SB	HBP
7	10	3	3	0	0	0	1	2	2	.300	.417	.300	0	0

How many pitchers hit a home run their first time up in the major leagues, in their only at-bat of their debut year, and without ever having played in the minor leagues?

Wilfrid Henry "Lefty" Lefebvre's home run came in the bottom of the eighth inning of a game the Red Sox were losing, 13-1. Lefebvre pitched the last four innings of the game, was touched up for eight hits and six earned runs, including a pair of home runs. The game was pretty much a lost cause and Lefebvre was doing mop-up duty, so he was allowed to bat in the eighth, facing Monty Stratton of the White Sox. How does he describe his first at-bat? "Bang-o!"

Home run! It was Lefebvre's first and final major league game and only major league at-bat in 1938. He's in the record books with a 1.000 batting average and a 4.000 slugging average. Given one at-bat, you couldn't do much better, But the Red Sox lost the game, 15-2. Stratton hit a grand slam in the second inning, and was 3-for-3 at the plate.

On November 11, 1915, Lefebvre was born in Natick, Rhode Island, a community in Warwick, about 10 miles southwest of Providence. The family later moved to Pawtucket. He first recalls becoming seriously interested in baseball around the age of 12 when he met a young man from the area named Pat Noonan. Noonan had traveled to try out with the Red Sox during spring training. He didn't make it but he talked about the experience after he came back and that kicked off Bill Lefebvre's interest in the game.

Bill played ball on the Pawtucket High School team, pitching and playing first base and in the outfield. He played on a good team. "We won the state championship two out of three years. The other time, we lost it in the finals," he recalled. Lefebvre's catcher was Hank Soar, who later played pro football for the New York Giants of the NFL for five years before taking up a career as an umpire. Soar was an umpire in the American League for nearly 25 years, from 1950 through 1973.

Lefebvre played during the summer in the Cape Cod

Lefty Lefebvre

League, and that led to his first contact with the Boston Red Sox, following his freshman year at Holy Cross. "I played in the Cape Cod League in '35. Hughie Duffy had come down. He was a coach with the Red Sox at the time. He came down because he wasn't feeling well and they sent him down the Cape for a couple of weeks to recuperate. He more or less scouted the Cape Cod League, and at the end of the season he took about 25 of us, you know like four guys from each team, to go work out at Fenway Park after Labor Day. Eddie Collins was the general manager."

"After being there 10 days, Eddie Collins called me in the office and he asked me if I wanted to play pro ball. I said, yes, but I want to finish school. He said, 'What kind of a deal is Barry giving you over there?'" Jack Barry, the former major-league infielder, was the Crusaders' baseball coach. "When I went to Holy Cross, they gave me a half a scholarship. I said, 'I gotta pay half, four hundred bucks a year.' Going to college in those days cost $800. (Collins) said, 'If you'll sign with us after you graduate, we'll pay the four hundred.' The next three years, you know. I says, 'Ok, yeah, but I owe the first year.' He said, 'How much do you owe?' I said, 'Five hundred dollars.' So he gave me the five hundred dollars. I had never seen *one* hundred dollars before.

"Every year, they'd give me $400 to pay for my tuition. That's how I came to sign with the Red Sox."

Lefty's father was a loomfixer who worked in the textile mills in the area. "My father was born in Canada, outside of Montreal. I'm a Frenchy. My mother, Philomene, was born up in Nova Scotia. She was French and couldn't speak a word of English. Peddlers would come around the house in the summertime—or in the wintertime—to sell something. My mother, the first thing she did when they'd knock on the door, she'd open the door and she'd say, "Can you speak-a the French?" If they said 'No,' Christ, bang! The screen shut. She slammed the door. My mother never worked. I had four sisters and they also worked in the mills doing some kind of work. I had a brother. He was older than I was. He never played baseball."

Lefty's parents encouraged him to play ball. He remembers a "bunch of kids about my age. We had an informal little league type of team, but it wasn't like it is today."

At Holy Cross in the spring of 1938, Lefebvre played left field against Brown, pitched against Fordham (2-for-4, with three runs scored on offense), threw a three-hit shutout against Providence College on May 21, and beat Colgate 14–1 on seven hits (2-for-5, with three runs scored) on May 26. The latter game was Lefebvre's seventh consecutive victory. On May 30, he held Boston College to three runs, but the Eagles shut out the Crusaders. A little over a week later, Lefebvre graduated—and the next day he was in uniform at Fenway Park. The day after that, he saw action in his first major-league game. "I graduated June the ninth of 1938 from Holy Cross, and the next day I went to Fenway Park and signed a major-league contract. Six hundred bucks a month."

He got in the lost cause of a ballgame, and pitched. "Then it came my turn to bat and Cronin said, 'Go up and hit, kid! Go up and hit!' So I went up and hit, and the first ball Monty Stratton threw to me, I hit it over the left-field fence. I was a left-hand hitter; I swung a little late. In those days, they didn't have the screen (on top of the wall). They had horns to advertise. They used to announce the lineups and so forth. Loudspeakers. And it hit in the loudspeaker, which was an automatic home run. But I don't know that. And the ball came back on the field. Mike Kreevich is playing center field, and he's taking his time. When I hit the ball, I figured I'd hit the wall and I'd make a double anyway. When I got to second base—he knew it was a home run, but I didn't—and I said to myself, 'Christ, he's not hustling,' and I went sliding into third base. Bill McGowan was the umpire and he hollered, 'Come on, kid. Come on in, you hit a home run.' I didn't even know it was a home run."

It was but a brief stay in the bigs. Lefebvre threw the four innings, hit the one homer, and was headed to Minneapolis to play for the American Association Millers under Donie Bush. "I only stayed with the Red Sox for a few days, and then they sent me to Minneapolis and I played with Ted Williams when he was 19 years old." When the Red Sox visited Chicago just over a week later, Joe Cronin called him in and explained that Bush needed a left-handed pitcher. He told Bill, "I think you'd be better off going over there, you'd be pitching regular, you know." So instead of sitting on the bench in Boston, he joined the Millers and became teammates with Ted Williams, Stan Spence, and Jim Tabor. Lefebvre's best pitch was the fastball, and he had a slider and a palmball in his repertoire, too.

"I had a good year. I won eight and lost eight, which was pretty good for a rookie." Lefebvre got in 127 innings and had a 4.25 ERA, striking out 45 while walking 35. Ted Williams won the American Association's Triple Crown that year, and after the season Lefebvre, Williams, Walter Tauscher, and Stan Spence did some barnstorming across the upper Midwest with their second baseman, Andy Cohen. Bill remembers falling asleep in the back seat, with Ted riding shotgun—literally. Every so often, a huge bang would wake him up; Ted had fired his shotgun at a jackrabbit or something. "Well, in about fifteen days, he emptied that whole case. By the end of the trip I think he was shooting at cats and dogs. He probably killed a couple of cows, I don't know. It's a wonder we never got pinched."

The following year, 1939, it was a choice between Bill and Jake Wade as to who'd be the left-hander taken to Boston, and Cronin chose the veteran Wade. The Red Sox had meanwhile bought the Louisville ballclub, and so sent Lefebvre to Louisville. He appeared in 30 games, throwing 116 innings, and ran up a record of 6–10 with a 5.51 ERA, walking one more than he struck out, 43–42. Despite the less than impressive showing, he got another call-up to Boston and worked 26 innings in five games, winning one and losing one.

His first start came on August 19 and he threw six innings against the Senators, in Washington, leaving the game a 3–3 tie for pinch-hitter Lou Finney. Finney doubled and scored, but the runs that made the most difference in the 8–6 Red Sox win came in the ninth inning when Ted Williams hit a grand slam off former Red Sox pitcher Pete Appleton.

The win came in Cleveland on August 29. Lefty started the game and it was scoreless after four innings, when the Red Sox scored a couple of runs and then Ted Williams broke the game open with another grand slam, off Harry Eisenstat, for a 6–0 lead. Lefty pitched through seven innings, got in a little trouble in the eighth, and was then relieved by Joe Heving. He recorded his first major-league win—and his only one for the Red Sox. He was 2-for-3 at the plate.

The loss came on September 4 in the second game of a doubleheader at Fenway Park. The Washington Senators beat the Red Sox, 7–6, in the first game, with Jake Wade getting knocked out in the second inning. Lefebvre started the second game and was staked to a 2–0 lead after three innings, but surrendered three runs in the top of the fourth and was knocked out himself during the seventh as the Senators scored three more runs on their way to a 6–4 win.

The day before, on September 3, Lefebvre had won another game, but with his bat, not his glove. The Yankees were at Fenway. It was the bottom of the eighth, with the score tied, 11–11, and the bases loaded. Elden Auker was due up, the third pitcher of the game for the Red Sox. Joe Cronin, remembering he had a good left-handed bat on the bench in Lefebvre, sent him up and Lefty singled in the one run that proved the game-winner.

Bill Lefebvre spent the next three years toiling in the

minors. In January 1940, he was sent on option to the San Francisco Seals of the Pacific Coast League in exchange for Dom DiMaggio. Lefebvre was just 1–4 with the Seals before being returned to the Red Sox, who assigned him to Little Rock in the Southern Association. He spent most of the season in Little Rock, appearing in 26 games and posting a 6–13 record, despite a very good 3.62 ERA. At season's end, he joined Scranton, appearing in seven games as a pitcher but also playing one game in center field and another in which he transitioned from pitching relief to fielding at first base. The whole of 1941 was at Louisville once more (12–7, 3.51 ERA)—again walking one more batter than he struck out (52–51). Minneapolis purchased his contract at the very end of 1941 and he played the '42 season for the Millers once more (9–11, 4.11 ERA, striking out one more batter than he walked (64–63). The Millers were now a Washington farm team.

In 1943, Lefty Lefebvre made it to the majors again. He spent most of the year with Minneapolis, compiling a 12–8 mark and an excellent 2.22 ERA. On the strength of that season, he was brought up to the Washington Senators in mid-August. He pitched 32 innings, finishing 2–0 (his first start was a complete game win over Cleveland) with a 4.50 ERA. In 1944, Lefebvre was with Washington all year long (2–4, 4.50 in 69⅔ innings of work.) Lefebvre led the league with 10 pinch hits in 1944. He ended his major-league years with five wins, five losses, and a lifetime batting average of .276.

Military service prevented him from playing at all in 1945. He served in an Army unit sent to Japan after the war ended and worked clearing minefields. It was in the Army that he suffered a strain that spoiled his prospects for future play—due not to an injury on a minefield, but to excessive work on a ball field. "We had a ball team. There were several camps around where we were. We won the championship—they called it the championship. I think the Army really ruined me. We had a guy that was a fanatic and he wanted to win the championship, in that league. I pitched Monday, Wednesday, and Friday. That was too much. I hurt my arm. I couldn't pitch any more. That's what ruined me. When I came back, I was washed up."

Lefebvre as a Red Sox scout

After the war, he gave it a try, though. Lefty pitched a full season for Minneapolis (167 innings, 11–12, but with a poor 6.41 ERA). His final year of pitching was with Providence and Pawtucket in the New England League in 1947 (3–3, 7.47 ERA).

At that point, he just quit, and went into teaching in Pawtucket. He stayed at it for 25 years, mostly fifth- and sixth-grade physical education instruction. Lefebvre coached soccer, basketball, baseball, track, and swimming. While teaching, he also scouted for the Red Sox. Lefebvre is credited with signing John LaRose, Mark Bomback, and Allen Ripley, and he contributed to the evaluations of Carlton Fisk and a number of other players. He saw his old Minneapolis teammate Ted Williams almost every year at spring training. Eventually Bill and his wife moved to Florida.

The couple had two boys. Bill Junior was signed by the Cardinals, and seemed slated to become their next catcher, starting at Class A and working his way right up to the top, but he was stricken with cancer and died before he was 26 years old. Their other son was Michael. "He's a Down syndrome boy. He's in a group home over here in Florida, but he's home right now," Bill said in early 2006. "He's with me right now. Michael. Great kid. We had taken him to Children's Hospital in Boston and at that time they said the Down syndrome kids don't live too long, maybe between 15 and 20 years old. My son is sitting right next to me right now. He's 51 years old."

Summing it all up at age 90, Lefty Lefebvre concluded, "I wasn't a great pitcher, you know. I was just an average guy." Reminded of his .276 batting average, he said, "That's right. I should have played first base."

Bill Lefebvre died in Largo, Florida, on January 19, 2007, at the age of 91.

Sources

Interviews with Wilfrid Lefebvre by Bill Nowlin on June 19, 1997 and January 29, 2006.

Lefty Lefebvre player file at the National Baseball Hall of Fame.

LEO NONNENKAMP *by Bill Nowlin*

G	AB	R	H	2B	3B	HR	RBI	BB	SO	BA	OBP	SLG	SB	HBP
58	75	12	18	2	1	0	5	12	6	.240	.345	.293	0	0

Red Nonnenkamp had to wait 1,702 days after his first major-league game to get his first base hit. After his September 6, 1933, debut with Pittsburgh in which he pinch-hit unsuccessfully, Leo came through on May 6, 1938 with his first big league safety. Nonnenkamp, in his 12th appearance for the Boston Red Sox, singled off St. Louis Browns pitcher Buck Newsom in a 7–3 Sox victory. Nonnenkamp got a chance to play in other than a pinch-hitting or pinch-running role, after regular Sox right fielder Ben Chapman was suspended. Leo took advantage of his opportunity and finally put some numbers up in the hits column.

Leo Nonnenkamp

Once Nonnenkamp got going, he put together a fine year, batting .283 for Boston. It was the best in a career that saw him hit .262 in 263 at-bats and drive in 24 runs.

Leo William Nonnenkamp was born in St. Louis on July 7, 1911, the only son of John Theodore Nonnenkamp (1877–1960) and his wife, Elizabeth Kruse Nonnenkamp (1881–1968.) He had two older sisters: Florence (b. 1906) and Lillian (b. 1909). Leo's father, John, had three brothers and four sisters. Leo's great-grandfather Joseph Nonnenkamp was born in Germany, near Hannover, and immigrated to the United States through the port of New Orleans, settling in St. Louis.

Leo picked up the nickname "Red" at some point along the line. He never played baseball in school and first played semipro baseball, at the age of 18, in the St. Louis Muny League in the summer of 1929. His .521 average earned him an invitation to join the St. Louis Cardinals' baseball school at Danville, Illinois. It wasn't a very exclusive invitation; the April 10, 1930, *Sporting News* reported that a full 50 rookies had already been released "but there are still enough newcomers present." Nonnenkamp rated a headline on a brief page five story, the left-handed left fielder dubbed "one of the outstanding rookies in the camp."

After further evaluation at Springfied, he was signed to a contract and assigned to the Waynesboro Red Birds in the Blue Ridge League, playing Class D ball in Branch Rickey's burgeoning farm system. Leo hit .297 over the course of 114 games, before the Red Birds lost the best-of-three league playoffs. Nonnenkamp went through a

couple of affiliate transactions during the offseason, on the roster of Houston and then Springfield, but by the time 1931 began he'd been advanced to Class C, playing in Pennsylvania's Middle Atlantic League for the Scottdale Cardinals. He was also on the roster of what he called a "traveling team"—Altoona, an independent team which began the season in Jeanette, moved again and became the Beaver Falls Beavers in the same league. He hit for an identical .297 average, this time hitting 10 homers as opposed to the two he'd hit the year before.

Sometime in the offseason of 1931–32, Nonnenkamp became part of the Pittsburgh Pirates system and was given a ticket to Tulsa in 1932, jumping to the Class A Western League. The Tulsa Oilers must have been glad to have him since he was hitting a spectacular .391 over his first 16 games when he broke his ankle sliding in an early May game and was forced to miss the rest of the season. He read in the newspapers of the Oilers' win in the league championship. He began 1933 with Tulsa (now in the Texas League) and was hitting .271 after 29 games but the Oilers needed some right-handed hitting and he was asked to go to El Dorado, Arkansas. Not surprisingly, he did better for the Class C Dixie League El Dorado Lions, batting .336 in 63 games and driving in 49 runs. He was rewarded with a late-season call-up to the big-league club, but with Paul and Lloyd Waner and Freddie Lindstrom (three future Hall of Famers) in the Pittsburgh outfield and with the Pirates hoping to secure second place, he did not get much playing time.

The one chance Red got in three weeks with the ballclub was at the plate when manager George Gibson asked him to pinch-hit for pitcher Bill Swift in the bottom of the ninth of the September 6 game. The Pirates were losing, 9–1, to the Giants and there was nothing happening. Hal Schumacher struck Leo out. Red had to wait more than four years to get his next major league at-bat.

The Pirates optioned Nonnenkamp to Little Rock (Class A) for the next couple of years. The 1934 Travelers finished in last place, but Red hit a respectable .278 over his 141-game season. Once again, he hit for the same average two years in a row, posting a .278 average in 1935, too. He seemed to suddenly find some speed in '35, leading the Southern Association in stolen bases with 36, four times as many as he'd stolen the year before. He developed a strong reputation as a patient hitter, drawing more than his share of bases on balls. Red played with Little Rock in 1936 and 1937 as well, hitting .326 and .332 respectively. Little Rock had meanwhile become a Boston Red Sox farm team, continuing in 1937 under manager Doc Prothro. Pittsburgh was out of options by this time and so had sold his contract outright to Little Rock. Prothro got Nonnenkamp to stop wiggling his bat while at the plate, and it made a difference. Nonnenkamp was voted MVP of the Southern Association in 1936, though the team still finished 17 games out of first place.

In 1937, the *New York Times* took note when Nonnenkamp won an exhibition game against the world champion New York Yankees with a two-run homer in the bottom of the ninth inning, to give Little Rock a 9–8 win. The home run snapped a 13-game Yankees winning streak. The paper noted Nonnenkamp as a "popular hero here," adding, "His mates mobbed him as he reached the plate." By August, *The Sporting News* predicted that he had a chance to make the Red Sox the following year. The Travelers led the league in 1937 and beat New Orleans in the playoffs; Red led the league in runs scored, with 145. *The Sporting News* reported in October that Nonnenkamp was the unanimous choice as the league's Most Valuable Player. The Red Sox were ready. And so was Red; after four years with Little Rock he was nonetheless "an incurable optimist, with a winning smile and a contagious laugh, believing that the service in the minors has done him a lot of good"—in the words of Edgar G. Brands, editor of *The Sporting News*.

During 1938 spring training the *New York Times* noted that Nonnenkamp's "lighting speed . . . brought a smile to [Tom] Yawkey's face" and a little power didn't hurt, either—the home run he hit over Sebring's right-field wall against the Newark Bears was said to be only the second to leave the ballpark over the 350-foot barrier; Lou Gehrig hit the other two years before. Nonnenkamp made the big-league club, and Ted Williams did not. Williams was sent to Minneapolis for more seasoning; Nonnenkamp joined the Red Sox as fourth outfielder behind Ben Chapman, Doc Cramer, and Joe Vosmik.

Leo traveled north with the ballclub and first saw action in Boston during the first of two City Series games in the Hub against the Boston Bees. He was asked to pinch-hit, but failed to connect. On Opening Day, Leo had

Nonnenkamp in an awkward pose

another opportunity, batting for Jim Bagby in the sixth inning. He walked to load the bases and scored on Doc Cramer's single, part of a six-run sixth. But then he appeared in nine ballgames (eight as a pinch-hitter and one as a pinch-runner) before he finally got his first major-league hit.

On May 5, Ben Chapman and Detroit's catcher Birdie Tebbetts tangled at the plate. Chapman, the Red Sox right fielder, drew a three-day suspension. Leo filled in for the final four innings of the May 5 game, going 0-for-2 but collecting his second RBI. The next day he started his first game and went 2-for-5 in a 7–3 win against the Browns at Fenway Park. He had two singles, drove in one run and scored another, and even threw a runner out at the plate for a double play. Fielding was a bit of a forte for Nonnenkamp. In an August 1938 clipping found in his Hall of Fame player files, sportswriter Vic Stout wrote, "Leo would much rather tear around the outfield chasing flies. In fact, Nonnenkamp is so wrapped up in his fielding that Manager Cronin has to keep after him to get him up to the plate in batting practice."

On May 7, Leo was 1-for-3, a triple, scoring one run and driving in another. On May 9, though just 1-for-3, he scored three times and drove in one. After Chapman returned to the lineup, it remained a tough outfield to crack but Leo got into 87 games for a total of 180 at-bats and hit .283 with 18 RBIs. The triple on May 7 was his only one of the year; he had four doubles but never hit a major-league home run.

A 3-for-5 game on June 2 and his 12th-inning game-winning single on July 30 were a couple of highlights of his season. After the season, Boston traded Ben Chapman to Cleveland for Denny Galehouse and Tommy Irwin (and secured Elden Auker and Jake Wade in another trade). *Washington Post* columnist Shirley Povich speculated that either Nonnenkamp or Fabian Gaffke would take over right field for the Red Sox. It was a rare lapse of forgetfulness for the usually solid sportswriter; he'd somehow forgotten that the kid who had won the Triple Crown in the American Association was the heir apparent: Ted Williams. There was no way to deny The Kid. He had a lock on right field. Nonnenkamp and Gaffke were outfield backups. Red, with his .300 average in pinch-hit duties, was kept on the team and Gaffke was the one sent to Louisville on option at the end of April.

Gaffke got into just one game in 1939, but Nonny accumulated 75 at-bats in 58 games, hitting .240. He drove in only five runs, but filled in as needed. Williams had an excellent year, his 145 RBIs setting a rookie record that has yet to be topped.

Leo didn't know it yet, but the handwriting was on the wall. His major-league career was almost over. The Red Sox had another couple of other outfielders coming up in their system: Dominic DiMaggio and Stan Spence. They'd purchased Lou Finney from Philadelphia early in 1939, and with Finney in right, Cramer in center, and Williams moving to left field, all three Sox regular outfielders hit over .300 in 1940. Nonnenkamp nonetheless trained with the team in spring training and even featured in a minor news story on April 5. During an exhibition game against Cincinnati in Greensboro N.C., with the score 12–10 in favor of the Reds, Red fouled an eighth-inning pitch out of Memorial Park. There simply were no more baseballs left with which to play. The game had begun with 96 baseballs available, but every one of them had been lost to fans in the stands or outside the ballpark. The game ended and Cincinnati won, with Nonnenkamp still at bat. Newspaper readers in Florence, S.C., the next morning might well have recalled the day precisely one year earlier when the two teams met the same fate in their town. On April 6, 1938, the game was called off with the score 18–18. That was quite a wild affair, too, but played with only four dozen balls. Doubling the number on hand hadn't spared them living out a bit of déjà vu.

Nonnenkamp's 1940 was even more frustrating than 1939. Red played in only nine games for the Red Sox during April and May, exclusively as a pinch-hitter. He was officially 0-for-7, was hit by a pitch once, and drove in his final run in major-league ball with a sacrifice fly to right field in the 11th inning of the May 11 game at Yankee Stadium. He drove in Jim Tabor from third, giving the Red Sox an 8–7 lead. Fortunately, Finney doubled and Cramer singled to give the Sox an insurance run. The Yankees scored once in the bottom of the inning.

On June 6, the Red Sox optioned Nonnenkamp to Louisville and brought up Stan Spence. Before the end of the month, Louisville had in turn sent Leo to Newark, with which, though it was a Yankees farm club, they apparently had a bit of an understanding. The Bears were desperate for an outfielder and the Colonels needed an infielder, so the Bears swapped Jim Shilling to Louisville. Nonnenkamp had hit .294 for Louisville, albeit in only 17 at-bats, but got more play in Newark. He felt that Johnny Neun was the best manager he'd played under. On August 27, it was announced that Nonnenkamp was to be brought back to the Red Sox when the rosters expanded in September, but on September 11, the Red Sox sold his contract outright to Newark. The International League season was still under way. By year's end, Red had hit .280 in 143 at-bats, and he helped the Bears win the Little World Series, beating—ironically—Louisville in six games, his sixth-inning single plating the game-winning run of the 6–1 victory.

Newark had Nonnenkamp for the entire 1941 campaign and he hit .301 with eight homers and 54 RBIs. His pinch-hit ninth-inning homer on May 6 beat the Rochester Red Wings. A three-hit game against Buffalo on July 11 and another three-hit game that included a pair of home runs on the 15th against Baltimore were big days in a torrid first half of July. His hitting through the rest of the year wasn't quite as spectacular. Early in 1942, the Kansas City Blues bid for his services and Leo joined the American Association in exchange for Bud Metheny. The move was prompted by new K.C. skipper Johnny Neun, who'd managed Leo in Newark. Neun was known to remain impressed with his strong arm as a fielder. He had a subpar season at the plate, though, batting just .227 over the course of 153 ballgames.

In the spring of 1943, Nonnenkamp was taken into the Navy, and right after finishing boot camp at Great Lakes Naval Training Station found himself playing for Mickey Cochrane's famous Great Lakes team. Cochrane had Leo lead off in a benefit exhibition game when Great Lakes visited Kansas City and played the Blues. Leo got two hits, but the Blues won the game, 1–0.

Nonnenkamp served in the Navy for the duration, stationed on New Caledonia in the Pacific for 1944 and 1945. He missed three seasons of pro ball, and returned with the Little Rock Travelers in 1946. It was his final year. He hit .231 in 65 at-bats and was finally released after 22 games, on May 13, the same day the Travs released Daffy Dean. The Travelers had him help run their baseball school in March, but this was the end.

Leo stayed on in Little Rock. While with the Red Sox, he had married Little Rock's Jill Young. The couple had no children, but they loved living in Little Rock and made it their lifelong home. "You could visit folks and not spend most of the evening traveling to get there," he told an interviewer. "You didn't have to lock your car and you could go fishing. It was more like living than in the big city." He was apparently an excellent local bowler. His wife, Jill, preceded him in death. The two were members of Holy Souls Catholic Church.

Nonnenkamp worked for many years as a post office mail carrier. Leo was inducted into the Arkansas Sports Hall of Fame in February 1993. He died at 89 on December 3, 2000.

Sources

Interviews with Marc E. Nonnenkamp, Don Nonnenkamp, Tommy Beck, Neil Dobbins, Jim Rasco, Danny Shameer, and Todd Traub, all in May 2007.

Traub, Todd. "Nonnenkamp's HR memorable" *Arkansas Democrat-Gazette*, August 31, 2006.

Leo Nonnenkamp player file at the National Baseball Hall of Fame.

FRITZ OSTERMUELLER *by John Green*

G	ERA	W	L	SV	GS	GF	CG	SHO	IP	H	R	ER	BB	SO	HR	HBP	WP	BFP
34	4.24	11	7	4	20	9	8	0	159⅓	173	86	75	58	61	6	2	5	701

G	AB	R	H	2B	3B	HR	RBI	BB	SO	BA	OBP	SLG	SB	HBP
34	56	4	9	0	1	0	4	3	5	.161	.203	.196	0	0

Fritz Ostermueller was 41 years old when he took the mound on September 30, 1948, to make the final start of his 15-year major-league career. The Pittsburgh left-hander had played with four big-league teams; his lifetime ledger was even at 114 wins and 114 losses. In early September the Braves, Cardinals, Dodgers, and the surprising Pirates had been involved in a four-team battle for the National League pennant, but in midmonth Boston caught fire and pulled away from the other three clubs.

On September 30, with four games left on the schedule, the Pirates and Dodgers trailed the second-place Cardinals by a single game. On that date Pittsburgh and St. Louis played a twin bill at Sportsman's Park, and the Cardinals took the opener, 6–1. In the nightcap, Pirates skipper Billy Meyer picked Ostermueller to oppose the Redbirds' 19-game winner, Harry

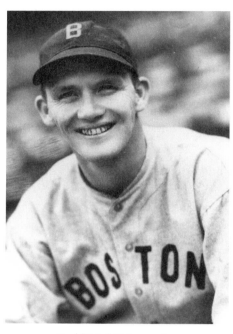

Fred "Fritz" Ostermueller

"The Cat" Brecheen. Called "Old Folks" or "Ostey" by teammates and sportswriters, Fritz had pitched in tough luck in his two previous outings, losing to the Braves and Warren Spahn in a 2–1 heartbreaker on September 18, and then going down to defeat, 4–3, to the Reds six days later.

It was a must-win situation for Pittsburgh, and Ostermueller, in the second game of the doubleheader; a victory would keep the Pirates' slim second-place hopes alive, and for Old Folks, it would restore his career record on the plus side of .500. St. Louis, however, touched Fritz for a run in the second inning, then added two more in the fifth, and Ostey was lifted for a pinch-hitter in the sixth. The Cardinals and Brecheen prevailed, 4–1; The Cat became a 20-game winner for the first time, and lowered his league-leading ERA to 2.24. Fritz took the loss, and three days later, Pittsburgh wound up the season in fourth place. The following week, Fritz Ostermueller announced his retirement from the game he had played professionally for 23 seasons.

Frederick Raymond "Fritz" Ostermueller was born on September 15, 1907, in Quincy, Illinois, to German

immigrants George and Anna Wink Ostermueller. The second youngest of nine children, Fritz grew up with his seven brothers and one sister on a dairy farm, and after the cows were tended to, the boys played baseball in the pastures and, eventually, in the area's Parish League.

Young Fritz attended St. John's College in Quincy for a while, but his talents on the diamond took precedence over academics, and in 1926, at the age of 18, he signed to play professionally with his hometown Quincy Reds in the Class B Three-I League. The local team soon came under the umbrella of the St. Louis Cardinals, and Ostermueller began an eight-year journey with Branch Rickey's "chain gang." The youngster was assigned to Quincy again in 1927, but in August was sent to Wheeling, West Virginia, of the Middle Atlantic League. Ostermueller pitched in only two games for Wheeling; one was in Cumberland, Maryland, where on August 16, he married Faye Simpson of Milan, Missouri. The two first met in Quincy, courted there, and were delighted when Fritz was shipped back to the Three-I League team to finish out the season. Overall, with Quincy and Wheeling, Ostey's record was eight wins and nine losses.

Ostermueller played in the Western Association in 1928 and 1929, and became a threat with the bat in addition to his growing skills on the pitching mound. In 1928 Eddie Dyer was the player-manager of the Topeka Jayhawks, and one day called on Fritz to start both games of a doubleheader against Joplin. The left-hander responded with complete game, 3–2 and 3–0 victories over the Miners, and his single plated the winning run in the first contest.

Ostermueller's record was 12–12 in 1928, and the following year he was a 20-game winner. From 1930 to 1933, Fritz moved up and down the Cardinals' farm ladder: St. Joseph, Greensboro, and Rochester. He was productive in his two seasons with Greensboro in the Piedmont League, winning 15 games in 1931 and 21 in 1932 to help the

Sox southpaw "Ostey" doing some tossing

Patriots become the circuit's playoff champions. Greensboro's regular lineup was riddled by injuries in the 1932 postseason; Ostermueller was called on to play right field and first base, and the left-handed hitter responded with two home runs and five RBIs.

Ostermueller sparkled with Rochester in 1933, posting 16 wins and 7 losses, and led International League pitchers with a 2.44 ERA. Fritz also hit .315, including a pair of four-baggers; his season was cut short, however, by an attack of appendicitis, and he was operated on in late July. Several major-league clubs were interested in obtaining him for 1934 delivery, and the Boston Red Sox won out in the bidding, sending three players and cash to Rochester. Rickey was banking on Dizzy and Paul Dean to anchor the St. Louis pitching staff, and willingly surrendered his longtime southpaw farmhand.

Tom Yawkey, who had inherited 7 million dollars in 1933 from the estate of his uncle, William Yawkey, purchased the Red Sox. The elder Yawkey had been a part-owner of the Detroit Tigers, and Tom had set his sights on one day acquiring his own major-league team. Four days after receiving his legacy on his 30th birthday, Tom Yawkey paid one million dollars to Bob Quinn for the Red Sox franchise, and hired longtime major-league standout Eddie Collins to become Boston's general manager.

Buoyed by the Yawkey bankroll and Collins's keen eye for baseball talent, the Red Sox acquired future Hall of Fame catcher Rick Ferrell from the St. Louis Browns in May 1933. In June they parted with $100,000 cash to add infielder Bill Werber and pitcher George Pipgras from the New York Yankees. And Collins dealt with the cash-strapped Philadelphia Athletics in December, giving up $125,000 and two players to obtain infielder Max Bishop and hurlers Robert "Lefty" Grove and Rube Walberg.

In addition to Ostermueller, the Red Sox added two other rookies from the International League to the spring training roster for 1934: Baltimore outfielder Julius "Moose" Solters and Rochester catcher Gordie Hinkle. Solters was the 1933 International League batting champion, and Hinkle was Ostermueller's batterymate at Rochester and several other stops in the Cardinals' chain. Two other important acquisitions were manager Bucky Harris, signed after being dismissed as Detroit skipper, and veteran left-hander Herb Pennock, a veteran of 21 seasons with three American League clubs.

Ostermueller was 26 years old, weighed 175 pounds, and was an inch short of 6 feet tall when he reported to the Red Sox training base at Sarasota, Florida, in February 1934. At the time Fritz threw mostly side-arm and had a good fastball, curve, and change, but had been plagued by wildness most of his minor-league career. Harris placed his rookie pitcher under the tutelage of Pennock; the two worked to improve Ostey's delivery and his control, and the student was impressive in spring outings. The Red Sox left training camp with Harris counting heavily on a pitching corps overloaded with lefties to carry the club. But Grove, with a sore arm, won only eight games; Rube Walberg triumphed just six times, and Pennock, in his swan song, logged just two victories. Southpaw Bob Weiland, after starting with just a single win and five losses, was traded to Cleveland on May 25 for right-hander Wes Ferrell, who became the staff ace. The time was ripe for Ostey to step in.

Ostermueller made his big-league debut on April 21, 1934, in a relief role in the fifth game of the season before the home folks at Fenway Park. The Yankees had a 6–5 lead when Fritz was summoned in the seventh inning with the bases loaded and two out. The rookie stymied the New Yorkers, recording seven outs, and Boston rallied to win, 9–6, giving Ostey his initial major-league victory. The freshman left-hander was spectacular again in relief on May 9, racking up the save with three scoreless frames in a 5–4 win over the Tigers. Entering the game in the seventh with the bases loaded and no outs, Fritz struck out Charlie Gehringer, and then induced a pair of groundouts.

Two days later he made his first start, hurling into the 11th inning at Fenway Park against Cleveland, only to lose, 6–5. Ostermueller faced the Browns on May 17, and took a 2–0 lead into the bottom of the eighth before allowing a two-run pinch homer to player-manager Rogers Hornsby; St. Louis rallied to win, 4–3. Fritz was on the beam in two straight complete games against Washington, winning 7–2 on June 3 at Griffith Stadium, and coming back five days later to post a 3–2, 12-inning victory. He also contributed two hits and scored the winning run in the final frame.

For the 1934 season, Ostermueller finished at 10–13, but he led Red Sox starters with a 3.49 ERA, seventh best in the American League. He pitched 198⅔ innings in 33 appearances, and completed 10 of 23 starts. Fritz's year was shortened on September 12 when he walked off the mound in the first inning at Tiger Stadium with an injury to his left shoulder. Ostey had some other memorable moments in his rookie year, including a Fourth of July triumph over the Yankees in relief of Wes Ferrell. Taking over in the fifth with bases loaded, no outs and the Red Sox clinging to a tenuous, 5–4 lead, he walked the first batter to tie the score but shut out New York the rest of the way and Boston rallied to win, 8–5.

On July 31 at Yankee Stadium, Ostermueller gave up Babe Ruth's 703rd career home run as New York triumphed, 2–1. The Bambino socked another round-tripper off Fritz on August 11 at Fenway (No. 705), but in a losing cause, as Ostey pitched all the way to record a 13-inning, 3–2 victory. It was Ruth's last season as a Yankee; after Fritz struck him out, he rewarded the rookie left-hander with an autographed baseball. The ball is now the centerpiece in the memorabilia collection of Sherrill Ostermueller Duesterhaus, the daughter of Fritz and Faye Ostermueller.

Eddie Collins parted with another $250,000 of Yawkey's bankroll in the winter of 1935, purchasing shortstop and manager Joe Cronin from Washington; Cronin's potent bat was needed to perk up the anemic Boston offense. Ostermueller enjoyed a good spring in Sarasota in 1935, but three physical maladies ruined his season. In April he was hit on the knee in batting practice, and on May 25 he took a shot in the face off the bat of the Tigers' Hank Greenberg, damaging his nose, jaw, and some teeth. And on August 18, a liner by the Browns' Moose Solters fractured a fibula in Fritz's leg. His season record was 7–8; he beat Cleveland three times, and lost to both the Yankees and Tigers on three occasions. Two of his victories were notable; on June 8 he triumphed over the Yankees and Lefty Gomez, 4–2, surrendering six hits and garnering three safeties of his own. And on July 30, he struggled to an 11–4, complete-game win over Washington, though he gave up a dozen walks, along with four hits.

A hitter of great renown joined the Red Sox in 1936: Jimmie Foxx. The power hitter from the Athletics added some needed sock to the Boston attack for several years; in '36 he batted .338, smacked 41 homers, and drove in 143 runs. Ostermueller saw more action on the mound that season, but his 10–16 record was disappointing. He started 23 games, completed seven, and worked 180⅔ innings; he still suffered dizzy spells from Greenberg's

smash of the previous year. The Red Sox finished the season in sixth place; Wes Ferrell and Lefty Grove notched 20 and 17 wins, respectively.

Ostermueller made only seven starts in 1937, and pitched just 86⅔ innings in 25 games. He was shut down at various times during the season by a chipped bone in his pitching elbow; Fritz didn't pitch after August 8, and went under the knife of Dr. Robert Hyland in St. Louis at the close of the 1937 season.

Red Sox hitters clicked in 1938, leading the league in team batting with a .299 average, and the club finished in second place behind the Yankees. Foxx led the AL in hitting (.349) and RBIs (175), and belted 50 home runs. The lowest batting average of the regulars was rookie second baseman Bobby Doerr's .289. The extra run support helped the pitching staff, including Ostermueller, who returned to form with 13 wins against 5 losses. He started the season strongly; on April 19, Fritz pitched six innings of one-hit ball in relief to beat the Yankees, 6–0. And six days later, he blanked the Senators, 7–0, on four hits.

Ostey batted .234 and totaled 175 hits in his major-league career without hitting a home run, although he belted several in the minors. On June 10, 1938, Ostermueller watched with irony as southpaw hurler Bill Lefebvre, signed off the campus of Holy Cross College by the Red Sox a few days earlier, made his big-league debut against the White Sox in a mop-up role. Lefebvre remained in the game to hit, and on the first pitch delivered to him in the major leagues, he lofted Monty Stratton's offering over the left-field wall for a home run.

Rookie outfielder Ted Williams was a welcome addition to the Boston lineup in 1939; he paced the AL with 145 RBIs, batted .327, and clouted 31 home runs. Foxx was the league leader with 35 homers, and batted .360 to finish second to Joe DiMaggio's .381. The Yankees took the flag again, distancing themselves from the runner-up Red Sox by 17 games. Ostermueller made 20 starts, won 11 games, lost 7, and recorded four saves. The left-hander was most effective against the Yankees, Browns, and Washington Senators, beating each club three times.

Fritz was ailing when he reported to Sarasota in February 1940. He arrived with influenza, along with a serious sinus condition, thought to be a delayed reaction to the line drive off Greenberg's bat in 1935. Ostermueller was left behind when the Red Sox departed Florida, worked out with the Louisville farm club, and didn't make his first start until May 12. He pitched seven innings against New York, allowed one earned run, yet it was all for naught; Red Ruffing shut out the Red Sox, 4–0. It wasn't until July 17 that Fritz recorded his initial victory, beating the Tigers in a relief role. In what would be his final season in Boston, Ostey won only five games and lost nine. He made 16 starts, going the route in five of them.

Ostermueller had three highlight games late in 1940. On August 1, he beat the Indians and Mel Harder, 5–2. Fritz logged a complete-game seven-hitter, and Foxx, filling in at his old position at catcher, slammed a two-run homer. Four days later, the same battery took on the Yankees, and led the Red Sox to a 4–1 victory. Foxx contributed another two-run round-tripper and the southpaw pitched a seven-hitter. On September 27, Fritz took the mound for his final start in a Red Sox uniform, and defeated Washington in a 24–4 laugher. In December, Ostermueller and right-hander Denny Galehouse were sold to the St. Louis Browns for $30,000.

In 1941 the Browns trained in San Antonio, Texas, where Ostermueller and Galehouse joined veteran hurlers Bob Muncrief, George Caster, Johnny Allen, and Elden Auker. The lone left-hander in the group, Fritz did well in spring games, but was plagued by a sore arm during the season; he lost three games without logging a win. In February 1942, St. Louis sold Ostey to their Toledo farm club, where he resurrected his career with 11 victories and a 3.23 ERA. The Browns bought his contract back on July 26, and the portsider worked in 10 games, contributing three wins against a single loss to St. Louis's rise to third place at season's end.

The Browns trained in Cape Girardeau, Missouri, in 1943, due to wartime travel restrictions, and Ostermueller's role was diminished when he was struck on the left elbow by a batted ball. Surgery followed to remove the elbow cap, and it forced a change in the left-hander's windup, as a "catch" developed in his elbow. Sportswriter Vince Johnson of the *Pittsburgh Post-Gazette* later wrote: "By bending low and swinging his arms in unison Fritz found that he could tell whether the elbow would 'catch' and then correct the trouble without interrupting his motion." Two of Ostey's future teammates also commented on the windup; Pittsburgh slugger Ralph Kiner said, "Fritz had an unusual windup; no one like it." And 1947 Pirates second baseman Eddie Basinski said, "It wasn't a true windmill; similar, but also partly a rocking motion."

Ostermueller worked sparingly for the 1943 Browns; he was winless in three starts, and was charged with two losses. On July 15 he was part of a trade to the Brooklyn Dodgers that brought much-traveled hurler Louis "Bobo" Newsom to the Browns. Ostey didn't want to go east because of the higher cost of living in New York, but Dodgers general manager Branch Rickey satisfied his demands, and the southpaw reported to Brooklyn. His baptism as a National Leaguer was spotty; Fritz relieved in six games before he injured his ankle while sliding into third base. Six weeks later, he started against the Braves, and was removed after pitching nine innings in a 2–2 tie. Also, because of his marital status, Ostermueller was classified 3-A in the military draft; then arthritis caused him to be rejected twice from military service in 1943.

Ostey's career took several more turns in 1944. He began the season in the Dodgers' rotation, and by May 14 had started four times, with three complete games and a pair of wins. Fritz's sole loss in those four appearances was a heartbreaker; on April 27 Jim Tobin of the Braves tossed a no-hitter to beat the Dodgers, 2–0. Ostermueller surrendered only five hits, one of them a solo home run by Tobin.

In spite of his creditable work, Fritz again was relegated to the Brooklyn bullpen, and on May 27, Rickey put him on waivers. The move was controversial, as the veteran left-hander was only six weeks short of 10-year status in the majors, and with several teams in need of help on the mound, Ostey went unclaimed on the waiver wire. On May 30, Rickey swung a deal with Syracuse; to obtain outfielder Goody Rosen, he sent cash and pitchers Bill Lohrman and Ostermueller to the International League team. The two Dodger hurlers didn't want to go back to the minor leagues, however, and refused to report to Syracuse. Two days later, Pittsburgh purchased Ostey's contract from the International League club, and he was back in the majors.

Pirates manager Frankie Frisch welcomed his new acquisition, and Ostermueller responded with 11 victories and a staff-leading 2.73 ERA. Fritz beat New York and St. Louis three times each. It was a nice turnaround for the veteran hurler, as Pittsburgh finished the season in second place, while the Dodgers wound up in seventh, 42 games behind the pennant-winning Cardinals.

It was snowing when Ostey joined the Pirates for 1945 spring training in Muncie, Indiana. And personally, a dark cloud was hanging over his head; word came that he had been reclassified 1-A in the draft, and to prepare for induction into the Army sometime in April. Fritz chose to stay with the team through spring drills, and was the Pirates' starting pitcher in the season opener in Cincinnati. The Reds' Dain Clay spoiled the afternoon for the southpaw when he hit a grand-slam; Ostey left after four innings, and the Pirates eventually lost in 10 innings, 5–4. Fritz made one more start, losing to Chicago, 3–0, before being inducted into the Army and assigned to Fort Leonard Wood, Missouri. He was discharged three months later, on July 24, and rejoined the Pirates the following week. The southpaw recorded an overall 5–4 record in the broken season; he defeated St. Louis and Boston twice each, and lost three decisions to Chicago. The Pirates remained in the first division of the NL, placing fourth.

Pittsburgh baseball spiraled downward in 1946 and 1947; the club dropped to seventh in 1946, but welcomed rookie outfielder Ralph Kiner to the roster. Kiner's 23 homers led the league, while Ostermueller topped the team's hurlers with 13 wins and a 2.84 ERA. Fritz had a bittersweet day in St. Louis on July 7, 1946. Five hundred admirers from his hometown took a special train 140 miles to attend Fritz Ostermueller Day at Sportsman's Park. Included in the gifts presented to the pitcher by the Quincy Boosters Club were a $500 check, a wristwatch, and a set of golf clubs. The Cardinals put a damper on the celebration two hours later, however, when they scored a run in the bottom of the ninth to beat Ostey and the Pirates, 4–3.

Frisch left as Pittsburgh skipper after 1946, and was succeeded by Billy Herman. A splurge in home runs couldn't keep the Pirates out of the basement in 1947; Hank Greenberg came over from Detroit to finish his career, and supplied 25 four-baggers. Kiner, batting in front of Greenberg, upped his homer total to 51, and tied Johnny Mize for league honors. The quote, "Home run hitters drive Cadillacs, singles hitters drive Fords," was originally credited as coming from Kiner, but the slugger later corrected the source. In October 2005, Kiner wrote, "Fritz was a great teammate and a good pitcher for us; he did coin the expression, not I." Ostermueller's 12 wins again were highest on the mound staff, and Pirates second baseman Eddie Basinski complimented his teammate by writing, "When Ostermueller pitched, I knew we had an excellent chance of winning."

Ostermueller's career came to a close in 1948; he finished the year at 8–11, but was a major factor in Pittsburgh's run for the pennant. Manager Billy Meyer spotted him against the league's best, and the veteran responded. In games with the Braves, he triumphed over Johnny Sain in 1–0 and 2–1 skirmishes, and was beaten 2–1 by Warren Spahn. Harry Brecheen of St. Louis beat Fritz twice, and in another classic game, the two lefties battled to a 10-inning, l-l tie halted by darkness. In his 1948 season debut, Fritz had a no-hitter going against the Reds until there were two outs in the seventh inning, but Hank Sauer ruined it with a homer. Fritz did gain a victory, 7–2.

Life after baseball was a busy time for Ostermueller. He and Faye had adopted a baby girl, Sherrill, in 1947, and retirement at home in Quincy allowed the couple to spend more time with their daughter. Fritz had other pursuits as well; he joined the American Legion, was a life member of the Quincy Lodge of Elks, and was an avid hunter. For several years he was part of the broadcasting crew for the minor-league Quincy Gems. Ostermueller was in the booth as color man on August 13, 1949, when Harry Caray, then the play-by-play voice of the St. Louis

Cardinals, came to Quincy to work the Waterloo-Quincy game on Gems' Boosters Night.

The Ostermuellers built a motel on their Quincy property, and Old Folks became the owner-operator of the aptly named Diamond Motel. The family took annual hunting vacations to the Rocky Mountains, and in 1956 Ostey was hospitalized in Missoula, Montana, after becoming ill. The first signs of colon cancer were discovered, and Fritz's health declined. On September 15, 1957, his 50th birthday, Ostermueller became eligible to receive his major-league pension. Daughter Sherrill said, "I can still see him walking out our little lane to the mailbox; he wasn't feeling good, but he would take that walk. He was so excited to receive his check."

The crafty pitcher, whose southpaw deliveries were received by some of the game's best catchers, including Hall of Famers Rick Ferrell and Al Lopez, succumbed to his illness, and died in Quincy on December 17, 1957.

For several years after his death, the Quincy Elks Lodge hosted an annual dinner to award the Fritz Ostermueller Memorial Trophy to a Quincy product who had gained national attention in sports. One of the recipients was Elvin Tappe, a graduate of Quincy High School and Quincy College, who later was a catcher and coach with the Chicago Cubs.

Faye Ostermueller took over as operator of the Diamond Motel after her husband's death, later sold the property, and worked for a time as a reservations clerk with Holiday Inns. She died in Quincy on July 14, 2001, at the age of 92, and was buried next to her husband in Quincy's Calvary Cemetery. Their only child, Sherrill Ostermueller Duesterhaus, resides in Missouri with her husband.

Sources

Fritz Ostermueller file at National Baseball Hall of Fame Library & Research Center

Scrapbook and clippings of Faye Ostermueller and Sherrill Duesterhaus

Conversations with Sherrill Duesterhaus

Eddie Basinski correspondence

Ralph Kiner correspondence

SABR ProQuest Historical Newspapers

Baseball Library.com (www.baseballlibrary.com)

Warren Corbett, SABR BioProject (Ralph Kiner)

Cleve, Craig Allen. *Hardball on the Home Front*. Jefferson, North Carolina: McFarland & Co., 2004.

JOHNNY PEACOCK *by Bill Nowlin*

G	AB	R	H	2B	3B	HR	RBI	BB	SO	BA	OBP	SLG	SB	HBP
92	274	33	76	11	4	0	36	29	11	.277	.347	.347	1	0

Mule trader, major league ballplayer, sawmill operator, college trustee—Fremont, North Carolina's John Gaston Peacock enjoyed a varied life. Johnny Peacock's work as catcher for the Boston Red Sox embraced six full seasons and parts of two others, his big-league career ranged from 1937 through 1945.

Born in Fremont, in the Piedmont region of central North Carolina, on January 10, 1910, Johnny grew up on a farm in an area where Peacock was a very common name at the time. He was born to Serena Aycock Peacock, a homemaker, and Frank Lee Peacock, a mule trader and tobacco farmer in and around Fremont. John was the middle of 11 children—five were born before him and five after.

John Peacock Jr., Johnny's son, says that among his father's brothers, there were two who were said to have been better ballplayers than Johnny, but they didn't have the desire or competitive spirit that Johnny had.

Johnny was an excellent athlete in high school and accepted a basketball scholarship to the University of North Carolina starting in 1929. In college, he lettered in three sports—basketball, baseball (primarily playing second base and right field, and catching occasionally), and football. In his first football game, he ran the opening kickoff back for a touchdown against Tennessee. But it was on the baseball field that he had the most success; he won one notable game against Penn in April 1931 with a two-run triple that accounted for all the runs scored in the game.

Peacock played some semipro ball for teams in Elizabeth City, North Carolina, and Culpeper, Virginia. He graduated from UNC in the spring of 1933 and was signed by Cincinnati Reds executive Larry MacPhail at a tryout camp held at Beckley, West Virginia. At this one camp, MacPhail also signed six other players who went on to major-league careers: Lee Gamble, Lee Grissom, Frank McCormick, Whitey Moore, Jimmy Outlaw, and Les Scarsella.

Peacock's first pro team was the Wilmington (North Carolina) ballclub of the Class B Piedmont League. A November 1933 summary of Piedmont League play described Peacock as an "above par" outfielder. He played

Johnny Peacock

some second base for Wilmington Pirates manager Blackie Carter as well, batting .285 with seven homers and 45 RBIs in 103 games.

Peacock played again for the Wilmington Pirates in 1934 (they were now a Cincinnati Reds affiliate), improved his average to .297 and played his first games as a catcher, though he wouldn't fully convert to catcher until 1937. His play earned him a promotion and his contract was purchased by the Toronto Maple Leafs, still in the Cincinnati system. In 1935, Johnny caught, played in the outfield, and played second base. At one time or another throughout his career, he played every position other than pitcher. He got into 92 International League games in 1935, with 255 at-bats, and hit for a .290 average. The next year Johnny went to spring training with the Cincinnati Reds but wound up playing for Nashville in the Southern Association, hitting .334 in 112 games. His accomplishments earned him a big payday, prompted by an unexpected ruling by Baseball Commissioner Kenesaw Mountain Landis on November 29.

Landis ruled that Peacock and infielder Lee Handley were both free agents, no longer under Cincinnati control, and that they were free to take offers from any ballclub other than Cincinnati. Normally, the sale of a player's contract would benefit the club making the sale; but because of Landis's ruling, the money went into Peacock's pocket—and he invested it well, buying three farms in North Carolina which he owned until 1965. Landis was upset at the transparent deception in player assignments of the day. In Johnny's case, as *The Sporting News* explained in its December 3, 1936 issue, his official file showed he had been "optioned by Toronto to Nashville early in 1936, with the option having been canceled, after which the catcher had been assigned by Nashville to Cincinnati for $500."

The chicanery concerned the commissioner, who wrote, "The record ought to speak the truth. The fact is, however, that to these players the whole record is a pure fake. Toronto never had any independent, real title to the contract of either player. At all times, the Cincinnati club, acting through its vice-president and general manager, completely dominated and controlled Toronto's attitude toward these players as well as Toronto's disposition of the players and their contracts. In plain truth, the Toronto club corporation had no more control over or title to either Handley's or Peacock's [contract] than did the Toronto bat boy." In Peacock's case, "Nashville acted only as a turnstile and so understood it." Landis nullified both contracts due to their "irregularities" (as it was politely reported in the press).

Three days after the Commissioner's ruling, Peacock signed for a reported $8,000 with Tom Yawkey's Boston Red Sox.

Yawkey had the money and made the deal, outbidding at least one other team, the Washington Senators. Shirley Povich reported in the *Washington Post* that Senators owner Clark Griffith was "thanking his lucky stars that he was unable to sign Peacock. . . . Griffith saw the lad in action for the first time at Orlando the other day. . . . He saw the Nats work a double steal against Peacock and generally outsmart him." It wasn't long before Griffith realized that Peacock was a player. The Red Sox assigned Johnny to the Minneapolis Millers, their top farm club, and by midsummer he was named to the American Association all-star game, held in Columbus, Ohio. By season's end, he was hitting .311, with seven homers and 54 RBIs in 109 games— and in August was formally added to the Red Sox roster for spring 1938 delivery.

In the meantime, after the Millers lost to the Columbus Red Birds in the American Association playoffs, four games to two, Peacock was called up to play in Boston and debuted on September 23, 1937, catching Jim Henry, with whom he'd worked in Minneapolis (Henry had earlier pitched in 21 games for Boston in 1936). Johnny batted eighth in the order and was 0-for-3 on the day. Henry threw a complete game, though, and the Sox beat the Tigers, 4–3. It was a tight 1–1 game through eight innings, Henry matching up against Elden Auker. The Tigers took the lead with two runs in the top of the ninth, but Ben Chapman hit a three-run homer in the bottom of the ninth frame to win it.

After another 0-for-3 day, Peacock collected his first hit on a bunt to lead off the third inning against the Yankees on September 26. It was the first hit of the game for the Red Sox, and he scored the first run. Johnny Wilson got the 7–2 win for Boston. In 32 at-bats in 1937, Peacock hit .313 (seven singles, two doubles, and a triple) and

Peacock, the mule trader who became a college trustee

drove in six runs. He became a full-time major leaguer beginning with the 1938 season. As a backup to Gene Desautels, Johnny batted .303 in 195 at-bats and drove in 39 runs. It was an all college-grad catching corps, with Desautels (Holy Cross), Peacock, and Moe Berg (Princeton). Near the end of the year, Johnny hit the only home run of his major-league career: a bases-empty homer off Philadelphia Athletics pitcher Buck Ross on September 27 at Shibe Park and drove in three runs during an 11–1 pasting. His batterymate, Bill Harris, was 2-for-3 on the day.

Peacock played more games than Desautels in 1939, getting into 92 games—up from 72 the year before. One might assume it was a platoon situation, with Peacock a left-handed hitter (he was not imposing—he stood 5'11"and weighed in at 165), but it was really just that the first-string catcher, Desautels, disappointed so Peacock was given the shot. Peacock, whose defense improved after coach Tom Daly suggested he use a more supple mitt, was better, but not sufficiently so to win the spot for good.

Early in the season, Joe Cronin more than once praised Peacock's pinch-hitting, "I think Johnny's the best I've ever seen. I think his record last year was something like 12 hits in 22 tries and about eight or 10 of those times Johnny's hit represented the tying or winning run." [*Boston Globe*, May 2, 1939] Cronin misremembered, but in a spirit of generosity. SABR's Maurice Bouchard found that Peacock was 24-for-99 for his career, a .242 average which was less than his overall batting average. Peacock himself said, "It seems that I've been doing nothing but pinch-hitting all my life." His formula was to "bear down that much harder than in an ordinary time at bat. If you'll notice, I use a wider stance at the plate when I'm tying to score a man and just try to punch the ball safely over the infield."

Desautels wasn't hitting as well as before, and more was asked of Peacock but his average ultimately declined, too, to .277, with fewer RBIs (36). Moe Berg even picked up a little more work. Peacock played an important role on the team, but never again matched his 1938 season. After the 1939 season was over, *The Sporting News* summary of the season tried hard to be understanding of Peacock's inexperience as a catcher, terming him "a better than fair hitter, but a reconstructed catcher who was not naturally a receiver and was learning the art the hard way—by catching big league games." Johnny had three years of catching under his belt, though. Another article in the same issue said, "Peacock did a lot of catching for the Red Sox, but did not develop along defensive lines as rapidly as had been expected." He'd committed a career-high 10 errors, but his .972 fielding average was not too bad. He improved. In 1940, he committed just one error and in the years 1941, 1942, and 1943 he erred just four times each. In 1942, his .988 average was third-best among major-league catchers, behind Al Lopez and Otto Denning.

By mid-1941, sportswriter Jack Malaney acknowledged that Peacock's catching "has improved to the point where he now is a very acceptable receiver" but he wasn't hitting as well early in the season. Then he reeled off a string of eight consecutive hits in mid-July and finished the year with similar numbers to 1940: .284 in 1941 to 1940's .282. He had twice as many at-bats in 1941 and his RBI totals were proportionate—but not large: only 27 in 1941. "He's my idea of a hustling ballplayer," said Lefty Grove in midseason.

Desautels, Foxx, and Peacock more or less shared catching duties in 1940, but Gene was clearly the first-string catcher. In 1941, Frankie Pytlak took over the first-string role. Come 1942, Pytlak developed a foot infection in the offseason then was called into military service. Peacock experienced some problems with his ankles and shins due to the soft and sandy soil in Sarasota. He shared catching duties with Bill Conroy in 1942, with Conroy getting just a bit more work. Johnny expected he'd be off to war, too, and had gone as far as giving all his clothes away to his brothers when John Jr. was born in January 1942. It was literally the day before he was to leave that he received the word that, because he now had two children, he was exempt. Johnny had married Julia Brown and they had two children, Julia Bates Peacock (b. 8/15/1937) and John Jr. (b. 1/20/1942).

John Jr. claims another sister, too: Mary Ruth Crawford. In 1944, Johnny and his wife were approached by the Methodist Church in Fremont and asked if 13-year-old Mary Ruth could come practice piano at their house because she had talent but had no piano of her own. Her mother had died when she was an infant and her father was "the town drunk," John Jr. says. "I loved Mary Ruth so much and my sister—who was older than I was—she liked her so well that my mother asked Mary Ruth to go to Boston with us that summer when school was out, to babysit us. She said she'd love to. Well, Daddy was traded to Philadelphia that year and during the war it was extremely hard to find housing. Mary Ruth was so disappointed that she wasn't going to Boston. Daddy told Mother, Why don't you just rent a beach cottage at Carolina Beach, North Carolina, for the summer? So Mother asked Mary Ruth to go with us, she did and she never

left. She stayed with us until she finished school and was married. My father never legally adopted her." Mary Ruth got married and had five children. Johnny's birth sister married as well, retired, and lives in Wilmington, North Carolina.

Johnny's average dropped in 1942, down to .266—still not bad for a catcher (and much better than Conroy's .200) The following year he dropped to .202, getting into only 48 games, and driving in only seven runs. Roy Partee handled most of the catching. Peacock was involved in an incident in 1943 that made headlines across the country. The Red Sox were playing at Washington's Griffith Stadium on May 9. The Senators' Ellis Clary was batting. For no apparent reason, Clary flung his bat away, ripped Peacock's mask off, and started hitting him. The two "sprawled all over the plate" and it took quite a few players to separate them. Peacock later admitted he had taunted Clary.

In 1944 the Red Sox had Partee at catcher, and added Hal Wagner. Peacock had only four at-bats in four games for the Red Sox before he was sold to the Philadelphia Blue Jays for the waiver price of $7,500 on a June 11.

With the Blue Jays, Johnny played in 83 games, hitting .225 in 253 at-bats. He drove in 21 runs. He even played one game at his old position, second base. Though he had been declared exempt from the draft earlier, with the increased need for men Johnny learned that he was called for induction on February 23, 1945. He was then given a 40- to 60-day extension, and so trained with the Phillies and began the season with them. His average drifted even lower; after 74 at-bats, he was hitting just .203. He had six doubles, six RBIs, six bases on balls, and scored six runs. With Mickey Owen in the Navy, the Dodgers needed a catcher, though, and several hours before the June 15 trade deadline, they swung a deal with the Brooklyn Dodgers, getting former outfielder and now converted pitcher Ben Chapman for the veteran Peacock. The transaction earned a headline in *The Sporting News*: "Peacock Added to Flock, All Brooklyn Preening." Writer Harold C. Burr offered his evaluation: "Peacock is what ballplayers call a good receiver. He hasn't any terrific plate punch, but he will hit for you in the clutch." Another assessment was less kind, calling it a "nothing for nothing trade" since Peacock had a broken hand at the time and Chapman a sore arm.

Johnny played well for Brooklyn and batted .255. In November, though, with so many ballplayers coming back from the service, he was sold to the New Orleans Pelicans, to become player-manager for the Southern Association club. He finished in the majors with a lifetime .262 batting average in 619 ballgames.

With the Pelicans, Peacock became a backup catcher. One of the first games he put himself into was an exhibition game against the Dodgers in New Orleans on April 7; Johnny won it with a pinch-hit single. He sent himself to bat 54 times during the season, and hit .259, but with three tobacco farms to run back in North Carolina, he decided to call it a career in baseball.

In fact, there was more business than just the three farms. While he was playing in Boston, a local hardware store declared bankruptcy and Peacock bought up the inventory and sent it home to North Carolina, opening a store in Fremont called Peacock Builders Supply. His oldest brother managed the store, selling building materials and hardware. In all, Johnny put four of his brothers in business. A sawmill and cotton gin came up for sale, the John C. Rose Lumber and Gin Company. Mr. Rose had lost his son, who was killed in the South Pacific, and he lost heart. Rose's daughter married Jimmy Peacock, one of Johnny's brothers—a pilot shot down and taken as a prisoner of war in Germany. Johnny and Jimmy bought out Rose, but within six months, Rose wanted back in so they worked out a three-way split. Johnny and his son John Jr. bought the company from Rose in the late 1960s. Peacock father and son were already operating a sawmill in Wilson. At one point, Johnny also ran a grain dealership buying wheat, corn, and soybeans. At the height of their varied operations, Peacock employed up to 180 people.

As a prominent businessman in Wayne County, Johnny was invited to serve on the board of trustees of the Wayne County Memorial Hospital. In 1963, he was appointed to the board of Wayne County Community College. He served five terms, becoming vice chair. His son says the college began as an industrial school and his father felt that it was very important to teach trades to young people who lacked either the means or desire to pursue a college education. The college has grown dramatically since the time he joined the board.

John Jr. and his father had worked together for 20 years before they sold the business and John Jr. went into public sector work. In his last few years, Johnny developed rheumatoid arthritis and suffered considerable pain. While in Wilson one day, he had a heart attack and died on October 17, 1981. Johnny's son was with him at the time of his passing. "It was not an easy thing," John Jr. says. "Pain all the time. It was just so bad that he was ready."

Sources

Interview with John G. Peacock, Jr., June 4, 2007
John Peacock player file at the National Baseball Hall of Fame

WOODY RICH *by Mark Armour*

G	ERA	W	L	SV	GS	GF	CG	SHO	IP	H	R	ER	BB	SO	HR	HBP	WP	BFP
21	4.91	4	3	1	12	4	3	0	77	78	46	42	35	24	2	5	0	344

G	AB	R	H	2B	3B	HR	RBI	BB	SO	BA	OBP	SLG	SB	HBP
21	27	2	7	0	0	0	1	1	4	.259	.286	.259	0	0

Woody Rich, all too briefly, was a pitching phenom. He entered his first major-league training camp, in 1939, barely noticed amid all the attention given to fellow rookie Ted Williams. By the end of March he was being compared to the great Pete Alexander, and reliable witnesses were predicting he would win 20 games. He roomed with Ted Williams, but only one of them would go on to major-league glory. The other, alas, would hurt his pitching arm. Rich never fulfilled the high hopes of March 1939, but he did go on to pitch 19 more years professionally, and make several minor-league all-star teams. Not so bad, really.

Woodrow Earl "Woody" Rich was born to David Henry and Callie Lane Rich on March 9, 1916, near in Morganton, North Carolina. The Riches

Woody Rich

had owned a family farm, and raised eight children—five sons and three daughters—with Woody being the fifth child in the batting order. Morganton is in the western part of the state, a rural area about sixty miles east of the Smoky Mountains. Woody had the typical childhood of a farm family in the 1920s and 1930s—hard manual labor, and recreation when time permitted.

Rich graduated from Morganton High School in 1935, and began his baseball career pitching semipro ball in nearby Valdese, North Carolina. According to a story told later by Red Sox farm director Billy Evans, he was in the area on a scouting mission when he ran into an unnamed former major-league player who was down on his luck. Evans gave him five dollars, and the grateful ex-player tipped him off to Rich. Evans sent scout Fred Hunter to look Rich over, and the Red Sox landed him for the cost of the five dollars.

In 1937 the big right-hander (6'2", 185 pounds) made his professional debut with Clarksdale, Mississippi, of the Class C Cotton States League. There he finished 12–15 in 32 games with a 4.42 earned run average. He was a

Though a sidearm pitcher, Rich adopts here the more traditional pose

straight overhand thrower, but the next year at Little Rock (Southern Association) he was made into a side-arm pitcher by manager Doc Prothro, and he flourished despite early-season wildness. He walked nearly twice as many hitters in 1938 as he had the year before, but still finished 19–10 with a stellar 2.48 ERA. On September 6 he fulfilled the dream of most pitchers by hurling a no-hit, no-run game against the Atlanta Crackers, the club that went on to win the league championship.

Rich attended the Red Sox training camp of 1939 in Sarasota with the idea that he was a year or so away from helping the club. Although fellow recruits Ted Williams and Jim Tabor were practically handed starting jobs in right field and third base, Rich was the unexpected sensation of the camp, enough so that he made the starting rotation. In his first two spring appearances, against the Braves and Reds, he allowed three hits, no walks, and no runs. Coach Tom Daly compared Rich's delivery—side-

arming and nonchalant—and his effect on batters to his old teammate Grover Cleveland Alexander. Bill Mc-Kechnie, the Reds manager, was equally impressed. "If he doesn't win twenty, I'll be surprised" said the Hall of Fame skipper.

Asked to explain how he got his strong right arm, he told writer Burt Whitman, "When I wasn't plowing, chopping wood or hoeing corn, I used to throw a lot of stones at snakes and birds. Maybe that's how I developed my arm. But if, as you say, I've got big, powerful looking wrists I reckon I got them from hoeing that corn and chopping that wood." He added, "We used to make bats out of hickory logs, but maybe we didn't have enough bats. But we had plenty of birds and snakes." He credited Herb Pennock, Red Sox coach, with working with on throwing the ball to the catcher's glove and ignoring the batter. But he reserved more praise for teammate Lefty Grove, who taught him control and confidence.

In early April the Red Sox and Reds broke camp and made their way north playing exhibition games in different towns. On April 7 they played a game in Lexington, North Carolina, about 90 miles from Woody's home town of Morganton. His neighbors took up a collection so that his father could come to the game in a taxi. Rich's father did not know anything about baseball, and said that Woody had learned the game by playing with "the Negro folk" in the area. Woody started and lost the game.

In his first regular-season major-league game, April 22 at Fenway Park, Rich beat the Athletics on a six-hitter, 6–2. Rich got two hits himself, and handled six chances on the mound. After pitching poorly in relief, he got his next start on May 5 and pitched the Red Sox into first place with a three-hitter, which beat the Tigers by a 4–1 score. By the end of May he had won four of his six starts and appeared primed for a big rookie year. Fellow rookie Ted Williams, Rich's roommate, was doing all right for himself as well.

On May 26 Rich won his fourth game, becoming the team's leading winner, by beating the Senators at Fenway Park, 4–2. Late in the game, while making a throw to first base, he hurt his arm and after just a few more pitches had to be removed from the game. It was first thought to be a strained bicep, and not overly serious, but the pain lingered. Within a few days he could not raise his arm.

Rich did not start again until July 4, but he didn't survive the first inning in a game the Red Sox won 18–12. On July 17 he lasted only into the third. After a few more rough outings, in early August, the Red Sox finally sent Rich down to Louisville. The Red Sox had only one reliable pitcher, Lefty Grove, and manager Joe Cronin felt that the loss of Rich was the primary reason they could not hang closer to the Yankees that season. Rich finished 4–3, 4.91 for Boston, and 2–2, 5.10 for Louisville.

Rich returned to Sarasota in 1940, apparently recovered. He introduced a new delivery in which he twisted his body away from the batter before throwing the ball, thus hiding the ball a while longer. "I'm pleased with this new development in Rich," said Cronin, "because it ought to make him a better pitcher, more effective against the general run of big-league batters." The skipper added, "When a pitcher feels confident that a new wrinkle will help him, the battle is half won." But Rich did not pitch as well, and was sent to Louisville, and then to Scranton. For the season he finished 1–2, 6.58 for Louisville, 6–4, 2.60 for Scranton, and then pitched well in 11⅓ September innings for the Red Sox, including a win when he started the season's final game.

After a few tough outings early in the 1941 season, Rich was released outright to Louisville. After pitching nine games for that club, and then 23 for San Diego (Pacific Coast League), Rich was sold to Indianapolis (American Association) in December 1941. After a 10–10 season for the Indians in 1942, the St. Louis Browns drafted Rich, but released him back to Indianapolis in April. Except for a brief stint with the Boston Braves in 1944, Rich spent five seasons at Indianapolis, 1942 through 1946. While there he won 26 games and lost 38. For the Braves, he split two decisions with a 5.76 earned run average in seven games.

Pictures from this time suggest that Rich was no longer the lanky pitcher he had been when he reported to the Red Sox. Hub Miller wrote about Rich in an article about players with weight problems in *Baseball Magazine* in 1947. "One of the most tragic cases in the memory of the writer is that of Woody Rich. . . . But Rich's fame was short-lived. He did stay with the club long enough to win a few games and, at times, showed flashes of greatness. But the boy had such an uncontrollable appetite that he soon was fat and well beyond big league hurling condition. It was not long before he even had trouble winning in the higher minors." A note in his Hall of Fame file from 1958 says he weighed 220 pounds, 35 more than his listed weight in the encyclopedias.

After the 1946 season, Indianapolis released Rich and he resurfaced the following season with Anniston, Alabama, of the Class B Southeastern League. In fact, he spent most of three seasons there. In 1947 he finished 19–10 with a league leading 197 strikeouts and a 3.32 ERA. The next season (during which he pitched 3 games for Shreveport of the Texas), Rich returned to Anniston and posted a 17–10 record while pacing the circuit in strikeouts (196) and ERA (2.48). In both seasons he was named to the post-season all-league team. In 1949 his record fell to 10–11, but he still had a 2.81 earned run average.

By the 1950 season Rich was 34 years old, but not finished playing baseball by a long shot. He pitched for Greensboro, North Carolina, of the Class B Carolina League that year, and finished 16–9 with a league leading

2.41 ERA. Again, he was all-league. In 1951 he moved on again, to St. Petersburg of the Class B Florida International League. This time he put up a 25–6 ledger and a 2.34 ERA. In 1952 he pitched for Memphis of the Class AA Southern Association, and finished 13–10.

The 37-year-old kept pitching. He pitched three more games for Memphis at the start of the 1953 season (1–0), then joined the Forest City Owls of the Class D Tar Heel League, where he finished 11–2, 2.65. Returning the next season (and managing the club briefly), Rich started 3–2 1.85, but the league folded in June, and he spent the rest of that season and the next two with High Point-Thomasville of the Carolina League. He had three more good seasons—13–6, 19–4, and 17–12, at ages 38 through 40. In the middle season he led the league in wins and was voted all-league.

Rich finally started to slow down at age 41. He pitched 29 games for Savannah in the Sally League in 1957, winning his two decisions with a 2.48 earned run average. The next season he started just 1–5 for Charlotte in the Sally League, then finished the year in Boise, Idaho, winning six and losing four in the Pioneer League (Class C). After pitching in the Deep South for so long, the move to Boise must have been an adventure for old Woody. At any rate, his career had come to an end. In his two decades of minor league action, Rich finished with 250 wins and 174 losses, to go along with his 6–4 major league record.

Woody had married Durline Walker (born in August 1917 to Wade H. and Sarah Ann Chapman Walker) in 1935, before he started his baseball career, and the couple had two children. They settled in Indianapolis sometime during his five-year stint there, and remained after his baseball career ended. Woody worked as an auto mechanic. He and Durline returned in 1968 to their hometown in Morganton, where they spent the remainder of their days.

Woody died on April 18, 1983, in Valdese General Hospital, after battling lung cancer for a year. He left behind Durline, his wife of 48 years, a daughter, Martha, and eight grandchildren. Late in his life Woody answered a note from the Hall of Fame that sent him his complete professional record. He thanked the sender, and sent a brief note saying that he hurt his arm pitching against Washington and "it never came around after that so that is about all I can think up." After his sore arm, Woody Rich pitched 19 more seasons, many of them pretty well.

Sources

Woody Rich player file at the National Baseball Hall of Fame.
The News Herald (Morganton, NC), April 20, 1983.
Baseball Magazine. March 1937.
Christian Science Monitor. May 17, 1939; May 6, 1940.
The Sporting News. March 30, 1939.
Boston Globe, 1939.
US Census, 1920.

BILL SAYLES *by Maurice Bouchard*

G	ERA	W	L	SV	GS	GF	CG	SHO	IP	H	R	ER	BB	SO	HR	HBP	WP	BFP
5	7.07	0	0	0	0	3	0	0	14	14	13	11	13	9	1	0	2	67

G	AB	R	H	2B	3B	HR	RBI	BB	SO	BA	OBP	SLG	SB	HBP
5	7	0	1	0	0	0	0	0	5	.143	.143	.143	0	0

It is fitting that Bill Sayles started his big league career in Boston. The Sayles family had come full circle. He may not have realized it, but he was not the first of his family to ply his trade in Massachusetts. His ancestors landed on Boston's shore before Boston was Boston. The Sayles family can trace their ancestry in America to John and Philippa Sayles, who left Sudbury, England, in 1625 or 1626 and settled in what was to become Charlestown, Massachusetts (now part of Boston). There, in 1626, they had a daughter, Phebe, and in 1633, a son, John. After Philippa died in 1635, the family moved to Providence, Rhode Island. The Sayles family became well established in Providence and the surrounding towns for five generations before Stephen Sayles (b. 1780) moved his family to Wallingford, Vermont. Stephen's grandson Willis G. Sayles (b. 1846) became a civil engineer and surveyor. He moved with his wife, Delia, and their young son, Clyde Otis, from Vermont to Oregon in the early 1880s to work for the burgeoning railroads. The family moved to Walla Walla, Washington, for a time, but Clyde was back in Oregon before 1916. It was in Oregon that Clyde met and married Nell (nee Ashton) Nisbeth. Their first child, William Nisbeth Sayles, was born on July 27, 1917, in Portland, Oregon. Another son, Robert C., came five years later.

Bill learned to play sports with his East Glisan Street neighborhood friends in the Russellville section of Portland. Young Sayles grew to become a three-sport star at Washington High School. He played basketball; he was the quarterback and punter[1] for the football team; and pitched for the baseball team. During his high school years, the 6-foot-2, 185-pound right-hander was something of a baseball celebrity in Portland. Sayles was a star pitcher for the Portland City League champion, Ballin Finance. In 1934 and 1935, Sayles was the leading pitcher on Portland City League all-star teams. These teams were notable because they included future major-league stars Joe Gordon and Johnny Pesky and were coached by former Red Sox and Yankees pitching standout Carl Mays.

Bill Sayles

Mays, winner of 207 major-league games, imparted much baseball wisdom to his young pitcher. Sayles credited Mays with teaching him how to pitch. After Sayles graduated from high school in 1935, he was named to the Oregon Prep All-Star Team. With these accomplishments, it is easy to see why the University of Oregon offered Bill a baseball scholarship. He was the leading pitcher for the Ducks freshman baseball team the following spring.

Bill Sayles has the distinction of being on the first United States Olympic baseball team. A former major-league outfielder turned promoter, Les Mann, worked tirelessly to make baseball an Olympic sport. He couldn't convince the United States Olympic Committee in 1932 (when Los Angeles was the host city), but managed to persuade the Germans to include baseball as an exhibition sport in 1936. Trials were held in Baltimore in July. Sayles made the U.S. team and joined the rest of the Olympians as they traveled to Berlin in August 1936. Unfortunately, no other country fielded a baseball team. Consequently, the "tournament" was reduced to a single exhibition game between two American squads, dubbed "World Champions" and "U.S. Olympics." About 100,000 mostly bemused people were in attendance.[2] At the time, it was the largest crowd ever to see a baseball game.

Although announcers were explaining the rules in three languages, the German audience could not make sense of the game. They would be silent for spectacular fielding plays but cheer wildly for high popups. The game was played on a poorly lit, makeshift field with no mound. One member of the team joked, "They hung a 20-watt bulb in the outfield."[3] Because the diamond was described on the infield of the track, the outfield dimensions were nonstandard, to say the least. The distance to right field was more than twice the distance to left. In later years, Sayles often told the story of Adolf Hitler's appearance at the game.[4] Before batting practice, Hitler's guards told the young Americans that Hitler would enter the stadium during batting practice and they were to stop batting while the German people recognized their leader. They also didn't want anyone hitting the ball to where their boss was sitting. Hitler chose to sit on the short side of the field, just beyond the left field "fence." It proved too tempting for the young ballplayers. Not only did they not halt batting practice when Hitler made his entrance, they purposely tried to hit balls in Der Führer's lap. The World Champions defeated the U.S. Olympics 6–5 in seven innings. Sayles pitched for the World Champions but was not involved in the decision.

The following spring, Sayles played for Oregon's varsity nine, coached by Howard Hobson, and became their leading pitcher. He pitched two no-hitters for the Ducks that season. He led his team to the Northern Division championship, was named the Pacific Coast Conference's outstanding pitcher, and was named to the 1937 conference all-star team. After the college season was complete, Sayles pitched in a semipro senior league in Vancouver, British Columbia, where he compiled a 14–4 record and was named to the all-star team. After the standout seasons with the Ducks and in Vancouver, major-league scouts were bound to notice. Earl Sheely, the Red Sox' West Coast scout, signed Sayles to his first professional contract. The 20-year-old, who was now married to the former Geraldine May of Portland, said the financial inducements to leave school had greater appeal after his recent nuptials.

Sayles' first assignment in the minor leagues was with the Little Rock Travelers, managed by Doc Prothro. The Travelers were part of the eight-team Class A1 Southern Association. Sayles compiled a 7–9 record in 1938 with the fifth-place Travelers. Sayles was a hard thrower (Ted Williams remembered his fastball to a reporter from *The Sporting News* nearly 30 years after the fact).[5] Like many hard throwers, Sayles suffered from control problems. He struck out 53 in 133 innings for Little Rock but he also walked 70. Even so, he had a respectable 3.32 ERA and four complete games in his initial professional season.

Sayles went to spring training with the Red Sox in 1939, and early in March manager Joe Cronin told Jack Malaney of the *Boston Post* he was impressed with his young pitchers (including Sayles).[6] Four years later, Sayles remembered it differently. In an interview with Frank C. True, Sayles said,

Sayles was on the 1936 Olympic team that Hitler watched take batting practice

"I know it's traditional for pitchers to howl about getting a raw deal, but, really, I don't believe Cronin saw enough of me to know the color of my hair." He went on to add, "The longest conversation I ever had with him [Cronin] was when he walked over to me during spring training in 1939 and said 'You'll never make the Red Sox.' What his basis for the statement was still is a mystery to me. I asked a question, but it went unanswered. Such a blunt rebuff took the heart out of me for several months."[7]

Whatever was said, by the end of March, Sayles was released to Little Rock to start another season with the Travelers. Sayles spent the first three months of the 1939 season with Little Rock where he "performed brilliantly."[8] In mid-July, when Jim Bagby Jr. was sent down to the Travelers, Sayles was called up to the Red Sox. He made his major-league debut, in relief, on July 17, 1939, at Briggs Stadium in Detroit. The Sox were losing 8–3 when Sayles was brought in with no one out in the fourth inning. Sayles pitched the last five innings, giving up five runs on four hits with one strikeout, four walks, and a wild pitch as the Sox fell to the Tigers, 13–6. It was not a great outing but Sayles did manage his first major-league hit, a single off Buck Newsom.

Sayles' next appearance came two days later, in the second game of a July 19 doubleheader against the White Sox in Comiskey Park. He came into the game, started by Fritz Ostermueller, with two outs in the fifth inning and Boston trailing 5–0. Sayles pitched 2⅓ innings and gave up three runs on five hits with a strikeout and a walk. The Red Sox lost the game, 8–0. Sayles didn't get into another game until July 28, when, yet again, he came in to relieve when the Red Sox were already behind. They were trailing the St. Louis Browns, 6–1, when Sayles relieved Elden Auker with one out in the top of the second inning. Sayles held the Browns scoreless over 1⅔ innings, allowing just one hit, with a strikeout and three walks.

On August 2, with the Sox trailing the Cleveland Indians, 8–2, at Fenway Park, Sayles pitched hitless, scoreless eighth and ninth innings. The lanky Oregonian's last major-league outing of 1939 came three days later in the same homestand, this time against the Tigers. The Red Sox were getting pounded, 11–3, when Sayles took the mound in the top of the seventh. The Tigers, fresh off a seven-run sixth inning, continued the onslaught against the rookie right-hander. Sayles gave up five runs, including a grand slam to Tigers catcher Birdie Tebbetts in the seventh. Sayles held the Tigers scoreless in the eighth and ninth innings but the damage had been done as the Red Sox succumbed to Detroit, 16–4. His earned-run average ballooned to 7.07 in 14 innings of major-league work. Shortly thereafter, Sayles was optioned to the Scranton Red Sox of the Eastern League. He appeared in seven games for the first-place Scranton team in August. Sayles had a 4–2 record, including four complete games with 24 strikeouts and 21 walks in 47 innings. His ERA was 2.30. Sayles was recalled to Boston on August 30, but did not get into any more games with the parent club.

Sayles was back with Little Rock to start the 1940 season. In 1939, before his stints with Boston and Scranton, Sayles had posted an 8–8 record for the sixth-place Travelers with a very respectable 3.13 ERA in 141 innings. Sayles looked to improve upon that record in 1940, but arm trouble limited him to just six games. When a tonsillectomy, undertaken to relieve arm problems, proved ineffective, Sayles was placed on the suspended list with a sore arm in late April or early May. Apparently this was not the first time Sayles had experienced arm trouble. According to Jack Malaney, writing in the *Boston Post* and *The Sporting News* in early 1941, "Several times Sayles has been bothered by a sore arm. It cropped up on him midway through last season."[9] Malaney described Sayles as a pitcher the Red Sox had been trying to develop over the prior three or four years and said Sayles went as far as writing a letter to Joe Cronin asking for advice on his ailing arm.

Sayles finished the 1940 season with a 3–1 record for the Travelers and a 3.04 ERA in 35 innings. He struck out 18 and walked 13. The 23-year-old hurler no doubt looked for bigger and better things in 1941, but it was not going to be in Little Rock. After visiting the St. Louis Cardinals, team physician Dr. Robert F. Hyland, about his sore arm, Sayles went to Red Sox spring training in Sarasota. He was in the Red Sox camp for about a month when his contract was sold outright (he was out of options) to the Louisville Colonels of the American Association in late March. Sayles won his first two starts for Louisville, although he had to leave one of the games with a stiff neck. The stiffness was "caused by the straining of several leaders [tendons] while emitting a yawn[!]."[10] By mid-July Sayles had fully recovered from the arm problems of the year before and was "turning in a consistently effective job."[11] He compiled a 13–12 record for the second-place Colonels in 1941. He had 11 complete games in 30 appearances with a rather high 4.37 ERA. He struck out a career high 107 batters in 169 innings; he issued 71 walks.

Sayles was back with Louisville in 1942. With solid pitching and timely hitting, the Colonels got off to a fast start. "Chick"[12] Sayles scattered six hits in a 4–3 win over Toledo in April, his "brilliant hurling offsetting the explosiveness of Louisville's young and inexperienced infield that made four errors."[13] Late in April, Sayles pitched all 14 innings in a 4–3 loss at Toledo. In early May, he pitched a one-hitter in a seven-inning game but lost 1–0 to the first-place Kansas City Blues. Overall, Sayles won 11 and lost 12 games for the fifth-place Colonels. He pitched a career high 183 innings and established a career high with 12 complete games. He struck out 90 and walked 79 while compiling a 3.44 ERA.

In December 1942, Sayles, who spent the winter in Portland working for the Zellerbach Paper Company, learned the New York Giants purchased his contract. The conditions of the purchase allowed the Giants to return Sayles to Louisville by May 1, 1943, without penalty. Further, the Giants would not have to pay Sayles if he was called up for military service. With that hanging over his head, Sayles signed his contract in early March and reported to the Giants' wartime spring training locale in Lakewood, New Jersey.

The Giants were coming off a third-place finish in 1942. All teams lost players to the military in those years and the Giants were no exception. First baseman Johnny Mize, outfielders Willard Marshall and Babe Young, and pitcher Bob Carpenter were all in the service. Combine that loss of talent with the off-years turned in by shortstop Billy Jurges and player-manager Mel Ott and the Giants were staring at a second-division finish. Sayles, a fastball/curveball pitcher in 1939, had been working on a changeup since he last appeared in a major-league game. He was likely anxious to test it against major-league hitters. Sayles was also motivated by Cronin's rebuff four years earlier. He wanted to make good to prove his old skipper wrong. Sayles pitched well in spring training. On April 19, he was the only effective pitcher of the three who pitched in a 9–3 exhibition loss to the Washington Senators.[14] Sayles apparently impressed the Giants management because the May 1 deadline came and went and Sayles was still with the big club.

After being out of major-league ball since 1939, Sayles got his first taste of National League action on May 1, the Giants' seventh game of the season. He relieved starter Cliff Melton in the sixth inning of the first game of a twin bill at the Polo Grounds. The Giants were already behind, 5–0, when Sayles entered the contest. He gave up one run in three innings as the Giants went on to lose, 9–2. Sayles pitched two innings in the nightcap as well. Again appearing in a losing effort, he got a no-decision in the 3–0 loss. Sayles made his first major-league start in the second game of a twin bill on May 5, appropriately enough in Boston against the Bees. It was the first time Sayles had entered a major-league game when his team was not behind. He was lifted for a pinch hitter in the top of the sixth with the Giants trailing 3–0 (his opposing pitcher, Manny Salvo, with a single, a triple, and two RBIs, did most of the damage to Sayles). The Giants, however, erupted for six runs in the bottom of the sixth and went on to a 7–3 victory. It was Bill Sayles' first major-league win; it was also his last.

Sayles was used as a reliever and a spot starter for the next three months by the fading Giants. He got one of those spot starts on May 18 against the Reds and pitched well. He gave up just one run through seven innings but wasn't involved in the decision as Cincinnati won, 3–2, in 10 innings. On May 30, Sayles started the second game of a doubleheader in St. Louis. He pitched well for seven innings but gave up two runs in the eighth and took the loss as the Cardinals prevailed, 3–2.

June 4, at Forbes Field in Pittsburgh, was a memorable day for Sayles and the Giants but for all the wrong reasons. New York starter Van Lingle Mungo lasted just 3⅓ innings and Sayles was called in with the Giants down 6–2.[15] An error by Sayles in the sixth led to two unearned runs and an 8–2 Pirates lead. The game appeared over but the Giants charged back with five runs in the top of the eighth to make it 8–7, Corsairs.[16] In the bottom of the frame, Vince DiMaggio singled. Sayles' first pitch to the next batter, Pirates second baseman Pete Coscarart, went through Ernie Lombardi. The Giants catcher was charged with "a world record passed ball."[17] The preternaturally slow Lombardi took so long to get to the ball that DiMaggio rounded second and took third. Sayles, for his part, was so disconsolate over Lombardi's effort that he failed to cover home and DiMaggio scored what proved to be the winning run. The Giants scored a run in the top of the ninth but fell short, 9–8.

By the end of July 1943, the eighth-place Giants were 36–57, 25½ games behind the first-place Cardinals. The Giants were in need of a change and the crosstown rival Brooklyn Dodgers' general manager, Branch Rickey, had a plan. Rickey coveted 6-foot-6, 20-year-old first baseman Howie Schultz, then the property of the St. Paul Saints in the American Association. For their talented first sacker, the Saints wanted Bill Sayles among others. Sayles had pitched well against the Saints while he was in the American Association and the Saints thought he would do a good job for them. Rickey had to get Sayles, pitcher Bill Lohrman, and infielder Joe Orengo from the Giants. Rickey offered the Giants first baseman Dolph Camilli, a Brooklyn fan favorite, and pitcher Johnny Allen. Because of league rules, the Dodgers and the Giants could not complete the swap as a trade.[18] The deal was constructed as five separate waiver transactions. While this might seem like a trivial technicality, the structure of the transaction kept Sayles in the big leagues. The Cubs, for reasons known only by them, twice refused to allow waivers on Sayles and Lohrman before eventually relenting. The delay prevented Rickey from providing the two pitchers to the Saints. He was forced to offer other players and $40,000 to get his precious Schultz. Consequently, Sayles

reported to the Dodgers on the road in St. Louis and remained with the club for the rest of the 1943 season.

Sayles made only five appearances for the Dodgers, all in relief. He had no record and compiled a 7.71 ERA in 11 innings. Sayles had made 18 appearances, including three starts, for the Giants, with a 1–3 record and a 4.75 ERA. He had 38 strikeouts and 23 walks in 53 innings.

After the 1943 season, the major-league portion of Bill Sayles' career was over. By early 1944, his professional baseball career was also over, at least temporarily, as world events finally caught up with him. In early February 1944, Sayles passed his pre-induction physical and then joined the Army Air Corps hoping to become a pilot. Sayles failed the pilot's test, however, and was assigned to be a tail gunner, a job with a very low life expectancy. Sayles had some friends and contacts in the military and was able to get reassigned as a physical education instructor in Fort Lewis, Washington.[19] There he guided, as player-manager, the Fort Lewis baseball team to a Ninth Service Command title.[20] Unfortunately, Sayles did further damage to his arm while in the Army and was no longer able to pitch.

Sayles was back with the Dodgers for spring training in 1946 but he was optioned to the Asheville Tourists of the Class B Tri-State League on April 13. Sayles played the outfield and managed the Tourists. The Tri-State League was a new circuit, one of many that cropped up after the war. Sayles guided the Asheville nine to second place (83–57) after spending much of the season in first place.[21] He was named the league's Manager of the Year and Most Valuable Player. In addition to having a great first season as manager, Sayles had an all-star year as an outfielder. He hit .334, which was second in the league. He led the league in RBIs at 105 and also had 24 doubles, 10 triples, and 6 home runs.

On July 26, 1946, the Tourists had held a day for Bill Sayles and it was a memorable one. Sayles was presented with a "flock"[22] of gifts, including a new car. League president C. Manley Llewellyn and even the opposing manager gave a speech. In the second inning, however, Sayles argued a little too vociferously with umpire Al Zingone about a strike called on a Tourist. Sayles refused to leave the field and arbiter Zingone took out his watch. Sayles remained on the field and Mr. Zingone declared the game forfeited to Charlotte. He then left the field in a shower of beer bottles. Because so many fans came out to see a baseball game, President Llewellyn persuaded Charlotte to stay and play an exhibition game. Asheville lost the exhibition contest as well, 9–3.[23]

Sayles, recently divorced, remarried on February 26, 1947, to Oregon native Eileen Prohaska[24], and was back as the Tourists' player-manager in 1947. The manager portion of his job was difficult in his second year. The team slumped to a losing record (65–74) and sixth place in the eight-team league. Also, Sayles was suspended for three games by President Llewellyn for an incident in Reidsville, Georgia, where Sayles again refused to leave the field and the police had to be called twice. In mid-July, Asheville forfeited the second game of a doubleheader due to "an all-night rhubarb"[25] in which three players were ejected. As a player, however, Sayles had another great year at the plate. He came in second again in the batting race with a .360 average. Sayles had 28 doubles, 8 triples, 12 home runs (fourth in the league), and 98 knocked in (seventh in the league). He was named to the All-Star team. The stress of managing, however, surpassed the success of playing; Sayles retired after the '47 season. Bill and Eileen Sayles went home to Oregon. Bill went to work for a forest products company and the two raised three children, Bill Jr., Karen, and Tammy.

Sayles was back in baseball by 1957, this time as an assistant general manager of the Vancouver (British Columbia) Mounties of the Pacific Coast League. He held this position until March 1959, when he took the same position for his hometown Portland Beavers, also in the PCL. The Beavers' general manager, Tommy Heath, was also the field manager. The combined responsibilities were too much for Heath and by the end of the 1959 season Sayles had taken on most of the general manager duties although Heath retained the title. Sayles, for example, was responsible for the very successful Kids Night at Portland's Multnomah Stadium. The event drew a record 24,109 fans including 17,000 youngsters admitted on special 50-cent tickets.[26] Sayles, who had the title of business manager in 1960, became the general manager before leaving the Beavers in 1962. From 1962 until 1982, Sayles was the West Coast scouting supervisor for the St. Louis Cardinals. His territory included California, Oregon, Washington, Idaho and western Canada. Sayles scouted and signed several quality major leaguers for the Cardinals, including Nelson Briles, Reggie Cleveland, Keith Hernandez, and Bob Forsch.

In 1982, Sayles retired from baseball and went into the men's clothing business. From 1983 to 1995, he owned the Esquire Men's Apparel shop at Salishan Spa and Golf Resort on Oregon's Pacific coast just south of Lincoln City. On November 20, 1996, at 79, Bill Sayles succumbed to cancer. His remains were cremated.

Notes

1. Interview with Bill Sayles Jr., May 30, 2008.
2. Estimates ranged from 90,000 to 150,000.
3. http://www.la84foundation.org/SportsLibrary/JOH/JOHv1n1/JOHv1n1e.pdf
4. Bill Sayles Jr. interview.
5. *The Sporting News*, July 15, 1967, p. 8.
6. *The Sporting News*, March 9, 1939, p. 6.
7. National Baseball Hall of Fame Library file on Bill Sayles. Article by Frank C. True in 1943. The publication is not known.
8. *The Sporting News*, July 20, 1939, p. 1.
9. *The Sporting News*, January 16, 1941, p. 4.
10. *The Sporting News*, May 1, 1941, p. 1.
11. *The Sporting News*, July 24, 1941, p. 5.
12. *The Sporting News*, April 23, 1942, .p 5.
13. Ibid.
14. New York *Times*, April 23, 1943, p. 25.
15. It's not possible to tell from the box score or the accompanying story whether Sayles allowed inherited runners to score, but Mungo was on the hook for the loss.
16. The Pirates were often called Corsairs by sportswriters of the 1930s and '40s.
17. Drebinger, John, *New York Times*, June 5, 1943, p. 21.
18. Most reference books, e.g., *The Baseball Encyclopedia* and web sites, www.baseball-reference.com, call it a trade.
19. Bill Sayles Jr. interview.
20. Before his assignment in Fort Lewis, Sayles also played baseball at Camp Lee, Virginia.
21. The Tourists lost to Knoxville in the first round of the Tri-State League playoffs.
22. Bisher, Furman, "Sayles Gets Car From Fans, Gate From Ump in Asheville," *The Sporting News*, August 7, 1946, p.30.
23. Ibid.
24. Bill Sayles Jr. interview.
25. *The Sporting News*, July 23, 1947, p. 32.
26. Gregory, "Beavers' Success Earns '60 Pact for Aid Sayles," *The Sporting News*, August 26, 1959, p.33.

Sources

The Sporting News, New York Times, Boston Post, New York Herald-Tribune, Worcester Telegram.
The Baseball Encyclopedia (New York: Macmillan, 1992).
Ballew, Bill. *Baseball in Asheville* (Charleston SC: Arcadia Publishing, 2004).
www.baseball-reference.com.
www.baseball-almanac.com.
www.retrosheet.org.
www.sabr.org.
www.ancestry.com.

JIM TABOR *by Maurice Bouchard*

G	AB	R	H	2B	3B	HR	RBI	BB	SO	BA	OBP	SLG	SB	HBP
149	577	76	167	33	8	14	95	30	54	.289	.337	.447	16	1

Jim "Rawhide" Tabor was a five-tool player before that phrase became part of the baseball vernacular. He was 6-feet-2 and played at 175 to 185 pounds. Often described as raw-boned and rangy, he hit from the right side for average and with power. He had great speed, was Mercury-quick, and had a terrific throwing arm. Tabor's arm was the standard by which all other infielders' arms were measured in the 1940s. When Red Sox first baseman Jimmie Foxx was accused of having an illegally reinforced glove, he pointed at third baseman Tabor as his defense. "He throws the ball like a cannon shot," Double-X asserted.[1] Unfortunately, cannon shot turned to scattershot all too often. Tabor wasn't always quite sure where the ball was going when he let loose.

Tabor earned his moniker with his hustle, his win-at-any-cost attitude, and his toughness. "He'd slide into second and knock you on your ass,"[2] said teammate Tony Lupien. Catchers blocked the plate at their peril. He once collided so violently with Detroit's Joe Hoover that the unfortunate Tiger infielder passed a kidney stone on the spot.[3] Rawhide was not above upbraiding his teammates. Early in Tabor's career, Lefty Grove came over to third to berate Tabor for an error the young third sacker had made. Tabor did not back down to the veteran Grove. "You're hired to pitch," he said. "I'm hired to play third base. Get out there and pitch."[4] Ol' Mose went back to the hill. Tabor had to be pulled off Minneapolis Millers teammate Ted Williams after one game in which Williams chose not to go after balls hit to left field.[5] Rawhide also earned his nickname off the field. Tabor was suspended several times in his career and in trouble countless other times. The usual reason given for suspension was "breaking training rules." Tabor liked the ladies, liked to smoke cigars (he usually had the stub of a cigar in his mouth off the field), and he liked to drink. Red Sox outfielder Doc Cramer said, "Jim Tabor was a twister. He would drink, get drunk and be half-drunk when he came to the park."[6] The Red Sox even hired two private detectives to follow Tabor in an effort to get him to stop drinking.[7] It didn't work. Jim Tabor had great talent and an undeniable will to win, but the wax melted quickly for this baseball Icarus.

James Reubin Tabor was born on a farm a mile south of Owens Cross Roads, Alabama, on November 5, 1916, the second son of John H. and Amy Olene Tabor. John Tabor was a schoolteacher who once had a contract to play in the Southern League but gave it up to get married.[8] John imparted his baseball knowledge to all of his

Jim "Rawhide" Tabor

sons. The Tabor troupe played together on an amateur team in Owens Cross Roads, playing surrounding town teams with "Pop" Tabor as the manager-catcher and a Tabor boy on first, second, and third base. The third baseman, Jim, was "the mightiest hitter ever seen down Owens Cross Roads way."[9] Jim was also a standout baseball and basketball player at New Hope High School in New Hope, Alabama. He attracted the attention of University of Alabama basketball coach Hank Crisp. Tabor received a full four-year scholarship to play for the Crimson Tide, the first incoming freshman to receive such an award.[10] In the summer of 1935, after high school graduation, Jim played for the Ozark, Alabama, nine in the Dixie Amateur League, and soon impressed major-league scouts. Tabor entered the university in the fall of 1935 and starred on the freshman basketball team, but when the baseball coach learned he was an accomplished baseball player, he made sure Tabor went out for baseball as well.

After classes were over in 1936, Tabor played in the semipro Coastal Plain League in North Carolina. His first assignment in that league did not last long. Tabor and his manager did not get along and Tabor was dropped from the team. His university came through with another assignment, Ayden, in the same league. Tabor thrived there and impressed the major-league scouts again. The Philadelphia Athletics were first to act, and scout Ira Thomas had Tabor all but persuaded to join his team, having Connie Mack send a contract and a $3,500 bonus check to Tabor. In the meantime, either Alabama baseball coach Happy Campbell or football coach Frank Thomas, or both, contacted people they knew in the Red Sox organization. The Sox promptly dispatched Billy Evans, the head of the Red Sox farm system, to Alabama with a blank check. Evans signed Tabor with a $4,000 bonus and was savvy enough to get dad's signature too (something the Athletics failed to do). Later the Athletics protested the signing but Commissioner Kenesaw M. Landis ruled in favor of the Red Sox. The Red Sox deal called for Jim to become a professional after he graduated from college, but young Tabor couldn't wait. He had difficulty focusing on his studies and by the spring of 1937 he was on the phone with Billy Evans. Evans tried to persuade Tabor to stay in school, but Jim would not be dissuaded. He prevailed and the Red Sox assigned him to the Little Rock Travelers in the Southern Association.

The 1937 edition of the Little Rock club, managed by former Red Sox third baseman Doc Prothro, was destined to finish in first place (97–55) and win the league championship in the postseason playoffs. Tabor was a key ingredient in the team's success. Prothro thought the Southern Association too big a jump for a kid with only a year of freshman ball under his belt, but Evans was sold on Tabor, and Tabor's enthusiasm swung Prothro around enough to get Tabor a look. Prothro needn't have worried. Tabor showed he belonged from the beginning. Possibly all the questions were answered early when the Cleveland Indians came to Little Rock for an exhibition game that spring. On the mound for the Tribe was 18-year-old star-in-the-making Bob Feller. The first time Tabor faced Feller he struck out. The next time, Tabor came up with the bases full. He timed one of Feller's storied fastballs and laced it for a home run to center field. Jim enjoyed national publicity for his grand slam off the future Hall-of-Famer.

By late April, the writers were convinced of Tabor's talent. The comment expressed in *The Sporting News* was typical: "Tabor, the University of Alabama recruit, an uncertainty at the opening of the season, has become a third base fixture. If he keeps up his good work, the Boston Red Sox need not worry about the future for a hot corner guardian."[11]. The sportswriter covering the Travelers

for *The Sporting News*, A.W.P., enthused, "Right now, the outstanding player of the entire circuit is young Tabor. Tabor does all things well and makes almost impossible plays."[12] Tabor stayed with Little Rock all season and was hitting above .300 for most of the year before finishing at .295. He impressed with his 94 RBIs, 93 runs, 25 doubles, 10 triples, 4 home runs, and 12 stolen bases. The once reluctant Doc Prothro was now a true believer. He predicted major-league stardom for Tabor.

For his efforts, Tabor was invited to Red Sox spring training in 1938. Tabor arrived late to camp and did not have much of an opportunity to show his skills. Once he arrived and started to play a little, he pushed Red Sox third baseman Pinky Higgins into raising his game.[13] Though Tabor had a good spring, it was clear he needed more experience. Tabor made the team's decision easier by breaking training rules. On April 1 he was optioned to Minneapolis of the top tier American Association.

Tabor had an excellent year for the sixth-place Millers. He started off quickly, hitting .452 in early series against Indianapolis, Louisville, Columbus, and Toledo. He was the early league leader in triples by "combining a ground-eating stride with a penchant for belting liners to left and right center."[14] He drove in six runs in a game in the early going and by June 9, he had already hit two game-winning homers.

When Pinky Higgins injured his knee in late July, Tabor, who was hitting .330 with 13 home runs and 72 RBIs in 103 games with the Millers, was called up to Boston. Tabor made his major-league debut in Cleveland on August 2, going 2-for-4 with two doubles, both off Denny Galehouse. By August 8, the Red Sox coaching staff was predicting Tabor would be better than the Indians' sensational third baseman, Ken Keltner.[15] Joe Cronin, who claimed he was not that impressed with Tabor in spring training, said he couldn't believe how much the rookie had improved. Cronin favorably compared Tabor's defense at third base to that of his old Pittsburgh teammate Pie Traynor, saying, "This kid knocks 'em down and throws 'em out just like Pie."[16] Sportswriter Vic Stout reported Tabor's play at third as "little short of miraculous" and wrote, "He has made plays which no third baseman in either league is making these days."[17] Expectations were high, but Tabor did not disappoint. On August 9, the Red Sox were at Shibe Park in Philadelphia for a three-game series. Athletics starter Nels Potter was perfect through six innings and had a 3-0 lead, but the Red Sox exploded for seven runs in the seventh. The big blow was a grand slam by Tabor, his first major-league home run. Higgins soon recovered from his injury and Tabor was to be sent back to Minneapolis, but American Association rules prohibited the move. Consequently, Tabor remained with the Red Sox through the end of the season. He was relegated to pinch-hitting and the occasional start. His teammates voted him a half-share of the 1938 second-place money. Overall, Tabor got into 19 games for the Red Sox in 1938 and hit .316 with one home run and eight RBIs. He showed well enough to cause a "problem" for Joe Cronin.

The problem was a "good" problem. The Red Sox had two good third basemen, Tabor and Higgins. The incumbent, Higgins, 29, was coming off two successful years with the Red Sox. He had been a consistent run producer since 1930, when he was with the Athletics. Tabor was only 21 at the end of the 1938 season with just two years of professional baseball on his résumé. It seemed risky to many Red Sox fans and the media to trade Higgins, but that is exactly what the Red Sox did.

Citing the dire need for pitching, on December 15, 1938, the Red Sox traded Higgins and pitcher Archie McKain to Detroit for pitchers Elden Auker and Jake Wade and outfielder Chet Morgan. Cronin told sportswriter Jack Malaney, "We will be gambling at third base and in right field next summer, but the extra pitching we have acquired possibly will offset the gamble we are taking." Cronin went on to say, "We'll be gambling, but, at least, we'll be gambling with two of the finest young players [Tabor and Ted Williams] in the country."[18] Malaney's tone in the article implied he was not convinced Tabor could make the grade. By the time the Red Sox broke camp in Sarasota, Florida, however, Malaney was picking Tabor over Williams to be the rookie sensation of 1939.

Tabor was impressive in spring training. The confidence he gained from knowing the third-base job was his must have been palpable. He was described as "cock-sure"[19] and "like a panther as a fielder."[20] He was "confident and game in a quiet way [as compared to Williams]."[21] He was the "Far Corner Phenom"[22] and "Freshman Star."[23] Time and again, his arm was described as the strongest in baseball, often with the "erratic" qualifier. He was enthusiastic about baseball regardless of the conditions. He was a "hustler"[24] and had "pep."[25] Many baseball experts predicted Tabor would eventually take his place among the great third basemen of the time. By the time the 1939 season started, there were few who thought Tabor was a gamble.

The Red Sox opened the 1939 season on the road at Yankee Stadium. The game matched future Hall of Famers Red Ruffing and Lefty Grove. Tabor, batting fifth, went 1-for-4 with a double in his first game as the Red Sox regular third baseman and played errorless ball as the Yankees won, 2–0. Tabor went 4-for-5 on April 24 against Washington. On the 25th, he singled to knock in Jimmie Foxx in the ninth to tie the game, and Foxx homered in the 11th to win it. On May 16, Tabor went 3-for-5 with five RBIs, and three days later he had a 4-for-4 day. On May 21, he went 2-for-3 with two runs scored and an RBI. While certainly not perfect, Tabor was more than holding his own in the early going.

On June 1, Jack Malaney wrote, "Bobby Doerr and Jim Tabor have been sensational in their infield play and both youngsters have been hitting hard and driving in runs."[26] By the end of June, however, Joe Cronin suspended Tabor for three days. The manager refused to give details, but said the suspension was "for the good of the club and to discipline him a little. He hasn't been acting too well lately."[27] Tabor "foolishly broke training much after the fashion of a high school boy who wanted to show off."[28] Tabor was back in the lineup against Philadelphia on June 29. On July 1 against the Yankees, he went 2-for-3 with a run scored and two stolen bases. He had a "mad plunge for a run in the third"[29] and spiked Yankee catcher Buddy Rosar, who was blocking the plate. Rosar had to leave the game and was admitted to a hospital.

Tabor had the game of his life on July 4 in Shibe Park. The Red Sox swept the A's in the holiday twin bill by scores of 17–7 and 18–12. Tabor was just getting warm in the opening game when he went 3-for-5 with a home run, a double, and two RBIs. In the nightcap, Jim Tabor had a record-tying performance. He came up with the bases loaded in the third facing A's starter George Caster. Tabor, who had a grand slam in Philadelphia the previous August, enjoyed Shibe Park one more time with a long ball off Caster. In the sixth, the bases were full again for Tabor and he hit an inside-the-park grand slam off Lynn Nelson. He touched Nelson again for a solo shot in the eighth to top off his nine-RBI game. Tabor was only the second major-league player to hit two grand slams in a single game.[30] The four home runs in a doubleheader also tied a record.[31] The next day, Tabor hit another home run against A's pitching for his fifth home run in three games.

Rookie Jim Tabor had a good year at the plate. He finished at .289 with 33 doubles, 8 triples, and 14 home runs in 149 games, while leading the Red Sox with 16 stolen bases. His 95 RBIs nearly replaced the 106 produced by Pinky Higgins the previous year. Tabor's power/speed number was fifth in the league.[32] His fielding was more of a mixed bag. He had 40 errors -- the most by any third baseman in the major leagues that season, though tempered by his 338 assists, also the most in either league. He was making more errors, mostly throwing, but he was getting to more grounders than anyone else.

Tabor started the 1940 season slowly, but broke out of his slump after about a dozen games. On May 3, he hit two home runs against the St. Louis Browns; the second tied the game in the ninth. In the 10th, Tabor singled with the bases loaded for the walk-off win. On June 1, Tabor knocked himself out in batting practice. He hit down on a ball that bounced back and hit him in the eye, cutting him badly enough for him to need two stitches. Rawhide missed the game that day but he was back the next.

On Sunday, July 14, the Red Sox had a doubleheader at home against the Browns. Tabor played in both games and went 4-for-8 with a double, three RBIs, and a stolen base. The Sox won both games. Some time after the second game, James Tabor married Bostonian Irene Bryan at St. Augustine's Church in Boston. Teammate Joe Heving was the best man. Shortly after the wedding, Tabor went on a home-run tear, hitting four in three games between July 23 and July 26. (He hit another on July 28.) Jack Malaney marveled at Tabor's hustle and enthusiasm even as the Red Sox were mired in an eight-game losing streak; he wrote, "If the other players could have followed Tabor's lead, it might have been different."[33] Tabor had eight RBIs in the three games, going 6-for-12. He had six hits in six plate appearances over the course of two games, July 25 and 26.

While opposing pitchers couldn't stop Tabor, his appendix did. Before a game against Cleveland at Fenway Park on August 21, Tabor collapsed on the field and was taken to the hospital for an emergency appendectomy. He was expected to be out a month. On September 21, precisely one month later, Tabor was back in the lineup and went 3-for-4 with an RBI. The Red Sox were 12-16 with Tabor out of the lineup and were eliminated from the pennant race.[34] Tabor, part of a power-hitting infield that hit 103 home runs, had career highs that season in home runs (21) and slugging percentage (.510). He hit .285 in 120 games with 28 doubles, 6 triples, and 14 stolen bases. He was second only to the Yankees' Joe Gordon in the power/speed category. He also improved in the field. He still had the most errors (33) in the American League, but his range factor[35] was the best in the league, up from third best the previous year.

Tabor, who had no lasting effects from the appendectomy, put on 10 pounds in the offseason and told *The Sporting News* he wanted to add five more (Joe Cronin had been trying to get Tabor to put on weight for at least the last two seasons). The new, bulkier Tabor got into trouble with Cronin early in spring training of 1941. "[Cronin] had to spank Jim Tabor, his young and playful third sacker, and did so by telling him he was no longer a regular on the team because of Jim's apparent disregard for training rules and lack of interest in the welfare of the team" Jack Malaney wrote.[36]

On March 21, 1941, the *New York Herald Tribune* reported that Tabor had been suspended indefinitely for repeated violation of training rules. On April 3, Malaney wrote that the incidents had been forgotten, although Tabor did not appear for the spring training game on March 31, in violation of team rules. Tabor did not let the spring training problems faze him, however (or maybe the suspension got his attention), because he had a great first half of the season. By July, he was hitting 30 points higher than any other AL third baseman. By year's end, Tabor's average had dropped off to .279, but he had a career high in RBIs with 101 in just 125 games (injuries curtailed his playing time). He also had a career-high 17 stolen bases, fifth best in the league. Tabor had 16 homers, 29 doubles,

and 3 triples for the second-place Red Sox. After a few weeks in the South, Tabor spent the winter in the Boston area working for the Gillette Safety Razor Company.

Though the Red Sox improved to 93 wins in 1942, Tabor's hitting and fielding dropped off. He was benched for a time because of a prolonged slump. He hit just .252 in 139 games, and all his power numbers were down: 12 home runs, 18 doubles, 2 triples, and 75 RBIs. He had just six stolen bases and was caught 13 times. In the field, he had 33 errors to lead all American League third sackers; his range, which had been a strength, was now diminishing. It appeared his hard living was catching up to him. Tabor spent the winter in Boston again. He and his wife purchased a home in East Milton and Jim worked as a riveter at the Fore River Ship Yard in Quincy. Tabor was able to work out at Tufts University often in the winter and reported early for spring training there (wartime travel restrictions barred spring training in the South).

Tabor started the 1943 season poorly, hitting just .158 through April 29. By May he was benched for poor hitting, and he hit just .243 through June 24. The season proved to be difficult for the Red Sox. Jimmie Foxx had retired and Williams, DiMaggio, and Pesky were in the military. The Red Sox finished seventh. Tabor finished the season at .242 in 137 games, his lowest average as a professional. His slugging average was just .299. Tabor committed 26 errors, a career low, in 133 games at third, but still high enough to lead the league for the fifth consecutive year.

The Red Sox held spring training at Tufts again in 1944. Manager Cronin told players who lived in warm-weather states to stay home and train on their own. Consequently, Tabor, who had again spent the winter in Boston working at the shipyard, was one of only four players to attend early spring training. His batting average and the Red Sox' fortunes bounced back a bit in 1944. Tabor was hitting .296 as late as July 27. On August 10, he passed his military pre-induction exam, making him eligible for call-up to the Army at any time. He was allowed to finish the season. Tabor finished the year with a .285 average in 116 games. He had 25 doubles, 3 triples, 13 home runs, and 72 RBIs. On October 26, Tabor got the call from Uncle Sam. He entered the Army at Fort Devens, Massachusetts. He spent the remainder of 1944 and most of 1945 at Fort Devens, then at Camp Croft, South Carolina.

Tabor was given a dependency discharge from the Army on December 14, 1945, and was ready to rejoin the Red Sox for the spring of 1946. The Red Sox looked like serious contenders for the American League pennant with Williams, DiMaggio, Pesky, Doerr, and Tabor set to return to their lineup. The Red Sox did win the 1946 flag, but Jim Tabor was not part of the team. Joe Cronin and general manager, Eddie Collins thought Louisville third baseman Ernie Andres was ready for the big time[37] and thought Tabor expendable. On January 22, 1946, after he cleared military waivers,[38] the Red Sox sold Tabor's contract to the Philadelphia Phillies for a reported $25,000. In 806 games with the Red Sox, Tabor had hit .273 with 90 home runs and 517 RBIs. Sportswriter Burt Whitman had these parting comments: "[H]e looked like a sure-fire big league star. He was very fast, had power at bat and while erratic of throwing arm, appeared to be about ready to blossom into stardom at any time. Annually, he failed to live up to this promise."[39]

Phillies general manager Herb Pennock knew Tabor well from his time as a coach and farm director for the Red Sox, and believed he could help the Phillies. It didn't hurt, of course, that the Phillies played their home games in Shibe Park, where Tabor had hit 16 home runs as a visiting player. Base-

Washington's Buddy Lewis in the Sox dugout with Jim Tabor

ball writer Stan Baumgartner had expressed concern about Tabor because all AL teams passed on him, but was impressed with Tabor's enthusiasm in spring training. Phillies management was not as sanguine about Tabor as Baumgartner. The Phillies tried to get Whitey Kurowski from the Cardinals because, after spring training, "they were not sure Tabor could help lift them out of the second division."[40] Tabor, however, got off to a hot start, hitting .344 in the early going. His performance "has made fans forget he was one of Joe Cronin's problem children."[41] He hit his first National League home run on April 21 off Johnny Sain in the bottom of the eighth. The hot hitting did not last, however. Tabor slumped to .266 through June 5 with just three RBIs and was then benched for a week. While he did show the occasional episode of greatness, like the walk-off home run he hit against Reds pitcher Joe Beggs on June 23, he could not sustain it for an entire season. Tabor hit .268 in 124 games for the fifth-place Phillies, with just 15 doubles, 2 triples, 10 home runs, and 50 RBIs. He finished the year with just three stolen bases.

Tabor's health and perhaps his fitness were becoming a concern. In late October or early November, Tabor visited the Lahey Clinic in Boston for an unspecified ailment. There were more injuries, specified and otherwise, during the spring and summer of 1947. He had sore ankles in spring training and was in Temple University

Hospital for X-rays and "further probing of his tonsils."[42] He had a bad spine bruise between the shoulder blades caused by an overly exuberant trainer. He injured his hip sliding into a base. He bruised two ribs and cracked another running over Walker Cooper in a play at the plate. Also, Tabor was suspended by the Phillies for six days, from May 13 to May 19, further limiting his playing time. He showed flashes of his former self from time to time. He had a walk-off home run against the Braves on April 27, but again he could not sustain it. He turned in the weakest offensive season of his major league career. Tabor hit a career-low .235 and played in only 75 games for the seventh-place Phils. His 14 doubles, 4 home runs, and 2 stolen bases were all career lows. In 1947, Tabor lost his job as the regular third baseman. He played only 67 games at third. He had a .915 fielding percentage, the lowest of his career. Back in Massachusetts after the season, Tabor spent the winter coaching the Pere Marquette basketball team in South Boston. It's likely he was contemplating his baseball future as well.

On December 11, 1947, the Phillies traded for outfielder-first baseman Bert Haas of the Cincinnati Reds. In early January 1948, they announced Haas would be their third baseman[43] for the coming season. When Tabor learned the news, he didn't hesitate to comment. "That means I'll have to knock him off," responded Tabor. "I don't think I'll have any trouble with him. I'll just have to go to work."[44] The 31-year-old Alabaman was as cocky as ever. In late January it looked as though Tabor might be dealt to another team. When he wasn't, it appeared doubtful he would be invited to the Phillies' camp in Florida. In the end, Herb Pennock left it up to manager Ben Chapman. The former Red Sox outfielder allowed Tabor to come to camp to compete for the position. Tabor did not earn the job, however, and was given his unconditional release on March 2. Owner Bob Carpenter tried to waive him to another team and then tried to sell his contract to the Pacific Coast League, but nothing came of either effort. Tabor was free to make his own deal. By March 22, he was on his way to Los Angeles after signing a contract with the Los Angeles Angels of the PCL. In early May, Tabor hit three home runs in a five-game series against the Hollywood Stars. One of the home runs won the game in the 10th inning. In late May 1948, the Angels sold Tabor to the league rival Sacramento Solons. Tabor finished the season with the Solons, hitting .273 overall with 17 home runs in 143 games. After the season, Tabor went to Mexico on a barnstorming tour, but because of mismanagement, very few games were played.

Tabor was ready for a full season in Sacramento in 1949, and at the plate he had one of the best seasons of his professional career. He went 11-for-21 in a series against the San Francisco Seals and, a week or so later, he went 15-for-24 against the Portland Beavers. He had newfound speed, Tabor claimed, after getting treatment from a Sacramento chiropodist. During the season he received a "substantial salary boost"[45] due to his outstanding play. In a doubleheader on August 28, Tabor hit a home run in the sixth inning of the first game to provide the winning margin over Portland. In the second game, he drove in four runs and started a triple play, snagging a low line drive with the bases loaded, stepping on third and firing the ball to first baseman Walt Dropo for the third out. Tabor's comeback was the single biggest improvement in the Solons' 1949 season. Sacramento had 27 more wins than in the previous year and finished third, improving on 1948's last-place finish. Tabor hit .318 with 38 doubles, 1 triple, and 21 home runs in 167 games. His 113 RBIs led the club. Tabor, who was still living in the Boston area, played winter ball in Puerto Rico during the offseason.

In 1950, Tabor was back with Sacramento. He missed the first four games of the new season with a sore elbow, but homered in his first at-bat on April 1. By mid-April, Rawhide Tabor was fined $100 and suspended for breaking training rules. Tabor settled his differences with manager Red Kress very quickly, though, and the suspension was lifted. The Solons played 190 games in 1950. Jim Tabor played in 178 of them. His average slipped to .266 but he again hit 21 homers. He also had 32 doubles, one triple, and 94 RBIs for the eighth-place Sacramento squad.

Former Yankees star second baseman Joe Gordon was the new manager of the Solons in 1951. The Solons also added former Indians all-star third sacker Ken Keltner to their team. In spring training, with regular first baseman Herman Reich holding out, manager Gordon gave Tabor a first baseman's glove and told him to work out at the position. By the end of May, however, there were three players and two positions. Tabor was the odd man out and his contract was sold to the PCL's San Diego team, where he finished the season. Tabor was impressive in his first week with his new team, hitting at a .571 (16-for-28) clip. For the season, he played a total of 112 games for both teams and hit .301. Tabor, who spent the winter in Sacramento, learned of his release from the Padres in January 1952.

Determined to keep playing baseball, Tabor got a two-week trial with the Portland Beavers in March. He made the club, but he jammed his shoulder while sliding. Tabor was just 1-for-13 in eight games with the Beavers when they released him in late April. With his baseball career over, Tabor went to work for a Sacramento construction company.

On August 17, 1953, barely more than a year after leaving baseball, Tabor suffered a heart attack. He remained unconscious and in an oxygen tent until August 22, when he succumbed to congestive heart failure. Jim "Rawhide" Tabor was just 36 years old. His wife, Irene; his father, John H.; his brother Ferrell; a daughter, Virginia; and a son, James Michael, survived him. He was buried at Beason Cemetery in Gurley, not far from Owens Cross Roads, Alabama.

Notes

1. Felker, Carl T. "Basket Glove Bar Affects Most Players," *The Sporting News*, June 15, 1939: p. 2.
2. Golenbock, Peter. *Fenway*. New York. G.P. Putnam's Sons, 1992: 140.
3. *The Sporting News*, October 5, 1944: 14.
4. Kaplan, Jim. Lefty Grove American Original, Cleveland: Society for American Baseball Research, , 2000: 228.
5. James, Bill. *The New Bill James Historical Baseball Abstract*, New York: Free Press, 2003: 581
6. Golenbock: 140.
7. James, op. cit.
8. Undated correspondence from Jim Tabor.
9. Marston, S/Sgt Gordon D. "Slugging Red Soxer Jim Tabor." *The Sporting News*, November 25, 1943: 14.
10. Undated correspondence from Jim Tabor.
11. A.W.P. "Travelers Riding On One-Way Ticket." *The Sporting News*, May 6, 1937: 12.
12. A.W.P. "Travelers Avoiding Detours in Spite of Injuries and Shifts." *The Sporting News*, June 3, 1937: 3.
13. Shannon, Paul. "Sergeant Jim's Son Gets Major Rating." *The Sporting News*, March 17, 1938: 10.
14. Ibid.
15. Stout, Vic. "Tabor's Play Gives Cronin Big Problem." National Baseball Hall of Fame Library file folder on Tabor, publication unknown. August 9, 1938.
16. Ibid.
17. Ibid.

18. Ibid.
19. Malaney, Jack. "Tabor Being Tabbed As Freshman Star." *The Sporting News*, April 13, 1939: 6.
20. Ibid.
21. Patterson, Arthur E. "Red Sox Brain Trust Banks on Williams, Tabor." *New York Herald Tribune*, March 17, 1939.
22. Malaney, Jack. "Tabor Flunked Out of School Teacher Role So He Could Use Hickory Stick for Red Sox." *The Sporting News*, April 20, 1939: 5.
23. Malaney, Jack. "Tabor Being Tabbed As Freshman Star." *The Sporting News*, April 13, 1939: 6.
24. Drohan, John. "Tabor to Dust Mike Higgins?" unknown publication, January 10, 1938.
25. Ibid.
26. Malaney, Jack. "Nub Of Hub Trouble Centers On Mound." *The Sporting News*, June 1, 1939: 5.
27. "Red Sox Suspend Tabor 3 Days 'for Good of Club.'" *New York Herald Tribune*, June 27, 1939.
28. Malaney, Jack. "Miller Snub Gives Bees Case Of Hives." *The Sporting News*, July 6, 1939: 6.
29. "Doerr Red Sox Ace As Yanks Bow." *New York Times*, July 2, 1939: S1.
30. New York Yankees infielder Tony Lazzeri hit two grand slams on May 24, 1936, also at Shibe Park
31. Earl Averill, Cleveland Indians, September 17, 1930.
32. Power/Speed Number, created by Bill James, is (2xHRxSB)/ (HR + SB). It indicates a player with good power and speed.
33. Malaney, Jack. "Hub Thumping Tub for Tabor's Labor." *The Sporting News*, August 1, 1940: 14.
34. The Red Sox were 7-3 in the last 10 games of the season with Tabor in the lineup.
35. (Putouts + Assists)/Games.
36. Malaney, Jack. "Cronin Sharpening Eye For Mound Cut." *The Sporting News*, March 27, 1941: 3.
37. He wasn't.
38. If a team claimed a player from military waivers, it had to keep the player for the remainder of the season, plus two weeks.
39. Whitman, Burt. "Sox Sell Jim Tabor To Phils on Waiver." *Boston Globe*, January 23, 1946.
40. "Kids Lose Out to Old-Timers." *The Sporting News*, April 4, 1946: 2.
41. Baumgartner, Stan. "Phils Flogging Ball, but Own Flinging Flops." *The Sporting News*, May 2, 1946: 10.
42. *The Sporting News*, June 18, 1947: 32.
43. Bert Haas had last been an everyday third baseman in 1942 for the Reds.
44. Birtwell, Roger. "Haas At Third For Phils? Not While Tabor's Around." *The Sporting News*, January 14, 1948: 19.
45. *The Sporting News*, August 17, 1949, page 26.

JOE VOSMIK *by Bill Nowlin*

G	AB	R	H	2B	3B	HR	RBI	BB	SO	BA	OBP	SLG	SB	HBP
145	554	89	153	29	6	7	84	66	33	.276	.356	.388	4	3

The Joe Vosmik story is the classic American tale in which the scion of an immigrant family falls in love with the national game of the family's adopted country. Vosmik's tale has all the required elements: precocious skills, early passion, an indulgent father, a disapproving mother who later relents and shares her son's ardor, obsession, truancy, and even an officious school administrator who proclaims: "the boy will never amount to anything." Not only did Joe Vosmik amount to something; he became a baseball star for his hometown team, and at his peak, one of the better players in the American League.

Joseph Franklin Vosmik was born in Cleveland, Ohio, on April 4, 1910, to Josef and Anna (Klecan) Vosmik, immigrants from Bohemia (then part of the Austro-Hungarian Empire, now part of the Czech Republic). Josef was a naturalized citizen who may have immigrated as early as 1879 (or as late as 1890, census

Joe Vosmik, Boston's "Bashing Bohemian"

records vary). He worked as a machinist, a "sawman," a stockroom manager, and even a cigar roller. Anna Klecan immigrated in 1890 and was naturalized the next year. The two married in the United States, likely in the late 1890s. Joe was the first son after the Vosmiks had five daughters (Anna, Amelia, Elsie, Lillian, Marie). Younger brother Edward came three years later. It was around the time of his brother's birth that Joe's future avocation started to percolate. It seems that young Joe Vosmik showed passion for baseball as a toddler.

Joe later told writer Harry Brundidge of the Star Chronicle Publishing Company, "Mother tells me she learned of my interest in baseball on the day I was three years old. During the afternoon of that day she heard me screaming and found me tugging at a ball bat, too heavy to lift. It belonged to the boy next door and I was enraged because he would not permit me to drag it home." One of his older sisters was dispatched to the corner drugstore to buy a 10-cent bat for little Joe. Joe's father had come to the country as a youngster and developed his own enthusiasm for baseball, so fully encouraged his son's interest in the game. Joe's mother knew little about the game, and disapproved of his interest at first because it seemed obsessive to the exclusion of everything else. Before too long, though, as John Drohan later wrote, Anna Vosmik could talk "inside baseball" with Joe—"and the blast she can put on an umpire is worthy of a veteran baseball bug." [June 2, 1931 clipping in Hall of Fame archives, publication unknown]

Joe started playing catch in the streets of Cleveland even before beginning school. He saw his first action at Dunn Field (later called League Park), starting around the age of 10. "When I was in the fourth grade I began playing truant to go to the Indians' ball park and watch the big league players," he recalled. "Soon after, I began finding ways and means of sneaking into the stadium but most of the time I was kicked out as soon as I got in. But I had made up my mind to be a professional ballplayer and nothing discouraged me." Not that many years later the Indians were paying him to play.

Vosmik pored over newspaper box scores and read what he could about baseball and ballplayers. Nabbed by a truant officer from time to time, he was given a "lively slapping" by one teacher who also beat him on the shins with a yardstick. Nothing could break his spirit for long, though it was disappointing when he progressed to East Technical High School, a school which didn't have a baseball team. Cutting school became more frequent, either to play sandlot ball or to go to Dunn Field. His principal admonished him, "Joe Vosmik, you will never amount to anything and you'll wind up in jail or in some lowly position in life."

For Vosmik, semipro play began just after he turned 15, pitching and playing first base for the Ruggles Jewelry team. He kept in school, though, and played basketball, football, handball, and skated. He graduated the following year—1926—both from school and to a higher level of play, pitching for Rotbart Jewelers in a municipal league. The team's manager, Ben Gotch, urged Joe to give up pitching and play the outfield. Joe was still trying to crack into baseball any way he could, but was turned down by the Indians when applying for jobs as an usher, an office boy, or a vendor. After the 1928 season in the city league, when Joe was spotted by Indians manager Roger Peckinpaugh, a graduate of the Cleveland sandlots, Vosmik was designated one of the top four prospects in the Cleveland Amateur Baseball Association. His signing was credited to Peckinpaugh, but it was Cleveland GM Billy Evans who gave him a $300 bonus (according to legend, Vosmik caught the eye of Billy Evans' wife at the tryout. When Evans needed one more local kid to sign, Mrs. Evans suggested "the good-looking blond boy"). Joe

had to be talked into taking the money; Evans urged him, "Take it home and give it to your mother." [*Cleveland Press*, July 17, 1931]

In 1929 Joe played for the Frederick (Maryland) Warriors, the Class D Blue Ridge League farm club of the Indians. With Frederick Joe hit .381 in 407 at-bats, with nine homers and 63 other extra-base hits for a .661 slugging percentage. He had good speed; his 24 or 25 triples (figures differ) set a league record. He was second in the league in batting average, but he admitted to Brundidge that he was an "awkward outfielder." The Cleveland newspapers, a bit confused geographically, dubbed him the city's "blond Viking."

In the following winter, Joe met Hall of Famer Tris Speaker and asked him for a few pointers on fielding, then worked on that part of his game. The Indians took him to spring training in 1930, and first placed him with their top farm club, in New Orleans, but by the time the season began, general manager Evans had second thoughts about jumping him three levels and assigned Joe instead to the Class B Three-I League's Terre Haute Tots, where the right-handed hitter played center field. Vosmik learned to cover ground in the outfield, seeing time in all three fields, and showed quite a good arm, recording 13 assists for the Tots. Joe flirted with .400 and wound up hitting .397, with 116 RBIs; he beat out Springfield's Pete Susko for the batting title in the final game of the season and earned himself a September call-up. Joe's dramatic diving catch of Susko's liner may have been the play that broke his rival's push. Evans observed of Joe's plate work, "Anybody who can hit .380 for two consecutive years, no matter what company he is in, strikes me as the real article." [Unattributed article by Ed Bang found in the Hall of Fame archives]

The *Hartford Courant* predicted that the "big, blond youngster" (Vosmik was an even 6 feet tall but weighed in at 185 pounds) "may be the find of 1931." His debut with the Indians saw him pinch-hit in vain in the ninth inning of the September 13, 1930, game against Philadelphia—facing Lefty Grove. Joe grounded out to second base, but collected his share of hits for manager Roger Peckinpaugh. Vosmik's first major league hit came on September 20, 1930 at home against Boston's Milt Gaston. He had a 2-for-5 game that day against the Red Sox (driving in two) and a 2-for-4 game against St. Louis on the 27th, again driving in a pair. Those were his four RBIs for his abbreviated season; his average took a big hit when he suffered through an 0-for-10 doubleheader. Vosmik finished his brief 1930 debut with a .231 average in 26 at-bats.

For the next 10 years, Vosmik was a major leaguer, though he confessed in August 1931 that he still ducked every time he saw one of the Cleveland ballpark's guards or gatemen come by: "I'm still afraid I'll be recognized and bounced out." [Brundidge's article appears in the *St.*

Louis Star, August 12, 1931.] With Tris Speaker in the stands on Saturday April 18, 1931, Vosmik went 5-for-5, with three doubles and a triple. The effort seemed to cement him as the team's left fielder. Joe blistered the ball in early going, hitting safely 14 of his first 22 times at bat, with eight of the 14 hits going for extra bases. Not surprisingly, he cooled off some and he rode the bench for just a couple of days, then got in about as full a season as one could hope for, playing in 149 games.

Vosmik hit .320 his rookie year (1931) and drove in 117 runs, a tremendous accomplishment and, at the time, the third highest single-season RBI total for a rookie in major league baseball history. He led his team in triples with 14, which was good enough for fourth in the AL. He, along with Averill, led the Indians in doubles with 36. His 189 hits were eighth in the league. Had there been a Rookie of the Year award in 1931, Joe Vosmik might have contended, though 22-year-old rookie Lefty Gomez, who was 21–9 for the Yankees would have been a pretty solid choice.

Vosmik had an equally fine sophomore season, driving in 97 runs and batting .312, while scoring 106 runs. He was honored in his hometown with Joe Vosmik Day on June 22, and went 2-for-4 with one RBI in an 11–2 shellacking of the Senators.

Joe failed to play full seasons in 1933 (119 games) and 1934 (104 games), hitting just .263 in '33. A number of articles in May 1933 discussed Joe's vision. He saw an eye specialist, but the more likely cause was a bout of the flu that affected his eyesight for a spell. Hit by a pitch, Joe suffered a broken right hand on Labor Day in 1933, which cost him the rest of the season. He shone in 1934, in more limited action, placing fifth in the race for the batting title, hitting an excellent .341. Joe was far and away the most difficult man in the AL to strike out in 1934, fanning only 10 times in 405 at-bats. In his career, Vosmik finished in the top 10 in this category five times.

He was primed for what became his best season, 1935. Vosmik put it all together in 1935, leading the league in hits (216), doubles (47), and triples (20), becoming the first player in the AL to lead outright in those three categories since Ty Cobb did it in 1919. He drove in 110 and just barely missed the batting title by percentage points on the final day of the season: .3483 to Buddy Myer's .3490, when Myer went 4-for-5 in the final game of the year. The All-Star Game had been held in Cleveland in 1935 and Joe received a two-minute standing ovation when he came to the plate, the hometown showering its appreciation on its native son. Vosmik came in third in the American League MVP race, finishing behind Detroit's Hank Greenberg and Boston's Wes Ferrell but just ahead of Myer. After the season, Vosmik signed a new three-year deal with the Indians for a reported $37,000 total, the Cleveland club turning down a purported offer from the New York Yankees to sell Averill and Vosmik for

$241,000—the odd sum said to be the total of losses over the eight-year tenure of Indians owner Alva Bradley. The Yankees denied making the offer.

Joe still lived at home, and had drawn extra crowds to the ballpark, attracting a number of Central European immigrants who had never before followed baseball. There was one discordant note: In August, he was sued for $100,000 by Minnie Barr, who alleged breach of promise, charging that back in 1928, when he was 18, he had promised to marry her. His "attentions ceased in August, 1934," according to the Associated Press. The suit was settled out of court.

In November 1936, Joe married Sally Joanne Okla. The couple had three children: Joseph Robert, Larry Earl, and Karen. Joe seemed to have lost some of his skill, suffering a serious slump, and a benching, early in 1936 before rebounding to a .287 average by season's end. Despite the lower average, he nonetheless drove in 94 runs. The Indians, though, had dropped to fifth place and decided to make a move. In mid-January 1937, they traded Joe, Oral Hildebrand, and Bill Knickerbocker to the St. Louis Browns for Ivy Andrews, Lyn Lary, and Moose Solters. Vosmik played for the eighth-place Browns just the one year, but performed well, batting .325 and driving in 93 runs. He was fourth in the league with 47 doubles.

After that fine year, in December 1937 the Red Sox shipped Bobo Newsom, Red Kress, and Buster Mills to the Browns to secure Vosmik as their left fielder. They'd tried hard to get him before the '37 season, offering third baseman Mike Higgins and more to the Indians, but were turned down. Now they'd bagged their quarry. A few days later, general manager Ed Barrow of the Yankees said, "We offered no fewer than five players for Vosmik, who is my idea of the type of left fielder we could use at the Stadium." [Dan Daniel, *New York World-Telegram*, December 9, 1937] Joe was 27, and looking forward to playing in Fenway.

In 1938 Joe again led the league in hits, with 201. He hit .324, drove in 86 runs and scored 121. The Red Sox played Vosmik in left for 1939 as well, despite having Ted Williams on the team (Ted played right). Joe's average dropped to .276 (84 RBIs). After the season, though, the team decided to move in another direction, and to shift Williams to left field. The Red Sox believed—correctly—that Dominic DiMaggio was ready for the big leagues. Boston took the $25,000 waiver price from the Brooklyn Dodgers for Joe and sold him in mid-February, 1940. Joe sported a lifetime .311 average at the time, but was said to have begun to have "bad legs"—an assertion not supported by his 1939 season, which saw him play 144 games in left. The Sox made it known they were dealing Vosmik to Brooklyn and would have pulled back Joe had any AL club offered the waiver price. The Yankees didn't need Vosmik, but skipper Joe McCarthy had more or less endorsed him, telling Brooklyn's Larry MacPhail, "There

Vosmik in action, 1938

wasn't a better left fielder in our league last year than Vosmik." [*New York Times*, February 13, 1940]

The sandy fields in Clearwater and in some of the other Grapefruit League ballparks weren't good for Joe, who did have concerns about his legs. His ailment early on, however, was a rib injury in May, suffered in a collision with Cardinals shortstop Marty Marion. Into mid-June, Vosmik was slumping. He hit .282 for Brooklyn but his productivity was down. He drove in exactly half as many runs (42) as the year before and scored only 45.

In late February 1941, Joe suffered a big scare while the team began to train in Havana. A bottle of medicine he'd purchased at a local *farmacia* exploded as he opened it, blinding him for more than two hours before a physician was able to treat his eyes sufficiently to restore his sight. He opened 1941 with the Dodgers, but was released on Independence Day. He was hitting just .196 and every one of his 11 hits had been a single. Gordon Cobbledick of the *Cleveland Plain Dealer* felt that the Indians should have scooped up Joe, and not just out of sentiment. He thought Vosmik still had some good baseball in him and that his disappointing play in the National League may have been in part psychological: "Joe was unhappy from the beginning of his connection with this Brooklyn club"—though Joe never said as much publicly.

Vosmik had already made it clear a year or two earlier that his ambition after his playing career was to become a manager in the minor leagues, but he wasn't ready to give up as a player yet. Herb Pennock, the Red Sox farm director, approached Joe and signed him to Boston's Double-A Louisville Colonels, where Joe appeared in 42 games, batting .292. He played for the Minneapolis Millers for the next two seasons, hitting .304 and .253 respectively. With World War II on in earnest, Joe took wartime work with Thompson Aircraft Products in Cleveland but became embroiled in a minor controversy. Lou Boudreau of the

Indians had said in January 1943 that Vosmik could be a great addition to the Cleveland club. But no one from the Indians ever contacted Minneapolis owner Mike Kelley. Joe, seeing the possibility of getting back to the majors, wrote Kelley to say he'd simply quit if he didn't wind up with a major-league team. Kelley wrote back, saying he didn't blame him, but then threatened to report Cleveland for tampering. As matters worked out, Joe played the full year with the Millers.

He began 1944 with the Millers, too, but refused to report in a salary dispute, continuing to work in a Cleveland defense plant. On June 7, Vosmik signed with the Washington Senators; he appeared in 12 games, batting just .194. He was released on July 25. Later reports suggest he may have suffered from "chronic leg trouble." He announced his retirement on February 21, 1945, leaving major-league ball with a lifetime .307 average. Vosmik produced 1,682 hits including 335 doubles and 874 RBIs in 1,414 games. Immediately after baseball, he continued to work in the war plant, and also with a local brewery.

In April 1947, Vosmik achieved his managerial ambition, named to skipper Cleveland's Class C Tucson Cowboys (Arizona-Texas League). The team finished in second place, with an 80–52 record. Joe played in 30 games, batting .354. He managed the Dayton Indians (Class A Central League) in 1948 and the Double A Oklahoma City Indians in 1949 and 1950. He even squeezed in another 20 at-bats for Oklahoma City in 1949, batting .350 with one final home run. In midseason 1950, he had to be hospitalized for stomach ulcers and was reported to be "seriously ill." A week later he was replaced as manager by Tom Reis for the rest of the season. Joe had already reportedly contracted pneumonia and needed the rest.

The Indians gave him work that winter, helping to sell season tickets. He said he'd help the organization in any way he could and later that summer, he filled in as temporary manager for the Batavia (New York) Clippers of the Class D Pony League when the manager there became ill. For three seasons, through 1952, he worked as a scout for the Indians.

Joe later took up work selling automobiles and then as an appliance salesman for Sears Southgate, an area department store, but developed a cancerous lung tumor and was operated on at age 51. The operation appeared to be successful, but after a week in the hospital, Joe contracted pneumonia and he died on January 27, 1962. In 1993, Joe Vosmik was honored by his home state with an induction into the Ohio Baseball Hall of Fame.

Sources

Thanks to Fred Schuld for supplying a great deal of information on Vosmik's career, including a copy of his Hall of Fame file. Maurice Bouchard added considerable insight to this biography.

"WHISTLING JAKE" WADE *by John Fuqua*

G	ERA	W	L	SV	GS	GF	CG	SHO	IP	H	R	ER	BB	SO	HR	HBP	WP	BFP
20	6.23	1	4	0	6	8	1	0	47⅔	68	34	33	37	21	1	0	2	234

G	AB	R	H	2B	3B	HR	RBI	BB	SO	BA	OBP	SLG	SB	HBP
20	12	1	0	0	0	0	0	0	5	.000	.000	.000	0	0

In the sandy soil of Carteret County, North Carolina, young boys were schooled in a tough brand of baseball. They emulated their fathers, uncles, and community leaders who held regular jobs during the week in the whaling and fishing community of Morehead City and played baseball in leagues on the weekend. The spirited local nine was tough, smart, scrappy, and hard-working, and on occasion settled slights and disagreements with their fists. These men played the game because they loved it. Baseball was not their occupation. It was their avocation. They shared this love with their sons.

Jacob Fields Wade, Jr. was born on April 1, 1912, in Morehead City, North Carolina. His father, Jacob Sr., was a whaler and shipbuilder in this Southern coastal community. He married Love Styron and together they raised a family of 11 children. The four boys were Rupert, Charles Winfield "Wink," Jake, and the youngest brother, Ben. The daughters were Carita, Maidie, Eudora, Duella, Eleanor, Hazel, and Josephine.

Jake Wade attended the Charles S. Wallace School in Morehead City from 1918 to 1929. He played high school baseball for Wallace, where he started as a first baseman because of his 6-foot-plus height, but the coach quickly moved him to the pitching staff where he developed into a dominant pitcher. His competitors hated to bat against him, and often spoke of his wicked curve and sinker, and how he would enhance his pitches with a special foreign substance often used by pitchers of his day.

Baseball was to become a family business for all three Wade boys. Older brother Winfield was the first to graduate from Wallace School. Wink, also known locally as "Croaker," was an excellent player and went to North Carolina State College to play baseball. Jake followed his brother to State College, which he attended from 1929 to 1931. Again, Jake started out at first base, but quickly became a pitcher based on the strength of his arm and his ability to get movement on his pitches.

After college, Wink played outfield in the minor leagues and spent eight seasons with eight different

Jake Wade

ballclubs; his final assignment was player-manager with the Richmond Colts in 1934. During 1930, he played in the Texas League with the Beaumont Exporters (he later worked in Beaumont as an engineer). It was there that he met Tigers scout Jack Zeller. Wink told Zeller of his little brother's high hard fastball and sweeping curveball. It did not hurt that the strapping 6-foot-2 Jake was a left-handed hurler at North Carolina State. Zeller signed Jake Wade and placed him with Raleigh in the Class C Piedmont League. Later, Jake assisted younger brother Ben in making the move from Wallace School baseball to becoming a right-handed pitcher in professional ball. Ben pitched in the National League during the 1940s and '50s for Chicago, Brooklyn (he was 11–9 with the 1952 pennant winners), St. Louis, and Pittsburgh. Ben worked as a scout for the Dodgers organization after 19 seasons in baseball.

In his pro debut, in 1931, Jake pitched in nine games for Raleigh, with a 1–0 record. In 27 innings he allowed 30 hits, struck out 23 batters, gave up 20 walks, and had a 4.67 ERA. During the season he moved up to Evansville of the Class B Three-I League, where he compiled a 4–3 record with a 3.43 ERA in 18 games, pitching 97 innings, allowing 97 hits, striking out 57 batters, and walking 60.

Before the start of the 1932 season, Evansville released Wade to Decatur of the Three-I League; in turn, Decatur released him to Moline (Illinois) of the Class D Mississippi Valley League. He pitched in 33 games for the sixth-place Plow Boys, with a 10–18 record, pitching in 221 innings, allowing 212 hits, striking out 200, walking 135, and finishing the year with a 3.87 ERA. His year included a one-hit, 2–0 shutout of Davenport on June 27. He was named a second-team league all-star. At the end of the season, Jake was promoted to Beaumont of the Class A Texas League.

As the Texas League season began, Wade pitched ineffectively. He won 1 and lost 5, giving up 58 hits and 40 walks in 52 innings, with a 6.23 ERA. In May he was released to Shreveport of the Class C Dixie League where his pitching improved at the lower level. In 30 games, he was 9–9 in 182 innings, allowing 206 hits, 107 strikeouts, and 84 walks. Jake finished with a 5.09 ERA, but pitched two shutouts.

The next year, 1934, was pivotal for Wade. He returned to Beaumont, and had his best year yet: 14–11, with an impressive ERA of 2.70. The next year, the Tigers invited him to spring training at Lakeland, Florida. An Associated Press story datelined March 6 says that manager Mickey Cochrane watched Wade "burn up the plate with a fastball this afternoon, but the rookie failed to satisfy." Though it had been thought he'd likely be returned to Beaumont, before camp broke, the big league club sent him on option to Portland of the Pacific Coast League. He pitched in 40 games during the Beavers' 173-game season, won 17 games and lost 15, struck out 153, with a 3.98 ERA in an impressive 263 innings. His best game was a June 15 one-hitter against the Hollywood Sheiks. He still allowed a large number of baserunners (235 hits, 166 walks, 8 hit batsmen). Dick Dobbins spins a delightful tale in his book *Nuggets on the Diamond:*

During the 1935 season, the Mission Reds were playing a series in Portland's Vaughn Street Park. It was "Jake Wade Day," with Wade pitching the first game of a Sunday doubleheader. Reds center fielder Lou Almada was having a field day against Wade. Anything Wade tossed up to the plate, Almada hit out of reach of the Beavers' defenders. The two began jawing at each other. Wade became angrier with each Almada success, and by the end of the game, he was angry and embarrassed. Between games, both teams retired to their respective clubhouses. After a few minutes, there was a knock on the Reds' clubhouse door. Outside stood John "Moose" Clabaugh, the burly Portland outfielder. Clabaugh was there as Wade's second for a showdown with Almada. Manager Gabby Street told both players to take off their cleats and go out to settle their differences. Almada made quick work of Wade as Clabaugh passively stood by. Beavers pitcher Sailor Bill Posedel later told the Missions' George McDermott that Clabaugh had urged Wade to challenge Almada. Clabaugh didn't care at all for Wade and was confident Almada could beat him. Ah, teammates.

Wade's nickname was Whistling Jake, which did not reflect his fastball but rather his fondness for imitating songbirds. A Detroit sportswriter once said of Jake, "He whistles like a mockingbird and he pitches like a kangaroo." The sportswriter was referring to Wade's lack of control. He fought his control his entire major-league career (440 walks in 668 innings).

In 1936 Wade again made the trip to Lakeland with the major-league ballclub. This time he broke camp on the Tigers' roster. He made his major league debut on April 22, 1936. He lasted just one inning pitching in relief in a 12–4 loss at the hands of the St. Louis Browns, giving up three runs on five hits, and was soon sent down to Montreal of the International League. There he compiled a record of 6–8 with a 4.88 ERA in 24 appearances. In late July, he was recalled by the Tigers because of injuries to the Detroit pitching staff. By year's end, Jake had pitched in 13 games for the Tigers amassing a 4–5 recording including four complete games and an August 6 shutout of the Indians among his 11 starts. Indicative of the difficulties he had with his control was the September 2 start against the Senators. He got the tight 3–2 win, allowing only three hits through eight innings, but walked seven batters. When he walked the first man he faced in the ninth, Vic Sorrell was called on in relief. Wade had a lackluster 5.29 ERA for his 78⅓ innings, gave up 93 hits, struck out 30, and walked 52.

In March 1937, Wade married the former Rosalie Watson. That year proved to be his best season in the major leagues; the whistling left-hander posted a 7–10 record for manager Mickey Cochrane in 33 appearances, including 25 starts, seven complete games, and one shutout; but his ERA was still a disappointing 5.39 ERA. Two of the wins were four-hitters thrown against the league-leading New York Yankees on June 7 and 26. And one of the losses was a heart-breaker. He dueled Wes Ferrell of the Senators in a 1–1 June 16 game through 11½ innings, only to lose it in the bottom of the 12th on a bases-loaded wild pitch.

Wade hurled his best game on the last day of the season, October 3, at home. Undefeated Cleveland Indians pitcher Johnny Allen was going for his 16th consecutive victory. A win would tie Allen with Smoky Joe Wood, Walter Johnson, Lefty Grove, and Schoolboy Rowe for the most consecutive wins in one American League season. Wade matched Allen pitch for pitch, and carried a 1–0 lead deep into the game. H.G. Salsinger, sports editor of the *Detroit News*, wrote, "It was about time for Wade to crack. He had a well-earned reputation as a crumbling pitcher. He got nervous and excited and tightened up in the tough going and the going on this afternoon was tough, if it ever was."

The Detroit press corps had been tough on Jake, who despite his major-league arm battled control problems throughout his career. But in this game, Wade had given up only one hit and no runs. The Tigers scored a run in the first inning and Wade held Cleveland at bay throughout the game. In top of the ninth, still nursing the 1–0 lead, Wade gave up his fourth walk of the game, to Lyn Lary. John Kroner sacrificed Lary to second base. Earl Averill hit a fly ball, leaving Wade with just one out standing between him and a win.

Hal Trosky, the only Indian to get a hit, was the next batter. Wade bore down and fanned Trosky for the victory that cost Johnny Allen his chance to tie the record. Jake later told reporters, "That's the way I should have been pitching in April. I do everything backwards."

But in 1938, the Tigers lost faith in Jake and his control issues. He pitched in 27 games with just two starts, winning three games and losing two. His ERA climbed to 6.56. In 70 innings he allowed 73 hits, walked 48 batters, and struck out only 23. On December 15, he was traded to the Boston Red Sox with Elden Auker and Chet Morgan for Pinky Higgins and Archie McKain. The *New York Times* noted that the principals in the trade were Higgins and Auker, but—recalling Wade's game against Allen—added, "Wade may well become an important member of Joe Cronin's pitching staff." He was dubbed "a rangy young fellow with a lot of speed but erratic in control."

Wade and Woody Rich were the two pitchers uncertain to make the team, but both saw action in 1939. They had high hopes for both, but neither really panned out. With the Red Sox, Wade pitched in 20 games including six starts, and had a 1–4 record with a 6.23 ERA, reflecting the 105 runners he put on base in just 47⅔ innings and including the two runners he forced in with bases-loaded walks in the July 29 game. The Sox had tried to send him down to Louisville in early May to get some more seasoning, but couldn't get him through waivers and so kept him on the ballclub. On September 6, the Red Sox sold him to the St. Louis Browns, on waivers, for whom he had an 0–2 record in four appearances, including two starts. Pitching in 16⅓ innings for the Browns, he gave up 26 hits and walked 19. His earned-run average soared to 11.02.

The Browns sent the 28-year-old Wade to the minors in 1940 to work on his control and try to rehabilitate his career. With the Toledo Mud Hens of the American Association, he was 2–2 with a 7.15 ERA. On December 5, the Browns sold Wade to the Cincinnati Reds.

Jake started the 1941 season pitching for Reds' Indianapolis Indians affiliate in the American Association. He recorded a 0–1 mark with a 9.00 ERA but before too long went home to North Carolina to rehabilitate his sore arm. He signed with the New Bern Bears in the Class D Coastal Plain League as a player-manager and went 12–9 with a 2.44 ERA.

In 1942, Jake got back to the major leagues, purchased by the White Sox on June 3 to help bolster their pitching staff after losing Thornton Lee to an injury and Johnny Rigney to the Navy. The *Chicago Tribune* noted, oddly, "In 1939 Jake lost his stuff and says he doesn't know why—no pain, or anything. . . . Jake claims he now is very deceptive and it was on this assurance the Sox signed him." Wade pitched 85⅔ innings in 15 games, starting 10 games and compiling a respectable 5–5 record with three complete games and a 4.10 ERA for the sixth-place White Sox. Jake struck out 32 batters, but allowed 84 hits and walked 56. Talk about long relief—on July 1, after White Sox starter

Wade with the 1939 Red Sox

Orval Grove had allowed seven runs to score in the first inning without recording an out, Wade was brought on in relief and pitched the rest of the game, securing 27 outs while allowing just three hits. The game, though, was a lost cause, 7–2. On the 12th of the month, he threw a complete game three-hitter against Philadelphia and was 3-for-5 at the plate, all singles. Wade batted .167 lifetime, with but seven runs batted in.

During the war year of 1943 with the White Sox, Wade pitched in 21 games, with nine starts, three complete games, and one shutout. He was 3–7 with a much-improved 3.01 ERA.

The White Sox continued to use Jake as a spot starter the following year, 1944; as always, he was occasionally brilliant in relief—pitching four hitless innings against the Senators on July 25, and seven innings of three-hit shutout ball against the Indians on August 4, but was 2–4 at season's end, with a 4.82 ERA. On December 15, 1944, he was traded by the White Sox to the New York Yankees for Johnny Johnson. In February of 1945, Wade, almost 33 years old, joined the Navy. He pitched for the Bainbridge Commodores before being detached and assigned to the Dahlgren Naval Proving Ground. In Fredericksburg, he threw a no-hitter on July 18, striking out 18 while blanking the Indian Head team. He was discharged in January, 1946, and reported to spring training with New York.

Wade pitched in 13 games for the 1946 Yankees with

one start, a 2–1 record and a 2.29 ERA. He was placed on waivers in midseason and was claimed by the Washington Senators. He made six appearances for his sixth major-league ballclub, the Senators, throwing just 11⅓ innings with no decisions and a 4.76 ERA. Jake appeared in his final major-league game on September 12, pitching in relief in a 9–6 Senators' victory over the Browns. The Senators sold him to the International League's Jersey Giants on December 16. In announcing the sale, Washington commented, "Wade looked good against us while he was with the Yankees, but didn't do so well after we bought him."

In 1947, Wade helped Jersey City in impressive fashion, compiling a record of 17–5 with a fine 2.52 ERA. The Giants ball club, managed by Bruno Betzel, won the International League pennant but was blanked by Buffalo, four games to none, in a playoff semifinal series. For the season, Jake pitched 197 innings in 32 games, 26 of them starts, with 18 complete games and four shutouts. Still battling control problems, he walked 108 batters. Jake and his brothers were honored by their local community, Morehead City, on August 14. The park behind the Charles Wallace School was named Wade Brothers Memorial Park.

In December, Wade was one of three players sent by the Giants, along with $65,000, to San Diego of the Pacific Coast League in exchange for first baseman Jack Harshman.

With San Diego, Jake was 0–4 with a 7.09 ERA, and was dealt to the Buffalo Bisons in midseason. With Buffalo, he was 8–11 with a 5.10 ERA. In 1949, he was 3–4 with a 6.70 ERA for the Bisons.

The 1950 season was Wade's last in professional baseball as he returned to record a 7–6 mark for Buffalo. One of his wins for the Bisons was a 2–0 no-hitter thrown against the Syracuse Chiefs on August 6. He ended the season with a 4.96 ERA, then retired. He was 38 and had spent almost two decades playing in the pros, with all or part of eight seasons in the majors. He completed his major-league career with a record of 27–40. He made 71 starts, had 20 complete games, and pitched three shutouts. He pitched in 668⅓ innings in 171 games. His major-league ERA was 5.00. Always fighting his control, Jake gave up 440 walks and 690 hits and had a career WHIP (walks plus hits per inning pitched) of 1.69. He struck out 291.

After returning to North Carolina with his family, he worked as an electronics repairs technician at the Cherry Point Marine Corps Air Station in Havelock, North Carolina. He retired in 1976. During 1999, he returned to Detroit for the last game in Tiger Stadium, where he was on the field with other former Tigers greats in old-style uniforms. In 2005, Rosalie Watson Wade, Jake's wife of 68 years, died.

Jacob Fields Wade Jr. died on February 1, 2006, at the age of 93 at his residence in the Newport Community of Wildwood, North Carolina. He had suffered a stroke about four years before. When he died, he was the oldest living former player for the White Sox. He was a member of Wildwood Presbyterian Church. Wade was interred at the Historic Bayview Cemetery. He was survived by two sons, Jacob Fields Wade III and William Albert Wade; two daughters, Rebecca Wade Davis and Sara Wade Wallace; eight grandchildren; and five great-grandchildren. He was preceded in death by a daughter, Jo Ann Wade Eaves.

Sources

SABR MiLB Database
Baseball-Reference.com
The Sporting News
Detroit News
Interview with baseball historian Joe (Boy) Willis, Carteret County, North Carolina, June 2008
Dobbins, Dick. *Nuggets on the Diamond* (Judith Dobbins, publisher, 1994)
Thanks to Bill Francis at the National Baseball Hall of Fame.

CHARLIE WAGNER *by Bill Nowlin*

G	ERA	W	L	SV	GS	GF	CG	SHO	IP	H	R	ER	BB	SO	HR	HBP	WP	BFP
9	4.23	3	1	0	5	2	0	0	38⅓	49	19	18	14	13	3	0	0	170

G	AB	R	H	2B	3B	HR	RBI	BB	SO	BA	OBP	SLG	SB	HBP
11	14	2	1	0	0	0	2	0	2	.071	.071	.071	0	0

Charlie Wagner logged more continuous service with the Boston Red Sox than any other person before or since. From his signing as a player in 1934 until the day he died while scouting for the Red Sox in the summer of 2006, Wagner spent more than 70 years with the Red Sox—parts of six of them in the 1930s and '40s as a pitcher with the "varsity." The only exceptions were the three years he spent in the Navy during World War II. Charlie was born in Reading, Pennsylvania, and died there 94 years later. And he was first signed by the Red Sox at Lauer's Park in Reading, in 1934. His was a long life in baseball. He laughed with writer Chuck Greenwood in 1997, "When I played, they didn't have baseball cards. I was born before the Dead Sea was sick."

Charles Thomas Wagner, born on December 3, 1912, was the third of three children in his family. His father, Charles Albert Wagner, was a meat inspector for the state of Pennsylvania. His mother, Mabel, was a homemaker. Neither his older brother, Henry, nor his sister, Elizabeth, had any real talent at athletics, but Charlie was a four-letter man at Northeast Junior High and in high school. Charlie said he was motivated to become a pitcher simply because so many told him, "You're not big enough to be a pitcher." Red Sox PR director Ed Doherty quoted Charlie as saying, "I was so small in school that the rest of the boys insisted I do the catching. I caught several games with a mask and a glove—we couldn't afford a chest protector—and right then and there I decided I was either going to be a pitcher or I would give up baseball entirely and study medicine."

He joined the Reading Athletic League and earned a position with the Ajax, a Midget (for younger boys) team. They won the championship two years running, and in the third year beat the competition in the senior division. Under coach Mead Remley, not one player changed position for the full three years. Charlie got some offers to play ball on Sundays, but his parents were opposed to Sunday baseball. He hid his baseball suit, made his way to the games, and picked up a little cash.

The 5-foot-11, 170 pound right-handed Wagner had no basis of comparison for how good he might be, but acknowledged, "You know you're pretty good because you were winning. I was winning all the time, around the town." Charlie played third base when he wasn't on the mound, but it was pitching he enjoyed most and where

we had his greatest success. Melvin "Doc" Silva was a former professional ballplayer, an outfielder, and he ran the American Legion baseball team in Reading at the time. Reading was a Red Sox farm club in 1933 and 1934 and Silva recommended Charlie to Reading manager Nemo Leibold: "I want you to watch this kid pitch." Wagner threw batting practice; Leibold was suitably impressed and kept his own eye on Charlie.

A bit later, Leibold approached Charlie and recommended him to a team near Pittsburgh. Charlie's reaction? "I was scared to go out because I had never traveled in my life before. Pittsburgh sounded like you could say it was over in England or something." Doc Silva was about 40 years old, but he and Charlie both played on the same semipro "Anthracite League" team in Lebanon, Pennsylvania, about 30 miles from Reading. Charlie was picking up $10 to $15 a game. That's where, as Charlie put it, "I started to sprout out from my little home town here." Silva liked the Red Sox and Charlie signed a contract proffered by Herb Pennock of the Red Sox and agreed to go to Charlotte in the Class B Piedmont League for 1935. Pennock was the GM with the Sox farm team in Charlotte and Frank O'Rourke the manager. Charlie was intimidated at first, but became friendly with Jim Bagby and pitched 201 innings in 44 games, with a 3.22 ERA and a record of 7-16. Charlie credited Pennock with giving him a great deal of assistance. For example, Pennock took Wagner into the Charlotte bullpen and told him to throw three straight strikes. Harder than it might seem, Pennock told Wagner the secret was never to take your eyes off the target. In his many years as a pitching instructor for the Red Sox, Wagner taught the same lesson to many a prospect. In 1935, Charlie had one of the best earned run averages in the league, but the problem was "our ballclub wasn't right. . . . I don't want to embarrass anybody but they couldn't put a team together to make up double plays like some of the other teams did. . . . I went back the next year and I won 20 games."

So he did, for Rocky Mount (North Carolina), in the Piedmont League: 20-14, with a 4.07 ERA in 254 innings of work for manager George Toporcer, under whom Wagner would later work in the Red Sox farm system. After his 20-win season, Toporcer told Charlie, "I'd like to get you to Minneapolis (in 1937)." Minneapolis was a Double-A team in the American Association, the highest classification at the time, and Wagner went there with some trepidation: "It seemed like 400,000 miles away. I couldn't get adjusted to traveling."

Apparently, he made the adjustment, and thrived, having an excellent year—20–14 again, with a 3.53 ERA in 278 innings, with 20 complete games. Donie Bush was his manager but Andy Cohen took over when Bush had to be treated for facial cancer. Bush "sure would wake you up. He was about 5 feet 4 but he talked like he was 7 feet 4. He was a great manager. And Andy Cohen was extremely good to me. He gave me all the opportunities in 1937."

In 1938, Wagner, who featured a curveball, fastball, and change-up, went to spring training (in Sarasota, Florida) with the Boston ballclub for the first time and made the team. His debut came in the second game of the season, the opener of a Patriots Day doubleheader at Fenway Park between Lefty Grove of the Red Sox and Lefty Gomez of the Yankees. In the seventh, with New York leading 2–1 lead, Eric McNair hit for Grove, but the Red Sox failed to score. Charlie pitched a scoreless top of the eighth and when Boston scored two in the bottom of the eighth he could have earned the win. Wagner, however, walked the first two Yankees in the ninth. Johnny Marcum then took over for Charlie. After a sacrifice and an intentional walk, the bases were loaded for pitcher Red Ruffing who came in to bat for Gomez. A good-hitting pitcher, Ruffing hit a single that scored two. Charlie took the loss.

He didn't get nearly enough work. Manager Joe Cronin, and most of baseball, greatly favored veteran pitchers at the time. "We were just growing up in the business of having a farm system, and I was part of it, thank God, because I enjoyed being with the Red Sox." After sitting around more than he wanted, Wagner approached Cronin and said, "I don't want to sit here and watch these guys play. I've gotta pitch." Cronin responded, "Well, if you do . . . " and shipped him back to Minneapolis. There Charlie developed a lifelong friendship with a young outfielder on the Millers by the name of Ted Williams. Charlie was 1–3 (8.35 ERA) with the Red Sox and 8–3 (3.90) with Minneapolis. Donie Bush had told him that he'd done enough pitching; Charlie was set to go to Boston in 1939.

During the years he spent with the big-league club, Charlie was Ted Williams' roommate. They'd known each other in Minneapolis, and roomed together—as they did for the time that Charlie spent with Boston through 1946. When he first arrived in Florida for spring training in

1938, Ted asked Cronin for someone who didn't smoke, didn't drink, and liked to get to bed early and wake up early. Cronin pointed him to Charlie Wagner and both ballplayers frequently said it was a very good fit.

Charlie was a snappy dresser, too, and that had an appeal to the young Ted. The "Broadway Charlie" moniker was first assigned to him by Boston sportswriter Johnny Drohan. "We used to walk at night," Charlie remembered. "Johnny Drohan and a few other guys. We had a great rapport with the newspaper guys. They were nice guys. Johnny was kidding me all the time: 'Hey, Broadway! You look like Broadway.' He put it in the paper and it started that way." It was important to Charlie to dress well. "When I was a kid," he explained, "I had one suit and that was for Saturdays and Sundays. I made up my mind that when I had enough money, clothes were going to be number one on my must list."

Charlie spent most of 1939 with Louisville. The Red Sox had just purchased the Louisville club and as the Boston-bound Red Sox prepared to board the train north from spring training, Joe Cronin took Charlie aside and asked him if he would pitch Opening Day in Louisville. It was a favor, he explained, a request from owner Tom Yawkey. "I was a little disappointed, but I said, 'No, if it's for Mr. Yawkey, I'll go over.' So I went over and we won the game in Louisville." Yawkey was present, and he told Charlie, "I'll never forget this day, and I'll never forget you." Charlie remembered the moment 66 years later: "We fell in love and that was where it started." He enthused, "There's no greater owner that's ever lived than Tom Yawkey. Nobody. There's not even a close match to him. He took care of his ballplayers."

Charlie's son Craig heard that Yawkey had run onto the field and hugged Charlie and told him, "As long as I'm with the Red Sox, you'll never have to look for another job the rest of your life."

Wagner stayed in Louisville, but Woody Rich hurt his arm in midseason and on August 13, the Sox sent Rich to Louisville and called up Wagner and Lefty Lefebvre. Wagner posted a 3–1 mark with the Red Sox in 1939 (4.23), after going 10–11 (2.90) for Louisville. In 1940, he began the season with the Red Sox but had to undergo a tonsillectomy early on and couldn't seem to regain his full strength, so was sent down to Louisville in July. He finished strong with the Colonels, losing his first game but then winning nine in a row (with a 1.84 ERA) and three playoff games to help bring the Colonels deep into the Little World Series between the American Association

Wagner as a Red Sox instructor

and the International League champions. Newark beat Charlie in the sixth game and took the title for the International League. By season's end he had only appeared in 12 major league games and held a 1–0 record (5.52). It wasn't easy to get a chance to pitch at the time. "They liked the older pitcher. The young pitcher had a hell of a time. Today they give that young kid a start. And then another start and another."

The following two years—1941 and 1942—Charlie spent the full year with the Red Sox. He pitched in 29 games each year, with records of 12–8 (3.07) and 14–11 (3.29) respectively. They were good years and Wagner was a solid part of the starting rotation. His record in 1941 could have been much better, but he lost quite a few games by the thinnest of margins. Perhaps his best games came August 25, 1941 (when he threw a four-hit 1–0 shutout opposing Bob Feller), and July 9, 1942, when he threw a complete game 2–1 win against Hal Newhouser, again permitting just four hits in 11 innings. Like most ballplayers, and most adult men, World War II interrupted his career. Wagner married Elynor Becker after the 1942 season and two weeks later enlisted in the Navy as a seaman second class. The couple had two sons—Christopher Charles, who died at three years of age, choking on a peanut while his parents were out and his grandmother's bridge club was gathered; and Craig, who works today as a tour director with a travel company. Craig went to college, roamed the country in the '60s, and then took a position with an insurance company before later moving into real estate and now the travel business. Charlie showed his son how to pitch, but Craig did not play beyond the high school level. "He taught me how throwing a curveball was, he used to say, like you're pulling a window shade down, the rotation you'd get," recalls Craig. "I was all right, but one baseball player in the family seemed to be quite enough at the time."

As the war dragged on, Charlie missed three full seasons (1943–45). He played some ball for the Navy at the Norfolk Naval Training Base, but not nearly as much as some players did during the war years. He was ultimately shipped out to the Philippines. He served there and in New Guinea and developed a serious case of dysentery which did him in as a pitcher. Teams were allowed five extra slots on their rosters in 1946, the first year after the war, to accommodate returning veterans. Wagner stuck with the pennant-winning Red Sox for the full season, starting four games in the middle of the season but threw only 30⅔ innings (1–0, 5.87). It wasn't a good year, though: "I was just weak as a cat." His last game was on August 8; he did not appear in the World Series.

After the year was over, Tom Yawkey offered Wagner a job as assistant farm director working under Specs Toporcer. Charlie felt he was getting better as the year went on and might have been able to pitch a few more years but he took the job and never regretted it. "I was 36.

[Wagner misremembered his age by three years in the interview.] When you lose three years and you're hitting 36 and you haven't thrown any, it takes a little bark out of you. Mr. Yawkey offered me the job. I took the job because I thought it was the best thing I could do." He said he didn't want to become a manager. "Managers just get fired."

In 527⅔ innings of work in the major leagues, he'd made only one error, in 1941. "I don't know where I made the error," he laughed. "Maybe somebody pushed me or something."

Charlie's second career with the Sox began in 1947. Charlie really enjoyed working with his old manager, but Toporcer lasted only one year because his sight was failing. "One of the sharpest guys you'll ever have in baseball," was Charlie's assessment. "He played with St. Louis for about eight years as a utilityman. He says, 'I don't know why I couldn't play second base.' I asked, 'Who was playing second?' 'Wait until I think of his name . . . Rogers Hornsby. I can't understand why they're playing Rogers and I'm sitting on the bench.' He'd kid about that. But he could fill in for third base or anyplace else, and he could run like a son of a gun. He was a good baseball man. Then he went blind. He used to make speeches, and I think the league should have hired a guy like that to keep him going. He was a beautiful man. A baseball man and smart as a whip. I learned a lot from him."

Johnny Murphy, who had finished his playing career with the 1947 Red Sox, replaced Toporcer as farm director in 1948. It was a different time. "At that time, you could just walk up to a kid and say, 'Do you want to play ball?'" recalled Charlie. "You didn't have to go through this draft stuff." For the most part, though, the farm director did the signings. Charlie made the rounds of all the team's affiliates—the Red Sox had an extensive system of 12 minor-league farm clubs. "That's where I was most of the time, with instructional work. I used to go around to all the farm clubs. My wife, I used to write her ' . . . Dear Friend . . . '" For somebody who had not liked to travel, Charlie was racking up mileage. "I learned," he said. "But then you have all winter to yourself. Of course, we had to go to all the meetings and so forth in the wintertime . . . which was a pleasure."

After 15 years as assistant farm director, he became a roving minor-league pitching instructor and scout beginning in 1962.

Though more an instructor than a scout, Wagner is still credited with signing a few players who made the majors: Dick Gernert (1950), Bobby Mitchell (1965), Wim Remmerswaal (1974), John Lickert (1978), and Danny Sheaffer (1981). But for the most part, he enjoyed teaching—which he did (admittedly to a declining degree) right up to his final year. "I didn't do much scouting per se. I didn't sign that many guys. I'd go out and OK some of them. We had such good scouts. And that's what makes baseball—the good scouts. And we had some great ones. Not good ones. Great ones. The Danny Doyles and those type of guys."

Charlie spent one year working again at the major-league level. In 1970, incoming Red Sox manager Eddie Kasko's first official move was to ask Charlie to serve as Boston's big-league pitching coach. Charlie enjoyed the experience and very much enjoyed working with Kasko ("one of the better managers that you'll see"). It was just the one year, and Charlie returned to his prior duties as Kasko brought in Harvey Haddix in 1971, their seventh pitching coach since the start of 1963.

Instruction was the work he truly loved, and it was a love he never lost. As late as January 2003, a few weeks before heading to spring training, he said, "I still do teaching when I go down to Florida, with the pitchers. I like that part of it." The Red Sox had honored their longtime loyal employee in March 1998 so for his last several years when Wagner went to the minor-league complex in Fort Myers, he could drive and park on Charlie Wagner Way. He laughed when asked about it: "It's a very small street!"

Looking ahead to the 2003 season, Wagner was still actively scouting three ballclubs—the Pittsburgh Pirates, the Philadelphia Phillies, "and then they give me another one sometimes. Each time you go down to the Phillies or you go to Pittsburgh, you're there a week or more, trying to get everything done. Sometimes you can't get it all done in a week." Charlie would write up his reports—longhand. "Most of the guys put it on computer. I don't do computer. I write it out. And I have good friends in the office that put it on the computer."

Charlie also scouted the Reading Phillies. In the hometown that had honored him in 1992 with induction into the Reading Baseball Hall of Fame, it was an easy task for Charlie. "I just fall out of bed and I'm in the ballpark. I like to go out there." In 2002, just a few months after the death of his old roommate Ted Williams, Wagner was crowned "King of Baseballtown" in Reading. On Opening Day 2005, at the conclusion of Fenway Park ceremonies celebrating the Red Sox' long-awaited world championship, it was Charlie Wagner who was asked to make the call to announce the start of the new season: Dapper as always, he spoke into the microphone, "Let's play ball!"

Wagner was in St. Louis to witness the Red Sox winning the World Series in October 2004. He'd been there in 1946, and again saw the final defeats in 1967, 1975,

"Broadway" Charlie Wagner

and 1986. It was nice to see the Sox win one, a full 70 years after Charlie had signed that first contract back in 1934.

Charlie lost Ellie, his wife of 60 years, shortly after the 2004 World Series triumph. He'd earlier discussed his marriage with *Philadelphia Daily News* writer Jim Salisbury and told him "every day with Ellie was like winning the World Series." He added, "Cherish your memories."

About this time Charlie began to experience a touch of dementia, his son Craig explains. "He would go out to the Reading ballpark, and they were nice enough to give him a ride out every day. He would say he was going to work, that the Red Sox wanted him out there. He *was* on the payroll, but he just sort of watched the game from the press box—which was named after him."

Charlie Wagner attended his last ballgame on August 30, 2006, in Reading. Coincidently, August 30 is Ted Williams' birthday. That evening, Charlie had presented the "Charlie Wagner Scholarship Award" between innings during the game. "And then, as he normally did, he would go out of the ballpark early, to avoid the crowds—he wasn't too steady walking. He just went out to the car, and waited for the driver, and that was it."

Sitting in his car after the game, Charlie expired at age 93. A tribute by Tony Zonca appears on the Reading Phillies website. Zonca wrote that Charlie "had an innate ability to leave each person feeling better for having met him. It is a rare trait he carried with him, like a cherished good-luck piece." After Ellie died, many had worried about him: "He went on the DL for a time, but he came back this season with the stride and bearing of a rookie. He still wins our vote as Comeback Player of the Year." Zonca concluded his piece: "Smile knowing in your heart that 'Broadway' Charlie Wagner has just inked a new, long-term contract with Mr. Yawkey, his revered old boss with the Sox, as he starts a new season. He is a rookie again. His long journey has just begun."

Sources

Quotations from Charlie Wagner come from interviews with Bill Nowlin on January 16, 1999, and January 14, 2003.

Interview with Craig Wagner, July 14, 2007.

Doherty, Edward. Untitled, undated Red Sox press release draft (1941) from the Wagner player file at the National Baseball Hall of Fame.

Greenwood, Chuck. "Longevity at its finest," *Sports Collectors Digest*, April 25, 1997.

Thanks to Rob Hackash and Jim Salisbury.

MONTE WEAVER *by Warren Corbett*

G	ERA	W	L	SV	GS	GF	CG	SHO	IP	H	R	ER	BB	SO	HR	HBP	WP	BFP
9	6.64	1	0	1	1	2	1	0	20⅓	26	15	15	13	6	0	1	2	99

G	AB	R	H	2B	3B	HR	RBI	BB	SO	BA	OBP	SLG	SB	HBP
9	4	0	0	0	0	0	0	0	1	.000	.000	.000	0	0

Sportswriters treated pitcher Monte Weaver as a curiosity during his nine seasons with the Washington Senators and Boston Red Sox. He was a college professor, a mathematician, a hypochondriac, and—most radically—a vegetarian, according to the sports pages.

Montie Morton Weaver was born on June 15, 1906, in Helton, North Carolina, a hamlet in the state's northwestern corner near the present-day Blue Ridge Parkway. His father, Wade, who was born in Virginia about 1872, had a blacksmith shop and later became a farmer. His mother, Mollie, was born in North Carolina. Montie was the youngest of their four children.

The Weaver family moved to nearby Lansing, a town that sprang up along the Norfolk & Western railroad tracks. In 1923 Montie entered Emory & Henry College, a small Methodist school in Emory, Virginia, about 40 miles from home. He pitched for the baseball team, played center on the basketball team, and, because he was 6 feet tall, joined the track team as a high jumper and pole vaulter. He graduated with honors in 1927 with a major in mathematics and a grade average of "90 or above." Weaver later told *Washington Post* writer Shirley Povich that he had applied for a Rhodes Scholarship, but lost his chance when the college failed to forward his transcript before the deadline.

He went on to graduate school at the University of Virginia in Charlottesville and taught geometry while earning a master's degree in mathematics in 1929. This became the defining fact of his life for sportswriters; they called him a professor, but the job description was probably more like today's graduate teaching assistant.

Weaver's master's thesis was titled "The companion to the litnus: the curve whose vectorial angle is proportional to the square of the arc length." Inevitably, sportswriters would connect this topic to the curveball, no matter how many times he explained that it was an investigation of curves on railroad tracks.

The right hander began pitching for pay in the summer of 1925 with a coal company team in Jenkins, Kentucky—"66 days for $660," he recalled. That paid his way

Monte Weaver

through college, since his expenses at Emory & Henry amounted to about $450 a year. While pitching semipro ball in Valdese, North Carolina, after graduation in 1927, he impressed several Duke University players. They recommended him to their coach, former major leaguer Possum Whitted, who also managed the Durham club in the Piedmont League.

Weaver pitched for Durham in 1928 and 1929, posting 12 wins and a 1.94 ERA in his second year, then moved up to the Baltimore Orioles of the International League, the highest minor-league level, in 1930. Weakened by appendicitis, he compiled only a 4–6 record. After offseason surgery he won 21 and lost 11 in 1931 and was named to the league's all-star team.

Washington owner Clark Griffith first spotted Weaver when the Senators and Orioles met in 1931 spring training in Mississippi. Griffith later traveled to Baltimore to scout the prospect. He paid the Orioles $25,000 for Weaver's contract, crowing, "I regard him as the best minor-league pitcher available today." In his first appearance for Washington, on September 20, 1931, the 25-year-old beat the White Sox, 6–4.

In a 1932 spring training profile, Shirley Povich wrote that Weaver was trying out professional baseball, rather than being tried out. The pitcher said he could make more money in the majors than teaching, but he would quit rather than go back to the minors. Povich described Weaver as a loner who spent most of his free time walking on the beach or reading the Bible in his hotel room rather than hanging out with his teammates.

The Sporting News headlined Povich's story "Professor Monte M. Weaver" and referred to him as "the erudite pitching recruit of the Washington Senators." Throughout the season most stories identified him as "'Prof.' Monte Weaver."

Weaver was the rookie sensation of 1932, winning 22 games, the most wins by a rookie pitcher in the "Live Ball" era. His manager, Walter Johnson (who knew a bit about pitching), commented, "He's got a great curveball, one of the best in the league, and enough speed to bust 'em by the batters."

Starting on July 4 Weaver won eight straight decisions. As the wins piled up, he was described as a "lucky" pitcher. His teammates backed him with more than five runs in 14 of his 22 wins, including scores of 15–4, 14–4, and 13–5. But his 4.08 ERA was better than the league average. He finished fifth in *The Sporting News* Most Valuable Player poll of writers, behind Hall of Famers Jimmie Foxx, Lou Gehrig, Earl Averill, and Charlie Gehringer.

The Nats came home in third place with more than 90 wins for the third straight year, but they trailed the pennant-winning Yankees by 14 games. Manager Johnson was fired after the season, though his won-lost record is still the best of any manager in Washington baseball history.

The new manager was Joe Cronin, the 26-year-old shortstop who was married to Clark Griffith's niece. Cronin and Griffith proceeded to turn over the roster. They dumped the last holdovers from Washington's pennant winners of 1924–25, pitcher Fred Marberry and first baseman Joe Judge; traded for Earl Whitehill and other pitchers; and brought back the best hitter in the franchise's history, Goose Goslin, who had a big nose and a big ego to go with his big bat.

New York sportswriter Dan Daniel later reported that the Yankees offered to trade their righthander Red Ruffing for Weaver in May 1933, but Griffith wouldn't bite. This tale is not as far-fetched as it sounds; although Ruffing went on to a Hall of Fame career, he was not yet an established star in 1933 and was pitching poorly. Daniel repeated the story several times to illustrate the importance of a trade not made.

On April 29, New York was torturing Weaver with "squibs, rollers, and pop-fly singles," Povich wrote. Cronin commiserated, "Don't worry, Monte, they're not hitting you hard." Weaver replied, "I know, Skipper, but they're tapping the hell out of me." Povich said that was the first curse ever to escape the pitcher's lips.

In that game, Weaver was the beneficiary of what Povich called "the play of the century." Lou Gehrig reached base on a topped ball that traveled only four feet. Gehrig was on second and Dixie Walker was on first when Tony Lazzeri hit a drive to right-center. Gehrig held up until he was sure Goslin couldn't catch the ball. Then he took off, with the speedy Walker close behind. The relay—Goslin to Cronin to catcher Luke Sewell—cut down

Weaver winds and throws . . .

Gehrig at the plate, and Sewell spun around to tag Walker for a double play at home. Clark Griffith said, "Forty-eight years in baseball and I've never seen the likes of it before."

The revamped Nats won the 1933 pennant, the last for a Washington team. Weaver pitched even better than in his rookie season—when he was able. He missed more than a month with a sore right shoulder. Without him, the Nats charged into a pennant race with the Yankees. When Weaver recovered, he contributed six wins to the club's successful stretch drive, two of them over the Yankees.

That summer Povich commented that Weaver was "given to worrying over every ailment, be it hang-nail or toe-nail." It was the first mention of what would become a familiar criticism. He also acquired a new sports-page nickname: "Brain Truster" Monte Weaver, after the college professors who advised the new president, Franklin D. Roosevelt.

Weaver finished 1933 with a 10–5 record in 21 starts; his 3.25 ERA was ninth best in the league. Cronin chose him to start the fourth game of the World Series, with Washington trailing the New York Giants two games to one. His opponent was Carl Hubbell, that season's National League MVP, who had beaten the Nats in Game One.

Weaver walked the first batter he faced, Jo-Jo Moore, who was then erased on a double play. The third batter, Bill Terry, singled, and Mel Ott popped out. The next two innings were perfect for Weaver, but in the fourth, with one out, Giants' player-manager Bill Terry smashed a drive into the temporary bleachers in Griffith Stadium's deep center field. Washington scored an unearned run in the seventh, and the two starters matched zeroes into extra innings. New York's Travis Jackson led off the 11th with a bunt single and was sacrificed to second, bringing up weak-hitting shortstop Blondy Ryan. His solid single to left sent home the go-ahead run. The Nats loaded the bases in the bottom of the 11th, but Ryan started a double play to end the game. The Giants won the Series the next day on Mel Ott's 10th-inning home run. Terry later said Weaver was the Senators' best pitcher.

Weaver started strongly in 1934 and had won nine games by mid-July. But the Nats lost 11 of his last 13 starts as they sank to seventh place, crippled by injuries to Cronin, catcher Sewell, and first baseman Joe Kuhel.

The sporting press turned on Weaver. He had been portrayed as an oddball, but a respected, educated one; now his quirks were blamed for his poor performance, an 11–15 record with a 4.79 ERA. In September *The Sporting News* labeled him a "hypochondriac" and made the first mention of his vegetarian diet: "addicted to the spinach habit."

The next spring *Washington Star* sports editor Denman Thompson wrote that Weaver "does not resemble even remotely the well-built pitcher bought by Griffith from Baltimore five [actually four] years ago. Monte sticks to peas and carrots and passes up the starches and meats so necessary to the profession that is his. As a result the gaunt Weaver has been unusually tardy in hitting his stride and fails to promise much improvement when warmer weather comes." The *Post* reported that his weight was down to 146 pounds, from 170 when he broke in.

Weaver once more

Other writers of the meat-and-potatoes school ridiculed Weaver. Dan Daniel of the *New York World-Telegram* wrote, "They tell a strange story about Weaver down in Washington. . . . [A] disciple of a certain school of bone manipulation and starvation came to Monte and sold him the idea of taking treatments—for $500." According to Daniel, the quack showed Monte an alarming x-ray of his sore back—actually an x-ray of a hunchback—and promised to cure him with a vegetarian diet. Months later he displayed an x-ray of Weaver's own straight back—"a marvelous cure." Daniel said Weaver was hooked on the diet, and his weight and his pitching declined.

"It seems you can't throw strikes on collard greens," the sportswriter-nutritionist concluded.

Whatever the merits of greens, peas, and carrots, Weaver was hammered in his first two starts of 1935. In May he was waived by all other American League teams and sent down to Albany in the International League. Clark Griffith said he was too weak to pitch in the hot weather at the Nats' other top farm club, in Chattanooga.

Weaver returned to the Senators in 1936, insisting that he felt fine, and made the team. But he was the "forgotten man" until July, when the pitching staff was struggling and manager Bucky Harris gave Weaver a "desperation" start. He won that game and his next start, then went back to the bullpen. He pitched only 91 innings with a 6–4 record and a better-than-average 4.35 ERA.

Weaver bounced back in 1937. During spring training,

Sporting News columnist Dick Farrington reported, "Trainer Mike Martin of the Senators talked like a Dutch uncle to Monte Weaver for three years before finally getting him off that vegetarian diet. After gormandizing [sic] steaks, Monte picked up ten pounds and his fastball this spring." The *Washington Star's* Francis Stan hailed him as "the big pitching surprise," and commented that he was "heavier and stronger than at any time since his great 'freshman year.'" As the Senators finished sixth, his 12–9 record was the best on the team and his 4.20 ERA was better than average. However, he completed only nine of his 26 starts, and the *Star's* Denman Thompson was still referring to his "frail physique" and "lack of stamina." Weaver also gave up 21 home runs in 188⅔ innings, a career high for home runs allowed. He could not repeat his success in 1938; starting only 18 times, he won seven games and his ERA swelled to 5.24.

During 1939 spring training in Orlando, Florida, the 32-year-old bachelor met Roberta Clifford, a local elementary-school teacher. "Good we met when we did—Monte was traded to the Boston Red Sox 10 days later," she would recall. They were married in October 1940. Monte Weaver told Shirley Povich, "[I] was the oldest bachelor in the league, I guess. Then I gave it a little philosophical thought and popped the question. I began to reckon that the older you get, the more particular you get. But also the less desirable you are. So I got hitched."

The Senators sold Weaver to Boston for less than the $7,500 waiver price. He started the first game of a Decoration Day 1939 doubleheader on May 30, beating the Yankees and Red Ruffing 8–4. It was the last of his 71 big-league victories. Weaver later said the Red Sox had bought him for their Louisville farm club, but could not waive him out of the league until July.

The onetime professor who had "tried out" baseball was not ready to give it up. He spent the 1939 and '40 seasons with Louisville before being released. In 1941 he paid his own way to the Baltimore Orioles' training camp in Haines City, Florida, and was signed by manager Tommy Thomas, his former roommate with the Senators. Pitching in relief for the Orioles, he went 7–4 and was hailed as "the International League's No. 1 comeback."

Weaver had worked for the United States Army at Fort Belvoir, Virginia, as a civilian logistics specialist in the winter of 1940–41. After Pearl Harbor he enlisted in the Army Air Force and was commissioned a second lieutenant. By 1943 he was managing the Eighth Air

Force baseball team in England. He was discharged as a captain.

When he came home from military service, the 39-year-old Weaver did not return to teaching because he had been away from it too long. Washington, swollen with war workers, was too crowded to suit him, so he and Roberta moved to her hometown, Orlando. He first had an awning business, a good investment in those days before air conditioning was common, then bought orange groves. He returned almost every year to the North Carolina mountains to see relatives and visited Griffith Stadium at least once for an old-timers game.

In retirement the Weavers moved to a house on Lake Adair in Orlando. Their daughter and son-in-law, Betty and Bruce Saulpaugh, and two grandchildren lived nearby. Their son, Brian, and his family lived in Vero Beach.

Montie Weaver died at age 87 on June 14, 1994.

Sources

Baseball encyclopedias give the player's full name as Montgomery Morton Weaver, but his daughter says he never used the name "Montgomery." He appears as "Montie" in the 1910 and 1920 census records and as "Montie Morton Weaver" in the alumni records of Emory & Henry College. North Carolina did not begin recording birth certificates until 1913, according to the state's Vital Records Office.

Most information about Weaver's life and career comes from *The Sporting News*, the *Washington Post* and the indispensable www.retrosheet.org.

Costello, Al. "Make Mine Beefsteak." *Baseball* magazine, June 1937: 322.

[Dan Daniel,] "Daniel's Dope." *New York World-Telegram*, undated (1935) and April 21, 1937. Clippings in Weaver's file at the Baseball Hall of Fame library.

Emory & Henry College archives, Emory, Virginia, provided by R.J. Vejnar II, archivist.

Kelley, Brent. "Monte Weaver and the Senators' last hurrah," *Sports Collector's Digest*, March 20, 1992: 270.

Thomas, Henry W., *Walter Johnson: Baseball's Big Train*. Washington: Phenom Press, 1995.

U.S. Census, Ashe County, North Carolina, 1910 and 1920.

University of Virginia Alumni Records, Charlottesville, Virginia.

Clarice Weaver of West Jefferson, North Carolina, interview, August 13, 2004. Mrs. Weaver's husband is Monte's nephew and she met him many times. She is a member of the Ashe County Historical Society.

White, J. Russell: "Math, Mound Both Part of Pitcher's Past," *Orlando Sentinel*, July 29, 1993: 13.

(No byline), obituary, *Orlando Sentinel*, June 16, 1994: B4.

TED WILLIAMS *by Bill Nowlin*

G	AB	R	H	2B	3B	HR	RBI	BB	SO	BA	OBP	SLG	SB	HBP
149	565	131	185	44	11	31	145	107	64	.327	.436	.609	2	2

Any argument as to the greatest hitter of all time always involves Ted Williams. It's an argument that can never be definitively answered, but that it always involves Williams says a lot. One could probably count the legitimate contenders on the fingers of one hand. Most would narrow the field to just two players, Babe Ruth being the other. One could make a good case for Lou Gehrig, and a very small handful of others. Ted himself ranked Ruth, Gehrig, Jimmie Foxx, Rogers Hornsby, and Joe DiMaggio as the top five (he elected not to include himself in any such ranking).

If the name of the game is getting on base, no one ranks above Williams. His lifetime on-base average was .482, and think what that means. He reached base safely 48.2% of the time he came up to bat—almost half the time. Ruth comes in second, at .474. One of the reasons Williams ranked first was his self-discipline; he refused to swing at pitches outside the strike zone. In time, he developed such a reputation that more than one catcher complaining about a pitch being called a ball was told by the umpire, "If Mr. Williams didn't swing at it, it wasn't a strike." But The Kid had the strike zone down cold from

Williams' 145 RBIs in his rookie year set
a record that still stands

the first. Even in 1939, his rookie year, Ted walked 107 times, ranking second in the American League (he led the league that first year in total bases—by a big margin). Across his entire career, which touched four decades (1939–1960), Williams had a walks percentage of 20.75. More than one out of every five times, he took a walk.

Even with a pitch in the strike zone, he wouldn't take a cut at it unless he felt it was a pitch he could drive. "Get a good pitch to hit"— the philosophy imparted to Ted in Minneapolis by hitting instructor Rogers Hornsby, meant more than just a pitch in the strike zone. If the pitcher dropped in a good curveball low and away (which he knew was his most vulnerable spot in the zone), he would figuratively tip his cap, take the strike, and wait for a better pitch. Unless there were two strikes on him, he would take his chances that there was a better pitch coming.

Ted had strong opinions about what made for a great hitter, and it involved hitting for a combination of average and power. Had he been willing to sacrifice power for batting average, one suspects, he could have

Another view of The Kid in 1939

ranked right at the top instead of just fifth among "modern era" (post-1901) players. Had he been willing to sacrifice average and just swing for the fences, he would have hit more than 521 home runs. As a young man, he knew what he wanted. At age 20, he said, "All I want out of life is that when I walk down the street folks will say, 'There goes the greatest hitter that ever lived.'" In conversation late in life, when someone asked whether he thought he'd accomplished that, he simply said he didn't know but that it was a great honor just to hear his name in the same sentence as a Ruth or a Gehrig.

Becoming a great hitter was a goal Ted set for himself at a very early age. Born in San Diego on August 30, 1918, he was the first-born son of professional photographer (and former U.S. cavalryman) Samuel Williams and his wife, a Mexican-American who dedicated her life to Salvation Army work, May Venzor Williams. It wasn't the happiest of marriages and both parents were frequently out of the home, often leaving Ted and his brother, Danny (two years younger), to fend for themselves. Fortunately, neighbors welcomed Ted in, but he spent endless hours playing ball on the North Park Playground in the Southern

California city where the climate allowed one to play pickup ball all year round. A dedicated playground director, Rod Luscomb, saw Ted's drive and took him under his wing. By the time Ted reached high school, he was an exceptional player who attracted the attention and support of coach Wofford "Wos" Caldwell.

It was his bat that first caught coach Caldwell's eye, but Ted excelled as a pitcher for the Hoover High Cardinals. He often struck out a dozen or more batters in a game, but he hit well, too, and found a place in the lineup for every game. Even while still a high school player, Ted signed his first professional contract—with the locally-based San Diego Padres, of the Pacific Coast League. With the Padres, Ted got his feet wet in 1936, hitting a modest .271 but without even one home run in the regular season. Ted completed high school and then played for the Padres again in 1937, upping his average to .291 and showing some power with 23 homers. Boston Red Sox general manager Eddie Collins had spotted Ted while looking over a couple of Padres players and shook hands with owner Bill Lane on an option to sign the young player, which he exercised in time for Ted to go to the big league training camp in Florida in the spring of 1938.

Williams was a brash and cocky young kid who was deemed to need a full year in the minors and he was assigned to the Minneapolis Millers, where he proceeded to win the American Association Triple Crown with a .366 average, 43 home runs, and 142 RBIs. There was no question that he would be with the Red Sox in 1939, and the buildup in Boston's newspapers was unprecedented. The Kid was all that had been promised, and then some. Playing right field, he hit 31 home runs and batted .327. Not only did he lead the league in extra-base hits and total bases, he also led the league in runs batted in in his rookie year with 145, setting a major league rookie record that has never been beaten. His fresh and evident love of the game won the hearts of many Boston fans.

The following year, 1940, Williams switched permanently to left field and improved his average to .344, though he dipped a bit in home runs (23) and RBIs (113). He placed first in both on-base percentage and runs scored. It was the first of 12 seasons that he led the league in on-base percentage; remarkably, he led in OBP every

Williams crosses home plate after homering on May 30, 1939

year through 1958 in which he was eligible. From his very first trip across country to spring training in 1938, Ted became known for his relentless questioning of other players about situational baseball—what was Ted Lyons' "out pitch" to a lefthanded hitter late in the game with runners on base? What would Bobo Newsom start you out on first time up? Williams seemed to live and breathe baseball and it rang true when he later acquired the nickname "Teddy Ballgame."

Maybe he seemed just too good to be true. After a brief honeymoon with the press in the highly competitive newspaper town that was Boston, the critical stories began to come out. Taking on Ted sold newspapers, and writers like Dave Egan and Austen Lake could get under Ted's skin, sometimes provoking a story where none had existed before. He was easy to mock, taking imaginary swings out in the field and letting a fly ball drop in. He was so cocksure that he turned off some of the crusty ink-stained wretches, and a little sanctimonious—declining an interview with one of the deans of the press corps, columnist Bill Cunningham, because the writer had been drinking. Some of the writers had it in for Ted, and let him have it. There commenced a feud with the writers that lasted Ted's whole career, and beyond. He enjoyed barring the scribes from the Boston clubhouse, sniffing the air distastefully as one walked by, and more than once spit toward the press box in contempt. He earned some other monikers—"Terrible Ted" and the "Splendid Spitter"—the latter being a reference to his widely-known nickname as a lanky, gangly kid—The Splendid Splinter.

There were fans who enjoyed egging Ted on, too, and during this second season he turned against the fickle fans. He later admitted he had "rabbit's ears" and could hear the one loud detractor over the hundreds of cheering fans, and he let it get to him. He admitted he was "never very coy, never very diplomatic. As a result I would get myself in a wringer. . . . I was impetuous, I was tempestuous. I blew up. Not acting, but *re*acting. I'd get so damned mad, throw bats, kick the columns in the dugout so that sparks flew, tear out the plumbing, knock out the lights, damn near kill myself. *Scream.* I'd scream out my own frustration." He just could not abide the fair-weather fans who'd be for him one day and against him the next. One thing he determined never to do was tip his cap to the fans; even though there were days that he truly wanted to, he just couldn't bring himself to do so. He was a complicated man and yet, despite all the tumult and turmoil, he never showed up an umpire by arguing a call and never got tossed from a game. And, though he preferred to keep to himself, he got along fine with other ballplayers, both on his own team and on opposing teams.

It was in 1941 that The Kid had a season for the ages—batting .406 despite the sacrifice fly counting against the hitter's average. Few players had achieved the .400 mark, and no one has done so since. Ted also set a single-season on-base percentage mark (.553) that was never topped in the 20th century. (Barry Bonds now holds the highest mark.) Williams led the American League in runs and home runs. Two months after the season ended, Japanese warplanes attacked Pearl Harbor.

As sole supporter of his mother (his parents had divorced), Ted was exempt but that didn't prevent some from questioning his courage when he chose to play baseball (and pay off an annuity he'd purchased for his mother) in 1942. He had already achieved national stature as a star baseball player at a time when baseball was unrivaled by any other sport. This made him a convenient target for criticism, but servicemen attending ball games cheered for Williams. Once he'd made his point, he signed up in the Navy's V-5 program to begin training as a naval aviator when the season was over. In his fourth year of major league ball, Ted hit for the Triple Crown in the major leagues, leading both leagues, as it happened, in average (.356, down a full 50 points from the prior year), home runs (36) and RBIs (137). And then it was off to serve. For the second year in a row, Williams came in second in MVP voting.

Ted Williams spent three prime years training and becoming a Navy (and then Marine Corps) pilot—and becoming so good at flight and gunnery that he was made an instructor and served the war training other pilots. The day he received his commission, he married Doris Soule—the first of three marriages. He kept active to some extent, playing a little baseball on base teams but only as time permitted given his primary duties. Lt. T.S. Williams ended his stretch at Pearl Harbor and never saw combat.

After the war, Ted returned to the Red Sox and received his first MVP award from the baseball writers, helping lead Boston into its first World Series since 1918. He led the league in OBP, total bases, and runs, but an injury to his elbow while playing in an exhibition game to keep loose for the upcoming Series hampered his ability to compete effectively in the fall classic. Boston lost to the Cardinals in seven games, and Ted's weak hitting helped cost them the championship.

In 1947, Ted had his second Triple Crown year, leading the A.L. with .343, 32, and 114. The Red Sox didn't come close to the Yankees that year, and in each of the next two years, they lost the pennant on the final day of the season. Williams led the league in both average and slugging both seasons, among other categories. In 1949, he earned his second Most Valuable Player award—and only missed an unprecedented third Triple Crown by the narrowest of margins. He led in homers and RBIs, but George Kell edged him by one ten-thousandth of a point in batting average.

The year 1950 might have been his best ever—he had already hit 25 homers and driven in 83 runs when he shattered his elbow crashing into the wall during the All-Star Game. He missed most of the rest of the season, and said he never fully recovered as a hitter—though one would hardly know it to look at the stats he posted. In 1951, he led the league once more in OBP and slugging.

Come 1952, as the war in Korea mounted, the Marines recalled a number of pilots to active duty. Among them was the less-than-pleased T.S. Williams, now a captain in the Reserve. He was to turn 34 that August, and Doris and he had a young daughter, Barbara Joyce (Bobby-Jo.) When it was clear there was no choice but to comply, Ted determined to do his best. He requested training on jets and was ultimately assigned to Marine Corps squadron VMF-311 which flew dive bombing missions out of base K-3 in South Korea. Capt. Williams flew some 39 combat missions, though he barely escaped with his life on the third one when his Panther jet was hit and had to crash-land. The plane burned to an irretrievable crisp but Williams was up on another mission at 8:08 the next morning. It truly was an elite squadron to which Williams was assigned; on more than half a dozen missions, Williams served as wingman to squadron mate John Glenn.

A series of ear infections consigned him to sick bay for two stretches and when it was obvious the war would be over in a matter of weeks, Williams was sent back Stateside and mustered out—in time to be an honored guest at the 1953 All-Star Game. He threw himself into preparation to play and he got in 91 at-bats before the season was over—batting .407 in the process.

Ted broke his collarbone in spring training in 1954 and missed so many games at the start of the season that come season's end, he fell 14 at-bats short of having the

Manager Pinky Higgins looks on as Ted points out his San Diego home town on the map in 1957; the Sox played three games there in 1959.

requisite 400 to qualify for the batting crown he would have otherwise won with his .345 average. Ted appeared in only 117 games, but still drew enough walks to lead the league (136). The walks hurt him, though, since the batting title was based on "official" at-bats alone. This seemed so unfair that the criteria were changed in later years to be based on plate appearances. After the 1954 season, he "retired" (the term is placed in quotation marks because it seemed as though retirement was a strategic move in a divorce) and did not make a start in the 1955 season until May 28. He completed the year with 320 at-bats, but hadn't lost his touch as indicated by his .356 average and 83 RBIs in the two-thirds of a season he played. In 1956, he had what by Williams standards seemed like a pedestrian, even somewhat lackluster year, accumulating an even 400 at-bats with 24 homers, but still hit at a .345 clip. A.L. pitchers were no fools; he drew over 100 walks and led the league in on-base percentage.

The year 1957 is what was arguably the year in which Ted Williams proved what a great hitter he truly was. No longer the Kid who turned 23 while hitting .406 back in 1941, Ted entered his 40th year in that season. He might have been "splendid" but he was no splinter. He'd filled out his physique, gone through war and divorce, suffered broken bones and pneumonia. Despite all the accumulated adversity, Ted hit .388 (just six more hits would have given him .400 again, hits that a younger man might have legged out) and led the league by 23 points over Mickey Mantle. His .526 OBP was the second highest of his career and so was his .731 slugging average. So, too, were the 38 home runs he hit. It was truly a golden year.

His final three seasons saw a decline, though batting .328 as he did in 1958 would for almost any other player be spectacular. In fact, it was enough to win Ted the batting championship even if it was some 16 points below his ultimate .344 lifetime average. The batting title was his seventh, not counting 1954 as per the rules of the day. 1959 was his one really bad year; he developed a very troublesome stiff neck during spring training that saw him wear a neck brace and have a very difficult time trying to overcome it. He never truly got on track and batted a disappointing .254 with only 10 homers and 43 RBIs in 272 at-bats. It was sentiment alone that placed him on the All-Star squad, one of 18 times he was accorded the honor. Everyone expected him to retire; even Red Sox owner Tom Yawkey, with whom Williams had a good if distant relationship, suggested it might be time.

Ted Williams didn't want to leave with a season like 1959 wrapping up his career. He came back for a swan song season, but insisted that he be given a 30 percent pay cut because of his underperformance in 1959. He felt he hadn't earned the money he was being paid, at the time—as it had been for many years—just about the highest salary in all of baseball, understood to be around $125,000. Williams had hard work in 1960 but he produced, batting .316 with 29 home runs—the last of which was hit in what had been announced as his very last at-bat in the major leagues.

In his latter years, Williams had played for a Red Sox team that offered him little support in the lineup, had not much in the way of pitching, and didn't draw many fans. Even Ted's final home game drew just over 10,000 fans to Fenway Park. How much better he would have done had he played in a park with a friendlier right field, like Tiger Stadium or Yankee Stadium, remains unknowable. How much better he might have done had he had a Lou Gehrig hitting behind him in the lineup, or had he not missed five seasons to military service, remains unknowable.

Leaving on such a high note, Williams couldn't resist a final shot at the Boston press corps with whom he had so frequently feuded since his second year with the Red Sox. The "knights of the keyboard" wouldn't have Williams to kick around anymore. And Ted Williams left town, though in lieu of any farewell dinners he quietly, and without publicity, stopped to pay a visit to a dying child stricken with leukemia. Teddy Ballgame, as he was known, had been the leading spokesman for Boston's "Jimmy Fund" for many years. Ted had appeared on behalf of Dr. Sidney Farber's children's cancer research efforts since the late 1940s, in fact since before Dr. Farber (the "father of chemotherapy") first achieved remission in

leukemia. Today, over 85 percent of children with leukemia are cured.

Save for appearances for the Jimmy Fund, Ted took time off and spent the next several years catching up on his fishing while bringing in some endorsement income through a long association with Sears Roebuck, which produced an extensive line of Ted Williams brand sporting equipment—all of which Ted insisted on testing personally, right down to the tents and sleeping bags that would bear his name. Ted married a second time, to Lee Howard of Chicago in September 1961. It was a short-lived marriage, perhaps in part because Ted had already met the woman who was his soulmate in life, Louise Kaufman. Though they never married, she loved Ted through both his second and third marriages (the third, to Dolores Wettach, occurred in 1968, when she was apparently already pregnant with the son who became John-Henry Williams.) Dolores and Ted later had a daughter, Claudia Franc Williams, born shortly after Ted and Dolores separated a few years into the marriage. Always in the background was Lou Kaufman, who—though six years older than Ted—was a fishing champion in her own right and apparently had enough salt to spar with Ted with the sort of banter he liked to dish out. There were other women, of course. In many ways, Ted Williams was a "man's man" and perhaps didn't have the patience for a relationship. Visiting one afternoon in the late 1990s at Ted's house in Florida, this author was presented with a blunt, candid, and unanswerable remark when—out of the blue—Ted declared, "Yeah, I guess I was a great hitter, but I was a lousy husband and a crummy father."

After the requisite five years following his playing career, Ted Williams was elected to the National Baseball Hall of Fame in his first year of eligibility. When he was inducted in the summer of 1966, Williams wrote out his speech by hand the evening before (the original is in the Hall of Fame) and after thanking those who helped him on his way, he devoted part of the core of his speech to an impassioned plea that the Hall of Fame recognize the many Negro League ballplayers who had not been allowed to play in the segregated major leagues prior to 1947.

He wrote in his autobiography *My Turn At Bat* (published in 1969) of his Mexican-American mother, "If I had had my mother's name, there is no doubt I would have run into problems in those days, the prejudices people had in Southern California." One can speculate that his own awareness of prejudice may have informed his remarks at the Hall of Fame. The first African American in the American League, Larry Doby, says that Williams went out of his way to make him welcome—not grandstanding but with the simplest of private gestures on the field. When the Red Sox finally integrated by adding Pumpsie Green to the big league roster in 1959, Ted chose Pumpsie as his throwing partner before games.

In the same year as his remarkably self-revealing autobiography was published, Williams became manager of Bob Short's Washington Senators ball club. The team showed a fairly dramatic improvement in team batting his very first year and, while on safari in Africa, Ted received word that he had been named Manager of the Year. It was good timing for Ted's second book (written as had been the first with author John Underwood)—*The Science of Hitting*. The book demonstrated the Ted Williams approach to the game and, as with *My Turn At Bat*, has remained in print ever since—no small feat in the world of books. Even in the 21st century, *The Science of Hitting* is often the book of choice for aspiring batters.

Ted had signed on as manager for five years, but he lost interest after the Senators failed to further improve (and some of the ballplayers chafed under his regime to the point of near-insubordination). Ted traveled to Texas with the franchise and served as the first manager of the Texas Rangers in 1972 but he begged out of the fifth and final year of the deal.

Throughout his years as player and as manager, he was always a colorful "larger than life" figure with a booming voice and a presence that defined charisma. He was often a lightning rod of sorts, loved or hated by fans, and a reliable source of controversial copy for sportswriters and reporters. He was loud and boisterous, but as he himself admitted in his autography, he was "never very diplomatic. . . . I did a lot of yakking, partly to hide a rather large inferiority complex."

After leaving full-time employment in baseball for good, Ted served for years and years as a "special assignment instructor" with the Boston Red Sox. Typically, this meant he would show up at spring training for a few weeks and look over the younger hitters, occasionally taking a player aside later in the year as well. When Carl Yastrzemski was struggling in his first year of trying to fill Ted's shoes as Boston's left fielder, the team flew Williams in from where he was fishing in Canada and he spent a few days working with Yaz. Yastrzemski says, "He really didn't say anything; he was just trying to build me up mentally. He says, 'You've got a great swing—just go out and use it.'" Yastrzemski realized he was trying too hard to emulate Williams as a home run hitter, but Ted helped him settle down and helped him become himself. Over time, Yaz says, "I think the big thing that I learned from him, which he talked about, was the strike zone, strike zone, strike zone."[1]

For many years, Ted lived in a small but comfortable cabin on New Brunswick's Miramichi River where he was able to fish for his beloved Atlantic salmon, a fish he so admired that he became a leader of the fight to preserve the species from overfishing and other encroachments on its habitat. An annual "Ted Williams Award" is presented to others who have joined in the cause. Ted enjoyed the companionship of Lou Kaufman in his later years.

Ted the elder statesman

Ted Williams was active on the Hall of Fame's Veterans Committee (and sometimes criticized for being too vocal an advocate for players he championed such as Phil Rizzuto and Dominic DiMaggio). As he grew older, many of the hard attitudes toward Ted softened and, in the words of Doris Kearns Goodwin, "It seemed like his stature . . . his stature was always there—I don't think anyone ever disputed how great he was—but the kind of emotions he generated in the fans got stronger as time went by rather than weaker, which is really nice. I'm glad he's lived to see all that. It seems to have mellowed and made him a happier person, too."[2]

He always engendered strong opinions and harbored many of his own. This was a man of many interests and an intellectual curiosity perhaps surprising in a ballplayer, a man whom his Marine Corps instructor could conceive of as a Shakespearean scholar and whom Tommy Henrich of the New York Yankees could envision as a brain surgeon or nuclear scientist. Biographer David Halberstam once said that Ted "won 33,277 arguments in a row . . . the undisputed champion of contentiousness"—but then went on to write a book about the friendship between Ted, Bobby Doerr, Dominic DiMaggio, and Johnny Pesky that endured for six decades.

For the last several years of his life, Ted became active in the memorabilia market, attracting very large sums to appear for occasional signings at industry shows. Some took advantage of his natural generosity and in one case Ted pursued a man who had defrauded him, the case becoming an episode on the *America's Most Wanted* television show. Ted's son, John-Henry Williams, took over management of the marketing of his father with mixed success. Many criticized John-Henry for being too zealous in his father's behalf and for some of his business schemes, but there was no doubt that Ted very much loved his son and was prepared to turn a blind eye to any faults. Ted suffered a stroke and a subsequent heart operation sapped his health, and he entered a period of decline that ended with his passing on July 5, 2002. In death, as in life, controversy swirled around Ted Williams as two of his three children had his body cryonically frozen for the possibility of some later revival if science someday learns a way to restore life to those who have been so preserved. Many of Ted's closest friends were aghast but efforts by his eldest daughter to reverse the decision were in vain. An outpouring of more than 20,000 people attended a memorial at Boston's Fenway Park later in July 2002 and the memory of the man they called The Kid lives on.

Notes

1. Interview by Bill Nowlin, August 31, 1997
2. Interview by Bill Nowlin, May 3, 1997

JACK WILSON *by Ryan Brodeur*

G	ERA	W	L	SV	GS	GF	CG	SHO	IP	H	R	ER	BB	SO	HR	HBP	WP	BFP
36	4.67	11	11	2	22	5	6	0	177⅓	198	109	92	75	80	10	1	4	797

G	AB	R	H	2B	3B	HR	RBI	BB	SO	BA	OBP	SLG	SB	HBP
37	63	6	10	0	0	0	6	0	17	.159	.159	.159	0	0

". . . for if ever a fellow rode to the top the hard way, it has been John Francis Wilson."—Vic Stout, August 28, 1937

Jack Wilson

The story of Jack Wilson could be the story of so many players who have passed through professional baseball over the past century. Known for his determination as much as his fastball, Jack used both talents to forge a nine-year career in the major leagues.

John Francis "Jack" Wilson was born on April 12, 1912, in the country of the Pacific Coast League, in Portland, Oregon. A blue-eyed, black-haired young man of Irish-German descent, Jack was one of two children born to James Wilson and Magdalen Weber, along with a sister, Mary.[1] As an adult, Jack stood 5 feet 11 and weighed 210. He batted and threw right-handed, and from an early age was pushed to choose sports over typical adolescent shenanigans, recalling that "[m]y parents figured it was a lot better for me to be playing ball than run the risk of getting into some kind of mischief."[2] Wilson elaborated a bit more for sportswriter Carl Felker:

"You see, my father is a red-hot fan, [and my] mother also likes to watch games. . . . My father told me to make an infielder of myself, and while I was in high school and Columbia (College, in Portland), I played third base. Dad was determined to make a big-leaguer out of me, and at his request I never even played football, basketball, or any other game while in school."[3]

That's not to say that Wilson was free of temptation to play those other sports. In fact, when he first reported to Columbia College for high school, he was immediately noticed by the football coach, who was determined to have Jack in the backfield. At the time, Jack was 180 pounds and would've been a welcome addition to any gridiron gang; for Wilson's father, however, there would be no replacing baseball as his son's greatest chance for athletic success.

Jack, playing third base for the school baseball team in 1930, came to the attention of Oscar Vitt, the manager of the Pacific Coast League's Hollywood Stars. Vitt brought Wilson to Hollywood for the summer of 1930, but upon arrival Jack found the hot corner occupied by former New York Yankee Mike Gazella. As a result, Wilson found himself released to the San Francisco Seals in August, where he wrapped up the fall of 1930 and began the spring of 1931. Unfortunately, Jack saw no playing time at third base in San Francisco because he was blocked by another big leaguer, ex-Cincinnati Red

Babe Pinelli.[4] Wilson was consequently farmed out to the Globe, Arizona Bears of the Arizona-Texas League, where he ended the 1931 campaign.

On all of his first three professional teams Wilson hit .300 or better as an infielder, but because of the former major leaguers manning third base in the PCL, Jack was unable to break through. In the spring of 1932, when Wilson was informed he would have to go back to Globe, he decided to return home to Portland, free from any commitments to professional baseball. His return to Oregon set in motion the events leading to his call-up to the majors as a starting pitcher.

"I wasn't hitting very well," recalled Wilson, "and when San Francisco wanted to send me back to Globe in the spring of 1932, I felt that it was useless for me to go on with an infielding career. . . . I still enjoyed playing ball, however, so I went out for a semipro team at home. It happened that the team needed a pitcher, and the manager asked me to take a shot at the job. I had never pitched before in my life and had no idea of ever becoming a hurler, but I could throw a fastball and was willing to try. I was rather surprised myself when I won my first game."[5]

Jack ended up winning his first four outings with his semipro team. Portland Beavers manager Spencer Abbott noticed Jack's newfound talent and brought him back into professional ball for the remainder of 1932, handing Wilson the ball on the second to last day of the season. As Wilson recalled, his PCL pitching debut was not without a healthy dose of well-deserved skepticism:

"In my first appearance on the mound in the Coast loop, I faced Seattle. Some Seattle players had known me as an infielder, so they began to give me a going-over. 'Look who's trying to pitch!' they yelled. 'We'll chase you clear back to Globe, Arizona.' I don't wonder that they thought I was easy pickings, for I was throwing like an infielder, without any follow-through, and I had little except a fastball.

"Naturally, I was rather unsteady, but I was mad, too, and I bore down on those birds. When the game was over, I was the winning pitcher."[6]

In throwing a complete game against the Rainiers, Wilson picked up not only a win, but also a 1933 contract with Portland. In his first full year with the Beavers, Jack was used primarily in relief, but in 1934 he was given the hill regularly as a starter, racking up a record of 9–9, with an impressive 13 complete games.

Thanks to his showing with Portland, Wilson and fellow starter George Caster were both asked to report to Connie Mack's Philadelphia Athletics in September 1934. Their contracts had been purchased from Portland on the recommendation of Mack's son Roy, who at that time was the secretary of the Portland club. Both pitchers met up with the Philadelphia club in Cleveland, where Connie Mack tabbed Jack to start the first game

Wilson with Bob Feller

of a doubleheader on September 9. In another stroke of unfortunate luck, A's catcher Charley Berry, who had been prepping Wilson for his first big-league appearance, broke his leg just before the game, forcing Jack to throw to 19-year-old backstop Frank Hayes, himself in the middle of his first full year in the majors. Wilson was opposed by Cleveland right-hander Oral Hildebrand, who pitched a much better game. Wilson was tagged for eight runs and 12 hits and took the loss. On top of losing the game, Wilson also suffered a sore arm. When the season closed, Connie Mack sent Jack back down to Portland, deciding to hold on to Caster instead.

The winter of 1934 turned out to be an eventful one for the young Wilson. On October 17, he married Rosalie Ellen Walsh in St. Andrew's Catholic Church while at home in Portland. As Jack signed one personal contract with the young Miss Walsh, he had no idea that he would soon complete a contract of a different sort. The Boston Red Sox, led by new manager Joe Cronin, traded infielder Bill Cissell to Portland for Wilson. It was the first player acquisition of Cronin's regime and, as Cronin himself recalled to sportswriter John Drohan in 1937, it was a move the young skipper was particularly proud of:

"You know that winter I became manager of the Red Sox, I was out home [in California], visiting my family. Earl Sheely, one-time White Sox first sacker, dropped by . . .

"Well, I got to quizzing him about the Coast league. Who's got the best arm in the league, I asked him.

"'There's a kid up in Portland,' said Sheely, 'who's got the strongest arm I ever saw. He's pretty wild, doesn't know a whole lot about it, but is as willing as they come. His name is Wilson, and I think you can get him.'

"A short time afterward, they had a meeting of the Coast league. I attended it just to see if I could do business with the Portland club owner. . . .

"Buddy Ryan put me in touch with the fellow who had just bought the [Portland] club and I proceeded to give him a sales talk. . . . All I wanted was Wilson in return. . . . Well, the upshot of it was that Mister Portland went for it; he had Cissell and I had Wilson. It was my first deal as manager of the Red Sox and I'm really getting more proud of it every day. I don't want to appear hoggish, but I wish I had a couple more."[7]

Having been acquired by the Red Sox, Jack used the offseason to give his arm a rest in an attempt to recover from the sore arm acquired in Philadelphia. When spring arrived in 1935, he went to camp with a healthy arm, a healthy outlook, and—most importantly—healthy job prospects as a reliever for the Boston Red Sox.

"Now Joe Cronin has me for the Red Sox," Wilson told writer Burt Whitman. "I hope my arm continues to feel as strong as it is right now. I never worried about it all winter and I never worked out until I got here. I played a little basketball and am in condition. And, say, isn't Cronin a great guy to work for? He makes you believe in yourself, and I only hope I can deliver for him."[8]

Cronin wanted the rookie to get a bit more experience in professional ball and so Wilson was farmed out to Syracuse in the International League for six weeks before being called up to the Red Sox. As Wilson himself was quick to admit, he had little more than a fastball and his rugged physique at his disposal on the mound. In Syracuse, Jack benefited from working with Al Schacht and Tom Daly, coaches who gave him time to work on his curveball mechanics.[9] After notching a record of 4–2, Wilson was called back to the majors.

Jack's first major-league win came on September 2, 1935. The Red Sox were playing host to the Washington Senators. Sox starter Wes Ferrell dug the Sox an early hole, giving up seven runs in just two innings before Cronin sent Wilson in to relieve in the third. Jack managed to hold the Washington hitters to just one run over the next six innings while the Sox sluggers mounted a comeback and tied the score at 8–8. Jack pitched the game through the top of the 11th, but when Boston failed to score the winning run it became Jack's turn to seal the deal. In the bottom half of the inning. Jack stepped in against reliever Phil Hensiek. With the bases empty, the former infielder stood quietly as the count ran full. On the sixth pitch, Jack stepped into one, and hit what the next day's *Washington Post* called a "screaming home run into the right-centerfield bleachers" for the game-winner. It was his first win, his first hit, and his first home run in

the major leagues. Sportswriter John Drohan of the *Boston American* sat down with Wilson after the game and discovered that the rookie attributed his storybook ending to an unlikely source.

"[Detroit scout] 'Wish' Egan is a pretty interesting gazabo, at that," recounted Wilson. "He was telling me about old Eagle-Eye Jake Beckley. It seems that whenever old Eagle-Eye was in a hitting streak, or felt he was going to hit, he generally wound up, kicked one leg up in the air and yelled 'Chickazoola.'

"Somehow or other when I was up at the plate I thought of that. It's funny how those things will run through your mind at times. Anyway, you recall how that young Washington pitcher pitched three balls without a strike. Naturally, [coach] Al Schacht gave me the 'take' sign, which means take the pitch regardless of where it is.

"He gave it to me twice. But I knew better than to take it the third time. I just decided I'd wind up a la Jake Beckley, give it the old Chickazoola to see if it would work. It did. And from now on there's going to be plenty of Chickazoola whenever I'm at bat."[10]

The rest of the 1935 season saw Wilson notch two more wins and secure a place for himself on the Sox pitching staff. He posted a record of 3–4, with a 4.22 earned run average, but walked nearly twice as many (36) as he struck out (19). In 1936, Jack doubled both his wins and his losses, going 6–8 to accompany a 4.42 ERA as he struggled to clear the biggest hurdle for all young pitchers: his control. Former Yankees star Herb Pennock, who came to work as a coach for the Sox that year, worked extensively with Jack on his follow-through in an attempt to improve the young hurler's accuracy. In particular, Jack credited Pennock with the development of a serviceable curveball.

One of the most interesting moments from 1936 involving Jack came on September 25, in a game against the Washington Senators. In the third inning, with the game scoreless, Sox starter Jim Henry was chased after loading the bases on two walks and a hit batsman and then allowing a two-run single to outfielder Johnny Stone. With nobody out and men on first and second, Henry dropped the ball during his windup, just as the baserunners took off for a successful double steal. Jack Wilson was called in to relieve the ineffective Henry, still with nobody out. After finishing the third inning, Jack got into more hot water in the fourth when Washington loaded the bases on a single and two walks. What happened next would be something Jack would certainly want to forget. As *Washington Post* writer Shirley Povich described it, Wilson "performed the trick of losing his balance on the rubber, falling to the ground and committing an automatic balk which permitted [Washington pitcher] DeShong to score from third unmolested."

Despite that particular incident, the work from 1936

paid off the following season. The 1937 campaign began a four-year stretch of double-digit wins during which Wilson racked up more appearances and more wins (54) than any other pitcher on the Red Sox including the notable Lefty Grove, who won 53. No other pitcher on the Sox staff during that period won more than 32.

As a single season, 1937 stands out as the best of Jack's career. While Cronin had primarily used him in relief roles, Jack was inserted into a regular starting slot when the struggling Wes Ferrell was traded to Washington. As a starter, Jack ended up winning 16 games, second only to Grove's 17. His final totals were 16–10, with a 3.70 ERA in a full 221⅓ innings of work. With 21 starts and 30 relief appearances Jack demonstrated his ability in both roles, and made himself one of the most important members of the 1937 Red Sox. Said manager Cronin on August 28: "I'd shudder to think where we would be in this American League race without our boy Jack. Right now I wouldn't swap him for any pitcher in the league. And that goes for [Lefty] Gomez, [Tommy] Bridges, [Roxie] Lawson, [Bob] Feller and the whole crowd of 'em. If we had had two more Wilsons on our club this year, we would win the pennant in a breeze."[11]

In the same article that quoted Cronin, Jack referred to the way Cronin used him that season: "I know a lot of people have criticized Joe for using me so much this year. In fact Joe comes to me every once in a while and asks me if I'm working too often. I tell him I'm ready to go any time. And it's the truth. I haven't had a sore arm all season. I think I could go every other day."

Jack was willing and able to step up for any game that needed his help, and after a successful 1937 campaign he hoped to repeat in 1938. Unfortunately, his good fortune did not continue. On the way back north from spring training in '38, he pulled a muscle in his leg. The injury hindered his efforts at the beginning of the season, though he still managed to pitch two shutouts in the first few weeks of the season, including a 5–0 win over Bob Feller and the Cleveland Indians on May 8. Wilson struck out 12 and induced many popups and flyballs. The Red Sox tied a record for fewest assists in a game—and the only assist came in the ninth inning.

While he was able to pitch through the nagging injury to his leg, Wilson's celebrated grit and determination came up against a more familiar challenge, the return of his sore arm. The pain in his elbow was so severe that Wilson was reportedly prepared to end his career. Cronin and the Sox sent the young hurler to see Dr. Robert F. Hyland, the surgeon for both the St. Louis Browns and St. Louis Cardinals, who found no serious injury. The prescribed regimen for Jack was a healthy dose of rest for his arm but he received little, returning to his regular turn in the rotation before long.

During the next three seasons, from 1939 to 1941, Wilson posted only one more winning record, going 12–6

in 1940, while his total innings pitched declined steadily. In each year from 1937 through 1940, his earned run average climbed. One of the few milestones of these three seasons was as a batter—he took White Sox pitchers deep twice in a game on June 16, 1940. He hit the first into Comiskey Park's upper deck off Jack Knott; the second came off Pete Appleton. The two home runs were the last of Wilson's professional career, but they made him one of only 23 American League pitchers to homer twice in the same game.

At the close of the 1941 season, during which Jack recorded only four wins against his 13 losses, the Red Sox began looking for ways to trade the now-ineffective pitcher.

That was a sad year when I was traded to Washington. That Cronin—I saw him in San Francisco after the '41 season. I played golf with him and Ty Cobb and Tony Lazzeri. I went down to see him on purpose 'cause I knew the newspapers were on me pretty bad. My arm wasn't so good and I knew they were *trying* to trade me.

I told him, "Do me a favor, don't trade me to St. Louis or Washington."

A newspaperman named Holly Goodrich called me up one night in Portland in the wintertime and says, "Well, what do you think of it?'

"Think of what?"

"Don't you know?"

"Know what?"

"You've been traded to Washington."

I couldn't believe it. I hung up the phone and I actually cried. I didn't have much of a year in '42 at all.[12]

The trade was made on December 13, 1941. Wilson and outfielder Stan Spence were sent to the Senators for pitcher Ken Chase and outfielder Johnny Welaj. Jack pitched 42 innings for the Senators in 1942 and surrendered 57 hits to opposing batters, a sign of his ineffectiveness. He was 1–4 with a 6.64 ERA. Nevertheless, the Senators were able to sell his contract to Detroit on July 17. He threw only 13 innings for the Tigers; they were the last innings of his major league career.

Wilson was exempted from military service when bone chips were found in his arthritic elbow during his examination. The surgery to remove the chips guaranteed that he would see no action. Unable to serve in the military, Jack returned to Portland. There he found work at Willamette Iron and Steel building ships for the Navy. Jack ended up making his shipyard job part time, as he signed on with the Beavers to pitch once more. Jack threw three more seasons in the Pacific Coast League, two for Portland and one for Sacramento, but the success he had in 1937 continued to elude him.

Wilson finished his professional playing career after appearing in just four games for the Sacramento Solons in 1945 and giving up 8 earned runs in 14 innings. His major league career totals were 68–72 with a 4.59 ERA.

He walked 601 and struck out 590 in 1131⅔ innings of work. As a batter, he hit .199.

After finishing his playing career with Sacramento, he returned to Columbia College, which had become the University of Portland in 1935, to coach its baseball team for the 1945 and '46 seasons. Jack was a coach with the Salem Senators in the Western International League in 1947 and '48. Unfortunately, like many former Sox players, Jack was never able to find a place in the Red Sox system. Wilson's feelings towards former manager Joe Cronin kept him on the outside looking in.

While Wilson enjoyed his time starting and relieving for Cronin's Red Sox, the constant and unpredictable strain on his arm ended up as the reason for the early end to his career. Wilson spoke about it to Brent Kelley for Kelley's book *In the Shadow of the Babe*:

> JW: I liked to start. I'd start and go nine innings, but Cronin ruined my career. I'd hurt my arm pitching today and tomorrow and the next day and then starting. It was nothing to pitch nine innings today and go down in the bullpen and go in and save one the next day, but they didn't count saves in those days.
>
> BK: Elden Auker said the worst year he ever had was the year he played under Cronin. He was not thrilled with him as a handler of pitchers.
>
> JW: You better believe it. Nobody else was. He ruined more good young pitchers than anybody. (Bill) Butland and (Woody) Rich and Mickey Harris—he didn't help him, either. Joe was a funny guy. He thought that nobody could have a sore arm because Walter Johnson never had a sore arm. Nobody could ever be hurt because Walter Johnson was never hurt.[13]

Wilson's strong feelings regarding what he perceived as Cronin's hand in the shortening of his career came back to haunt him. A confrontation with Cronin in 1942, when Jack was with the Senators, forever soured their friendship. Cronin never forgot Jack's bitterness, and when Joe was promoted to the general manager position in 1948, he prevented Jack from finding a spot in the Red Sox system.

"[T]hat was the end of everything," recalled Jack. "Ed Doherty was in public relations, then he went in the service and then they gave him a ballclub—Scranton—to run and he asked me if I'd manage it and I said, 'Yeah.' He called me and told me I had the job and then he wrote me a letter and told me that Cronin, who was then the general manager of the Red Sox, said that I wasn't gonna manage the ballclub and that was it.

"Bobby Doerr was scouting for the Red Sox and he asked me over in Spokane one day, 'What in the hell ever happened? All these donkeys get jobs around someplace. All you did for him, why didn't he give you a job?'

"I told him [about the confrontation with Cronin]. He said, 'That's the reason!' (Laughs)"[14]

After the 1948 season, Wilson left the Salem team to pursue work in the pinball machine and jukebox industry. In 1949 Jack and his aunt bought a tavern in Forest Grove, Oregon. They sold it three years later, when Wilson went to work for the Lucky Lager Brewing Company as a salesman in Portland, Salem, and Spokane.

Jack left his salesman position to work for the Lucky Lager distributor in Spokane, where he and his family settled down. In 1964, he moved to San Rafael, California, to run his own Lucky Lager distributorship, though he sold it five years later, returning to Portland and eventually Spokane, where he resumed his job at the Lucky Lager distributor. He remained in that position until his retirement in 1977.

The Wilsons moved to Lynnwood, Washington, to be closer to their daughters and three grandchildren. Although Jack had been out of professional baseball since 1948, he left a legacy in the national pastime that was carried on by his grandsons Joe and Andy. Both boys played high school and college ball, with Andy playing shortstop for the University of Utah; they also taught and coached baseball at Edmonds-Woodway High School in Edmonds, Washington. Andy coached the JV team for eight years, and his older brother Joe coached the varsity team to 200 wins over the course of a 15-year tenure.[15] As a fitting denouement to his professional baseball career, Jack was inducted into the Oregon Sports Hall of Fame in 1994.

John Francis "Jack" Wilson died of a stroke on April 19, 1995, in Edmonds, Washington. He was 83 years old.

Notes

1. "Descendants of James Walsh, Generation No. 4," http://familytreemaker.genealogy.com/users/w/e/b/Bruce-J-Webster-Jr/GENE5–0006.html (accessed May 3, 2008).
2. Carl T. Felker, "Jack Wilson, Flop as Third Sacker in Minors, Gets to Majors by Turning Hurler Over Dad's Protest," February 20 1941. Jack Wilson player file, National Baseball Hall of Fame and Museum.
3. Felker, op. cit.
4. Henry P. Edwards, Press Release from American League Service Bureau to Sunday Papers, Jack Wilson Hall of Fame player file.
5. Felker, op. cit.
6. Ibid.
7. John Drohan, "Joe Cronin Enthuses As Wilson Wins Ninth," July 17 1937. Jack Wilson Hall of Fame player file.
8. Burt Whitman, "Jack Wilson, Who Started as Infielder, Looms as Red Sox Ace Relief Pitcher," March 8 1935. Jack Wilson Hall of Fame player file.
9. John Drohan, "Syracuse Star Is Expected to Join Regulars," July 15 1935. Jack Wilson Player File.
10. John Drohan, "Home Run Hero Was Confident of Ability," September 4 1935. Jack Wilson Hall of Fame player file.

11. Vic Stout, "Lefty Grove, Poffenberger Pitch Today," August 28 1937. Jack Wilson Hall of Fame player file.

12. Brent Kelley, *In the Shadow of the Babe: Interviews with Baseball Players Who Played With or Against Babe Ruth*, (Jefferson NC: McFarland & Company, 2001), p. 162.

13. Kelley, op. cit, p. 160.

14. Kelley, op cit., p. 163.

15. Kathie Webster, personal email, May 27, 2008.

Sources

1938 Boston Red Sox regular season game log, http://www.retrosheet.org/ (accessed April 28, 2008).

"Cards Win 2; Nats Split Pair with Red Sox." *Washington Post*, September 3, 1935. ProQuest Historical Newspapers for the *Washington Post* (accessed June 17, 2008).

"Descendants of James Walsh, Generation No. 4." http://familytreemaker.genealogy.com/users/w/e/b/Bruce-J-Webster-Jr/GENE5-0006.html, (accessed May 3, 2008).

Drohan, John. "Home Run Hero Was Confident of Ability." September 4 1935. Jack Wilson player file, National Baseball Hall of Fame and Museum.

Drohan, John. "Joe Cronin Enthuses As Wilson Wins Ninth." July 17 1937. Jack Wilson player file, National Baseball Hall of Fame and Museum.

Edwards, Henry P. Press Release from American League Service Bureau to Sunday Papers, Jack Wilson player file, National Baseball Hall of Fame and Museum.

Felker, Carl T. "Jack Wilson, Flop as Third Sacker in Minors, Gets to Majors by Turning Hurler Over Dad's Protest." February 20 1941. Jack Wilson player file, National Baseball Hall of Fame and Museum.

Howe Bureau Player Card for John Francis Wilson. n. d. Personal email from Rod Nelson, January 16, 2008.

"Jack Wilson." *Baseball-Reference*. http://www.baseball-reference.com/w/wilsoja01.shtml, (accessed September 20, 2007).

"John Francis Wilson." *Seattle Times*, April 20, 1995.

Kathie Webster, personal email, May 27, 2008.

Kelley, Brent. *In the Shadow of the Babe: Interviews with Baseball Players Who Played With or Against Babe Ruth*. Jefferson NC: McFarland & Company, 2001.

Kelley, Brent. "Jack Wilson: Former Red Sox hurling ace speaks out." February 14 1992 Jack Wilson player file, National Baseball Hall of Fame and Museum.

Povich, Shirley. "Nats trample Sox, 9–3; Sure of 4th." *Washington Post*, September 26 1936. ProQuest Historical Newspapers for the Washington Post (accessed May 7 2008).

Spink, J.G. Taylor. *1942 Baseball Register*. New York: The Sporting News, 1942.

Stout, Vic. "Lefty Grove, Poffenberger Pitch Today." August 28 1937. Jack Wilson player file, National Baseball Hall of Fame and Museum.

Untitled Summary of Jack Wilson Call-up to Philadelphia. September 14 1934. Jack Wilson player file, National Baseball Hall of Fame and Museum.

Whitman, Burt. "Jack Wilson, Who Started as Infielder, Looms as Red Sox Ace Relief Pitcher." March 8 1935. Jack Wilson player file, National Baseball Hall of Fame and Museum.

1939 Season Timeline

by Bill Nowlin

The Red Sox had finished the 1938 season in second place, their highest finish since winning the pennant in 1918. The investments Tom Yawkey had made seemed to be starting to pay off, and the picture looked bright for 1939. They'd finished behind the Yankees, 9½ games back, but after almost two decades of being in last place, second place was a heady height. There was every reason to think that 1939 was going to offer the possibility of rising even higher, and maybe even battling for first place.

It really had been a horrible 20 years. The Red Sox had won the World Series four times in seven years, from 1912 through 1918, but then things fell apart. Or were taken apart. In 1919, Boston finished in sixth place, with a record of 66–71, their first losing record since 1908. Owner Harry Frazee sold Babe Ruth to New York over the holidays, and the team stagnated for a couple of years as more and more Red Sox were sold off or traded—often to New York—until the Sox hit rock bottom in 1922 (while New York finished first for the second year in a row.) With eight teams in the league, the Red Sox finished eighth in 1922, 1923, 1925, 1926, 1927, 1928, 1929, and 1930. The year they didn't finish last, they finished next to last, just a half-game better than the eight-place Indians in 1924.

In 1931, was there a glimmer of hope? The Red Sox finished sixth—but they were 45 games (!) out of first place. In 1932, they dropped back to last place. In 1933, again, they climbed out of the cellar, finishing seventh, but 34½ games out of first. Owner Bob Quinn couldn't bear the losses any more. He sold the team to Tom Yawkey, who had just come into an inheritance that made him one of the wealthiest men in America at the time the rest of the country was sinking deeper into the Great Depression.

Yawkey began to pump money into the Red Sox and they began to rise in the standings, finally reaching second place, in 1938. The team looked ready to turn the corner.

Heading to spring training

The advance guard of the Red Sox party left Boston for Sarasota, Florida at 8 AM on February 27, arriving 36 hours later at the Sox spring training camp. Some had begun to work out with Joe Cronin at Hot Springs, for instance Lefty Grove, who admitted he hadn't thrown a baseball since August 11, 1938 when he'd walked off the mound in mid-game with an arm that felt dead. He was still resting his arm, and it was thought it might be several weeks to a month before he would be ready to begin throwing. The first team workout was set for the first of

March. Cronin was said to have "never looked better in his life."

The players arrived from all directions. Charlie Wagner joined the southbound train at Richmond. Pitcher Bill Sayles came in from Portland, Oregon after five days on the rails. Pitching prospect Wayman Kerksieck took four days to come from Ulm, Arizona. He joined the train at Jacksonville, as did trainer Win Green (fresh from work with the Boston Bruins hockey team) and prospect Frank Dasso, the Eastern League strikeout king of 1938. By the time the train from Boston arrived, they found coaches Tom Daly and Herb Pennock already at the Sarasota Terrace Hotel, as well as players Berg, Berger, [Paul] Campbell, Carey, Desautels, Foxx, Grove, [Tommy] Irwin, Lefebvre, Ostermueller, Peacock, Rich, Tabor, Vosmik, and Wilson.

March 1

Grove excepted, Cronin found most of his players in good shape. Elden Auker had been in Sarasota three weeks already. "My job appears to be not one of getting these boys in shape, but to keep them from overdoing it," he commented just prior to the first light workout. It was the largest Red Sox squad he'd ever had to work with, large enough to field two full teams without having to ask pitchers and catchers to pull outfield duty. The only pitcher he hadn't heard from was Joe Heving, but Cronin wasn't at all worried about the veteran Heving.

Paul Campbell was set to be Jimmie Foxx's "understudy," a .333 hitter for Little Rock in 1938 and the "hustlingest player" in the game. Moe Berg was fresh off an appearance the previous week on the *Information Please* radio show; Al Schacht turned up in the studio audience wearing the "loudest polo coat" Berg had ever seen. Schacht hung out with the Red Sox throughout spring training, entertaining fans though not officially part of the Red Sox party. He could afford to; he reportedly pulled in $65,000 the year before with his clown act, more than Cronin, more than Bill Terry or Joe DiMaggio.

The Red Sox started workouts early in the morning. By noontime, the fields and clubhouses were nearly deserted. Several played golf, several fished, and several took to the Lido Beach. The *Boston Globe*'s Victor O. Jones characterized the Sox as "essentially a club of established stars." He added, "At the moment there probably isn't more than a single position on the Sox which hasn't already been assigned. The one exception perhaps is right field, where Ted Williams, the sensational rookie, still has to prove he's better than Leo Nonnenkamp. Jim Tabor seems a cinch for third. Gene Desautels and Johnny Peacock will undoubtedly share the catching, and there's no doubt about the rest of the team until you get down to picking the fifth or sixth-string catcher."

The first workout began at 10 AM and lasted 90 minutes. Cronin said, "I had to warn several of them today to take it easy." They were an enthusiastic group. They were also taller than many teams of the day, with only 5'8" Tom Carey being under six feet tall.

March 2

Lanky Jake Wade, obtained from the Tigers for Mike Higgins over the wintertime, "entered the second day of Red Sox practice the most discussed player in camp." Cronin liked his build, and had thought he was older than he was—he would turn 26 on April 1. Wade said he'd been under-utilized with Detroit, adding, "I don't know if there were cliques on the Tigers or what, but I was always the last guy in the bull pen they'd call upon." He admitted he needed work. Catcher Gene Desautels said that Wade should benefit from throwing to a smaller catcher such as himself and Johnny Peacock, rather than the larger Rudy York.

Red Sox traveling secretary Phil Troy with Donie Bush and Joe Cronin in early days of spring training, 1939.

Minor league manager Donie Bush turned up and predicted that Ted Williams, who he'd managed in Minneapolis to a Triple Crown season in 1938, was "sure to stick" and that Williams was a "wonderful hitter, with mountains of confidence in his own ability, that he knows the game and will be a great help to the Red Sox."

March 3

Somewhat unexpectedly, Grove began to throw off a mound, working out 10 or 15 minutes with Tom Daly. Working for the second day on fielding bunts, Jake Wade stepped on the ball and sprained his ankle slightly for the

first casualty of the young spring session. Grove felt good and left the workout in high spirits. The Sox pinned high hopes on Jack "Strong Boy" Wilson becoming a 20-game winner; a 1938 leg injury (stepping in a hole while shagging flies during a Columbia SC sandlot session while the team headed north) recurred again later in the year, and then Wilson hurt his arm while favoring his leg. This all had held him back, but he'd still won 15 games.

Ted Williams was, as the March 3 *Evening Globe* headlined, "Most Talked of Rookie Since DiMaggio." Bush noted Teddy's 43 homers in 1938 and added, "I lost track of the home runs he hit over 400 feet." Fielding? "He didn't throw to the wrong base a single time last season . . . and I'd remember if he did. Of course, there were a few times last summer when I could have cheerfully wrung his neck. Like the day when the opposition had the sacks drunk, two out and the count three and two on the batter. I looked out to right field and there was Williams waving to some kid who was perched on a building outside the fence and paying no attention whatsoever to the ball game. A couple of other times I caught him out there with his back to the plate going through the motions of swinging an imaginary bat."

Bush also praised Lefty Lefebvre. "Lefebvre was much better than his record showed with me last year. His biggest asset is needle-eye control of his curve ball. He can put that wrinkle anywhere he wants to and if he just improves his fast ball, he's got a great chance."

March 4

The Sox worked out for two hours, with Auker and Bagby getting in their first work. Wade's ankle was still tender. Joe Vosmik was hitting well. Leo Nonnenkamp got married in Little Rock and sent a telegram advising traveling secretary Phil Troy to make appropriate hotel arrangements for his arrival.

March 5

Sunday was a day off for the Sox. Bobby Doerr and his bride Monica, married in the autumn, both arrived in camp.

March 6

Lefty Grove turned 39. The squad was divided into a first-string (Cramer, Vosmik, Williams, Foxx, Cronin, Tabor, Doerr, Desautels, Nonnenkamp, and Peacock, with pitchers Grove, Auker, Bagby, Wilson, Heving, Galehouse, Wade, and Ostermueller) and a second-string (Campbell, Irwin, Berger, Spence, [Chester] Morgan, Carey, Gaffke, Berg, [Pat] Colgan, and pitchers Dickman, Dasso, Rich, Sayles, Wagner, Lefebvre, and Kerksieck.) Two workouts a day began. At the last moment, though, Cronin put Charlie Wagner into the first squad, apparently to try and improve the confidence which may have been shaken in him early in 1938 when we was put into a game, in relief, too early in the year. Gerry Moore wrote that Wagner "seemed to lose more and more confidence with each succeeding start. . . . Even Cronin himself humbly admits that he gave young Wagner too tough a baptism of fire."

In Dickman's case, Cronin felt he needed a "little mental jolt" to try to get him to bear down more.

He'd been assigned to the first-string squad, but where *was* Ted Williams? He earned himself a six-column headline in the *Globe*: "Ted Williams Unreported at Red Sox Camp." He'd been scheduled to take the train with the Doerrs, but decided to drive cross-country by car and hadn't told anyone what his plans were. Cronin sounded unperturbed: "If Williams isn't piled up in a Georgia ditch or something, he should appear sometime tomorrow, too, and we'll be ready to go with all hands accounted for."

March 7

Ted Williams arrived at camp around noon, a little more than 48 hours late, having spent a couple of days with the flu and a 102-degree temperature in a New Orleans hospital, as he'd driven across country with San Diego family friend Les Cassie. Cronin, perhaps pointedly, remarked that Stan Spence looked like "quite an outfielder." In the fall of 1937, Spence had been rated the top outfield prospect in the Red Sox system. But Leo Nonnenkamp jumped from Class-A1 Little Rock to the big leagues in the spring of 1938 and then Ted Williams stole the spotlight. It sounded that Spence might have spoken with a bit of an edge when he called Ted a "sho nough screwball" explaining, "Why plenty of times last season ah had to play right field as well as center when Williams would be talking to the boys running the scoreboard with a fly coming his way." He softened his comments, however, adding, "But don't worry about that boy hitting. He'll murder that potato."

Cronin had a word with Ted. "I told Williams not to worry about his hitting in training camp; that I did not care if he did not make a hit in Florida this Spring, that I have confidence in his ability to hit and what I wanted him to specialize on here was the perfection of his defensive play."

Fabian Gaffke arrived, too. He'd missed a train connection on his way in from Milwaukee.

The Red Sox uniforms first bore the patch on the jersey sleeves celebrating the nominal centennial of baseball, 1839–1939. Trainer Win Green was said to have stayed up half the night sewing the patches on.

March 8

There were as many as 1,000 watching the workout. Jim Tabor hit a high foul ball which shattered one of the arc lights which the field used for summer softball games, and some of the glass fell on patrons below.

A visiting physician offered the glum assessment that because of a diagnosed blocked blood vessel in his arm, he didn't see it as medically possible that Lefty Grove could ever pitch more than three innings at a time again.

Both Tommy Irwin and Gene Desautels wore #2 and were said to be look-alikes who even ran in almost identical fashion.

Williams worked out only in the morning session, still recovering from the flu—which had left him even more slender than usual. It was noted that Ted used an uncommonly light 34-ounce bat.

Wilson said the new American League baseball had the seams raised a bit more and this was helping his curve ball.

March 9

Third base coach Tom Daly said that Woody Rich reminded him of Pete Alexander (Grover Cleveland Alexander), according to the morning's *Boston Globe*. Grove took Jake Wade under his wing and worked with him on "how to flex his knees, how to stride and how to pivot"— a private tutorial that soon attracted most of the rookie Red Sox pitchers. A couple of Wade's offerings, though, were hit for 500 feet by Ted Williams, all the way to the deep right-field fence. A quirky notion: Cronin ordered that there should be no drinking water near the Red Sox bench. "What's the use of sweating off two pounds in a workout and then putting it all back by drinking water every five minutes?" Water would be available in the clubhouse.

March 10

Jimmie Foxx declared that the Red Sox "have definite pennant possibilities . . . for the first time since I've been a member of the Red Sox, we've got manpower at every position. . . . If they all click at once, we're going to be very tough to beat." He saw the pitching as the team's most vulnerable point, but much improved from the year before when the Sox had lost their two best pitchers— Grove and Wilson—at the same time, with several players capable of blossoming. Third base and right field were the question marks, but he expected Tabor to become a good ballplayer and felt Williams was a pretty sure bet. "Any kid who can step into Class A1 ball and hit .291 like he did on the Coast and then move up into the highest minor league classification and add 75 points to his average can't miss at the bat."

The first intrasquad game of the spring saw the Joe Cronins beat the Hugh Duffys 4–2. As Victor O. Jones put it, the two question marks turned into exclamation points as Tabor had four hits—two of them doubles—while Williams had two hits including a "towering triple to right." Both of Ted's hits came off Auker, as had one of Tabor's two-baggers. Player-manager Cronin was 3-for-5, with a triple.

Cronin characterized his team as a "high-class bunch of fellows, with no sore heads, no percentage guys, no prima donnas. Maybe this sounds like being a Boy Scout, but I think that sort of thing is important."

March 11

Coach Hugh Duffy's team beat Cronin's, 7–5, in another 9-inning intrasquad game. Ted Williams duplicated his hitting of the day before, right down to the 400-foot "towering triple" that would have been a home run at Fenway Park. Moe Berg played third base for Duffy's Yannigans. Colgan, playing for Cronin's Regulars, was 4-for-4 with a triple of his own. Gaffke drove in four runs for Duffy's team.

March 12

There was only a short Sunday batting drill, with many of the Sox pitchers throwing b.p.

Cronin said that he would use Ted Williams as much as possible during the exhibition season to expose him to as much big league pitching as he could. Williams "already enjoys the status of a regular," the *Globe* observed. Cronin's plan to use Ted frequently was to some extent contrary to his usual practice of using spring training to look over the rookies while not pushing the veterans too hard.

A blizzard hit Boston, killing 20, while it was unseasonably hot in Florida.

March 13

The Joe Cronin Regulars scored three times off Jack Wilson in the sixth and final inning of the day's scrimmage, tying Hugh Duffy's Irregulars, 3–3. Joe Vosmik was used three times as a pinch-hitter, hitting for both teams, but still failed to get a hit. You can do that sort of thing in an intrasquad game. After the game, there was some fun as golfer Walter Hagen pitched to fellow golf pro Sammy Snead.

March 14

The first Grapefruit League game of the year saw the Dodgers beat the Bosox, 6–3, in Clearwater. Tom Yawkey had driven down from his estate in Georgetown, SC and sat in the stands with both Cronin and Donie Bush. Williams was 1-for-4 with a double, oddly dubbed a "cheap double" though it hit the right-field fence. Most of the first-string players sat this one out. Frank Dasso allowed three home runs. Tom Carey hit a two-run homer for the Red Sox. Lefebvre threw hitless ball during his portion of the game.

The only three players to rate single rooms were Cronin, Grove, and Moe Berg. In Grove's case it was because he went to bed so very early; in Berg's it was because "he fills the room up with so many books, magazines and papers that there isn't room for any roommate."

March 15

The Sox held a long session, working on fundamentals such as cutoffs and rundowns. And Grove began to open it up off the mound. Cronin said Williams was a better thrower than Ben Chapman, who played right field in '38. Former Yale second baseman Tom Yawkey played some in the field and commented on the success of the team's scouting efforts: "When we started our farm system, we didn't figure it would do us much good for four or five years. . . . It gave us Bagby last year and it looks as though from now on we'd be getting good talent from it."

It was reported that Frankie Frisch would succeed Fred Hoey as radio broadcaster for both the Bees and the Red Sox home games, over the Colonial Network. "It is the first I've heard about it," said Hoey.

A Chinese checkers craze was sweeping the beach and the hotel lobby. Joe Cronin's favorite drink was 50% ginger ale and 50% grape juice. He said the habit of chewing tobacco was dying out among players. "Jack Wilson is pushing young Charley Wagner hard for the Beau Brummel honors." Ted Williams' wrists were the source of his power, nearly as thick as his legs. "That's the only place I'm strong," he told Victor O. Jones.

The March 16 *Globe* has a wonderful Gene Mack cartoon of the lobby of the hotel.

March 16

In the first game of the Florida city series, pitting Boston's two major league teams against each other, the Red Sox beat the Boston Bees, 8–7, in 10 innings. Jimmie Foxx hit his first homer of the spring, a long 430-footer. Fabian Gaffke was hit hard in the face by a Dick Errickson pitch and it was thought his jaw might have been fractured. X-rays the next morning proved negative. Woody Rich made the team with three perfect innings from the fourth through the sixth. In the 10th, Peacock singled and Lefebvre laid down a perfect bunt that didn't even draw a throw. Then Spence bunted and Peacock would have been out at third, but the ball went right through Bob Kahle at third and the winning run scored.

March 17

The St. Louis Cardinals hosted the Red Sox in St. Petersburg and Boston played 12 innings before going down to a 5–4 defeat. It was a back-and-forth game that was tied four times, before a single and a triple off Dasso spelled defeat.

March 18

The Red Sox came from behind to beat the Cincinnati Reds at Sarasota, 5–4. Bagby threw the last five innings, allowing just one run. Foxx and Tabor each drove in a pair. Already showing good plate discipline, Williams drew a couple of walks, scoring once. His error looked like it could have opened the gates for the Reds, but

Tabor executed a sensational double play to squelch the rally.

Jimmie Foxx asked a couple of writers if they'd seen Gehrig. "He looks 45 years old," Foxx said. Word was that he was distinctly slowed in the field.

March 19

The Sox welcomed the Dodgers to Sarasota, but both Joe Heving and Jack Wilson struggled, walking six and allowing 10 hits. Two Brooklyn runs in the top of the eighth broke a 4–4 tie and made for a 6–4 final.

March 20

Boston beat Louisville, 10–7, with Wade and Dasso both being hit hard by the Colonels.

After the first week of games, Tom Yawkey marveled about Paul Campbell, but being a backup to Foxx put him in the Babe Dahlgren category: backing up Foxx and then, in the Yankees' system, backing up Gehrig. The Sox had a hot shortstop prospect in Pee Wee Reese; Boston had bought the Louisville ballclub just to hold onto him. He was the heir apparent to Cronin at short. Cronin bemoaned letting the Bees get Sibbi Sisti away from him while farm director Billy Evans was preoccupied with the bonus money he'd not received for securing Emerson Dickman. Ted Williams' smart play in the field received some praise. Both Ted and Jim Tabor were seen as surpassing expectations. All in all, though, Sox spirits were a little low because of their inconsistent mound work. This proved to be a theme for the season.

March 21

GROVE'S SHOWING IS MOST ENCOURAGING. Paul Campbell made three hits and the Sox beat Kansas City, 4–1, with Kerksieck, Dickman, and Wagner combining on a six-hitter and Tabor making three great plays at third base, but the big news was the 15-minute b.p. thrown by Lefty Grove and the feeling that he might have fully recovered. Dasso was cut from the big league camp and sent down the road about 50 miles to Arcadia, Florida where Louisville trained.

March 22

RICH AND AUKER STOP THE REDS FOR SHUTOUT. In Tampa, the two held Cincinnati to just four hits. The Sox scored all their runs in the sixth. Williams walked, as did Foxx, and Cronin tripled them both in, scoring on Doerr's sacrifice fly to center. 3–0, Red Sox. Doc Cramer had been sick with a bad cold for several days, and Vosmik stayed in Sarasota because of sore feet occasioned by the sandy outfield in Sarasota. Later accounts said the Sarasota outfield was subpar "tufted sand."

March 23

The Red Sox beat the Bees in Bradenton, 7–6, at Ninth Street Park—though the two runs the National Leaguers put across in the bottom of the ninth made it close. Galehouse allowed no runs and just four hits in the first five innings of work, but Ostermueller was not nearly as effective and three Red Sox errors were costly.

March 24

FLUKE PLAY LEADS TO RED SOX DEFEAT. The Sox got six hits; the Cardinals only got four off starter Jack Wilson. Joe Heving threw three hitless innings, striking out seven. But two unearned St. Louis runs in the third were all that either team scored. The error was charged to Joe Cronin, though it was a freakish throw that "broke sharply to Joe's left" about three feet from his glove.

Manager Joe Cronin offered an assessment on the team's prospects: "I would be foolish to say that our club will win the pennant this year, and say it definitely, because the Yanks are a high-class club, and everybody knows it. They've won for three straight years, they have a smart manager and a great organization, they have hitting, pitching and a good, fast defense—in fact, they are champions, until somebody knocks them down, and that will take some doing. But I won't give you any of that 'wait till next year' stuff about the Boston club. We have a good chance of winning this year, if things break right. These boys are not intimidated by the Yankees. If we miss it will

Boston's 1938 infield: Bob Doerr, Joe Cronin, Pinky Higgins, and Jimmie Foxx. All but Higgins were back for 1939

be because a better club beat us. No jitters. No discouragement. Nothing like that. We have a real good spirit, and we think we can win.

"It's no secret that our weakness last year was pitching. We were the best hitting club in the league—a sock at every position. This year we've strengthened the pitching. Auker and Galehouse are two good men. Bagby won 15 for us in his first year. Watch that kid. He has more heart than a lion, and he's learning fast. Wilson should go better. He has all the stuff to be a 20-game winner. Jake Wade, who came from Detroit along with Auker, could be one of the best southpaws in the business.

"Looking ahead, I'm not even counting on Lefty Grove for a win. Anything he wins for us will be velvet. He's been going easy on that arm that went dead last Summer. There's no telling how he'll got until the season starts. But all you have to do is talk to him to know how he feels. He expects to take his regular turn. And that means—well, you know what it means. I've got my fingers crossed.

"The rest of the club is pretty well set—a good front line, good reserves. We wouldn't have traded Ben Chapman and Frank [Pinky] Higgins if we didn't think we had boys just as good to take their places. Jim Tabor will play a good third base for us. And that Ted Williams, in the outfield—have you seen him hit? He really leans on it."

March 25

Jim Tabor drove in four of Boston's five runs as they beat the International League champion Newark Bears, 5–0, at Sarasota. His bases-clearing triple in the fifth was the big blow. Bagby and Wade combined to throw a seven-hit shutout.

Tom Yawkey played third base during batting practice and "showed up well." Cronin was still talking about Jack Wilson's game the day before, and said he was going to give Auker a full game to let him show what he could do.

March 26

REDS JUMP ON AUKER TO BEAT SOX, 9 TO 5. It was a gusty day with a lot of dust flying about, but that wasn't really a good excuse. Auker gave up 11 hits in four innings, Lefebvre five in the next four. Doerr homered for Boston and played well in the field. Ted Williams hit a triple and a single and drove in two, as did Campbell, but Auker only lasted the four frames and was touched up for seven runs.

March 27

To try and bolster their pitching staff, the Red Sox bought eight-year veteran Monte Weaver from the Washington Senators for cash. "Used sparingly, I think he'll help us," said Cronin. Lefty Grove said he was ready and was anxious to pitch a game. He'd given up his trademark cigars and worked on his legs throughout the offseason and felt his arm was in fine shape.

RED SOX BATS ROUT COLONELS, 24 TO 2. The game at Arcadia was, shall we say, one-sided, as the Red Sox jumped on Dartmouth's Ted Olson for 11 runs in the first four innings. Williams, Foxx, and Cronin all homered. It was Ted's first homer in a Red Sox uniform.

(During the brief time Williams was with the Red Sox in 1938 before being assigned to the Minneapolis Millers, he'd not hit a homer.) Even Chester Morgan collected three RBIs for the Red Sox. Denny Galehouse held Louisville to five hits and one run in his seven innings. Lefebvre pinch-hit for him in the eighth, and singled, but was optioned to Louisville after the game and simply stayed behind as the bus pulled out for Sarasota. Stan Spence was told to report to Colonels manager Donie Bush as well. Cronin had 11 hits in his last 23 at-bats.

March 28

Boston 3, Newark 2 at Sebring. Rich and Dickman combined in a 6½-inning game shortened by rain—the first rain the Red Sox had seen in four weeks in Florida. Cramer had two hits and made the play of the game, but there were others. Mel Webb of the *Globe* wrote that Rich threw better to the more experienced Gene Desautels, and when Peacock was catching he worked faster, "pushed" his pitches, and suffered some loss of control.

March 29

Cincinnati beat Boston 1–0, with fine four-hit pitching by two of their rookies, but the big news for Boston was the start for Lefty Grove. He gave up just one single (to Joost, who was thrown out trying to stretch it into a double) in three innings, before turning the game over to Wilson after facing just nine batters. "A foul tip off Joe Vosmik's bat hit the rubber plate and, bounding sharply, struck Joe on the right ear, nearly knocking him out." Outfielder Chet Morgan was sent to Louisville; Louisville sent pitchers Dasso and Sayles on to Little Rock. Tom Yawkey declared, "I am sure that this is the best ball club I have had since I purchased the Boston American League franchise back in 1934. I think we have more power, the finest of all round spirit, the chances for a stronger attack than we have had, and, in addition, the opportunity to see better and more consistent pitching. We had to gamble by sending Higgins to Detroit and Chapman to Cleveland in order to get this more experienced pitching."

Of Tabor and Williams, he said, "Both of these boys have shown us a lot in the three weeks of Spring drilling." Yawkey was appreciative of Bobby Doerr, saying, "Personally I look to see Bobby Doerr keep on paying the classiest ball at second base of any man in the league, and I also am predicting that he'll hit even better than he did last year when he showed a big improvement." Yawkey believed Desautels was one of the most improved players on the team. "It took some time for Gene to arrive, but he is due for a fine year, in my opinion, not only as a backstop but as a clever handler of pitchers, who have all kinds of faith in him."

Yawkey said he felt they'd made the moves to close the gap of 10 games with the Yankees, but acknowledged that New York had tried to improve as well. "There's no sense in making predictions. What I am aiming for is to have a better team each succeeding year. It's a slow job. Still I am now satisfied that the team which Joe Cronin will operate is the best of any that has appeared at Fenway Park since I have been the owner of the club."

Charlie Wagner and Paul Campbell were sent to Louisville, and Morgan from Louisville to Little Rock. Boze Berger was to be the backup for Foxx at first base.

March 30

FARMHANDS TRIM RED SOX, 5–4. Elden Auker went the distance but lost the game. It was getaway day before the team left for the long road trip heading north. Auker gave up 11 hits, including three to Campbell and two to Spence. Yank Terry and Ted Olson held the Red Sox to eight hits. Cronin was nonetheless satisfied with Auker's work. After the game, 26 players and a retinue of newsmen, coaches, and team officials took the train for Moultrie, Georgia to play the Class-D Georgia State League Moultrie Packers.

March 31

CRAMER HITS HIS ANNUAL HOMER. The Red Sox beat the Packers, one of their former farm teams, 13–3, in "what is optimistically called the municipal stadium." It was "nothing more than a light workout" for the Red Sox. The Moultrie team was now a Phillies affiliate but was only two weeks old in its new incarnation. It had been a full year since Cramer hit a homer (against the Dodgers in the spring of 1938) and "as he rounded third base he paused to doff his cap to the entire Sox bench." He added a double and two singles from the leadoff spot. The 500 fans on hand saw Jimmie Foxx strike out three times, but saw Ted Williams triple. Heving and Galehouse shared mound duties. Gaffke was hit on the back of the head, but was OK. There weren't more fans on hand (the town was 12,000 strong) because many had driven to Tallahassee to see the Yankees play.

Joe Cronin said he hadn't decided on his rotation yet, but the problem was a good one: he felt he had enough pitching to pick and choose. Rich, Bagby, Auker, Galehouse, Wilson, Heving, and Grove looked to be the core of the staff. The biggest disappointment? Ostermueller. "He hasn't looked good to me," confessed Cronin—though Ostermueller's 13–5 mark in 1938 was second-best on the Red Sox. Cronin wondered out loud whether Rich might benefit from another year in minor league ball. Kerksieck was still hanging in there, largely on the strength of his unexpectedly good curveball and much to the surprise of many of the newsmen who'd derided his promotion from Little Rock.

April 1

Throughout his long career, Ted Williams was never thrown out of a major league game by an umpire—but

Joe Cronin yanked him out of the game in Atlanta as he "cracked down with a flourish on the screwball tendencies of Ted Williams. . . . Without a moment's hesitation, Cronin waved Williams out of the game in the middle of the eighth inning as the result of an untoward act which saw the 20-year-old slugger misjudge a short foul fly to right field then pick the ball up and fire it clear over the grandstand roof into Ponce de Leon av., a busy thoroughfare that adjoins the ball park." It was deemed Ted's "first real outward display of temperament" despite the screwball reputation that preceded him. "Hitherto his unusual conduct has been confined to a constant line of senseless chatter," remarked the *Globe*'s Gerry Moore. Ted had loafed a bit the prior day, but Cronin had let that one pass. Cronin swore that he'd continue to crack down on him "until all the 'bush league' is out of him and he begins to act like a major leaguer." Though he had tripled once in five at-bats, Ted had struck out in the game, and committed an error, so was already on edge. Cronin met with Williams privately, and in the evening Moore said he was a "thoroughly chastened young man."

Jake Wade was hit hard, and Atlanta won it, 10–9.

Later in the season, in August, Williams admitted, "I really was so ashamed after I threw that ball over the grandstand that if the ground opened up and swallowed me, it would have been perfect with me."

April 2

BAGBY, OSTIE BLANK ATLANTA TEAM, 3–0. And Jim Bagby, Sr. got to see his son pitch in a major league uniform for the very first time. Gerry Moore's game account in the *Globe* began, "Ted Williams, the glorious screwball, celebrated his return to the Red Sox lineup today by belting a well-smacked homer that accounted for the first run of the contest, drawing a walk with the bases loaded to force across the second tally and contributing the most spectacular fielding play as the Hub hose squared their two-game series against the Atlanta Crackers with a snappy 3–0 win." A 400-hit drive by "Titanic Ted" was hauled in by an outstanding Johnny Rucker catch, or Ted might have had another one. The homer that Ted hit struck the third tier of billboards, stacked one above the other, in deep right center.

April 3

The Red Sox and Cincinnati began the first of 10 scheduled games against each other that some thought might be a "World Series preview." The first game was at Macon and the Reds scored five times in the eighth to take a 7–4 victory. Auker and Rich had allowed only three hits in the first seven frames, but the Reds landed hard on Rich in the eighth. He couldn't get his curveball down; it was the first time he'd really been hit hard all spring. The two teams played before a segregated audience. Billy Werber's "blood-curdling war whoops" intended to distract Red

Sox infielders "only served to tickle the colored gentry who sit in their private bleacher over back of third base and keep up an amusing chatter back and forth with the athletes." Come 1960, the Red Sox would integrate New Orleans baseball in a spring training game.

April 4

REDS STAGE A REAL MASSACRE. Cronin Pitchers Suffer—Score 18 to 7. Cincinnati accumulated 37 total bases on 22 hits, and annihilated the Red Sox in Augusta. Heving gave up six runs in the fifth before being relieved; Cronin just left him in and let him get battered, as he did while Dickman was touched up in each one of his innings, and as Kerksieck was hammered for seven runs in the top of the ninth. The *Globe* said that "Bucky Walters actually struck out on purpose for the final out in the ninth for fear some of his mates would collapse from running in the heat." The only bright light for Boston was Vosmik's 4-for-5 day, with a couple of RBIs, on his 29th birthday.

Grantland Rice wrote from Augusta that he liked Cincinnati for the NL flag. He added, "I still don't think the Red Sox can whip the Yankees, but, if any team turns this trick, it should be the hired men from Boston." He highlighted Tabor and Williams, and said the Red Sox had more punch, with Foxx, Cronin, and Williams, but "it all gets back to the pitching."

April 5

Playing in Columbia, SC, Lefty Grove started and pitched four strong innings, giving up one run on four hits—a solo homer to Eddie Joost in the first. This despite a poorly-prepared pitcher's mound at Dreyfus Field. Vosmik's arm was sore, but the Sox batted out 12 hits and beat the Reds, 9–4. Coach Tom Daly marveled how Grove had made the transition from a fireballer to a control pitcher: "I'll take Lefty as the greatest control artist in the game today."

April 6

RED SOX AND CINCI IN DUSTY 18–18 TIE. The game was called in the beginning of the ninth because they ran out of baseballs. All 72 balls had either been lost in the unrelenting winds ("a baby tornado and a series of dust storms that would have frightened the hardiest Dust Bowl resident"), or grabbed by the spectators who crowded the all-dirt field in Florence SC, encroaching on both the first and third base foul lines. The Reds got 24 hits and the Red Sox got 22, with some 37 players taking part. Nonnenkamp played both left field and first base (not at the same time), and had four hits, including a home run. Of the dust, Gerry Moore wrote, "The press box was erected on the ground about 20 feet behind home plate and at times it was impossible to see the shortstop."

April 7

Lexington, NC was the venue and the Red Sox apparently put on quite an exhibition of home run power during batting practice—every regular in the lineup hit at least one out of the park—but they only made four hits during the game itself and lost to Cincinnati, 7–2. North Carolinian Woody Rich started and took the loss. His father had made the 120-mile trip to the park by taxi, with funds raised by his neighbors. He said he didn't know a thing about baseball himself, and that nobody ever showed his son how to pitch but that Woody had taken up the game in earnest after playing with "the Negro folk" around the farm.

April 8

The Reds beat the Red Sox, 13–5, in a game at World War Memorial Stadium in Greensboro, North Carolina. Ostermueller and Galehouse were the victims, with Galehouse's error in the ninth creating an opening for the final three Reds runs. A feverish Ted Williams played the game but couldn't get the ball out of the infield. Tabor and Vosmik each drove in two for Boston.

April 9

With three games yet to go, Cincinnati clinched their barnstorming spring series against the Red Sox with a 7–5 win in Durham. Ted Williams, still getting over a fever, was dropped to sixth in the lineup and was collared with an 0-for-4. Jack Wilson gave up all seven of the Reds runs in his six innings of work. "Grove is the only one who hasn't taken a shellacking now," said Cronin. "The pitching is disappointing, but I guess there's no other way out of it except to work these babies and see if they can pitch their way out of the doghouse."

Jimmie Foxx said that one of the reasons his legs had held up so well over the years was his long-term love of dance. Many of the ballplayers attended a tri-fraternity dance at Wake Forest College and "James Emory trod the light fantastic, putting all the young collegians in the shade." The Sox drew large crowds in the North Carolina games, with several Tarheels on the team: Peacock, Rich, Wade, and Weaver.

April 10

FOXX' HOMER GIVES RED SOX WIN IN 10TH. It was his first home run since leaving Florida, and it came on a 3-2 count with two outs on a pitch from Jumbo Jim Weaver. Boston beat Cincinnati, 4–3, in a game played on the home field of the Rocky Mount Red Sox farm club. Jim Bagby started the game for Boston, allowing just three hits in seven innings—but every one of them was a home run—though the field was noted as a small ballpark. Williams hit a solo homer off Johnny Vander Meer earlier in the game, the only one of the five likely a homer at Fenway. NC native Woody Rich got the win in relief, and the *Globe*'s Moore wrote that he was "considered one of the greatest pitching prospects ever to hit the major leagues." Red Sox farm director Billy Evans had signed both Rich and Tabor. In the hotel lobby, Ted Williams was quoted as saying, "I'm 3000 miles from home, 800 miles from my best girl in Minneapolis and I'm not hitting, but I'm happy." Moore observed: "Which only shows you how you can't help liking the glorious screwball."

April 11

Petersburg, Virginia offered wind and dust "almost as bad as last week's fiasco at Florence" and the Reds hammered the Red Sox for an 11–9 win at Roland Day Park. "Good baseball again was out of the question" and the day was dubbed as "nothing more than a good workout." There wasn't one home run, mainly because the crosswind kept knocking balls down. Williams had two singles and walked twice, showing the plate discipline that would set a rookie record by year's end.

April 12

Johnny Peacock hit a grand slam off Bucky Walters in Roanoke, and Boston beat Cincinnati, 17–14, in another windy, dusty game that included nine home runs among 37 hits. Williams was 4-for-4 with two singles, a double, and a home run. Cowboy Jim Tabor hit the other Red Sox homer. Auker and Wade shared the pitching duties and the burden of the Reds' barrage. Seven runs in the Red Sox eighth won them the ballgame.

Cronin continued to express worry about his pitching staff. "Right now, we haven't got a single outstanding hurler on whom we can count to win 20 games. Unless there's a sudden turn for the better, that means we'll have to do plenty of juggling with our pitching staff like we did last year." He said he knew Williams would hit. "He stands up there against left-handers better than any left-handed batter I know, and that goes for the Gehrigs, Gehringers, Travises. . . . As I said before, Tabor is a revelation. He can hit a ball a country mile." Physically, Cronin said, the only problem was Vosmik's arm, which was bad but improving. It was only the pitching that worried him. Cincinnati had hit .353 off Red Sox pitchers during the series of games.

April 13

The Sox were due to play in Newark, but the weather didn't cooperate. They were "frozen out" of the contest and most of the team took the train all the way to Boston. Tom Daly took Ted Williams for a walk around Boston.

Cronin said, "All things considered, we had a great training session. We didn't miss a game until we hit the cold of Newark this morning. While our pitchers haven't done very well, I really think they'll improve now that we will be playing on good diamonds." Tabor was greatly improved, he said, and Rich more than lived up

to expectations. About the youngster from San Diego, he said, "Ted is still a kid at 20 and you really can't expect him to be a great player this season, but I'm sure some day he'll be one of the greatest hitters in the game." Williams led the team in spring hitting, at .394 (13-for-33), with three homers and nine RBIs. Tabor drove in 15 runs and had the most extra-base hits—four doubles, two triples, and two homers. Hy Hurwitz opined, "It appears that Williams and Tabor will make Boston fans forget about Pinky Higgins and Ben Chapman before the season is very old."

April 14

WILLIAMS LEADS OFF WITH HOMER. In his first at-bat in the Commonwealth of Massachusetts, Ted Williams hit a first-inning grand slam at Holy Cross's Fitton Field in Worcester and drove in another run later in the game, as the Red Sox beat Holy Cross 14–2. Mike Klarnick was Ted's victim of the long inside-the-park home run to dead center field. Grantland Rice reported that baseball writers almost unanimously picked the Red Sox to finish second to the Yankees, with a few picking them for first place. Rice called Cronin a "brilliant actor" as a manager.

April 15

Casey Stengel's Boston Bees hosted the Red Sox at National League Park before 6,100 fans and beat the Red Sox in the first of two City Series games by a convincing 7–1 margin, all due to a six-run sixth off Joe Heving. Ted was 0-for-3 in his first game in the city of Boston, but made a sensational catch close to the "Jury Box" in deep right. Pitching prospect Kerksieck was optioned to Louisville.

April 16

SOX WIN SERIES, NOSING BEES, 1–0. Three wins to one, the Red Sox took City Series honors, beating the Bees in "one of the most stubbornly contested Spring series ever played by the two clubs." All three wins were by one-run margins, and the March 16 game had gone into extra innings. Some 15,300 paid to see the game, staged at Fenway Park. It was Ted's first game at Fenway, and he was 1-for-3 with a seventh-inning single (Ted was cut down trying to steal second). Woody Rich pitched a complete nine-inning five-hitter.

April 17

Interest in Boston was higher than it had been for years. Rather than sit idle, waiting for Opening Day on the 18th, the Red Sox stopped by New Haven on their way to New York to play against the Yale team coached by former Red Sox pitcher Joe Wood. Jake Wade was roughed up by the Elis, while Joe Wood Jr. played right field and pitched for Yale. Joe Jr. "drove in the first Yale run, scored the second, made the only extra-base hit of the game, pitched one perfect inning, and robbed Ted Williams of a homer."

Williams otherwise struck out three times in a row, 0-for-4, and was booed by the crowd. The Red Sox won the 6-5 game with a run in the ninth. Another Red Sox relative in the game was center fielder and Yale team captain Eddie Collins Jr., son of Boston's GM, who was hitless but made two excellent catches. It was later remarked that the Red Sox had fewer college players than any other team, prompting Tom Carey to question, "Since when can a guy think his way to first base?" Cronin counted seven collegians, three of them being the catchers: Berg, Desautels, and Peacock.

April 18

Rain, cold, mist, and fog combined to cause the postponement of the scheduled Opening Day at Yankee Stadium. The Lefty Grove vs. Lefty Gomez matchup was pushed back a day—but the Dodgers played the Giants at Ebbets Field nonetheless, and many of the Sox players took in the game.

April 19

Lefty Grove was the first man in the lobby, waiting for the breakfast room to open. Ted Williams was the second, said the night porter. But the game was postponed yet again due to rain and wet grounds. Ted Williams went to visit his three aunts in Mount Vernon, while Woody Rich visited the Stadium. "It's bigger than my home town," he allowed.

April 20

Mayor Fiorello LaGuardia threw out the first pitch, and Commissioner Kenesaw Mountain Landis presented the 1938 World Series emblems to the Yankees. Despite having the start pushed back two days, Cronin stuck with Lefty Grove, calling him "the most remarkable pitcher of all time. For 11 years, he depended on his fast ball. Then his arm went dead and the big southpaw had to start pitching all over. When he broke in he didn't have any control and the guy wound up with the best directed delivery in baseball." Cronin was "overboard" regarding Woody Rich. GROVE STAGES REAL COMEBACK was the *Globe*'s headline, though the Yankees had won the game, 2-0, behind the pitching of Red Ruffing. Both pitchers allowed seven hits, and one of the runs New York scored was unearned. Even the Yankees fans cheered for Grove. Ted Williams struck out his first time up, but doubled off the right-field fence about 400 feet distant in the fourth inning. Lou Gehrig was "sloppy in the field. He couldn't get off a dime and he allowed a couple of thrown balls to escape him, which he would have caught in his back pocket during his prime." He hit into a pair of double plays. Ominously, Hy Hurwitz's game summary concluded with comments on Grove and Gehrig: "Grove

showed himself to be the guy who was the inspiration for that well-known song 'Ole Man River, he just keeps rollin' along.' As for Gehrig, poor Lou has just passed away."

April 21

Jim Bagby Jr. and Doc Cramer were the stars as the Red Sox opened the season at home, beating Philadelphia, 9-2. Bagby threw a five-hitter and Cramer's bases-clearing double in the sixth inning broke a 2-2 tie. The buildup for Ted Williams had been tremendous. It was the rookie's first appearance at Fenway in a regular season

Bagby won the home opener with a 9-2 win over the Athletics.

game, and he received a bigger ovation than any of the established players; he also had more fan mail waiting for him than any of the others. Fans "shouted his name every time he came up." Ted batted sixth, and was 1-for-5 with a seventh-inning single and RBI off reliever Ed Smith.

The entire park gave A's manager Connie Mack a rousing and prolonged round of applause before the game.

April 22

Roommates Woody Rich and Ted Williams were the stars at Fenway as 10,300 saw the Sox win one, 5-2. Rich threw a complete game six-hitter, and Ted was 2-for-4 with a double high off the left-center-field wall near the flagpole, and one RBI—the exact same line as Doc Cramer, though The Kid got the headlines. It was Rich's first big league start, and he proved a complete player with a couple of singles at the plate and six assists as a fielder. Four of the Red Sox runs were unearned, but it still goes in the books as a W.

April 23

TED WILLIAMS REVIVES FEATS OF BABE RUTH. The front page of the *Boston Globe* featured a photograph of "Fans' Idol" Williams and the game story which detailed his first big league home run, a "towering two-bagger" and "a pair of wickedly-hit singles" capped off by a sensational running catch. He was 4-for-5 with three more RBIs, but the Red Sox lost the game, 12–8. The weather was damp and cold, but "every man's son among the spectators sat through the inclement conditions when the game was obviously lost to await titanic Ted's final appearance at the plate in the ninth inning." That was the one time the A's got him out, but "he nearly drove left fielder Bob Johnson through the left-field scoreboard before Johnson finally speared a line drive that was prevented from landing up against the barrier only by the unfavorable East Wind." The home run came off Luther "Bud" Thomas in the first inning, and sailed into the right-center-field bleachers into a spot where only a handful of hitters had ever hit one before. His double just missed going out over the Wall by a matter of inches. The game got off to an inauspicious start as Elden Auker walked five of the first seven batters he faced and Cronin was forced to bring in Galehouse during the top of the first. Galehouse pitched 6⅓ innings but the six runs Philadelphia scored in the eighth off him, Ostermueller, Heving, and Dickman spelled defeat for the Red Sox.

That the fans had stayed to see Ted hit one more time, and then leave immediately after his at-bat, reminded writers of Ruth. More than an hour after the game, Ted was reported to be "surrounded by a hundred urchins in the parking lot near the players' entrance . . . He was shivering in the cold, but still showing the kids how he broke his wrists to buggy-whip that ball. Guys that are that screwy about hitting always can hit, and guys who take time out to be nice to kids usually last a long time in baseball." (Victor O. Jones)

April 24

A sports page cartoon showed that Ted Williams had won the hearts of New England fans, with not one but three stories featuring Ted in the headlines—and an ad for Wheaties depicting him eating the cereal, too. Williams played right field at Fenway Park in 1939 and Melville Webb's story was headlined "Sox' Sun-Field Rookie Most Popular Since Hooper." Ted was 8-for-18 on the young season—but what goes up inevitably comes down and Williams was 1-for-6 on the day (0-for-5 with runners on base, leaving 11 men stranded) in a 10–9 loss to Washington that very day. He doubled once his first time up, the one time there was no one on base. Wilson, Wade, Auker, and Weaver all pitched but a hastily-summoned Jim Bagby pitched the top of the 10th and gave up three singles and bore the 10–9 loss. It was the second day in a row Cronin had used five pitchers. Despite Auker having

walked the five batters on the 23rd, the ever-optimistic Cronin actually brought him on in relief to face a batter with a 3–0 count. Cecil Travis hit the ball back to the mound and off Auker's arm, to drive in a run.

April 25

Jimmie Foxx hit his second homer of the year, to win one for Joe Heving (the fourth Red Sox pitcher of the day) in the bottom of the 11th inning, 6–5, off Senators starter Joe Krakauskas. The ball went out just inside the left-field foul line but some 20 feet over the Wall, bouncing off a Lansdowne Street rooftop and onto the railroad tracks beyond. Jim Tabor had tied it with a single in the bottom of the ninth after walks to Foxx and Cronin. There were runners on first and second with nobody out, and Cronin asked Williams to sacrifice but Ted hit into a double play instead and the inning ended a moment later.

Ted stories abounded. Hugh Duffy had been hitting fungoes before a game, and yelled to Ted, "You looked like Mother Hubbard on that one," to which Ted inexplicably replied, "Don't bring sex into this." The bright light of the day for pitching was that Ostermueller had allowed just five hits in his six innings.

April 26

The Red Sox decided that Ted didn't need backup from both Nonnenkamp and Gaffke, so Gaffke was sent to Louisville (the Red Sox having transferred their Triple-A franchise from Minneapolis to Louisville) despite being the only powerful right-handed pinch hitter the Sox possessed.

The day's game against Washington was rained out. Williams was ordered to bed with a slight cold. It was the third time Ted had been bedridden since he got sick heading for spring training. "Still the kid refuses to wear a hat or tie," wrote the *Globe*'s Gerry Moore a few days later. "No wonder managers go nuts."

April 27

The scheduled game against the visiting New York Yankees was postponed due to cold. A rumored Jake Wade for Jake Powell trade was denied. Manager Joe McCarthy declared he was satisfied with his club as it stood, but "if I were considering a deal, you can rest assured the Red Sox would be the last club in the world with which I'd take a chance of strengthening." The Indians had expressed interest in Ostermueller, but Cronin couldn't find a fit. All he really was looking for was minor league pitching. Foxx was confined to bed with a cold, too.

April 28

Yet another game postponed, which was to have been a 3 PM Ladies Day game with free admission for all women, the Red Sox took the 10:35 train to Philadelphia. On the train was Hugh Duffy, who had just been named first-base coach, succeeding Herb Pennock, who'd been relieved of those duties so he could become assistant supervisor of the Red Sox farm system.

April 29

PEACOCK'S PINCH HIT IN 9TH WINS FOR SOX. It was a cold afternoon at Shibe Park, and threatening to become the third extra-inning game in a row for the Red Sox. Grove started for Boston and allowed but one run in six innings. Doc Cramer's two-run single gave the Red Sox the lead in the fifth, but Philadelphia tied it in the bottom of the seventh. Peacock had tied the game on the 24th in the ninth inning, his last time up as a pinch hitter. This time, he drove in Bobby Doerr from second with a solid single into left. Jim Tabor's brilliant stab of Bob Johnson's liner inside the bag at third base almost certainly spared the Red Sox seeing the game tied up again in the bottom of the ninth. Ted Williams insisted on playing, and was 1-for-4 with a single. Despite being under the weather, he stole a base—one of just two in 1939.

May 1 *Globe*: "It is now revealed that the foolish ground rule which robbed Double-X of a well deserved homer yesterday was in vogue only one day and was the brain child of Earl Mack . . . Papa Connie saw the unfairness of the rule after Jimmy's belt and decreed today that all drives henceforth hitting as high as Jimmie's did against the lighting towers will go as home runs." [Yes, it was Jimmy and Jimmie in the same sentence.] "Today" was April 30.

The previous day's paper described it thus: "Still another circumstance which cost Grove the decision today is a weird ground rule which is in vogue here because of the recently erected towers for night baseball and which also robbed Jimmie Foxx of a well-merited home run . . . Jimmie opened the third inning with a terrific 425-foot liner that landed right at the juncture of the top of the wall and screen which surrounds the light tower in right center. The ball dropped down behind the screen . . . If it had hit the structure first, it would have been a home run had it cleared a yellow line which designates a ground-rule four-master on the screen, but the umpires ruled it dropped down behind the screen without touching the iron girders and held Jimmie to a ludicrous two-bagger. The blow, which would have made the center field bleachers at Fenway Park, should have added another run to the Sox total and would have been enough for Grove to win."

Jimmie Foxx's hit out of the park in center field was ruled a double under a ground rule that lasted exactly 24 hours, and was changed the very next day.

Hugh Duffy coached first base during the game, the first time he had ever served as a coach during a major league game.

April 30

The Red Sox took first place after winning another game against the Athletics, 3–1. Bobby Doerr hit his first homer of the year, but the story was more that Jim Bagby scattered seven hits for a complete game win, and hit a solo home run himself to provide the winning run, a third-inning drive that went some 400 feet off the façade of the upper tier in dead center field. Williams missed another game, ill and confined to quarters. Nonnenkamp was 0-for-3 in his place. Ted was left behind when the team traveled to Cleveland.

May 1

Now it was Cronin's turn to take to bed with the grippe, as did his backup shortstop Boze Berger and Emerson Dickman. A Victor Jones column blamed Williams for not wearing a hat, getting sick, and seeing the sickness spread to Foxx and now three more players.

Scheduled off day.

May 2

Cleveland GM Cy Slapnicka called the game due to cold, but most of the Red Sox said it was the best weather they'd seen since Florida. The Sox worked out, and worked up a good sweat. Suspicion abounded that the Indians called off the game because of a "beleaguered pitching staff"—but for the Red Sox it gave them another day for Williams and Cronin to get better.

In Detroit, Yankees first baseman Lou Gehrig took the day off—after playing 2,130 consecutive games—and every batter in the New York lineup hit exactly two hits except center fielder Tommy Henrich, who had to settle for one, as the Yankees beat the Tigers, 22–2.

May 3

AUKER PITCHES RED SOX TO 5 TO 1 WIN. Allowing just five hits, the submarine specialist threw a gem. "It was easily the best pitched game we have ever seen a Red Sox pitcher unfold in League Park," wrote Moore of the *Globe*. "And how!" added Moe Berg, saying it would give the Red Sox confidence for their remaining 10 games in Cleveland. Cronin did sit the day out, and Carey played shortstop. The only Red Sox run until their three-run seventh came after Auker singled in the fifth and advanced on a force play, a single, and Foxx's sacrifice fly. Ted was 1-for-4 with an RBI; Foxx hit two doubles. Williams stole another base, and made two good catches, but wasn't strong at the plate, making the final out three times in the first five innings. "Well, I'm glad to win that first game," said the self-effacing Auker, and Lefty Grove said, "Yeah, and you mightn't have won it if I hadn't gone up to the boys before the seventh inning and told them it wasn't me pitching out there and for heaven's sake get some runs."

May 4

TED WILLIAMS SCORES FIVE RUNS WITH TWO HOMERS, blared the front page headline. Before the game in Detroit, Foxx had told Williams he could be the first to hit one entirely out of the park, but Ted just laughed. Then Ted did just that—three times, accounting for "the two longest home runs Briggs Stadium has ever seen." The right-field grandstand had three tiers and no one had ever hit one on top of the third tier. It was 325 feet from home plate, but stood 120 feet tall. The first ball Ted hit out and over was foul by inches. He then lined out. The next time up, in the top of the fourth, the Red Sox were down 4–0, but Ted hit one out on top of the right-field roof "nearer centerfield than right." That one came off starter Roxie Larson. The Red Sox tied it up in the top of the fifth and Ted came up as the first batter to face reliever Bob Harris. There were two runners on base, and Harris ran the count to 3–0. Ted told Rudy York, catching for the Tigers, that he was going to swing on the 3–0 count, and Cronin gave him the sign. Ted hit the ball out about a dozen feet inside the right-field foul line. Witnesses outside the park said it landed on the other side of Trumbull and bounced against a taxi garage wall. The crowd, and players from both teams, were said to be awestruck. The "irrepressible string-bean rookie" had driven in five runs. Hank Greenberg sent word into the Red Sox clubhouse that he wanted Ted to come out early the next day and show him where he gets such power.

"There goes the kid that makes us a real pennant contender," said Foxx in a jubilant clubhouse as the Sox celebrated their fifth win in a row. "We didn't have any business to win that game today . . . the big difference was we've got that new kid who can put us right back in the ball game with one swish of the bat." Foxx added, "And don't overlook Jim Tabor."

May 5

Woody Rich pitched a three-hit masterpiece and both Foxx and Cronin hit homers for a 3–1 win in Detroit against Schoolboy Rowe. Rich's sidearm fast ball, and his "cagey manipulation of curves and change of pace" carried the day. Rich's roommate Ted Williams was 0-for-3, striking out his first three times up before drawing a walk. Rich said Ted had locked him out of their room the night before, and he struck back taking it out on the Tigers. Sportswriters looked on amused at the "friendly feud between these two great and temperamentally opposite rookies for command of their room."

The National League Boston Bees were also in first place. For the Red Sox, it had been a long time since 1918 and fans envisioned the first time in 21 years to have a chance to win the pennant.

May 6

LEFTY GROVE IS WINNER BY 5 TO 4. It was Grove's first win since the previous July 14 and gave the Red Sox their seventh win in a row. Cramer, Vosmik, and Foxx all singled to start the first. An error by Detroit's Chet Laabs allowed a run to score, and Cronin's infield out brought in another. The Tigers tied it in the second, but Vosmik's two-run homer (with Grove on base) gave Boston the lead in the fifth, and they added one more in the sixth on a single by Doerr, a walk to Grove, and a single by Cramer. They needed the extra run, as the Tigers scored once more in the bottom of the sixth and once again in the bottom of the ninth.

A photograph in the *Sunday Globe* showed a closeup of Ted Williams' hands gripping a bat. The caption read, in part, "It has been predicted that Williams will become the biggest hitting sensation since Babe Ruth."

May 7

Williams struck out three times in a row once again, but it was the three throwing errors by Tabor, Auker, and Galehouse that really aided the Tigers to score six runs and beat Boston, 6–3. The Red Sox fell a half-game behind the Yankees and into second place.

The loss, though, freed up the Red Sox to live life normally again instead of sticking slavishly to the routines that might or might have seen them through a seven-game winning streak. Cronin had insisted that Gerry Moore and A. Victor Stout ride in the cab, sitting in the same seats, always walking into the hotel elevator in the same order. Hugh Duffy no longer had to submit to Jimmie Foxx kissing him on the head after every win. Moe Berg wouldn't have to keep pitching batting practice every day. And Joe Vosmik wouldn't keep calling up Moore at "ungodly hours" to have breakfast with him, a tradition that the "Bashing Bohemian" initiated in Cleveland after getting four hits in a game.

May 8

The game at St. Louis was postponed due to rain. The Red Sox made a move nevertheless, though, with GM Eddie Collins purchasing backup outfielder Lou Finney from the Athletics for a bit over the $10,000 waiver price. Finney also offered protection at first base in the event Foxx needed to be out; Foxx called his former teammate a "hustling Alabama cotton picker" and said he seemed to be over the "delicate health" that had often troubled him. Cronin announced, "We're not in the market for any more deals. We're all set to go with the 25 men we have." Finney joined ex-A's Grove, Cramer, and Jack Wilson, too.

Despite not playing, the Red Sox regained first place because the Yankees lost their game.

Gerry Moore, writing in the *Globe*, saw the purchase "chalked up as another step in a budding campaign being waged by the 36-year-old millionaire Sox owner to build up a baseball empire to surpass the now outstanding Yankee system." He saw the Finney deal as the third and final transaction in strengthening the ballclub. First was getting Auker, Wade, and Morgan for Higgins and McKain. Second was trading Ben Chapman to get Galehouse and Tommy Irwin.

May 9

WILLIAMS RESCUES SOX WITH A HOMER. Seconds after the Sportsmans Park scoreboard posted the news that the Yankees had won and thereby retaken first place, Jimmie Foxx hit a three-run homer to give the Red Sox a 7–3 lead. But the Browns drove Bagby from the box and tied it up on a couple of homers. When the game went into extra innings, Ed Cole took over pitching for St. Louis and gave up singles to Joe Vosmik and Jimmie Foxx. Cronin whiffed, and up came Williams (0-for-5 on the day, twice striking out with the bases loaded.) Word was that Williams could be gotten out on high inside fastballs. Before the game, Cronin had denied he was going to bench Ted. Faith rewarded: on a 3–2 count, Ted hit a three-run homer that just cleared the roof in right. The Browns got one back off Boston pitching but when Joe Vosmik ran down Harland Clift's long fly ball, Cronin "fired his cap away and raced out to hug" him. The team flew to Chicago after the game in two American Airlines airplanes. They'd first flown, the same route, two years earlier, but it was still a rare occurrence. Ostermueller was the one who'd made the suggestion this time, though he'd been one of three who refused to travel by air in 1937. He'd been left behind during a switch of trains, and had to catch a plane to risk a fine. The experience converted him to air travel. Foxx, though, was airsick and declined the steak dinner.

May 10

Despite having rushed to Chicago, the Sox vs. Sox game in Chicago was called off due to rain. Moments after the postponement, the sun came out and "the afternoon burned off into as pretty a matinee as the Croninmen have seen during their entire trip." They took advantage and got in a "snappy workout." Word was the White Sox had some banged-up players who needed a little rest. Foxx hadn't eaten for 48 hours and needed rest, too. Joe Cronin was hit with a $10 fine for fraternizing with Charley Gehringer before the May 6 game in Detroit. "It's a silly rule," Joe grumbled. "Why, Charley and I just mentioned a new automobile he'd bought."

The Red Sox announced that the Memorial Day game against the Yankees was already sold out of reserved seats. Large numbers of items continued to arrive at League headquarters from old-time ballplayers as the request had gone out for items to stock the planned Baseball Hall of Fame.

May 11

Pitching in temperatures around 45 degrees, the veteran Ted Lyons dealt Woody Rich his first loss, in a 3–2 game in Chicago. Boston scored once in the first, when Williams hit a Texas Leaguer to drive in Foxx. Had Vosmik, who'd singled, not been cut down when Foxx missed on a hit and run play, it would have been a bigger inning. Chicago scored twice in the bottom of the first—and that was all the scoring until the White Sox got another in the eighth. Rich had been taken out in the eighth so Finney could pinch hit. It was Galehouse who gave up the third run in relief; a leadoff double kicked off the inning. A grounder moved the runner to third and he scored on a ball that accidentally bounced off Ollie Bejma's bat as he was ducking a pitch. It rolled to Doerr and a run scored. Boston got a run back in the top of the ninth, but fell one short. The Red Sox ended their Western road trip with a 7–2 W-L record, but dropped out of first place once more. The Bees fell out of first place, too.

May 12

On their way to Washington, the Red Sox played an exhibition game against the Louisville Colonels. Jake Wade came out of the bullpen to get a start and pitched a complete game 7–3 win. Williams hit the game's only homer. He also hit a 395-foot double. Louisville's star shortstop Pee Wee Reese looked good in the field for the Red Sox farm club. Chet Morgan had three hits, and both Paul Campbell and Fabian Gaffke had two, all making positive impressions on the Sox with whom they'd trained in Florida.

Lou Finney played first base for Foxx and was 2-for-5, flawless in the field. The Red Sox would have sent Jake Wade to Louisville where he could get more work, but couldn't get him through waivers so kept him with the parent club.

May 13

The first of three planned in Washington was rained out. This cost the Red Sox some revenue, since there had been a large advance sale "because of the growing conviction that the Back Bay Busters stand as real threats to the champion Yankees this year and a great build-up given Ted Williams." The advance sale had been larger than any other than a World Series or Opening Day game in Washington.

May 14

RED SOX RALLY FOR GROVE IN 12TH TO EDGE NATS, 5–4. It was 2–2 after seven innings, with Lefty Grove locked in a battle with Venezuela's Alex Alexandra. Cowboy Jim Tabor singled in the top of the 12th, and Bobby Doerr doubled him home. Gene Desautels doubled (when left fielder Johnny Welaj overran the ball) and so did Doc Cramer. It was 5–2, Red Sox. Grove was beginning to grow a blister, and tiring, so he was taken out of the game after getting one out but a walk, a single, and another single scored one run and put a runner on third. Cronin brought in Jack Wilson to relieve. A sacrifice fly made it 5-4. A walk put runners on first and second, so Cronin walked over from shortstop and waved in Joe Heving to take over from Wilson. Buddy Myer ran the count to 2-2, fouled off a couple, but then grounded harmlessly to Doerr at second base. Desautels had saved the game in the bottom of the 11th, expertly blocking the plate to squelch Welaj's attempted two-out steal of home plate.

Alexandra was born as Alex Carrasquel.

May 15

RED SOX PILE UP EXTRA BASE HITS TO ROUT SENATORS IN WINDUP OF BEST ROAD TRIP OF CRONIN REGIME. The eight-column headline stretched across the *Globe*'s first sports page. OSTIE HOLDS NATS IN 9-2 VICTORY read the story headline, and "Vosmik Makes Four Hits as Hose Show Signs of Batting Power" read the subhead. Vosmik's 4-for-4 day bumped his average up to .320, with a triple, a double, and two singles driving in two. He scored thrice. "Der Fritz" Ostermueller walked two and allowed eight hits, all singles. He'd now beaten the Senators in 16 of his last 21 starts. The Sox had five doubles and Vosmik's triple, and started piling up the runs early, leading 6-0 after three innings. The only two Sox to go hitless were Williams and Tabor.

The Red Sox road trip record was the same as the score of the day's game, 9-2.

May 16

RED SOX GIVE RICH PLENTY OF SUPPORT, Pile up 19 Hits For an 18 to 4 Win Over the White Sox. What more could you want to kick off a 15-game homestand?

Ted Williams, Woody Rich, and Lou Finney during the 1939 season.

They were Foxx-less, with Jimmie in St. Elizabeth's Hospital, but Vosmik drove in five more runs (with a 3-for-6 day) and Tabor matched those five (going 3-for-5). Doerr hit a homer, and both Cronin and Finney doubled twice. Williams was 2-for-4 with a double, coming off back-to-back hitless games. Foxx's condition was "acute exacerbation of a chronic sinusitis," and it was thought he might be out for a week. Finney filled in admirably. The Red Sox were hanging in just 1½ games behind the first-place Yankees.

May 17

HIT FAMINE FOLLOWS FEAST, SOX LOSE 6-3. To be precise, it was the Red Sox who lost, when the White Sox scored three times in the top of the 10th. Boston only had five hits all day, and Jack Wilson had only allowed three through the first nine frames. Come the 10th, though, four straight Chicago singles spelled defeat. All of Boston's runs came on a three-run home run off Joe Cronin's bat in the bottom of the fourth, giving the Red Sox a temporary 3-2 lead after Gee Walker's two-run homer in the top of the inning. It was a game filled with bench-jockeying, and even a complaint to the umpire about the way Lou Finney had taped his first-baseman's mitt. He was forced to use one of Foxx's.

May 18

Elden Auker won the game, 5-3, over Chicago but was carried from the field in the top of the eighth after Luke Appling's liner hit him on the instep and bounded up to hit him on the elbow. Ted Williams, who had gone hitless the day before and was 0-for-4 in this day's game, was pulled from right field in favor of Leo Nonnenkamp during the couple of minutes Auker was on the ground. Ted hadn't hit the ball out of the infield in either game. Doerr was 3-for-3 with a sacrifice to boot, but the deciding hit was Cronin's clutch triple that drove in both Finney and Vosmik in the bottom of the seventh. Complimenting the player-manager, first base coach Hugh Duffy called Cronin "the most old fashioned ball player" he'd seen in years.

Auker was expected to be OK, and drove himself home. Foxx was recovering more quickly than expected.

May 19

FOXX WATCHES RED SOX ROMP. Foxx was out of hospital and seated in a box seat, enjoying the game with the Friday afternoon Ladies Day crowd of 7,500. Williams was back in but dropped to batting seventh. Ted grounded to second his first time up, but then broke out with three hits and drove in two, as the Red Sox poled 16 hits to beat the Browns, 15-7. They were clearly more effective than St. Louis which rapped 15 hits off Jim Bagby, who went the distance for Boston. Tabor was the batting star, with a 4-for-5 day that included a home run and a double as he drove in four runs. Another Williams mental lapse in the field saw him throw his glove away after only two outs had been recorded in the top of the eighth; Ted had to go and collect the glove and put it back on. (In these days, fielders left their gloves on the field while up at bat.)

A photograph in the *Globe* showed four male students from Tufts who had entered the park dressed as women to gain free entry; it was said to be a fraternity initiation stunt.

May 20

RED SOX COLLAPSE IN SEVENTH INNING. Denny Galehouse's first start in a Red Sox uniform was a wasted opportunity, with Boston leading 5–3 after six innings. Jack Kramer went the distance for the Browns, benefiting from the five-run seventh inning. Poor defense cost Boston, and Galehouse was getting hit. Weaver came on in relief but only got one out; Dickman relieved him and let in another run with a wild pitch before retiring the side.

May 21

The Yankees won their 11th in a row, but Lefty Grove helped the Red Sox keep up by holding the Tigers to three runs, while hitting a home run of his own into the left-field screen to lead off the seventh inning. Bobby Doerr drove in three, and both Williams and Grove drove in two. Foxx was back, still under the weather, but managed to steal a base nonetheless, after singling. Tabor walked, putting runners on first and second. Doerr tried to bunt, but unsuccessfully—then crossed up the defense by hitting away, slapping a slow ball past third base to drive in both runners. Ted Williams "thereupon crashed another dead fish, a first pitch, into center to rescue Bobby."

May 22

The game against the Tigers was rained out, disappointing Cronin who'd seen his team flourishing while Detroit was floundering in last place. And the Red Sox now were looking ahead to 16 doubleheaders, 10 of them due to postponements. Hank Greenberg commented that Grove was harder to hit than when he'd relied on his blazing speed. "You could get set for his fast ball then."

After the first month of the season, Mel Webb discussed the "Three Musketeers" (Doerr in his second full year, Tabor, and Williams) and found that 55 of Boston's first 140 runs had been driven in by the trio of youngsters. They had a combined average of .312, with Tabor at .337, Doerr at .308, and Williams at .290. Williams had no errors in 39 chances, Doerr had just one in 140, but Tabor had made eight errors already at third base.

May 23

The Sox slipped another notch, to 4½ games behind New York, as the Yankees won their 12th in a row while the Tigers beat Boston (and Woody Rich), 7–2. Greenberg homered and doubled and drove in three runs. Foxx relapsed a bit with his sinus condition, and Finney had a 2-for-4 day. Johnny Peacock caught the game and was 3-for-4. Both teams had 11 hits, but the Tigers made theirs count for a lot more.

May 24

SINKER BALL TOO MUCH FOR SOX. Cleveland's Willis Hudlin threw a four-hitter and kept Boston from regaining a game on the Yankees, who'd finally dropped one—to the Tigers who, with back-to-back wins over Boston and now New York, inched out of the cellar. Hudlin even drove in the first two Indians runs with a double in the second inning and the last run with a homer in the eighth. Red Sox starter Jack Wilson was taken out of the game in the third inning, and Joe Heving finished it up. A collision at home plate landed Peacock in the hospital a day later.

May 25

Former Red Sox pitcher Red Ruffing earned his 200th career win for the Yankees, and Bob Feller one-hit the Red Sox while Elden Auker and Emerson Dickman were bombed, 11–0. The only hit the Red Sox got off Feller was Bobby Doerr's second-inning single, a clean hit to right field. Feller walked five and two other Bostons reached base on errors, but he struck out 10 and the Sox hitters were helpless. It was Feller's first win ever at Fenway. Cronin's men were in a bit of a doldrums.

May 26

RED SOX SHAKEUP MARKS 4 TO 2 WIN. Woody Rich became the first Red Sox starter to win four games, but had to leave the game in the eighth inning with what the next morning's paper called a "mysterious arm ailment." It was quickly diagnosed as a "strained bicep muscle" and it was thought he'd make his next start. Rich admitted he'd felt the pain back on the 23rd but not mentioned it. Doerr was put into the leadoff slot, Williams was moved back up to fifth, and Cronin dropped himself to sixth and Tabor to seventh. Cramer, batting second, had two doubles, as did Tabor. Foxx tripled. Attendance was "2600 paid, 2200 ladies." The Saturday afternoon paper more or less conceded the pennant to the Yankees: "Flag Race Looks Like Open Road for Yankees. A.L. Champions Are Too Classy." The Red Sox were still in second place, but 5½ games behind.

May 27

RED SOX GET SIX HOME RUNS. Win Two From Senators by 11–4 and 7–6. Foxx and Vosmik both homered in the first game; Vosmik drove in three, while Foxx, Williams, and pitcher Lefty Grove each drove in two. Both teams had 11 hits, but Washington scored far fewer runs.

"Mr. Williams was just about the whole show in the lamplighter's end of the program." Even though both Doerr and Cronin homered, too, "terrific Teddy's three-run round-tripper" was "easily the grand-daddy of the local season." It landed about 450 feet from the plate, a half-dozen rows up in the dead-center-field bleachers. Ted had six RBIs on the day, but the crowning blow of the day was Jolting Joe Vosmik's walkoff home run in the bottom of the ninth of the second game. It was 6–6 after 8⅓. Vosmik was the first man up in the bottom of the ninth, and he hit Pete Appleton's pitch over the Wall in left-center.

The sports page cartoon showed Ted doffing his cap to the fans and picking up his glove in the same motion.

May 28

SLUGGING SOX ROUT SENATORS, 12 TO 7. Williams, Cronin Clout Homers As Galehouse Gets First Win. The Red Sox beat the Senators for the seventh time in a row. Foxx drove in four, while Cronin and Williams drove in two apiece. Ted's homer went into the ramp entrance to the center-right-field bleachers. His two RBIs saw him tied for the league lead (32 in 30 games) with Taft Wright. Galehouse got his first win; Denny had come on in relief of Ostermueller as the Indians built up a 4–0 lead through three, a lead that was immediately wiped out by a six-run Red Sox bottom of the third. The Yankees arrived in town at 11 PM, ready to play the next day. Gehrig was on the trip, as was the still-ailing Joe DiMaggio, but their absence hadn't cost New York much: they were 27–6.

May 29

The Yankees made three errors ("and almost as many errors of omission"), and Yankees pitchers doled out nine bases on balls, but Boston only made three hits off Bump Hadley and Johnny Murphy and went down to a 6–1 defeat. Twice the Red Sox left the bases loaded, failing to score, leaving 10 runners on base in all. The Yankees' Bill Dickey ("one of the slowest runners in the business") even stole home as part of a double steal; Cronin's throw back to the plate struck catcher Desautels in the back and rolled all the way to the backstop, allowing Charley Keller to move up to third.

Bagby, Heving, and Wade all pitched. The only earned runs were the four scored off Bagby. Woody Rich remained unavailable; he couldn't even raise his arm about waist level, though X-rays were negative.

May 30

RED SOX WIN 8 TO 4, THEN LOSE 9 to 17. Williams Gets Fourth Homer in 4 Days. Fenway was sold out for the Memorial Day doubleheader and the Red Sox split with New York. Ted Williams hit one home run in each game; Cronin and Foxx both had one in the first game,

as Monte Weaver went the distance. The Red Sox scored four runs in the first off Red Ruffing, and three more in the second. Titanic Teddy hit "the longest home run ever witnessed at Yawkey Yard . . . like a meteor zooming out of the heavens the ball went steaming fully 75 feet up into the right center field stands, just to the left of the little alleyway that separates those open bleachers from the covered pavilion." It went out above a 402-foot sign on the wall.

Moe Berg played in his first game of the year, catching the second game (and batting 1-for-3, driving in Boston's first two runs). Cronin tried Wilson, Ostermueller, Heving, Dickman, and Wade in the nightcap, but they collectively gave up 17 runs on 17 hits, while the Sox hit safely 15 times but only scored nine. Eight walks by the Boston moundsmen did not help. The surprise of the day had been giving Weaver the start; heretofore, he'd only thrown 1⅓ innings of work.

After the game, both Foxx and Cronin came into the press box "instead of rush for the feed table" and let it be known that they felt they could well have won all three games, that they weren't intimidated by the Yankees. "There's no questioning the hitting ability of the Yankee individuals," commented Cronin. "But it is a fact that we drove the Yanks' leading pitchers, Ruffing, Pearson, and Hildebrand to cover—and made a very thorough job of it. It is a long season. Four months to go. It is still anybody's race."

May 31

An off day for the Red Sox. They took the 4:50 afternoon train to Detroit, though left Woody Rich at home because of his "heavily bandaged" sore arm. The Red Sox finished May in second place, 6½ games behind New York (which had won 19 of its last 20 games), and 2½ above third-place Cleveland. There was some thought that shortcomings in the Sox pitching staff could be laid at the feet of the catchers, and the team was reportedly looking for an experienced catcher but that they were not to be had.

A few days later, the *Globe* gave the Red Sox a "good hit, no pitch" label.

June 1

Elden Auker pitched against his former Detroit ballclub and held them to eight hits; despite giving up a three-run homer to Hank Greenberg in the bottom of the first, he held them to just two more runs the rest of the game, while the Sox piled up 14 runs on 18 hits. Jim Tabor hit three doubles, Cronin hit two doubles, and Foxx, Williams, and Doerr each hit one. Doerr hit a triple and a home run, too, lacking only the lowly single that would have completed the cycle. After the game, Ted Williams spent time in the hotel lobby soaking up stories from Harry Heilmann of the Tigers, who filled Ted in on some of the great hitters like Cobb and Speaker.

In New York, the Yankees announced that Lou Gehrig would go to the Mayo Clinic to try and determine why he was in such a weakened state. Gehrig said such a visit was "just another rumor."

Another oddity—the announcers at Boston's two ballparks (Fenway Park and National League Field) were both named Bill Daly—but not related—though the Bill Daly who announced for the Bees was also the scoreboard operator at Fenway. There was a dedicated telephone line to the scoreboard at Fenway, and the two Bill Dalys had spoken on the phone for three seasons—but never met.

June 2

Doc Cramer was 5-for-5 and Joe Cronin hit two home runs. The Red Sox had one more hit than the Tigers, but lost, 8–5. Galehouse was tagged with the loss, though the winning runs actually came in the three-run seventh on two errors while Jack Wilson was pitching and a home run by Tigers third baseman Pinky Higgins off Emerson Dickman.

June 3

Lefty Grove had already beaten the Tigers 56 times, but his scheduled start in Detroit was rained out by a cloudburst just prior to the game.

June 4

Jim Bagby Jr. faced Bob Feller and lost the first game of the doubleheader in Cleveland, 10–2, but Lefty Grove held the Indians to seven hits and one run, while Boston took the second game, 7–1. Between them, Bagby (11) and Wade (4) gave up 15 hits in the opener. Bobby Doerr wrenched his back in the second game, and had to come out. Tommy Carey came in to take over, made a couple of nice plays, and beat out an infield hit. Carey had hit .297 for the Hollywood Stars in 1938 and was described as "a player who has been through the mill without making quite the top grade, yet a fine competitor, a willing worker and a man whose presence in the lineup would in no way upset the general infield morale." He was content in his role as a reserve.

June 5

The Indians scored twice in the first and five times in the second, enough damage off Ostermueller and Weaver to win a 7–5 game, though the Red Sox inched close enough to make it interesting late—with one in the seventh, two in the eighth, and one more in the ninth. Earl Averill (HR, two doubles) and Ken Keltner each had three RBIs. Tom Yawkey was on hand and scoffed at arguments the Yankees should be forced to break up their team: "The Yankees spent money for years and took chances on players which other clubs refused to take a gamble on—and they have been winners. It's a great idea for somebody to tell a fellow to break down the business he has built

with some good luck, some good judgment, and some real gambling." Of course, Yawkey was hardly among the miserly magnates.

Several Red Sox fielders were upset at a league ruling that prohibited the way many players had strung lacing with knots to create a web in between the thumb and fingers of their gloves. A long story in the June 6 *Evening Globe* detailed the sorts of adaptations that were permissible and those that were not.

June 6

SOX WILT IN 8ᵀᴴ, BOW 8–7. Auker was cruising through seven innings, even had a home run to his credit, and Boston had a solid 7–2 lead. With a runner on first and one out, Jeff Heath lucked out by a broken-bat hit dropping in for a double, and the Indians ultimately added three more doubles, a triple, and some singles to tie the game in the bottom of the eighth, then win it in the bottom of the ninth on a double, an infield out that moved up the runner, and a sacrifice fly. The Sox had lost four of their last five.

Foxx was hitting an even .333, with seven homers and 32 RBIs. Williams led in runs batted in with 38 in the team's 39 games, and in homers with eight; he was batting .288. Cronin had 34 RBIs and seven homers, batting .289. Vosmik had an even 30 RBIs.

June 7

The game in St. Louis was rained out. Doerr was close to coming back and might have played had there been a ballgame.

June 8

PINCH HOMER BY FINNEY BRINGS SOX 8–7 VICTORY. They needed this one. The Red Sox had a 5–0 lead after three innings in St. Louis, with Foxx having homered twice in the first three frames. With two in fourth, two in the sixth, and three in the seventh, the Browns built a 7–5 advantage, driving out Galehouse, then Heving—though a wild throw by Tabor allowed the score to become tied. Three walks in a row by Heving forced in another run, and Dickman came on in relief. He promptly walked in the seventh St. Louis run. Boston got two in the eighth to tie it on Finney's home run while batting for Desautels, and Tommy Carey's double (Doerr started the game but had to come out partway through; X-rays proved negative, but another week's rest was prescribed) and two sacrifices (Cramer and Vosmik) won it. The scheduled second game was rained out before it got underway.

June 9

SOX CLIP BROWNS TWICE, GAIN GAME ON IDLE YANKS. Ostermueller's Blow in 8th Wins First, 4–3—Nightcap Is 18–7 Spree—Foxx Hits 2.

Gaining on New York was no big deal; the Red Sox

The Kid and The Beast (Williams and Foxx, likely talking hitting)

remained eight games out, but taking two (even from the last-place Browns—now 23 games behind after only 46 games played) still had to feel good. Bagby started the first game but gave up thee runs in the first inning, and Ostermueller took over from the second inning on. Foxx hit one home run in each game, for 11 on the season. Ted Williams hit one on the right-field roof in the second game. Ostey's blow was a "clean chop to left field" and drove in Cronin, who'd doubled, giving the Red Sox the 4–3 edge.

By the end of five innings, the Red Sox led game two 16–3 and Jack Wilson enjoyed a picnic of a game, even going 2-for-5 at the plate, driving in three runs. Williams was the RBI leader with six runs batted in, on the homer and two doubles. He led both leagues with 44 RBIs. Cramer was 3-for-4 in the first game, and 2-for-5 in the second, enjoying 21 hits in his last 41 times at bat.

June 10

For the second Saturday in a row, the Red Sox were rained out, this time in Chicago.

June 11

JIM TABOR HITS HOMER, TWO TRIPLES IN CHICAGO. It was a doubleheader, but that's still good production during a 4-for-8 twinbill. Tabor drove in four in the first game, and two in the second, though Boston lost the opener, 7–5, on Joe Kuhel's two-run homer in the bottom of the ninth off Lefty Grove. The Red Sox won the second game, 4–3, with Auker going the distance.

By finishing with a bit of a flourish, Boston was able to come home having taken six of 11 games on the road trip. Finney had gone 3-for-6 in pinch-hitting situations. The new regulations on gloves was finally published, and it really affected few except for a couple of first basemen who had strung "fishing nets" in their gloves.

June 12

A travel day on the train, and then a day off with a light 10:30 AM workout at Fenway on the 13th gave the Red Sox a break. Former Red Sox players Cy Young, Babe Ruth, and Tris Speaker, and Sox GM Eddie Collins were among the 11 players honored in Cooperstown in ceremonies celebrating what was declared the 100th anniversary of the invention of baseball.

Bagby and Galehouse were the disappointments on the mound. Williams was hitting better on the second road trip than the first—a good sign. He was still batting just .281, though his 45 RBIs placed him second in the league behind only Hank Greenberg. And Tabor, whose underhand throws across the diamond to Foxx were remarkably accurate, was living up to his potential. Woody Rich and Bobby Doerr were the two hurting players.

June 13

Just the afore-mentioned workout—which turned out not to be as light as advertised—filled the day for the Red Sox. Rich had won four games of his first six, and his loss was the biggest of the season to date. The *Globe*'s James C. O'Leary wrote, "With an improvement in the Red Sox pitching, they will be pennant contenders. They are still in the race." Rich did some throwing on the side and reported feeling good.

June 14

SOX BEATEN TWICE BY TIGERS, 9–8, 6–2. It was not the way they wanted to start the homestand. "Boston Pitching Staff Crumbles" read a subhead. The Red Sox actually had an 8–4 lead in the first game after four innings, but Bagby was chased without recording an out in the top of the fifth, and Dickman allowed three runs to score in the seventh, enough to win the game. Dizzy Trout held Boston to just six hits in the second game, even picking up the game again after a 55-minute rain delay. Newsom finished the game. The *Evening Globe*'s banner sports page headline read "Red Sox' Very Wobbly Pitching Endangers Second Place Spot."

June 15

Pete Fox hit a grand slam off Jack Wilson and the Red Sox faced a four-run deficit in the top of the first inning from which they never recovered. Wilson then pitched well for the rest of the game, with Dickman taking over for the final two innings, but the final was 6–3 Tigers.

June 16

The Tigers completed a four-game sweep at Fenway, breaking a 3–3 tie with five runs in the top of the fourth and then withstanding a four-run Red Sox rally in the bottom of the seventh.

June 17

The stretch of postponed Saturday games became three in a row, when the game in Boston was called off due to wet grounds and threatening weather; the result was a Sunday doubleheader against the Indians. Boston held to a slim half-game lead over the Indians for second-place standing. Ostermueller had pitched quite well two times in reliefs and won a role back in the starting rotation.

Joe Cronin's contract was due to expire at the end of the 1939 season and there were rumors of his return to Washington. Yawkey had sunk an estimated $4,000,000 into the Red Sox at this point; he expressed complete satisfaction with Cronin and said that he could stay with the Red Sox as long as he might want.

"What's wrong with the Red Sox?" asked the *Globe*. "Loss of Rich and Doerr Big Cause of Sox Dive" was the headline. Cronin saw it as a slump, pure and simple, "a normal condition in baseball. Teams have been in slumps before I came into baseball and teams will slump long after I've left baseball." He rued losing Rich, and wasn't sure when he might be able to return. He didn't want to rush him. As to Doerr, he said that Carey had filled in very nicely and he had no complaints whatsoever, but "Doerr just happens to be one of the best infielders in the league. Bobby is not only brilliant defensively but he's a dangerous man at that plate. Any team who loses such players as Rich and Doerr can hardly help but go into a tailspin."

June 18

WILLIAMS' 2-BAGGER DUMPS INDIANS, 5–3. Smash Unloads All Bases in Finale—Finney's Pinch Hit Wins 1st, 5–4. The Sox swept two from the visiting Indians. First things first, Lou Finney hit a pinch double in the bottom of the eighth to break the 4–4 tie Cleveland had just achieved by scoring twice in the top of the eighth. Peacock was on second after a walk and Ostermueller's sacrifice bunt. Batting for Carey, Finney doubled to left-center field. Ostey held the Tribe scoreless in the ninth and got the win. In the second game, Cleveland scored three times in the first. Tabor hit a solo homer in the third. An error, then a single by Tabor, and a squeeze bunt by Gene Desautels earned another in the fourth. In the fifth, Cramer reached on a one-out infield hit. Vosmik singled, putting runners on first and third. Foxx was walked intentionally to get to the rookie Ted Williams, who hadn't a hit yet in either game. Ted hit a three-RBI double into left-center. Lefty Grove got the victory. The games were enjoyed by a Sunday sellout crowd. "We can't get any more people in here," declared executive Phil Troy.

June 19

The Sox had a day off, and brought in a very few players for a light workout, including Doerr (Cronin was encouraged by how he was progressing) and Woody Rich (whose arm seemed to offer hope of coming back.) Cronin also had Bagby in to try and work on his control problems; Bagby hadn't won a game since May 19 and won that one despite giving up 15 hits.

June 20

VOSMIK DRIVES IN THREE RUNS FOR THE RED SOX. Elden Auker pitched very well, allowing the Browns just one run, but the story was Vosmik on offense. He stroked two singles and two triples, 4-for-4 on the day with three RBIs. Williams and Foxx each drove in two in the 8–1 win.

You can't tell the players even with a program? The *Globe* reported that the jersey numbers worn by Browns players were all mixed up, "so the fans got very little information by reference to the scorecards."

Yankees president Ed Barrow read a statement, explaining that Lou Gehrig had played his last game, a victim of amyotrophic lateral sclerosis, "Lou Gehrig's disease." It was the lead headline in the *Boston Evening Globe*: GEHRIG IS PARALYSIS VICTIM.

June 21

KRAMER, A ROOKIE PITCHER, SETS RED SOX DOWN 6 TO 0. The Sox would later acquire Jack Kramer. Their initial impression was the shutout dealt them by the Browns' new hurler, despite the 10 hits they achieved. Joe Heving started for Boston and was driven early from the box.

June 22

WILSON HAS STUFF AND RED SOX WIN. Joe Cronin decided to assign himself the leadoff slot in the batting order, but it was the very good game thrown by Jack Wilson (six hits for St. Louis) combined with a couple of RBIs each by Foxx and Tabor that made the 7–3 win a fairly easy one.

June 23

The game against the White Sox was postponed due to rain.

June 24

It was a "most humiliating 14-to-6 setback" in the first game hosting the White Sox. The star of the game was Chicago pitcher John "Footsie" Marcum, who allowed 13 hits to Boston batters but held down the score—and drove in four runs to help his own cause, with three singles. He baffled Ted Williams, who was 0-for-5 on the afternoon, though one ball that looked certain to reach the right-field bleachers was visibly blown back in at the 402-foot mark for a long fly out. The Kid "roamed all over his right field patrol to retire the side in the sixth." He ended the day with five putouts. Bagby gave up five runs in the top of the second, and Galehouse let another two in before the inning concluded.

June 25

A doubleheader against the White Sox was rained out.

June 26

GROVE HOLDS NATS TO SEVEN SINGLES. In Washington, Lefty Grove won his seventh game of the season with a shutout of the Senators. Ted Williams doubled and tripled and drove in two of Boston's three runs. Boze Berger starred on defense, and drove in the first—and winning—run for the Red Sox. Berger was playing third base because Jim Tabor was suspended by the team, "sent home for breaking training rules." Translated, this probably means he was hungover. Tabor was sent back to Boston. "He has been disciplined before for a similar offense," remarked the *Globe*. "He had been admonished to watch his step, but it appears he did not heed the advice." As for Berger, James C. O'Leary said, he "did surprisingly well and looks like a better ball player than he has generally been given credit for." It was his first start and he was "as cool as ice." Williams was 4-for-4.

June 27

AUKER SMEARS SENATORS AS RED SOX GET 8 RUNS. Auker pitched in with a shutout of his own. Finney played first for Foxx, who was sick in bed with a high temperature, and doubled twice and singled, driving in three of Boston's eight runs.

June 28

The game in Washington was rained out, and the ballclub returned to Boston. Foxx was taken from the train on a stretcher and delivered to St. Elizabeth's Hospital for observation. In the meantime, the Yankees continued to win with 23–2 and 10–0 victories over Philadelphia, extending their lead over the second-place Red Sox to 12½ games.

June 29

After their disastrous dual defeats at the hands of the Yankees the day before, Connie Mack's A's did some hitting of their own, punching out 17 hits off a quartet of Red Sox pitchers (Wilson, Galehouse, Bagby, and Heving) and took the game, 8–6. Ted Williams hit his 10th home run of the year, slammed off the seats in straightaway center so hard it bounded 100 feet back onto the field.

June 30

Philadelphia planned to play the Red Sox in Boston, but the game was rained out. Bobby Doerr, out of action for four weeks with a wrenched back, was due to return on July 1. Foxx was discharged from the hospital. Red Sox were set to host the Yankees for three games starting July 1, but trailed them by 13½ games (still holding second place) in the standings.

July 1

Four Red Sox were named to the All-Star Game squad: Lefty Grove, Jimmie Foxx, Joe Cronin, and Roger Cramer.

There is a reference in the July 1 *Globe* to "likable Ted Williams who won myriads of additional friends by his wholesome act towards the bed-ridden Roxbury youngster." The paper was referring to Ted's kindness toward young Donald Nicoll. The 12-year-old's appendix had burst, and doctors believed there was no hope he would survive. Nicoll's father, a real sports fan, reached out to Ted Williams and was thrilled he said he'd visit Donald. Years later, Donald, who survived, recalled asking his dad, "Who's he?" Ted befriended the family and visited them for at least a couple of years afterward.

OSTIE'S STUFF HAS YANKEES BAFFLED. New York got eight hits, but Ostermueller pitched a complete game 5–3 win over New York, knocking one game off their 13½ game lead. Cronin drove in two, as did Doerr. Bobby was 3-for-4. Williams scored two runs, one of them after a triple into Fenway's right-field corner.

July 2

SOX SPLIT WITH YANKEES AS INJURIES FELL THREE. The two games "turned out to resemble a minor war" as Lefty Grove won the first game, 7–3, and then lost, 9–3. Elden Auker only lasted three innings, by which time New York had a 6–1 lead. Joe Cronin drove in two runs in each game, a two-run homer in the first. Tommy Henrich was lost to the Yankees in the first game, crashing into Fenway's right-center-field wall in a futile effort to grab Ted Williams' home run, which broke open a 3–3 tie in the seventh inning. He had a concussion with lacerations and was held overnight at St. Elizabeth's. It was Henrich's second collision of the game; back in the top of the first inning, he had collided with Boston catcher Gene Desautels and knocked him unconscious at home plate. Though out cold, Desautels held onto the ball and Henrich was out. Desautels took the rest of the day off and Johnny Peacock caught both games.

Bobby Doerr, just back from a month out of action, was initially though to have a broken arm after being hit hard on the elbow by a Lefty Gomez ball. He was hit hard enough he had to leave the game for X-rays.

Lou Gehrig was traveling with the Yankees and between games Tom Yawkey came out to shake his hand near home plate, triggering a loud ovation.

July 3

No game was scheduled; the Red Sox prepared to take on the Athletics in an Independence Day doubleheader, with Rich and Dickman the starters. Joe Vosmik stayed behind, rather than travel with the ballclub, as the Vosmiks expected a child at any moment.

July 4

RED SOX CRUSH THE A's MAKING 35 RUNS ON 35 HITS. Tabor Equals Two Home Run Records. It was to be an interesting debut for Eddie Collins, Jr., playing left field for Philadelphia against his father's team, but it was completely overshadowed by the scoring—and the Athletics didn't do badly at the plate, either. In fact, the A's scored seven runs in the first game and 12 in the second. Normally, that would be enough but the scores were 17–7 and 18–12. Emerson Dickman started the second game and was staked to a 10–0 lead, but saw the game get tied up before Boston eventually prevailed.

Cowboy Jim Tabor hit one homer in the first game and three in the second—two of the latter being grand slams. The only other man to have hit two grand slams in a game was Tony Lazzeri. And previously only Earl Averill and Jimmie Foxx had hit four in a day. Tabor had 11 RBIs on the day; his second grand slam was an inside-the-park one. Tabor said he was using a different bat than the one he'd been using, a lighter-weight bat than his Ben Chapman model, "one I snitched from Ken Keltner."

Needless to say, Boston pitching didn't have its proudest day. It was his first start since May 26, but Woody Rich didn't even last the first inning. But the fireworks off the Boston bats ruled supreme. Collins pinch-hit in the first game, and fouled out to the catcher on the first pitch he saw. Collins came into the second game as a pinch runner, scored, and played the rest of the game, 1-for-3 with a single, and stole a base, but with all the hitting, he didn't even make the game story until the evening edition.

July 5

Jim Tabor hit another homer to help the Red Sox beat the A's, 6–4, behind the pitching of Auker, Bagby, and the last-minute squelching of a rally by Fritz Ostermueller. Lou Finney, filling in while Joe Vosmik Jr. was being born, had two hits in each one of the three games in Philadelphia. The Red Sox were now 20–8 on the road, but only 18–17 at home. They moved on to take on the Yankees for a five-game series.

July 6

Ted Williams had hit .500 over the last nine games, boosting his average to .302, and *Globe* writer Gerry Moore lamented that it was a mistake not to have named him to the All-Star team. Ted visited his father's three sisters who lived in Mt. Vernon, New York.

July 7

DICKMAN COOLS YANKEES WITH GREAT RELIEF JOB. Jake Wade started the game and left after 5⅓ innings just after the Yankees had tied it up, 3–3. In came "the Buffalo adonis" Dickman with men on second and third and only one out. He walked Keller intentionally, then struck out both Dahlgren and Ruffing. And held New York scoreless for 3⅔. With one out in the eighth, Williams singled, Cronin walked, and Vosmik was hit by a pitch. Tabor hit a ball to shortstop that could have been a double play, but Crosetti was playing a little deep and Tabor's speed just earned him the base as Williams scored what would prove the winning run.

July 8

SOX TAKE YANKEES TWICE FOR FIRST DOUBLE DEFEAT. As he had the previous Sunday, Ostie beat the Yankees—this time at the Stadium. And Denny Galehouse won the second game. In both cases, their games were said to be "the greatest performances of their respective careers." Ostie allowed four hits in a 3–1 first game win, and Galehouse allowed five in the 3–2 nightcap. There wasn't an extra-base hit among them. The Red Sox never trailed in either game, but both were obviously tight ones. It was pitching under hot and humid conditions, wearing the flannels, and Ostermueller in particular was noted as having a "uniform saturated with perspiration and appearing on the verge of collapse." The Yanks only got one runner past first base off him.

Foxx's home run in the top of ninth gave the Sox a 3–1 lead in the second game, and Galehouse walked Henrich leading off the bottom of the ninth. Joe DiMaggio singled off Tabor's chest. Bill Dickey hit the ball to Doerr at second, who retired Joe D. Doerr made a brilliant stop on Keller's drive and got Dickey at second as Henrich scored. Had the Yankees not already had three players tossed out of the game, they could have called on Joe Gordon to pinch hit. Or Jake Powell. But they had to use Billy Knickerbocker and he hit a "harmless short fly to Teddy Williams, who after making the final putout, did a snake dance through the spectators who stormed on the field in order to throw his arms around Galehouse."

July 9

SOX SWEEP 5-GAME YANKEE SERIES. It was a front page banner headline in the morning *Globe*. "Win 4–3, 5–3 on Homers by Cronin, Foxx" read the subhead. The Sox had indeed taken five in a row from New York, cutting the Yankees' league lead to striking distance: 6½ games. Boston came from behind in both games, Cronin's two-run homer in the top of the eighth won the first game off Monte Pearson after Pearson had walked Williams intentionally. Cronin had already tripled in Boston's second run his previous time up. Dickman allowed just two hits in the last three innings.

Auker gave up one run in the first, and after giving up two solid singles in the second, Jack Wilson was brought on in relief, and later, so was Joe Heving. Wilson got the win.

July 10–11–12 All-Star Break

There was a larger-than-usual advertisement for Wheaties in the July 11 *Globe*, depicting Cronin, Tabor, Williams, Foxx, and Ostermueller, reviewing the five-game sweep and attributing it, of course, to their consumption of the Breakfast of Champions. One expects that General Mills didn't run the same ad in the New York newspapers.

On the first of July, the Yankees had led by 13½ games. Their lead had been cut by more than half. "They can be had!" crowed Joe Cronin. "They opened a wicked lead on us there, but if we can knock off half of it in a week, why can't we wipe out the rest in three months?"

On July 11, the American League won the All-Star Game, played at Yankee Stadium, 3–1. Doc Cramer played right field, and was 1-for-4. Cronin was 1-for-4 at shortstop. Neither figured in the scoring. Bob Feller got the win.

On July 12, there was an Old Timers Game planned at Fenway Park, sponsored by the Veterans of Foreign Wars to help needy ballplayers. Hopes were that Hooper, Speaker, and Lewis would play in the game, reuniting the great Red Sox outfield of the teens. They did. Joe Wood hit a homer over the left-field wall. Bill Carrigan was in attendance, but did not play since he had hurt his back saving two people from drowning a couple of days before. Others with Red Sox background in the game included Dick Hoblitzell, Chick Shorten, Walter Lonergan, Bill Barrett, Jimmy Collins, Eddie Collins, Stuffy McInnins, Hal Janvrin, Larry Gardner, Herb Pennock, Jack Barry, Freddy Parent, Ray Collins, and Buck O'Brien. The game also featured Walter Johnson, Grover Cleveland Alexander, Fred Mitchell, Fred Tenney, Home Run Baker, Howard Ehmke, Chief Bender, Ed Walsh, and a host of others.

71-year-old Jack Ryan played catcher and second base in the Old Timers Game. The 71-year-old was 1-for-4 at the plate and "put up a great game in both positions and did some fine stickwork."

Monte Weaver was optioned to Louisville.

July 13

The Red Sox were riding an eight-game winning streak that took them from 12½ games out of first place on July 3 to just 5½ games out after the close of play on the 13th. The team rolled into Cleveland for a scheduled 10 PM (!) game at Municipal Stadium. ["Boston time" was an hour different from Cleveland time in 1939.] Tabor, Doerr, Williams, and Peacock all had experience playing under arc lights, but Cronin, Foxx, and Vosmik had not. They expected to face Bob Feller, who had thrown a one-hitter in his previous night game start.

The "baptism under the bulbs" began well for the Red Sox, scoring five times in the fourth inning and driving Mr. Feller from the field. It all started when a Tabor fly ball was lost in the lights and dropped safely. An infield hit by Peacock and a single by Sox starter Jack Wilson brought in the first run. Doerr's liner to left scored Peacock—and got away from Jeff Heath. Cramer singled in Doerr, Foxx moved Cramer to third with a single, and Feller was taken out of the game. Williams scored Cramer on a deep sacrifice fly. But the Indians tied it with five runs in the bottom of the ninth, driving out both Wilson and Dickman. Mel Harder came on to pitch the 10th for Cleveland and got Williams. Cronin walked, though, and stole second as Vosmik struck out. Sliding into second with great force, Cronin lay on the ground looking "lifeless" for nearly a full minute and the "entire Boston bench rushed out on the field to see what was ailing their skipper." Cronin got up and brushed himself off, staying in the game. The Indians walked Tabor intentionally, but then Harder couldn't find his way back to the strike zone and walked Peacock, too. Lou Finney batted for Heving and singled in a run, which held up when Rich retired the side in the bottom of the 10th, and the Red Sox had their ninth win in a row. It was the third game Finney had won as a pinch-hitter.

Ten Red Sox batters had struck out in the game that took nearly three hours to play. Both Cronin and Yawkey expressed their dislike of night baseball. Yawkey made it sound like he was dead-set against it, but the next day relented a bit: "I don't want it myself, but if the public wants it, there's nothing I can do but give it to them."

The winning run scored at 12:45 AM. Shortly after they got back to the hotel, some 20 awnings were destroyed in a fire that woke up several of the players at 2:30 at their Cleveland hotel. Elden Auker broke into one of the rooms where the awnings were on fire and put it out with a fire extinguisher, clad in his pajamas. "Someone made the crack that the Red Sox were so hot that they set the hotel on fire."

Cronin said, before the game, "I don't wish to talk about the pennant, but I will say . . . we have shown that the Yankees aren't the invincible team they have been cracked up to be. It's the Yankees and not the Red Sox who are on the spot . . . ."

July 14

An off-day for the Red Sox. The Red Sox began to lose ground in the standings once more, though they crept back to 5½ back on August 10 before fading yet again.

July 15

WILLIAMS PUTS RED SOX OVER FOR 10 IN ROW. For the second game in a row, the Red Sox jumped out to a five-run lead and then blew it. This time they scored all five in the first inning on a series of walks, singles, and Cleveland errors. Johnny Broaca replaced Willis Hudlin and pitched 7⅓ innings of relief, allowing just two singles. In the meanwhile, the Indians scored three times in the third and twice more in the fifth. Ostermueller was driven out in the fifth, and then it was Dickman's turn to pitch exceptional scoreless relief. The Sox finally got to Broaca in the eighth for a pair, the first coming on a long Ted Williams home run (his 13th of the season), and two more in the ninth for a 9–5 victory. Greenberg had 17 homers, Foxx had 14 (as did both Gordon and Selkirk of the Yankees), and Ted had 13. Williams led both leagues with 71 runs batted in.

July 16

RED SOX TAME DETROIT TIGERS, 9 TO 2, 3 TO 0. Almost 50,000 fans in Detroit saw the "sleepy Tigers" drop two, as the Red Sox ran their streak to 12 straight. It was their third consecutive doubleheader sweep. They had closed the gap to six games behind the Yankees. Lefty Grove won his ninth game with a six-hitter in the first. His catcher, Red Desautels, led the RBI list with three. Only a spectacular catch in the eighth inning kept him from getting two more. The Tigers committed an astonishing 12 errors on the day, eight in the first game alone. (The Tigers still held onto their major league single game record—12 errors, back in 1901.) Denny Galehouse was stingier with the hits, allowing just four, while shutting out Detroit. He'd won four of the 12 games in the Sox streak, after losing his first three games of the year and seemingly unable to work well in relief.

July 17

Despite being staked to a 2–0 lead by Ted Williams' 14th home run of the year, the disappointing Woody Rich continued to disappoint, driven from the mound during a six-run third inning as the Tigers snapped Boston's win streak with a 13–6 victory. Mike Higgins ran over Joe Cronin on the basepaths; Cronin stayed in the game but in the later innings took himself and several other regulars out of the game.

Columnist Victor O. Jones credited the spectacular Sox winning streak to the demotion of Jim Bagby to the minors. After winning 15 games in his rookie year, Bagby experienced a true sophomore slump. Expected to be the ace, he "couldn't lick anyone unless he had a 10-run backing." Jones felt that showing Bagby was expendable served as a wakeup call to the other pitchers, and they responded.

Bill Sayles debuted for the Red Sox after both Rich and Heving were battered about. He came into a difficult situation and pitched pretty well for four innings. "I was as nervous as a newlywed," he said after the game. "I really was scared stiff. It took me a couple of innings to get my curve ball to break . . . .To tell you the truth, I don't know who I pitched to, with one exception. I could pick out Greenberg."

July 18

The Red Sox were going for their fourth doubleheader sweep in a row, but that string was broken as well. After beating the White Sox, 13–10, in the first game, they dropped the nightcap, 8–5. The powerful trio of Ted Williams, Jimmie Foxx, and . . . Elden Auker (?) hit home runs in the opener, where the hits came early and often. The score was 9–7, Boston, after just 2½ innings. Auker, in fact, never made it past the first inning, officially; he was taken out in the bottom of the second before recording an out. He came back in late relief in the second game, and was roughed up for two more runs. Ted was the offensive star, with six hits and four RBIs; with 77 RBIs, Ted was now eight runs batted in ahead of second-place Greenberg. There were no stars among the pitchers, though Heving gave the best account. He only gave up two runs. Dickman, like Auker, worked in both games. Not that it helped. Auker was in a rough stretch; even during Boston's 12-game winning streak, he'd been knocked out of the box all three starts.

July 19

The White Sox took two from the Red Sox, 4–1 and 8–0. Only Foxx's 17th homer prevented a double shutout. Jake Wade could have used some run support in the first game. Boston had now, rather quickly, dropped back to nine games behind the Yanks. Hy Hurwitz said their play was "lackadaisical" and that they "played as if they had no chance to catch up." Finney's pinch-hit streak stopped at six, with one out in both games.

July 20

Chicago took four of the five games with a 4–0 shutout of the Red Sox, getting all four runs in the first inning off Denny Galehouse who left after retiring only two batters. Thornton Lee became the first left-hander to win against the Red Sox all year. Boston batters had nine hits, but hit into four doubleplays. Auker swore he'd go the distance the first game in St. Louis.

July 21

Auker didn't go the distance—but he almost made it through the third inning. When he left, the Browns held a 4–0 lead. The Sox worked their way back, though, tying the game in the ninth on Foxx's triple and Williams' single, then won it, 6–5, in the 11th when Ostermueller led with a single and Doerr singled. Cramer tried to bunt them over but failed twice, saw Ostie picked off at second, then struck out. Foxx singled off the pitcher's glove to load the bases. Williams banged one that struck the first-base bag, then the first baseman's glove, and caromed to the second baseman, who—rather than hold the ball—threw to first base. It was Ted's fourth single in a row. The moment Doerr saw the throw was going to first base, he bolted for home with the run that won it to the disappointment of the 714 fans who'd come to watch their hometown St. Louis Browns.

July 22

WILSON GOES DISTANCE BEATING BROWNIES, 6–3. Red Sox batters drove 14 hits, two each by Doerr, Finney, Cronin, Vosmik, Tabor, and Peacock—who was the only one with two RBIs. Jack Wilson gave up half as many hits and allowed half as many runs, despite a shaky start. He gave up all three runs in the eighth, but with a 6–3 lead still in place, Cronin kept him in the game and—for the second time in the game—was bailed out when Browns right fielder Myril Hoag hit into a double play.

Cramer had hurt his thumb badly in the July 21 game, and while there was no fracture, he was also nursing a cold so Cronin gave him the day off and put him on an earlier train back home.

July 23

SOX BOMB BROWNS TWICE, GAIN GAME AS YANKS SPLIT. The Red Sox concluded "their greatest road trip of all time" with 13–5 and 11–3 wins over St. Louis. They'd taken 17 of 22 on the long road trip, and were back to 7½ behind New York. They'd picked up five games during the course of the three-week excursion. The 24 runs and 31 hits included homers by Foxx, Williams, and Doerr. Doerr had seven hits on the day, four in the first game and three in the latter. Ted led the day with five RBIs, though Bobby had four and so did Foxx. Heving and Dickman were the two winning pitchers, in relief of Rich and Wade respectively. St. Louis had scored two runs in the first inning of each game, but the two relievers did their jobs, Heving throwing four full frames and Dickman throwing 7⅔. With more than two months left in the season, the Red Sox returned home with a "touch of pennant fever" according to the July 24 *Evening Globe* headline.

July 24

The Bosox returned home from the long road swing and prepared to play five against the visiting White Sox, hoping to turn the tables in back-to-back doubleheaders against the only team that gave them a hard time on the road.

July 25

With a 1:30 start for the first game, the *Globe*'s evening edition was able to inform readers with the headline SOX WIN, 3–2, CRONIN STAR. The next morning, readers learned RED SOX BEAT CHISOX TWICE; FOXX GETS HOMERS 20, 21. Lefty Grove won the first game. Boston broke a 2–2 tie when Williams tripled off the right-field wall, missing a homer by inches, and then came home on Cronin's double. Cronin had homered for Boston's first run. The second game saw Galehouse start and go 7⅔

innings, but the White Sox took a 5–3 lead in the eighth and he had to be replaced. With one out in the bottom of the ninth, Doerr homered. Finney hit a vicious liner, but it was caught for the second out. Foxx homered to tie the game. Cronin led off the bottom of the 10th with a walk, and Joe Vosmik's bunt was so good that he reached base safely, too. Tabor fouled out twice, trying to bunt the baserunners along, then gave up and singled to score Cronin standing up with the winning run.

"Nonchalant Ted had acted the villain twice" allowing two of the White Sox runs to score, but was only charged with one error.

July 26

FOXX GETS 2 HOMERS DRIVING IN 5 RUNS. The Red Sox lost the first game, though, 8–1, with Wilson and Wade both victims of aggressive White Sox batters. Chicago touched up Ostermueller and held a 5–1 lead after 4½ in the second game, with Foxx's homer accounting for the lone Red Sox run. He doubled in two more in the fifth, hitting the center-field wall, then homered over everything in left-center to tie it up in the bottom of the

Desautels with Williams and Doerr

eighth. Foxx had driven in all five runs. Chicago loaded the bases with nobody out in the top of the ninth. Heving struck out Gee Walker and fielded a ball hit back to him, starting a 1-2-3 double play. In the bottom of the ninth, Desautels singled. With two outs, Doerr singled and advanced Desautels to third. Finney, who had three hits on the day, added a fourth single and won the game. It was the seventh time that Finney had either tied or won a game for the Red Sox. For Heving, it was his fifth win in relief in his last nine jobs in relief. Foxx now had

23 homers, five more than any other major league batter. Williams, Finney, and Vosmik were all credited with "sensational catches."

July 27

Ted Williams was checked for possible appendicitis, but seemed OK and took part in the game. And went 2-for-3 with a triple, while making three more "sensational running catches"—all in the sixth inning. Foxx hit another homer, but the White Sox won, 12-7, with two runs in the eighth and four in the ninth. Galehouse bore the loss, in relief.

July 28

The lowly Browns, already 39½ games out of first place, and arriving in Boston with a 10-game losing streak, beat Boston 11-6, with "the inept Elden Auker" giving up seven runs in the first two innings and losing another one. Though the Sox closed the gap to 7-6, St. Louis added insurance runs in each of the final three innings.

July 29

The Red Sox dropped another one to the Browns, 4-3, with St. Louis scoring all of its runs in the fourth. The Red Sox scored twice in the seventh, and looked ready for a big inning in the eighth when Williams and Cronin both singled, then advanced to second and third on a balk by pitcher John Whitehead. The only problem was that home plate umpire Johnny Quinn at first affirmed but, after a strong protest by several Browns, overruled Bill McGowan and declared that the fake to first was no balk, sending the runners back. Needless to say, the "lantern-jawed local leader" (that would be Joe Cronin) had to have his say, too, "and the only wonder from his aroused appearance is that the Sox skipper didn't swing on the arbiter." After seven minutes of disruption, play resumed and Vosmik sacrificed the two forward. Whitehead walked Tabor. Leo Nonnenkamp was sent up to pinch hit for Ostermueller, but when Browns manager Fred Haney brought in a lefty, Cronin pulled Nonnenkamp and sent up Boze Berger, who struck out on three pitches. Tommy Carey was hit by a pitch, forcing in the only run the Red Sox got. Doerr flied out.

July 30

FOXX DRIVES IN FOUR RUNS IN SOX VICTORY. Jimmie hit a homer (# 25), a double, and a single. Desautels and Doerr each drove in runs, and the Red Sox won, 6-4, over the Browns, with Galehouse (relieved by Dickman) getting the win.

July 31

There was no game scheduled.

The Red Sox were considering bringing part of the right-field wall closer to help Ted Williams hit more homers. Though leading the league in runs batted in, he was far more effective on the road. At 402 feet, Fenway's right field was the deepest in the league. The trouble the Sox were having, though, really came from the "uncertainty of the pitching."—Victor O. Jones

August 1

A Bob Feller/Lefty Grove matchup saw Feller fold in the fifth as the Red Sox scored four times on their way to a 7-5 win. Leadoff batter Bobby Doerr hit a home run on the third pitch he saw, and added a two-out grand slam in the fifth inning. Feller threw six innings, and only surrendered five hits, but four of the five were for extra bases and he left with the score 6-3.

August 2

The Sox and Indians swapped wins with Cleveland taking the first game, 8-2, and Boston the second, 5-4. Jimmie Foxx drove in both Red Sox runs in the opener, but seven runs in the top of the fifth drove out starter Johnny Wilson (who walked two and allowed a two-run double), reliever Emerson Dickman (who gave up three singles and a double), and reliever Jake Wade, who saw an inherited runner score on a sacrifice fly before retiring the side. Woody Rich opened the nightcap and threw 5⅓ innings, with Joe Heving getting the win in relief when Boston scored twice in the bottom of the eighth for a come-from-behind win. Finney singled, advanced on an error, and Foxx doubled him in. Williams walked, and Cronin bunted both runners up a base. Vosmik was walked. Tabor hit a grounder that saw Foxx out at the plate, but Tom Carey batted for Peacock and beat out an infield single as Williams scored the go-ahead run. Doerr had a 16-game hitting streak going; Williams hadn't had a hit for four straight games.

The *Evening Globe* featured a cartoon honoring Lou Finney. In his first 10 pinch-hitting assignments in 1919, he'd reached base nine times (six of them with base hits) and in six of the 10 times, he had driven in either the tying or winning run. When acquired on May 7, he'd been hitting .095 (2-for-21). His average was now up to .331. Finney credited coach Hugh Duffy, who told him he wasn't bringing his bat back far enough. Adjustment made, Finney started hitting.

After a strong first month, it was Rich's failure to win that "has wrecked the Cronin pitching staff."

August 3

RED SOX WALLOP THE INDIANS. The Sox scored nine times in the bottom of the eighth, building on their 9-6 lead. Some 19 Sox hits and a "county fair fielding exhibition by Cleveland's Indians" enlivened a Ladies Day crowd which additionally welcomed 1,000 conventioneers from the Disabled Veterans. Cleveland was tagged with six errors, and all nine eighth-inning runs were unearned. Joe Cronin doubled twice in the inning. Williams broke into the hit column with a high fly single that dropped in among three fielders right behind third base, but drove in two and scored three times. Doerr was 4-for-6.

August 4

Friday's game was postponed to build for a Sunday doubleheader, but rains would likely have washed it out in any event.

August 5

Red Sox pitchers gave the Tigers a 16–4 win by walking 12 (!) and allowing 13 hits as "what is generously called Red Sox pitching sank to a new low." Two of the Detroit hits were big ones—Birdie Tebbetts' grand slam and Pete Fox's bases-clearing triple. "Single-X" Fox had four RBIs. "Double-X" Jimmie Foxx hit a solo homer. Vosmik doubled twice. In the free pass department, Auker walked five, Dickman walked one, Ostermueller walked two, and Chick Sayles walked four.

August 6

The Red Sox were chewed up by the Tigers, 10–1, but tore back with a convincing 8–3 win. Featuring a doubleheader worked; an estimated 12,000 to 15,000 fans were turned away when the gates were closed. Three extra mounted policemen had to be brought in to control the crowd outside. 20-year-old Freddy Hutchinson held the Red Sox to six hits and one second-inning run. Galehouse, Rich, and Wade threw for Boston for the first eight. In a bit of showmanship, Joe Cronin had Jimmie Foxx pitch the ninth inning for the Red Sox; Double X held the Tigers hitless in his major league mound debut, striking out Pinky Higgins. "I wanted to give the crowd a treat," acknowledged Cronin after the game. "They didn't have a thing to cheer about in those first eight innings." The crowd had been on the Red Sox pitchers all day and booed Foxx for a misplay in the bottom of the eighth. His moundwork turned the fans around and brought forth the loudest ovations of the season.

Johnny Wilson pitched and Moe Berg caught in the second game, both going the distance. Doerr was 0-for-7 on the day, Williams just 1-for-7. Vosmik and Cronin, though, each hit a home run and each drove in three. The Red Sox were in second place, eight games behind the Yankees but a secure seven games ahead of the third-place White Sox.

"I'm ready to start a game anytime Cronin tells me," Foxx declared. "I didn't get much chance to warm up today and I couldn't really put much on the ball, but I really can do tricks with it when I'm warmed up."

August 7

No game scheduled.

August 8

LEFTY GROVE WINS SEVENTH STRAIGHT. Foxx homered twice, his 28th and 29th of the year. Boston beat Philadelphia, 9–2. Foxx, Vosmik, and Williams each had two RBIs. Only a last-minute two-run homer robbed Grove of a shutout. Despite two hits and the two runs batted in, Williams was yanked out of the game for running listlessly to first base on a Texas Leaguer that he well could have turned into a double. Cronin immediately pulled him from the game, inserting Lou Finney in his stead. Ted showered and left the park. Cronin said, "Don't get the idea I'm worried about Ted. He's a great kid and will be around tomorrow as cheerful as ever. That's what I like about him best . . . But when he pulls these little bursts of temperament now, you've got to consider his disposition for the future." He added that he understood Ted was slumping and feeling down, but "all he's got to do is look two lockers down from his for an example of the way to take a batting slump . . . Until the last two games, Vosmik has experienced the toughest luck up at that dish of any player I've ever been with in baseball. In the past two months, I bet he's hit a 'million' line drives that have been caught. They didn't help Joe's average either, but you never saw him once dog it. He just kept on doing his job day after day in the hopes of helping the club in some manner." Cronin said he would bench Williams for two or three days.

August 9

BATTING RALLIES BEAT A'S TWICE. The Sox closed the gap to 6½ games behind New York by taking 5–3 and 6–5 wins from Philadelphia. Foxx broke open a tie game with a two-run homer in the bottom of the eighth to give Galehouse a win (Rich had started, and Dickman

Grove, Foxx, and Yawkey getting in some offseason hunting

relieved.) In the second game, it was Ostermueller in relief of Heving who got the win, as the Sox came from behind in the bottom of the ninth with a two-run rally. Peacock singled, Ostie sacrificed him to second, and Doerr tied the game by driving in Peacock. Cramer singled. Foxx was walked intentionally, loading the bases for Ted Williams, who hit a walkoff drive that hit the center-field wall, officially a single but which would have scored two more runs had they been needed. It was Ted's 94th RBI of the season.

Why hadn't Cronin benched Williams? He said he'd talked to Ted before the game and learned that "some outside circumstances of a private nature which do not permit of printing here" were on Ted's mind. Ted wanted a chance to prove himself, and came through. Years later, speculation suggests the difficulties may have involved Ted's divorcing parents or his younger brother Danny, who was often in minor scrapes with the law.

An hour after the game, Tom Yawkey took to the field and had clubhouse man Johnny Orlando throw him batting practice. It had become a bit of a nightly ritual.

August 10

The Red Sox won again and shaved another game off New York's lead, as they beat the A's, 7–5, behind the pitching of Jack Wilson and Emerson Dickman. Philadelphia scored twice in the top of the first, but Boston responded with three. The A's made it 5–3 in the third, but the Red Sox added three more of their own in the sixth, and a bonus run in the eighth. Vosmik drove in two. Finney pinch-hit successfully again, now 10-for-16 as a pinch-hitter.

August 11

No game scheduled. The Yankees won and made it a six-game lead.

August 12

RED SOX' 16 HITS BEAT SENATORS 9–5. The Sox kept pace with the Yankees as the Red Sox beat the Senators for the 10th time in succession. Without benefit of a home run, the Sox racked up the nine runs, most coming in their five-run fifth. Doerr and Williams each doubled twice. Excepting the pitchers, every Red Sox batter—except the league-leading Ted Williams—drove in at least one. Ted scored two runs, though. Cramer and Cronin each drove in two. Dickman earned the win in relief of Auker and Rich.

August 13

HOSE, NATS DIVIDE; WILLIAMS ON SPREE. The Red Sox won, 9–1, then dropped the second game, 6–3. Ostermueller threw a strong seven-hitter as Williams went 3-for-3 in the first game, scoring twice. Cronin drove in three and Foxx drove in two. In the second game, Ted homered (his only homer of the 22-game homestand)

and tripled, and added another single for a perfect 6-for-6 day, but Galehouse, Wade, Heving, Wilson, and Dickman all had to pitch, and to no avail.

Ted was 8-for-8 in his last eight official at-bats. "I should be doing a lot better," said "toothpick Ted" the following day, talking about the difficulties of hitting at Fenway with its deep right field. He hit much better on the road, he said. His goal before the year had been to hit .300, he mentioned, and to drive in around 100. Since then, he'd upped his ambitions.

August 14

No game scheduled. The Red Sox took the train to Philadelphia. The Sox were doing better on the road than at home, having a 34–13 away record on the year.

The Sox shipped Woody Rich to Louisville, and brought up two pitchers—Charlie Wagner and Lefty Lefebvre. They'd be put to work at once, said Cronin. "Between the two of them we might discover a pitcher. We had to do something." Wagner was only 10–11 at Louisville, but appearances were deceiving; he'd only been scored on 72 times in 177 innings. With unearned runs deducted, he was close to a 2.50 ERA. Auker was demoted from the starting role which had seen him knocked out of eight straight, his last win coming on June 24. Galehouse was similarly due to be demoted, not having won even one of his last five starts. Sink or swim with the recruits seemed to be Cronin's plan.

The bullpen was a busy place, and Washington and Lee graduate Dickman appreciated Moe Berg the most. "It's like going through college to sit with Berg in the bullpen. That Berg knows everything," he said. "He's best when he's talking about his travels and he's already taken us around the world four times this season." Heving added, "He should have been a salesman."

Desautels hadn't been working of late. He had a "lame arm" and had been undergoing daily treatment.

August 15

The Red Sox played under the lights—a night game at Shibe Park—and were shut out, 3–0. Wilson and Heving combined to hold the Athletics to just seven hits, but the Sox only got four (two each by Doerr and Williams) and none produced a run. The Sox didn't like playing at night. "Confidentially," declared Tom Yawkey, "it smells." Cronin added, "You can't judge the speed of the ball. I'm not trying to alibi for the defeat as I felt the same way about night ball after we won our only other night game in Cleveland." He admitted that fans liked night games, and that they provided good revenue, but the shadows of night make "the lowliest Philadelphia hitter just as dangerous as Jimmie Foxx." Black Jack Wilson lamented, "I finally pitch a good game and get beat. I'm not blaming it on the lights, it's just my luck. I'm beginning to believe it's better to be lucky than good." Ted Williams ran his

Boston's catching corps: Peacock, Berg, and Desautels

consecutive hit streak to nine in a row before his long fly ball was caught right at the fence on his 10th time up. Hugh Duffy blamed that on playing at night, asserting it would have carried for a home run during the daytime. "I've issued orders to my scouts not to judge any player by his performance under light. I've seen two games now and I still can't follow the ball."

August 16

No game scheduled. Lefty Grove took Ted Williams out fishing. Some of the others took in Atlantic City. A few worked out at the park. Some of the sportswriters tried to get Johnny Peacock to comment on the notion that the Red Sox catchers bore some blame for the disappointing performers of Boston's pitchers. Had he heard the idea? "That's all I've been hearing," he said. "All I can say is that as long as they've been playing baseball the pitcher has usually been credited for making the catcher. Why, it's a cinch to handle pitchers like Grove and Ruffing. They'd make anybody look good behind the plate." The farthest he would go was to say, "The catcher doesn't stand on the rubber and throw the ball up to the batter."

August 17

GROVE BEATS THE ATHLETICS FOR HIS 13TH WIN OF YEAR. He allowed 10 hits but they were well-spaced, as Philadelphia scored just once in the second inning. The Red Sox, meanwhile, scored seven times, with both Vosmik and Tabor hitting homers. Both had been struggling at the plate, and both changed their batting stance while taking b.p. from Lefty Lefebvre before the game. Bobby Doerr laid down a perfect squeeze bunt to drive in Tabor, who'd doubled and advanced on Desautels' sacrifice. Grove was now 13–2 on the year.

August 18

The Red Sox won again, 6–2 over the Washington Senators. Ostermueller went the distance. Vosmik drove in two more, and so did Cronin. Ted Williams climbed into the top 10 AL hitters with a .322 average.

August 19

TITANIC TED HITS A FOUR-RUN HOMER. Ted Williams came up with the bases loaded and the Red Sox trailing 5–4 in the ninth inning at Griffith Stadium, and hit his first grand slam home run—and reached exactly 100 runs batted in. Ted's drive off Pete Appleton—his first homer in Washington—gave Joe Heving the 8–6 win (the Senators got one off Dickman in the bottom of the ninth.) Lefty Lefebvre started his first major league game and went six innings and gave up three runs.

Washington won the second game, a tight 2–1 win with Jake Wade taking the loss. He walked two batters in the third and an RBI single, leaving the game with runners on second and third and nobody out. Auker allowed just one run in 5⅔ innings—his best outing in two months—on Cecil Travis's grounder to Doerr that scored Johnny Welaj only because Doerr was playing so deep. The Sox only managed four hits off Washington's lefty Kendall Chase.

August 20

Playing before a near-capacity Griffith Stadium crowd, the Red Sox were blanked in the first game, 2–0, as the Senators scored twice in the first off starter Wilson while knuckleballer Dutch Leonard kept the Red Sox from scoring. Both teams had seven hits. In the nightcap, Charlie Wagner got his first start of the season and pitched well, taking a 9–2 lead into the eighth inning before needing help. Foxx homered, driving in two. Tabor drove in three. And Wagner even knocked in a pair. Williams was 0-for-8 on the day.

August 21

No game scheduled, but Hitler and Stalin made a move, agreeing on a Nazi-Soviet nonaggression pact.

Between them, the quartet of Foxx, Williams, Cronin, and Doerr had 76 homers, more than any other foursome in the league. On the long 22-hour train trip to St. Louis, Cronin heard from his new two rookie pitchers, both of whom said that their Louisville teammate Pee Wee Reese was superior as shortstop to any other in the American Association.

August 22

Galehouse threw a complete game victory, losing a shutout when Walt McQuinn connected for a three-run homer in the bottom of the ninth. Both Foxx (33) and Williams (19) hit home runs, and Williams tripled, Jimmie now with 99 RBIs and Ted adding four more runs batted in for a league-leading 104. Final score: Sox 10, Browns 3. Paid attendance was in three digits: 997.

August 23

Ostie won his fifth game in a row, as starting pitching continued to do the job. The Sox beat the Browns, 9–1, as Ostermueller scattered four hits while the Red Sox hit four times as many. Cramer and Cronin helped the offense with two RBIs apiece. Foxx was 4-for-4 and scored three times. That the Sox trailed New York by eight games was disappointing. The Red Sox were 72–41. It was the other clubs which failed to beat the Yankees that discouraged the Bosox.

August 24

RED SOX HAND THE WHITE SOX TWO CHEAP RUNS AND LOSE, 3–1. Such was the story, ruining a "courageous comeback effort" by Elden Auker at Comiskey. Doerr booted one ball and Cramer misjudged another, accounting for one run. Williams bobbled a ground ball, allowing the other. The Red Sox only mustered six hits, though, none for extra bases. Foxx struck out four times in a row during the game, played at night. He admitted it was a "putrid exhibition"—the worst in his career—but did fix some of the blame on night baseball, which he deemed "all wet."

August 25

The White Sox scored seven times in the bottom of the eighth, and that made all the difference in their 9–2 win. Lefty Grove started for Boston, gunning for #14, but left after six full. It was Dickman who absorbed the defeat. Meanwhile, the surging Yankees extended their lead to 10½ games by taking two games from St. Louis.

Grantland Rice said he'd been told that if Williams played in Yankee Stadium, with its short right-field porch, he'd likely finish the year with 55 home runs. Though Ted was "a bit of a busher" when the season began, Rice credited Cronin for smoothing out the wrinkles and noted that Ted "has the entire league chasing him for top place at batting in runs, a remarkable start for a first-year entry."

August 26

LISTLESS RED SOX DROP ANOTHER TO WHITE SOX. Foxx walked three times, but struck out twice, bringing his K's for the series to seven. It was the seventh loss in a row for the Red Sox in Chicago. Though Ted Williams got Boston off to a 2–0 start in the first inning with a single driving in Cramer and Foxx, the White Sox got five runs early with "some of the sloppiest fielding of the campaign" by the Red Sox; they were charged with four errors. The final score was 5–4 and the Red Sox were happy to take the midnight train to Cleveland.

August 27

SOX, BEATEN TWICE BY TRIBE, FALL 13 GAMES BEHIND YANKS. After dropping five in a row, it was dawning on the Red Sox that their pursuit of the pennant was likely in vain. They were still seven games ahead of third-place Chicago, but a full 13 behind New York after dropping two to the Indians while the Yankees won one from the Tigers. The pitching had improved; now it was the lack of hitting that was hurting them.

The first game was a close one, a 1–0 loss to Bob Feller (who four-hit the Red Sox), despite a valiant performance from Denny Galehouse. Bruce Campbell's triple in the bottom of the eighth drove in Cleveland's only run. In the second game, Ostermueller pitched well, too, and the score stood 2–1 Cleveland through 7½. Then Hal Trosky took the starch out with a three-run homer. The final was 5–3 as Boston added single runs in the eighth and ninth.

The *Globe*'s game summary suggested it may have been Jeff Heath who sparked the Indians when, after striking out in the second inning of the first game he was so angered he blindly flung his bat. It nearly went into the Indians' dugout, but instead hopped into the box seats hitting a woman. He was immediately ejected and the minute he got back to the bench got into a fistfight with his best friend teammate Johnny Broaca.

August 28

WILLIAMS' 3-RUN HOMER IN EIGHTH TRIPS TRIBE, 6–5. Finally, a win as Ted hit his 20th homer of his rookie year and Jack Wilson held back the Indians with a "courageous hurling job." Heath was back in action, this time punching a fan after fouling out to end the game with two runners on base. Umpire Bill McGowan had a rough game, calling Heath safe at home earlier on when Heath hadn't even touched the plate (according to the *Globe*'s Gerry Moore.) That was just part of what Moore termed "some of the most ludicrous umpiring of the season." Elden Auker got the win.

August 29

TED WILLIAMS POLES HOMER TO WIN FOR RED SOX, 7 TO 4. The homer was a grand slam off Cleveland's Harry Eisenstadt, wrapping up a six-run Red Sox sixth. Ted drove in five in all. Lefebvre got his first major league win. Though Foxx had 13 more homers, 23 of his were solo home runs; Williams' four-baggers had driven in 51 to Foxx's 49.

Earlier in the morning, as it was raining a bit, the players were looking out their windows and talking when the men rooming above Williams called for him to look up. The Kid was rewarded with a "thorough dousing from a pitcher of ice water." Who had the room above the rookie? It was a suite where owner Tom Yawkey and Secretary Phil Troy were breakfasting.

The Red Sox recalled 12 players from various teams,

including Woody Rich, Jim Bagby, and Monte Weaver. Others brought up were Ted Olson, Paul Campbell, Frank Dazzo, Fabian Gaffke, Tom Irwin, Chet Morgan, Alex Petrushkin, Chick Sayles, and Stan Spence.

August 30

WILLIAMS A HERO, BUT HIS ERROR COSTS GAME. They were calling him "Timely Ted" after he'd won the last two games with late home runs. Playing in Detroit, Williams hit a three-run homer in the third to give the Red Sox a 3–2 edge. The Sox added three more runs in the fourth as both Jim Tabor and—of all people—Moe Berg also hit homers. It was Berg's first home run since 1935.

Jack Wilson went the distance for the Red Sox, and the Sox failed to convert some other scoring opportunities. Ted made a "spectacular" catch in the sixth, but in the bottom of the eighth, Wilson walked two. Pete Fox hit a Texas Leaguer, scoring one. With two outs, Birdie Tebbetts singled to right field and the ball skipped right through Williams as two runs scored for a 7–6 final score.

Lefty Grove "started a rumor" that the day was Ted's birthday. "Ted was so mad this evening he wouldn't even discuss it. His listed birthday was October 30." In fact, Grove was correct. Williams disguised his true birthdate so it would never fall during the baseball season, and perhaps somehow interfere with his focus on the game.

August 31

The Tigers won again, scoring six times in the eighth inning and sticking Grove with a loss. Though the score was a lopsided 11–4, the Red Sox blew a large number of opportunities to even things up. Grove left for a pinch-hitter in the sixth, down by 5–2. Boston scored twice in the seventh to make it 5–4. Then Dickman and Galehouse combined gave up the six runs that made it a rout. Williams had a double, a single, and a sacrifice fly. His 120 RBIs were 15 more than second-place Joe DiMaggio.

Though the Sox and Yankees had 10 head-to-head contests remaining, the Yawkeymen were discouraged and down after a disappointing road trip. The New York team was on a roll, though.

September 1

TIGERS SLUG 14–10 WIN OVER HAPLESS RED SOX. Williams was 5-for-5 in on-base work, with two singles, a double, and two walks. Johnny Peacock had three hits as well. Tom Carey led the Red Sox in runs batted in, with three. The Tigers scored four in the first off Auker and scored repeatedly in the fourth through the seventh. The Red Sox offense made it respectable, but it was still a loss.

September 2

RED SOX MAKE IT 6 IN 6 FROM WORLD CHAMPIONS. The Red Sox roughed up Red Ruffing for 19 hits and 12 runs for a 12–7 win, starter Ostermueller getting the W. Yankees manager Joe McCarthy left Ruffing in for the whole game, despite giving up four runs in the first and two more in the third. Vosmik, Williams, Cronin, and Carey all had three-hit games for Boston, with Tabor leading the RBI department with four. Cronin's three hits were all doubles and he drove in two, as did Johnny Peacock. It was more runs than any team had scored against the Yankees all year, and the sixth in a row the Red Sox had taken from the New York team. The Yankees' train from Cleveland had only arrived at 2:00 PM and the start had to be pushed back from 2:30 to 3:00 in consequence.

The Red Sox inaugurated their first aid room on this date; the room still exists under the grandstand at section 12.

September 3

RED SOX WIN OPENER, THEN LOSE ON FORFEIT. Fans Chuck Bottles, Yankees Given Nightcap. The first game was a slugfest that saw the Sox come out on top, 12–11, beating the Yankees for the seventh time in a row. The Yanks scored three times in the first, but Boston put across two. New York scored three more times in the fifth, but the Red Sox took the lead with five in the bottom of the fifth. Then New York scored five times to lead off the sixth. Boston added two in the sixth, two more in the seventh, and the tie-breaker in the eighth. Galehouse and Dickman had really been banged up, but Auker threw two hitless innings and got the win, with a save by Heving who tossed a hitless top of the ninth. Cronin had five RBIs, Cramer two, and Carey two.

Charlie Wagner started the second game for the Red Sox. The Yankees scored first, in the first, and the Sox countered with one of their own. The game went back and forth a bit, but was still tied 5–5 after seven innings. Ted Williams had hit two homers and Cronin had hit one. There was a 6:29 PM Sunday curfew in effect, and when the Yankees scored twice in the top of the eighth, Cronin started slowing down the game. There were runners on first and third with one out, and he asked Heving to walk Babe Dahlgren intentionally. Trying to speed up the game, Dahlgren swung at a pitch nowhere near the strike zone and Cronin protested, killing more time. George Selkirk then ran home from third base, purportedly trying to steal but getting himself tagged out by Peacock at the plate. On the very next pitch, Joe Gordon did the same thing, having advanced to third on the earlier play. Three out. At this point, angered that the umpires had done nothing to counter the Yankees' tactics, the "crowd took matters into their own hands. From almost every section of the enclosure, articles ranging from Sunday skimmers to undevoured hot dog rolls were thrown until the park was beyond playing condition. The barrage lasted for fully three minutes, despite several requests by the Sox management to halt the demonstration." At 6:26, the umpires declared a forfeit, and hence a 9–0 Yankees victory.

September 4

The Red Sox lost both games of the Labor Day doubleheader against the visiting Washington Senators, 7–6 and 6–4. Wade and Lefebvre were the two Boston starters, facing "Carrasquel, the mysterious Venezuelan" and "piano playing Pete Appleton." Appleton, the former Red Soxer, threw a four-hitter. The Sox were termed "sluggish" and "inept" but stayed in both games though never quite able to catch up.

September 5

No game scheduled. The Red Sox were 14½ games behind New York, heading into Yankee Stadium where—if nothing else—they had taken the last five games they'd played.

September 6

Lefty Grove threw a complete game, holding the Yankees to seven hits. The Red Sox took the lead when Ted Williams drove in a run in the top of the third after hits by Cramer and Vosmik. But that was the only run the Red Sox scored. The Sox committed four errors, Cronin's in the third leading directly to a run that tied it up. Joe DiMaggio's eighth-inning homer off Grove gave Lefty a 2–1 loss. Charlie Keller's leaping catch prevented a three-run homer from Foxx and effectively saved the game for the Yankees.

The sinking Red Sox began to look over their shoulder and notice that Chicago was not far behind. The White Sox hadn't made much progress; they were still 19 out, but now Boston was 15½ behind. The Sox had finally given up on Jake Wade and sold him to the Browns.

September 7

RED SOX FADE BEFORE YANKS AS WHITE SOX PRESS HARD. Boston lost to New York again, 5–2, with the New Yorkers hitting safely 11 times to Boston's three. And the White Sox won two games against St. Louis, putting them just two games behind the Red Sox. Williams sat out the game after bruising his hand with a crash into the Stadium's right-field wall the day before. The only way the Red Sox scored was thanks to four consecutive bases on balls in the fourth inning, courtesy of Monte Pearson, which forced in one and then Vosmik's double play, which saw the other one score on the back end.

September 8

The Red Sox had a loss removed when American League President Will Harridge declared the September 3 game a 5–5 tie, not a forfeit, and scheduled a replay for September 26. Selkirk and Dahlgren were each fined $100.

Another loss was added, though, when Red Ruffing held the Red Sox to one run on six hits, while Galehouse and Ostermueller allowed four runs on seven hits. Williams took some batting practice, but was still out with the sore wrist. Tabor's home run was the only score for Boston.

September 9

Elden Auker threw a complete game, but lost a 2–1 heartbreaker when Bobby Doerr's bottom-of-the-ninth-inning error opened the door wide enough for Dario Lodigiani to reach. Wally Moses singled him in for the tie-breaker. To make matters worse, Jimmie Foxx had to leave suddenly and was hospitalized, undergoing an emergency appendectomy at St. Joseph's Hospital in Philadelphia. He was expected to miss the rest of the season.

September 10

WILLIAMS HITS TWO HOMERS AS SOX TAKE A'S TWICE. Ted also hit two triples on the 5-for-7 game, adding three more RBIs to his total. He had a triple and a homer in each game. The Red Sox had broken out of their torpor with 10 runs in the first game, fortunate because Wagner and Dickman were touched up for seven. In the second game, Joe Heving threw a complete-game four-hitter for a 5–1 win.

September 11

The Sox hopped out to a 4–0 lead in the top of the first but the final score was 11–9. Boston scored five more times in the fifth, then withstood a three-run Philadelphia rally in the bottom of the ninth. Jim Tabor homered and tripled and drove in five. Williams was hitless but, drawing walks as usual (three on the day), scored twice. Jim Bagby got the win in relief. Cronin's wrenched ankle was so bad he didn't even dress for the game, and managed from the dugout. Foxx remained in the hospital.

September 12

GALEHOUSE PITCHES RED SOX TO WIN OVER TIGERS. Holds Them To Five Hits With No Passes Besting Bridges for a 2 to 1 Score. Tommy Bridges came out on the short end as the Red Sox opened their final homestand of the season. Bobby Doerr knocked in both Boston runs, one in the fourth and one in the sixth, driving in Ted Williams both times, first with a single and then with a sacrifice fly.

September 13

GROVE PITCHES BEST GAME OF YEAR. It only took one hour and 36 minutes for the Red Sox to dispose of the Tigers, in part because Grove only gave up four hits and walked nary a batter. The Red Sox scored one fifth-

Lefty Grove had a 15-4 season with an ERA of 2.54

inning run—all they needed—after Gene Desautels doubled. He took third when a pickoff throw hit him in the ankle, and then Lou Finney hit a long sacrifice fly to bring him home. 1–0, Red Sox.

September 14

RED SOX COME CLOSE BUT INDIANS NOSE THEM OUT. After building up a 7–0 lead off Auker and Dickman, the Indians saw the Red Sox score five times in the of the sixth. They added one more in the top of the seventh, just barely enough to edge Boston which scored twice in the bottom of the inning. Williams had three more RBIs. They fell one short: 8–7.

September 15

Both the Indians and Red Sox scored once in the first inning, but that was all the scoring—until the Indians scored three times in the eighth and three more in the ninth. 7–1. It was Ostermueller's game, throwing $7\frac{2}{3}$ innings. A missed third strike call by umpire Quinn seemed to open the floodgates, as the next pitch was hit for a Cleveland double and give them the lead. The Red Sox retained their three-game lead over the White Sox, though.

September 16

With both Cronin and Foxx out, the Indians took their third game in a row from the Red Sox, as Mel Harder out-dueled Broadway Charlie Wagner for a 2–1 win. Only a solo home run by Ted Williams in the ninth inning spared the Red Sox a shutout. The Indians had pulled three games closer to the Red Sox and now trailed the White Sox for third place by just half a game.

September 17

On the date the Yankees clinched, the two Sox teams met at Fenway to try and settle second place. A second-place win would mean about $1,200 extra pay per player. Boston lost to Chicago, 6–1, in the first game, but won the second, 11–7. The Red Sox only got three hits off Thornton Lee in the opener, one of them a Ted Williams solo homer (years later, Ted would homer off Thorny's son Don). The Red Sox got 18 hits in the second game, though, having to come from behind three times before finally taking the lead in the bottom of the seventh—and adding three bonus runs in the eighth. Heving had started but Bagby got the win, allowing just three hits in the final three frames. Cramer and Tabor both had three hits in the second game, and Doerr, Finney, Tabor, and Heving each had a pair of RBIs. A further downside to the first game was when Cramer and Vosmik crashed into each other going after a base hit in the fifth; Vosmik was spiked on his left foot and was expected to be out for a few days. Nonnenkamp took over in left.

September 18

No game scheduled. Had the Red Sox not pulled out the second game on September 16, they would have been just one game up on the White Sox. The win stabilized their increasingly tenuous hold on second; Boston had lost 18 of its last 28 games. Chicago had picked up 7½ games and the Indians (now only ½ game behind the White Sox) had gained 9½.

The Sox awaited the opportunity to play three games with last-place St. Louis, while the White Sox had to play in New York. St. Louis was 58 games out of first place. X-rays revealed a possible fracture of Bobby Doerr's heel, however, the result of another injury involving a collision with Cramer on September 16. Cronin, Foxx, and Vosmik were all still out. That meant Boze Berger would play short and Tommy Carey play second, with Nonnenkamp still going in left field. There were 13 games left for Boston, and five of them would be against New York.

In the September 19 *Globe*, the columnist known as "Sportsman" declared, "It is a very rare thing in baseball to find a catcher with the speed on the base lines of Johnny Peacock. I do not recall a catcher who could show the pace Johnny uncorked when he made his three-bagger Sunday."

September 19

Joe Cronin put himself back in the game at shortstop, and had a 3-for-4 day before letting Berger pinch run for him in the seventh. Finney and Cramer both drove in two and the Red Sox (behind Jack Wilson) beat the Browns, 6–2, while the Yankees took care of Chicago and Washington beat Cleveland. Boston now had a four-game lead with 12 to play. Doerr's X-rays were negative, so he played, too. Both Cronin and Doerr had one RBI. Doc Cramer was on the receiving end of an injury this time, hit hard in the head by a relay throw as he was streaking toward third base for a triple. He reached and he stayed in the game, but was down on the ground for quite a while, unable to get up and score even though the ball caromed off his cranium and rolled quite a ways.

September 20

RED SOX LOSE TO THE BROWNS IN 16 INNINGS. Had they held out one inning more, the game would have been called an 8–8 tie due to darkness, but Ostermueller (the fourth pitcher of the day for the Red Sox—Grove started) gave up three runs in the top of the 16th and his teammates were unable to score in the bottom of the inning. Ted Williams had hit a two-run homer in the third to give Boston a temporary 2–1 lead. It was Ted's 29th and his 138th and 139th RBIs. He was walked four times in all, and hit once. Chicago beat New York.

September 21

Cold weather saw a sparse "crowd" of 598 paid attendees watch the Red Sox win the rubber game against the Browns, 6–2. Gene Desautels was 3-for-3 and scored three times. Joe Cronin's two-run home run in the seventh was the disheartening blow that out the game more or less out of reach, as Galehouse was cruising, giving up two runs on seven hits. Cronin's homer was #18, a personal best. The Indians leapfrogged the White Sox into third place as the Yankees completed their sweep of Chicago.

September 22

Wagner and Dickman pitched for the Red Sox against the visiting Athletics, and the Red Sox bats (Cramer was 3-for-5 and had three runs batted in) provided seven runs. Wagner got credit for the 7–5 win.

September 23

RED SOX WIN BUT A'S THROW SCARE INTO PICTURE. The Red Sox piled up the runs with two in the third (two-run Ted home run) and seven more in the fifth, and "Strong Boy" Jack Wilson was sailing along. He gave up one in the sixth, and then surrendered four singles in succession in the seventh. A sacrifice fly followed, and it was 9–4 Red Sox. After Wilson ran the count to 3–0 on Hayes, Cronin pulled him in favor of Bagby, who worked his way out of the inning. The Indians scored twice more (off Bagby) in the eighth with a two-run homer and twice yet again with another two-run homer in the ninth. Cronin called in Ostermueller, who put down the uprising. Final was 10–8, Red Sox.

September 24

It was dubbed "Finney's Revenge" when Lou hit an eighth-inning double to break a 4–4 tie and kick off a

Add your own caption?
Herb Pennock, Doc Cramer, and Moe Berg

five-run Red Sox rally that led to their 9–4 defeat of Connie Mack and the A's. Disappointed with Lou's hitting, Mack had sold Finney to Boston. He was batting .314 for the Red Sox after some 255 at-bats. Cramer, Williams, and Doerr each had three hits. Finney and Doerr each drove in two. Dickman got the win, in relief of Heving. Boston now held a sturdy 4½ game lead over the White Sox and 5½ over the Indians in the battle for the second-place purse.

September 25

No game scheduled.

September 26

Rains washed out the planned Fenway doubleheader between the Red Sox and Yankees.

September 27

For the second day in a row, the Yankees and Red Sox saw a doubleheader get scrubbed due to rain and the Red Sox had to catch the 9 PM overnight train to Washington. With no more games planned at home, and their positions in the standings unlikely to be affected, it was seen as likely that one game would simply be canceled, with another one made up by playing back-to-back doubleheaders on the weekend in New York City. The Red

Sox only needed to win one of their remaining games to clinch second place.

September 28

Clinch second place they did, with a 4–2 win over Washington as Lefty Grove threw a complete game six-hitter, settling down after giving up one run in each of the first two innings. Grove gave up just one single in the final seven innings. The Red Sox got one in the second, and three more in the top of the fourth. Finney's two-run double made the difference, but it had been a good game for Jim Tabor, too, with a 2-for-4 day including a double, an RBI, and successfully pulling off a double steal with Desautels.

There was a second game—anticlimactic given the clinch—a 6–1 loss with Ostermueller giving it up. Tabor drove in the Red Sox run for a short-lived Red Sox lead, but the six unanswered runs that followed . . . well, that was the ballgame.

Though a year earlier, taking second place had set off a "succession of celebration excesses topped off by Joe Cronin's famous Parker House party," this year there was nothing other than congratulatory handshakes. Both Grove and Galehouse were allowed to leave and return home.

September 29

No game scheduled.

It was announced that Joe Cronin had signed a five-year extension to manage the Red Sox, and Tom Yawkey revealed early contract renewals with Doerr, Foxx, Tabor, and Williams. Boston's back-to-back second-place finishes seemed to solidify a foundation on which the team could hope to build.

September 30

The Red Sox lost the first game of the day, 5–4. Bagby began it, but it was Bill Dickey's seventh-inning homer off Dickman that won it for the Yanks. The second game lasted just seven innings, due to darkness, but saw a 4–2 win for the Red Sox. Ted Williams homered, his 31st, giving him a home run in every park—including both parks

in Cleveland (League Park and the July 13–15 games at Municipal Stadium). Jack Wilson held the Yankees to just five hits. Should the Red Sox win either of the two games in the October 1 doubleheader, they'd have 90 wins on the season—which had been Cronin's stated goal.

October 1

Cronin's hope to win 90 games fell short by one, as the scheduled twinbill with New York was rained out by an all-day drizzle. Within half an hour of cancellation, the Hotel Commodore was "practically bereft of ball players." The Sox had headed for their various destinations, save for Ted Williams—who wanted to stay and see the World Series—and manager Cronin and his coaches Daly and Duffy.

Had they played a full 154 games, they probably would have made it. Their final record was three games shy of a full schedule: 89–62. It was a very good year, spoiled only because the Yankees won 106 games and lost but 45. The Red Sox finished 3½ games above third-place Cleveland. The Sox had finished second for the second year in a row, their highest finishes since World War I and the 1918 season. But they'd finished with a .589 winning percentage instead of the .591 they'd posted the year before, and the Yankees had been so much better (106–45) that instead of being just 9½ games behind New York, they were 17 games back. It was a less than satisfying season, since hopes had soared higher.

Joe Cronin declared, "My most vivid memories of the 1939 season will always be recalled by the cry of 'Take him out!'." He was referring to the Red Sox pitching staff.

The biggest bright spot was the success of Ted Williams, though 1939 also say "the blossoming of Bobby Doerr into a real star, the handy stunts of Lou Finney, and the creditable first-year feats of Jim Tabor." For Ted, the accolades were abundant, with comparisons to Babe Ruth commonplace among them. The five-game sweep of the Yankees in Yankee Stadium was a highlight, but the inability of any Red Sox pitcher—save venerable Lefty Grove—to win even 12 games was the greatest disappointment.

After the 1939 Season

If they could bolster their pitching crew, maybe they could make a run at it in 1940. As it turned out, the league was more competitive and after four pennants in a row, the Yankees finished third. Detroit captured the flag and the Indians came in a close second, one game behind. The Yanks were one game behind them. Boston finished the 1940 season just eight games out of first, but that saw them tied for fourth place with the White Sox. And 1941 was like a reversion to 1939: New York first, Boston in second and again 17 games behind.

After that came the war. Ted Williams had hit .406, but a mere 39 days later came the Japanese attack on Pearl Harbor. Wartime exigencies resulted in large numbers of players going into military service or defense work. Predictability and planning in baseball became casualties of the war effort. Boston finished second, seventh, fourth, and seventh. It was only when the war was over that rosters could begin to reflect the work that player development staffs put into trying to staff a good team. The Red Sox had a number of great players returning, and a number of strong pitchers seeming to mature. They won the 1946 pennant with ease, 12 games ahead of second-place Detroit—and that's where we'll leave off.

All quotations are from the *Boston Globe*, unless otherwise noted.

Looking ahead to the year that followed: Joe Cronin and Tom Yawkey during 1940 spring training.

Contributors

Mark Armour grew up in Connecticut but now writes baseball from his home in Oregon. He is the co-author of *Paths to Glory*, editor of *Rain Check*, the director of SABR's Baseball Biography Project, a contributor to many websites and SABR journals, and, most importantly, Maya and Drew's father.

Anthony Basich comes from behind enemy lines as both a lifelong Yankees fan and a resident of New Jersey and New York City. But don't hold that against him. He considers himself a baseball fan first and foremost. He has been a SABR member since 2006 and has been a contributor of book reviews to the Deadball Committee's newsletter, *The Inside Game*. He previously contributed to the bioproject on the 1959 Chicago White Sox chronicling the career of third baseman Bubba Phillips.

John Bennett has been a member of SABR since 1993. His published works include *Johnny Podres: Brooklyn's Yankee Killer* (Rooftop Publishing, 2007) as well as contributions to a number of SABR publications. A graduate of the University of Vermont and Georgetown University, he has been teaching in Vermont for fifteen years. John manages to see 15–20 Red Sox games around the country each season, and once listened to a Red Sox game broadcast over the phone while studying abroad in Leningrad, USSR.

Ralph L. Berger lives with his wife Reina in Huntingdon Valley, Pennsylvania. He has contributed many articles to the SABR Biographical Project. Ralph has been a diehard Phillies fan, for all of his life. Ralph and his wife Reina are both graduates of the University of Pennsylvania. They share a passion for art, world travel, and collecting.

Maurice Bouchard, who lives in Shrewsbury, Mass., with his wife Kim, has been a baseball fan since Sandy Koufax struck out Bob Allison for the final out of the 1965 World Series. Bouchard, who grew up in upstate New York, was originally a Yankees fan but George Steinbrenner cured him of that. Since 1987, he has rooted for the Old Towne Team. He has two children, Ian and Gina, both of whom are inveterate Red Sox fans. Bouchard has been a member of SABR since 1999.

Ryan Brodeur grew up a Red Sox fan in the hotly contested Connecticut River Valley. He holds a B.A. in French Language and Literature from Trinity College, Hartford, and has been teaching high school French since 2005. In the fall he will pursue a master's degree in Educational Administration at Boston College. Ryan moonlights as a baseball writer on his blog, TheHotCorner.org and has been a SABR member since 2006. He currently lives in Newton, MA with his wife, Kathleen DiSanto, and their two dogs, Nora and Declan.

Warren Corbett is the author of a forthcoming biography of Paul Richards and an editor for SABR's Biography Project. A former NBC news reporter and minor league play-by-play broadcaster, he is the editor of *Set-Aside Alert*, a trade publication in Washington.

Jon Daly is a life-long resident of the Greater Hartford area. His father introduced him to baseball and the Red Sox during the 1975 season. Because he was a young lad at the time, he expected the Red Sox to play in the World Series every year. Boy, was he wrong! In his free time, he works in the financial service industry. Jon has been a SABR member since 2001. He has contributed several bios to SABR and is currently striving to become the world's leading expert on Bowie Kuhn.

As a lifelong Phillies fan, **James E. Elfers** knows what pain is. A member of SABR since 1986 he is the author of *The Tour to End All Tours: The story of Major League Baseball's 1913–1914 World Tour*, which won the 2003 Larry Ritter Award for the best book about the deadball era. It tells the story of a an around-the-world baseball tour which included Boston's Tris Speaker playing as a temporary member of the Chicago White Sox. He works as a library assistant at the University of Delaware.

John Fuqua grew up in rural Tennessee, about halfway between Graceland and the Ryman. A life-long National League and St. Louis Cardinals fan, he can recall listening to Harry Caray and Jack Buck broadcasts from KMOX on the old transistor radio. In the interest of diversity, he adopted the Boston Red Sox as his American League Nine and is a proud member of the Red Sox Nation. John and his wife Beth live in Franklin, Tennessee, along with their three children, Ben, Rachel, and Rebecca.

John Green is a native of San Diego and became a baseball fan in 1936, when teenagers Bobby Doerr and Ted Williams wore the uniform of the PCL Padres. When the two were purchased by Boston, he became a Red Sox rooter, and in the fall of 1941 John was a spectator as barnstorming Boston teammates Jimmie Foxx and

Williams smashed home runs in an exhibition game at San Diego's Lane Field. John made it to Boston in 1982; he saw the Blue Jays and Bosox at Fenway, and ran in the Boston Marathon. He has remained a long-suffering Padres fan, and feels fortunate to have witnessed the baseball skills of Tony Gwynn over the 20 seasons he played in San Diego, and to be in Cooperstown for his Hall of Fame induction in July 2007.

Donald J. Hubbard is a trial attorney from Boston and SABR member who lives in that city's West Roxbury district with his wife Lori and children Billy and Caroline. He is the author of *The Heavenly Twins of Boston Baseball*, a dual biography about Hall of Famers Tommy McCarthy and Hugh Duffy, and he is currently under contract with McFarland Publishing to write a book about the early Red Sox. By way of heresy to baseball, he is also working on a book about the Notre Dame football teams of the early 1950's.

Jim Kaplan grew up in Cambridge and saw Ted Williams countless times at Fenway Park. He considers the highlight of his sportswriting career the day he spent with the Thumper while working for *Sports Illustrated*. Kaplan wrote the biography *Lefty Grove: American Original* for SABR and recently, with Bill Chuck, published *Walkoffs, Last Licks and Final Outs: Baseball's Grand (and not-so-grand) Finales* (ACTA Sports). Kaplan and his wife, poet Brooks Robards, divide their time between Northampton and Oak Bluffs.

Len Levin was told by his parents long ago that he was taken to a Red Sox game before he knew what baseball was, and that Jimmie Foxx hit a home run. Maybe by osmosis, that made 'Double X' one of his favorite Red Sox players of the past. When not thinking about baseball, Len is a semi-retired newspaper copy editor.

Bill Nowlin is national Vice President of SABR and the author of more than 20 Red Sox-related books, including *Red Sox Threads: Odds and Ends from Red Sox History*. Bill is also co-founder of Rounder Records of Massachusetts. He's traveled to more than 100 countries, but says there's no place like Fenway Park.

Robert H. Schaefer was born and raised in the shadow of Yankee Stadium. He believes that this proximity altered his genetic structure, as he has been wild about baseball his entire life. He now lives on a small island on Florida's west coast. After retiring from the aerospace industry, he began researching baseball's past and has published numerous articles describing various aspects of 19th century baseball.

Doug Skipper is a marketing research, customer satisfaction and public opinion consultant from Apple Valley, MN, who reads and writes about baseball, and engages in father-daughter dancing. A SABR member since 1982, he researched and wrote biographies of Connie Mack, Willie Keeler, Wild Bill Donovan and Danny Murphy for *Deadball Stars of the American League*, and a profile of Norm Siebern for *The 1967 Impossible Dream Red Sox: "Pandemonium on the Field."* He has followed the Red Sox from afar since his grandfather escorted him and his two brothers to see their first major league game, on Thursday, August 3, 1967 at Fenway Park (a 5–3 win).

Glenn Stout has been a fulltime author since 1993. He has been series editor of *The Best American Sports Writing* since its inception and is author of the text for *Red Sox Century*, *Yankees Century*, *The Dodgers*, and *The Cubs: The Complete Story of Chicago Cubs Baseball*. He recently edited *Everything They Had: Sports Writing of David Halberstam*. His next book is *Young Woman and the Sea: How Trudy Ederle swam the English Channel and Changed the World*, and he is currently working on a book about the 1912 Red Sox and the first season in Fenway Park. He lives in Vermont.

Trey Strecker is the editor of *NINE: A Journal of Baseball History and Culture*. He teaches English and sport studies at Ball State University in Muncie, Indiana. He has edited *Dead Balls and Double Curves: An Anthology of Early Baseball Fiction, 1838–1923* (Southern Illinois UP) and *The Collected Baseball Stories of Charles Van Loan* (McFarland).

Acknowledgments

This book about the 1939 Red Sox team is the fifth in a series of books which grew out of a project of the Boston chapter of the Society for American Baseball Research (SABR). Chapter member David Southwick conceived of a publication to honor the 30th anniversary of the 1975 Boston Red Sox team that won the American League pennant and took the quest for a world championship to the seventh game of the 1975 World Series. That work was published by Rounder Books as *'75: The Red Sox Team That Saved Baseball*. It was edited by Bill Nowlin and Cecilia Tan. In 2007, Rounder published *The 1967 Impossible Dream Red Sox: Pandemonium on the Field* (edited by Bill Nowlin and Dan Desrochers), a book that drew on the collective efforts of more than 60 members of SABR, as well as contributions of photography from the Boston Herald and the Boston Red Sox and numerous others.

In 2008, two more books joined the list: *When Boston Still Had the Babe: The 1918 World Series Champion Red Sox* is the work of an even 30 SABR members who contributed a biography or editing work, as well as many other SABR members who helped out here or there in one way or another. The 1918 book was edited by Bill Nowlin with Mark Armour, Len Levin, and Allan Wood. *Spahn, Sain, and Teddy Ballgame: Boston's (almost) Perfect Baseball Summer of 1948* featured 74 biographies of the 1948 Boston Braves and Red Sox teams and was edited by Nowlin, with Mark Armour, Bob Brady, Len Levin, and Saul Wisnia.

In the works for years to come are two more Sox "team books"—one that covers a decade, with 50 biographies of players from the 1950s, and one on the 1912 team, the first team to play in brand-new Fenway Park.

All photography courtesy of the Boston Red Sox except as noted. Thanks to Mike Ivins and Megan LaBella with the Red Sox.

Photographs on pages 11, 21, 22, 24, 27, 42, 60, 71, 77, 78, 80, 81, 86, 88, 89, 91, 92, 102, 106, 108, 114, and 115 are courtesy of George Brace Photos. Thanks to Mary Brace.

The photograph on page 74 is courtesy of Lefty Lefebvre.

The photograph on page 116 is courtesy of the Weaver Family.

Additional thanks to: Bob Bailey, Thomas Beck, Dick Daly, Neil Dobbins, Judy Magerowski, Ray Nemec, Steve Netsky, Max Pokrivchak, Jim Rasco, Rev. Monsignor Royce R. Thomas, Craig Wagner, Joe Wargo, Richard Weaver, and Jim Wrobel.